Uncertain Warriors

Modern War Studies

Theodore A. Wilson
General Editor

Raymond A. Callahan
J. Garry Clifford
Jacob W. Kipp
Jay Luvaas
Allan R. Millett
Series Editors

Uncertain Warriors

Lyndon Johnson and
His Vietnam Advisers

David M. Barrett

 University Press of Kansas

Published by the University Press of Kansas (Lawrence, Kansas 66049), which
was organized by the Kansas Board of Regents and is operated and funded by
Emporia State University, Fort Hays State University, Kansas State University,
Pittsburg State University, the University of Kansas, and Wichita State
University

Library of Congress Cataloging-in-Publication Data

Barrett, David M., 1951–
    Uncertain warriors : Lyndon Johnson and his Vietnam advisers /
David M. Barrett.
        p.   cm. — (Modern war studies)
    Includes bibliographical references and index.
    ISBN 0-7006-0612-2 (cloth) ISBN 0-7006-0631-9 (pbk.)
    1. Vietnamese Conflict, 1961–1975—United States. 2. United
States—Politics and government—1963–1969. 3. Johnson, Lyndon B.
(Lyndon Baines), 1908–1973. I. Title. II. Series.
DS558.S88   1993
973.923'092—dc20   93-15654
                                                             CIP

British Library Cataloging in Publication Data is available.

Printed in the United States of America
10 9 8 7 6 5 4 3

Produced digitally by Lightning Source Inc.

With admiration, to my mother
Frances S. Barrett
and in memory of my father
Edward J. Barrett
and my uncle
John M. Barrett

No man will wish to be a mere cypher at the head of government: the great object of each president then will be to render his government a glorious period in the annals of his country.

—*Federal Farmer*, no. 14, January 17, 1788

Men make their own history, but they do not make it just as they please; they do not make it under circumstances chosen by themselves, but under circumstances directly encountered, given and transmitted from the past.

—Karl Marx, *The Eighteenth Brumaire of Louis Bonaparte*

Contents

Preface   ix

1 Lyndon Johnson, His Vietnam Advisers, and the
American Political Environment   1

2 1965: "Our Last Clear Chance"   13

3 1967: Waist Deep   62

4 1968: Tet   109

5 The Evolution of Johnson's Vietnam Advisory System   160

6 Secrecy and Openness in the White House: An
Interpretation of Johnson's Political Style   172

Afterword: On Rationality, Johnson's Worldview,
and the War   190

Appendix: Significant Advisers to Johnson
on Vietnam—1965, 1967, 1968   195

Notes   197

Bibliography   261

Index   271

Preface

ABOUT THE VIETNAM WAR there has been neither a lack of passion nor a dimming of interest on the part of millions of Americans since 1965, when the U.S. government sent combat troops by the thousands to Southeast Asia. Memories of Lyndon Johnson have continued to be intriguing for a more select group of people including historians, political scientists, and many longtime Washington journalists and policymakers. David Halberstam, a severe critic of Johnson in many ways, has written that the thirty-sixth president was the single most fascinating political figure of the 1960s. For the public, though, Johnson has been the object of much less curiosity and attachment. References to the Johnson years do not touch a responsive chord among the public, with the exception of those who share writer Ralph Ellison's view of Johnson as "the greatest American president for the poor and the Negroes." For the most part, biographies of Johnson have not topped the best-seller lists, and the public interest in and regard for Johnson that historian Vaughn Davis Bornet foresees does not yet exist: "It seems altogether likely that Americans in coming years will find it necessary to thank this president, even as they still feel forced to blame him." The memories of war, riots, assassinations, and a White House without John F. Kennedy may keep Johnson from ever becoming a popular historical figure. Even the domestic achievements of the Johnson presidency — in particular, Great Society and civil rights legislation — are controversial to this day, whether the judgments are made in think tanks or corner bars.[1]

In this book I address one aspect of the Johnson presidency — the evolution of the president's circle of Vietnam War advisers from 1965 to 1968. I hope and believe that an exploration of the interactions among those uncertain warriors can shed light on why the United States fought in a terrain described with remarkable prescience by Senator Richard Russell as "the most unfavorable place in Asia to fight a war (unless it be Afghanistan)."[2] I also hope that this book will influence future understanding of Lyndon Johnson, one of our most complex presidents. A president can choose virtually anyone to be an adviser ("even his chauffeur," Dean Rusk used to say). It is tempting to believe that presidents' advisory systems are, therefore, simply reflections of their personal inclinations. But a rational president will seek out critical and diverse views, especially in troubled times. Here I will argue that any sensible chief executive's advisory circle is a reflection not just of his possibly shallow personal preferences but also of his understanding of conditions in the American political environment.

War is central to this book; it is a phenomenon I do not approach casually. In part, this is because of my father. After parachuting into Normandy and taking part in one of the landmark battles of World War II, he wrote from a hospital bed in England to his brother, a fellow soldier in the U.S. Army. Due to the secrecy requirements of fighting a war, neither knew where the other was most of the time. Still, the events begun on D Day were, as the saying goes, in all the papers. Captain Edward J. Barrett wrote of the invasion to his brother, John: "No doubt you knew we were in there. The papers don't tell much though of the things that really happen. . . . Sherman was a man of understatement." From one Southerner to another in the 1940s, the latter statement carried a lot of weight. I found the letter after my uncle and father were dead. Sometimes I tell my students about it. When I do so, I remind them who Sherman was (the great Civil War general), what he did (blaze a trail of destruction through the South), and what he said (memorably, "War is hell."). I have never forgotten that my father suffered for decades after facing harsh combat in World War II. Truly, if unoriginally, I believe that all wars, even "good" ones, are abominable. Although I focus in this book on powerful individuals who sent young men into battle, and I describe those leaders as, on the whole, rational and well intentioned, I do so with the knowledge that many people are still in pain because of the Vietnam War.

I HAVE LONG looked forward to the time when I would write an acknowledgment of the assistance I have received while writing this book. One reason, of course, is that it would signify the near completion of a long, often fascinating, but sometimes difficult task. But beyond that, it is a pleasure to contemplate the tremendous help, encouragement, and friendship I have encountered these past six years as I pondered the complexities of Vietnam and Lyndon Johnson.

Professor Peri E. Arnold encouraged me to pursue my questions about this topic years ago, when I was a graduate student at the University of Notre Dame. He also read successive drafts of the book. I am grateful for his time and careful attention. I also am indebted to Professors John Roos, Alan Dowty, and George Lopez of Notre Dame. At Villanova University, Professor John Schrems has, as chairman of the Political Science Department, shown unfailing kindness to me. Two

Villanova colleagues in particular, Craig Wheeland and Matthew Kerbel, have offered helpful comments. To these and other political scientists and historians who have helped me, I offer my thanks.

I have always relied on the kindness of close friends, as well as the intimacy, honesty, and joy of such relationships. For me, it is the best thing in life. It is impossible to rank such friendships and would be unseemly to do so, but I want to mention some of them, in no particular order. The Kolskis—Cindy, Philip, Joey, and Chrissy—are my "family" in every sense of the word, except that we are not related by blood. They finally convinced me after some years that I really was a full member of their family, with all the delightful privileges and obligations that membership entails. Alan Gibson has been like a brother since our days together in graduate school. Donna Hunter has been a very close friend since the wonderful year I spent at the University of Essex in England. Michael Bridgeman and John Foster are two of my oldest and best friends; another is Kathy Foster. Along with them, for special achievement in the category of frequent encouragement, I want to thank other friends publicly: Bret Kincaid, Barbara Bartosik, Frank Guliuzza, Dan Reagan, Dennis and Noreen Moran, Marlene Spletzer, Caryll Vicsik, Elizabeth Kovacs, Hildie Bennett, Ted Gladue, the late Ed and Mary Fischer, Tom Holbrook, Ronda Hughes, Mary Stuckey, and all the gang at St. Francis House in Philadelphia.

The oldest and some of the richest relationships in my life are those with my mother, Frances S. Barrett, my brothers, Edward J. Barrett, Jr., and Stephen Barrett, and my sisters, Frances B. Coleman and Mary Louise Barrett. Edward (a Vietnam veteran) and Mary Louise deserve special thanks for helping me with problems ranging from unwieldy prose to financial crunches. To my mother and to all my siblings and their respective spouses (Sharon Barrett, Bobbie Barrett, and James P. Coleman) and children, I am much obliged.

I am also grateful to the staff of the Lyndon B. Johnson Library and to the Lyndon B. Johnson Foundation in Austin, Texas. From the latter (relying on the recommendation of an anonymous faculty committee at the University of Texas) I received a Moody grant. I also want to acknowledge the University of Notre Dame Graduate School's Zahm fund; the staff of the Richard Russell Library in Athens, Georgia; the staff of the Dwight D. Eisenhower Library in Abilene, Kansas; and those at the Minnesota Historical Society, the National Archives, and the Library of Congress's manuscript division. In particular, having compared experiences with researchers who have used various archives, the Johnson Library seems especially attentive to the needs of researchers without attempting to influence what will be written about Lyndon Johnson.

George McT. Kahin, George Herring, and Brian VanDeMark criticized earlier versions of this book. Each in his own way will disagree with parts of what I have written, but I appreciated the opportunity to draw on their substantive suggestions. Mike Briggs, acquisitions editor at the University Press of Kansas, has been helpful at every step of the way toward publication. A special word of thanks must also go to Tom Johnson, former deputy press secretary in the Johnson administration (but no relation to the late president) for granting me access to notes he took during many Vietnam advisory sessions. Mr. Johnson retains copyright on the notes but granted me permission to use them in this and in a forthcoming project. *Political Science Quarterly* and the *Review of Politics* also granted me permission to use portions of articles of mine that they published.

Three research assistants at Villanova University have reliably and graciously helped me on this and related work—Kevin Greer, Marcella Shinder, and Charlie Erwin. Diane Mozzone and Susan Burns, secretaries in the Political Science Department, have also contributed to this project. So have members of the staff of Pratt (Kansas) Community College, when I was on working vacations and faced computer problems. Pat Burke, from the University of Wisconsin–Milwaukee, shares my interest in Vietnam and presidents and has contributed to my now substantial personal archives.

I thank all these people. Obviously, they are not responsible for any flaws that undoubtedly exist herein. There will be no final word on Johnson and Vietnam. I accept full responsibility for the imperfections of this book and take no small pleasure in claiming some credit for its merits as well.

1 | Lyndon Johnson, His Vietnam Advisers, and the American Political Environment

ON JULY 25, 1967, a hot and humid day in Washington, D.C., President Lyndon Johnson opened one of his periodic unpublicized meetings with Democratic leaders of the U.S. Senate. The talk, in a mercifully cool White House, was to be of politics and the prospects of pending legislation. Johnson was having a hard day; he was still mad at Congress for voting down — even making fun of — legislation to spend $20 million on rat control in urban areas a few days earlier. Despite finding funerals unduly depressing, Johnson had been in the front pew at the National Cathedral for a service for his Secretary of the Navy–designate and longtime Pentagon official John McNaughton and his wife and son, all killed in a plane crash. He had slept very little the night before, having reluctantly ordered 4,700 soldiers into the city of Detroit, where the most destructive riots and looting in U.S. history were continuing nightly. After announcing the troop deployment at midnight, he had been up until two in the morning and was reawakened at 2:30 and 5:30 before rising again at 7:00 for the latest riot news. Republicans blamed Johnson for the disorder, and the *New York Times* sharply criticized his reluctance to send in the troops while reporting that many members of the Senate — friends and former friends of the president — were nearing "open revolt" against his Vietnam War policies. Columnist William Shannon wrote that Johnson, the "master politician," had "painfully little room in which to maneuver."[1]

The president opened the session with the legislators placidly enough, saying that he had nothing particular in mind — "I want to give you a chance to make any comments you wish." In the ensuing discussion, senators told Johnson, his assistants, and one another about probable forthcoming actions of their respective committees.

It was all rather businesslike until it was the turn of intellectual and acerbic Senator J. William Fulbright (D-Ark.). Once fellow senators, Fulbright and Johnson had enjoyed a "friendship out of the ordinary, a psychic attraction of the opposites" in the late 1950s. Fulbright had admired few if any men more than he did the majority leader, Lyndon Johnson. That friendship had died a painful, bitter death in late 1965, well after Johnson's accession to the presidency, each man feeling betrayed by the other over Vietnam. Fulbright, chairman of the Foreign Relations Committee, was now prepared to discuss a pending foreign aid bill, but only in the context of the larger problem of Vietnam. The senator had come to believe that Johnson was determined to seek a military victory in the unending conflict. He minced no words:

> Mr. President, what you really need to do is stop the war. That will solve all your problems. . . . I think there is a change of attitude on the war. Sen. Lausche changed his mind and said he thought the bombing should be stopped in the North. The Vietnam War is a hopeless venture. Nobody likes it . . . Vietnam is the root of many of your troubles. I don't want to speak for my colleagues, but I think this is in the minds of Senator Russell and some of my colleagues. Vietnam is ruining our domestic and our foreign policy. I will not support it any longer. I expect that for the first time in twenty years I may vote against foreign assistance and may try to bottle the whole bill up in the Committee.

It was an interesting challenge to the president, in part because Fulbright had long supported foreign aid as a tool of an enlightened U.S. foreign policy. For a moment, it seemed that the challenge to Johnson might pass, as it was the turn of Senator John Pastore (D-R.I.), head of the Joint Committee on Atomic Energy, to speak. But Pastore, setting aside protocol, solicited Johnson's response to Fulbright.

Focusing on Fulbright's threat to oppose the foreign aid bill, the president said that the $3.2 billion in the bill was the minimum necessary "to perform our obligations" in the world, then added sharply that if Congress wanted to tell the rest of the world "to go to hell," that was its prerogative. Johnson, who sometimes intimated to associates that Fulbright was a racist, then directed angry eyes and words to the senator: "Maybe you don't want to help the children of India, but I can't hold back." The president declined to launch into a full-scale defense of his Vietnam policies, saying, "I understand all of you feel like you are under the gun when you are down here, at least according to Bill Fulbright."

Fulbright countered, his Arkansas drawl and voice rising to match Johnson's famous Texas accent and volume: "Well, my position is that Vietnam is central to the whole problem. We need a new look. The effects of Vietnam are hurting the budget and foreign relations generally." With his temper rising rapidly, Johnson responded, "Bill, everybody doesn't have a blind spot like you do. You say 'Don't bomb North

Vietnam' on just about everything! I don't have the simple solution you have." Referring to diplomatic overtures of recent months, he added:

> We haven't delivered Ho yet! Everything which has been proposed to Ho has been rejected. As far as stopping the bombing in North Vietnam, I am not going to tell our men in the field to put their right hands behind their backs and fight only with their left. General Westmoreland told me when he was here that the bombing is our offensive weapon. And it will be just like tying his right hand behind him if we stop it. If you want me to get out of Vietnam, then you have the prerogative of taking the [Tonkin] resolution under which we are out there now. You can repeal it tomorrow. You can tell the troops to come home. You can tell General Westmoreland that he doesn't know what he is doing!

There, unresolved, the confrontation ended. Majority leader Mike Mansfield diplomatically suggested that the meeting proceed to a discussion of the Government Operations committee.[2]

THERE IS A STRIKING conflict among the existing accounts of Lyndon Johnson, his advisers, and the Vietnam War. Was Lyndon Johnson's character so flawed, were his "ego, stubbornness, and pride" so central in guiding his conduct that he did not rationally, honestly seek and listen to diverse views on how to deal with Vietnam? Did he "use" his advisers or verbally bludgeon those with dissenting views, communing mainly with counselors who never questioned the U.S. commitment in Vietnam?[3] This is the predominant understanding of Johnson and his advisers, widely recounted in memoirs, histories, and political analyses. Yet other scattered but respectable accounts of the thirty-sixth president and the war in Indochina give another view. Former Under Secretary of State George Ball, who opposed U.S. escalation in Vietnam in 1965, says that Johnson was "shaken" by his memoranda against the war and "insisted that we sit down and start arguments" about Ball's views. Another author writes that Johnson was not surrounded by "intimidated, acquiescent advisers," was "clearly reluctant" to increase the American presence in Vietnam in 1965, and did so only after "vigorous and extended debate."[4]

U.S. participation in the Vietnam War is widely and sometimes angrily seen as a monumental mistake, even an abomination. Because many analysts believe that Johnson's flawed advisory style was largely responsible for U.S. intervention and persistence in Vietnam, the discontinuity among portraits of this president, his advisers, and Vietnam decisionmaking is no small problem. In this book I draw on archival sources to examine and compare advisory interactions during three distinctly different periods of the war that nonetheless shared an important characteristic—the president was studying proposals to increase significantly the U.S. military presence in Southeast Asia.

There are obvious questions to ask about Lyndon Johnson and those who counseled him on the war: Who advised him? What types of advisers were they? Could and did they present unpleasant news and critical advice? What was their advice and when did they present it? Organization theory (which guides my thinking in this analysis) leads us to look at advising systematically, to ask questions that were inadequately answered before: How was Johnson's set of advisers—what I call his "advisory system"—structured? Did this change over time? What was happening in the American political environment as Johnson consulted his advisers? Was Johnson closed off from opinion outside the White House?

Answers to such questions and an exploration of the surprising paradoxes of Lyndon Johnson's political style suggest the need to think again about presidents' (not just Johnson's) advisory systems. Further, they reveal the weaknesses of accounts that "explain" Vietnam on the basis of the U.S. leadership's "willful, deliberate disregard of all facts."[5] The evidence that follows supports instead the sobering, perplexing thesis that rational advisory and decisionmaking processes can produce tragically flawed policies.

"The war bewilders": Explanations of Vietnam

Senator Mike Mansfield (D-Mont.) despised the Vietnam War. With a passion equal to that of Senator Fulbright but belied by his calm exterior, the majority leader of the Senate hated seeing President Johnson devote vast amounts of time and energy to Vietnam. A former professor of Asian history (and a one-time protégé of Johnson in the Senate), Mansfield lobbied the president almost desperately in face-to-face meetings, opposing most military options on Vietnam promoted by more hawkish advisers. "I think it is about time," he once wrote to Johnson, "that you got an accounting from those who have pressured you in the past to embark on this course and continue to pressure you to stay on it."[6]

When Johnson ultimately chose escalation in 1965, Mansfield dissented from the decision, yet he never joined those who blamed and castigated Johnson for the war. Paradoxically, he sometimes viewed the president as a victim, pushed into what Mansfield once called the war that "bewilders." There was, Mansfield observed, a "certain inevitability" to escalation in Vietnam. As he wrote to Johnson in early 1965, "In my judgment we were in [Vietnam] too deep long before you assumed office."[7] There was a duality to Mansfield's assessment of Johnson and the war: As a politician, Mansfield tried untiringly to turn a fellow political actor away from what he saw as a foolish and doomed policy; as an analyst of history, he saw forces larger than Lyndon Johnson pushing the nation toward war.

Debates have raged for more than two decades over what forces impelled Johnson toward war. Though there are variations, most published accounts addressing the topic fit into two groups. *Personalistic* analyses say that the war in Vietnam occurred largely because of the flawed character of Lyndon Johnson and/or the pathological advisory system he created. Analytically, they parallel Mike Mansfield's political frustrations as an on-the-scene observer of Lyndon Johnson's decisionmaking. *Structural* analyses emphasize factors such as ideology, a commitment to the containment doctrine in a time of Cold War superpower competition, and domestic political pressures.[8] These factors existed across presidencies and led the United States into war. Such explanations resemble Mike Mansfield's historical understanding of Vietnam.

An early manifestation of this debate arose during the war itself when Leslie Gelb and Richard Betts suggested an essential continuity of Indochina policy from the Truman administration through the height of the war in the Johnson era. Each president was committed to the containment doctrine and the derivative domino theory. Each feared an outcry similar to the "Who lost China?" debate in Truman's second term if South Vietnam went communist. But each also wished to avoid the trauma of a major war in difficult terrain, with attendant chaos in the United States and possible intervention by the Soviet Union or China. Therefore each president did just enough to prevent the fall of Vietnam but not enough (if such could be done) to win the war: "If they escalated to avoid defeat, they would be criticized. If they failed to escalate, they would be criticized for permitting defeat. Theirs was the most classic of all dilemmas: they were damned if they did and damned if they didn't."[9]

This picture of U.S. presidents virtually trapped by environmental constraints was too much for James David Barber, who responded in *The Presidential Character*, "If any 'system' was moving inexorably down the track toward tragedy in Vietnam, it was Johnson's own system — his character — not some structure or set of abstractions."[10] An aggressive and militaristic yet insecure Johnson would not allow critical advisers within his White House, writes Barber. Johnson's pathological character produced an operating style and advisory system that gave the world a war in Vietnam.

The debate has not abated in the intervening years.[11] Many analysts have followed Barber with other personalistic explanations of the war.[12] Larry Berman's *Planning a Tragedy* charges that Lyndon Johnson used his advisers in a sort of charade to give the impression that he was struggling with options in Vietnam. In fact (says Berman), Johnson was set on escalation, fearing that the "fall" of South Vietnam to communism would ruin his domestic political agenda.[13] More recently, other authors have written that Johnson possessed but ignored "substantial evidence" that he was going to lose in Vietnam, and that he did not "press for alternatives or question incisively the direction in which his administration's policies were headed." Richard Goodwin, a former Johnson aide, writes of Johnson under the stress of Vietnam decisionmaking: "If the world was beginning to slip from his control, he would construct a tiny innerworld that he could control, barricade himself not only from disagreement but from the need to acknowledge the very existence of disagreement except among the uninformed and hostile."[14]

By contrast, others, whether they applaud or decry the United States' role in the war, find (like Gelb and Betts) that something much more important than Lyndon Johnson's character or political style led the United States into war — namely, conditions in the American political environment and/or the international system of nation-states.[15] Gabriel Kolko's *Anatomy of a War* presents the war as the culmination of the United States' post–World War II effort "to halt and reverse the emergence of states and social systems opposed to the international order Washington sought to establish." Kolko denies that Johnson's personal conduct or "boorish manners" were crucial to Vietnam policymaking.[16] Even so staunch a foe of Johnson as North Vietnamese former commanding General Vo Nguyen Giap recently said of him, "throughout history, even the most intelligent leaders have not always been masters of their fate." Similarly, George Ball says of the early days of the Johnson administration, "I think it would have been terribly difficult for him to have disengaged immediately, because it would look as though he were repudiating the policy of Kennedy. . . ."[17]

The vast literature on presidents, advisers, and Vietnam (only briefly sampled here) displays fierce disagreements concerning Johnson and his advisers and reveals sharply differing theories about *why* the United States fought the long, tragic, and ultimately unsuccessful war in Indochina.[18] Systematically assessing Johnson's encounters with advisers (and the information and advice they wished to present) can clarify our thinking about Johnson's performance as president and the roots of the U.S. struggle in Vietnam.

Who Counts as an Adviser?
Measuring Access and Influence

In *The Adviser*, Herbert Goldhamer wrote that, because political studies have failed to create a well-established meaning, it has not been self-evident "who is to be included as an adviser."[19] Analysts have often written about "advisers" without defining the word, assuming that a president's cabinet and staff essentially constitute his advisory system.[20] Certainly, presidents' formal advisory systems for national security affairs have developed considerably since World War II. In the early days of the Cold War, Congress passed the National Security Act of 1947, which created many of the agencies (the Department of Defense, the Joint Chiefs of Staff, the Central Intelligence Agency, the National Security Council) that administer national security policies and whose leaders are supposed to advise presidents on those issues. But what about other less formal counselors to the president? Edward Corwin was enough of a political realist to know that "there are advisers *and* advisers," including (among others) those in presidents' "kitchen cabinets" without official status. The National Security Council (NSC) itself has had a decidedly uneven history as an advisory body. Many presidents, Lyndon Johnson included, preferred smaller, informal advisory groups (or one key adviser, as in the case of President Richard Nixon and his national security adviser Henry Kissinger) to assist them in devising crucial policies. Among the problems that presidents have had with using formal meetings of the NSC to discuss major issues are leaks to the press over contentious policy debates and the unwieldiness of large meetings.[21]

Assuming that only formal foreign policy advisers are significant counselors is misleading. It treats an administration's personnel chart as if it were the whole of a president's advisory system.[22] I assume that any individual viewed by the president as having individual characteristics and/or official position meriting access to the president (and who uses that access) is a presidential adviser with some influence. (A list of formal and informal adviser types is set forth in Table 1.1.[23]) In other words, an adviser's status depends on his or her official position, personal relationship with the president, or a combination of these.

Unfortunately, this definition of adviser and my assumption about advisory relationships do not precisely determine the cast of Johnson's advisers on Vietnam. I must also address (1) access to and influence with the president and (2) issues about which the president and adviser regularly talked.

As an operational definition for this study, an "adviser" is a person who could request and reasonably expect to communicate with the

Table 1.1. Types of Advisers to President Johnson, with Examples

Executive Branch	Nonexecutive Branch

Cabinet/Subcabinet
  McNamara, Rusk, Ball, Clifford
  from 1968, Helms
White House Staff
  Moyers, Valenti through 1966,
  McPherson, Rostow, Bundy
The Vice President
Military
  Westmoreland, Wheeler
Diplomats
  Goldberg, Lodge, Taylor
	Congress
	  Fulbright in early 1965,
	  Mansfield, Russell
	Government Elders
	  Eisenhower, Acheson, Harriman
	Personal Intimates
	  Fortas, Valenti after 1966,
	  Mrs. Johnson, Clifford until
	  1968

president — in person or by electronic media — on matters pertaining to the Vietnam War on a day's notice or less. This is not a perfect standard, for reasons related to measurement difficulties, but it moves us in the right direction: Those who talked with Johnson on scattered occasions about the war but were not influential are eliminated from consideration as advisers. For example, Senator Claiborne Pell (D-R.I.) requested a meeting with Johnson in 1967 to discuss, among other things, reasons behind his growing opposition to the president's leadership on Vietnam. Pell did so through national security adviser Walt Rostow and saw Johnson some days later. Using my operational definition, Pell is not treated as an adviser: An expectation that he would see Johnson within hours of his request would have been unrealistic and out of character for Pell, who was a knowledgeable student of foreign affairs but a relatively junior member of the Senate and no intimate friend or counselor of the president. My definition of "adviser" excludes persons who communicated in some limited fashion with Johnson on Vietnam and leaves them to be considered as either (1) representatives of the political environment or (2) parts of the foreign policy bureaucracy contributing to the information flow to the president.

There is no foolproof method to judge Vietnam advisers' access to Johnson and their influence with him. Certain advisers obviously meet the operational definition's standards — Robert McNamara, General Earle Wheeler, and other top administration officials clearly could talk to the president on short notice about war-related matters. The greater difficulty arises in treating subcabinet members, personal intimates of the president, and members of Congress.

I use multiple types of evidence to limit this problem. First, I use "reputational" evidence showing how others viewed the relationship between Johnson and a particular adviser. A second type of evidence indicates what the president and each adviser thought about their advisory relationship and, in particular, about Johnson's openness to the adviser's views. In pursuit of objectivity in describing Johnson's advisory system, I trace changes over time in these perceptions. Third, I use the paper trail of memoranda, letters, diaries, and notes to show the substance of advice offered. Such written evidence is usually superior to other sources, especially fallible human memories.[24] The fourth type of evidence indicates whom Johnson conversed with and the length and type of such encounters.[25]

How Do Advisory Systems Evolve?

Both the literature on presidents' Vietnam advisers and that of organization theory feature conflicts between personalistic theories emphasizing leaders' influence and freedom to maneuver and structural (situational) ones that stress environmental control. Stephen Hess's *Organizing the Presidency* assumes that the organization of the White House depends primarily on presidential style.[26] But Charles Walcott and Karen Hult write that such analyses "are not truly organizational at all, but rather studies of the behavior or strategic preferences of presidents."[27] Walcott and Hult, like other situational organization theorists, see human organizations as analogous to biological organisms: Organizations, like organisms, "interact with their surroundings, usually exchanging something . . . inside their boundaries for something beyond their boundaries." The actions of leaders are, according to another theorist, not simply "the result of conscious, foresightful choice" but rather of "external constraints, demands or forces that the social actor may have little control over or even cognizance of." These analyses reject, as I do, the assumption that a president's personal attributes are the only significant determinant of his advisory structure's makeup and explore the relationship between the environment and political organizations such as the White House.[28]

Situational organization theories usually assume that leaders are rational.[29] For this study, I define presidential rationality as responding to the environment by developing an advisory system to help determine and reach policy goals, seeking diverse views and information, and connecting means to ends. An irrational president fashions an advisory system that does not efficiently help him reach his political or policy goals, is closed off from diverse information, and fails to connect means to ends.[30] (On the concept of rationality, one political philosopher has written that the "whole subject, while of the greatest importance, remains shrouded in darkness."[31] I return to this problem in the final chapter.) Given the popularity of portraying Johnson as a substantially irrational president—either in choosing his advisers or in other, more colorful ways—there is a certain originality in employing a theory with a rational actor assumption to explain his leadership.

How might changes in the American political environment be expected to affect a president's shaping of his advisory system? Here are three propositions:

1. When certainty over a president's goals and the means to achieve those goals is at its highest in the American political environment, collegiality and regularized decisionmaking will be at their highest in the advisory system. Such a collegial system is "clanlike"—friendly and cohesive, featuring orderly interactions between president and advisers—and is comparatively indifferent to the limited dissent in the environment.

2. By contrast, when the administration's goals and means are controversial or downright unpopular in the environment, the advisory system will be "marketlike"—competitive and less orderly, featuring procedural competition among advisers and substantive competition of divergent ideas. There will be greater openness to outside political currents, with an increasing number of advisers and advisory bodies constituting the advisory system.

3. Under environmental conditions of relatively high certainty over goals but low certainty over means, advice seeking and decisionmaking will take place in a hybrid system with mixed elements and moderate levels of collegiality and competitiveness.

These propositions are empirical, predicting conditions that will exist rather than prescribing ideal advisory relations. Under these propositions, change in an advisory system over time is caused by choices that are made by the president but that reflect conditions in the political environment.[32] In laying out evidence relevant to the propositions, I describe the range of advice as well as advisers—their types, their interactions with one another, and their access to the president. Also, I note (1) evidence of Johnson's willingness or unwillingness to listen to new or unpleasant information or viewpoints and (2) assessments by the president and his advisers of the state of the environment. I also necessarily examine the level of certainty, uncertainty, or controversy in the American political environment over Johnson's goals in Vietnam and the means he employed to reach those goals. Although they do not constitute the entirety of the environment, I rely on votes and debates in the U.S. Congress and public opinion data as major barometers. Occasionally, I present other indicators of opinion in the environment—views of elites, news reports, and demonstrations.

ANY TREATMENT of a president's advisory relations must assess his political style and character.[33] Clearly Johnson's style affected the makeup of his advisory system, but did character flaws shape that style? Chapter 6 addresses that question and interprets Johnson's "theory" of presidential power, finding conventional (if now controversial) roots to Johnson's White House style. For now, it will suffice to keep in mind something of the essence of Johnson's political background and his seemingly contradictory character and colorful political operating style. Lyndon Baines Johnson gave rapt attention to politics even as a child, observing his father's political discussions at home and in the Texas legislature. As a young adult, Johnson became a congressional aide, then the leader of the Texas branch of the New Deal's National Youth Administration (NYA), and eventually a member of the U.S. House of Representatives before entering the Senate, where he became its majority leader in the Eisenhower era. The vice presidency in John Kennedy's administration was, of course, Johnson's last office before he assumed the presidency under tragic circumstances. Along the way, he had many mentors, including the masterful politicians Franklin Roosevelt, Speaker of the House Sam Rayburn, and Senator Richard Russell (D-Ga.). He learned much about politics from these and other mentors and from his years of operating in a congressional environment.

As president, Johnson fervently shrouded his decisionmaking in secrecy. Was this the result of a character flaw? Or were there rational, even compelling political reasons for his insistence on secrecy? It has also been widely reported that Johnson, though sometimes generous to a fault, was at other times obstinate and obnoxious toward advisers who offered critical views on any topic. Was there, in fact, a pattern of close-mindedness on Johnson's part, as in the encounter with Senator Fulbright? And what about the famous Johnson temper? Did it turn advisers into sycophants? These are questions to keep in mind and revisit after exploring the evidence in the next three chapters.

Rather than tracing advisory relations during the entirety of the Johnson presidency, from November 1963 to January 1969, I present three "deep cuts" into discrete periods of the war. This allows for a "thick description" of Johnson's interaction with advisers and permits a structured, focused comparison of advisory relations across time.[34] Chapter 2 examines deliberations in the first half of 1965, when the president and his advisers faced the prospective collapse of the internally unstable South Vietnamese government, under pressure from Vietcong guerrillas and North Vietnamese troops. (In that chapter and the two that follow, I italicize the names of significant advisers to Johnson on Vietnam as they are introduced.) Chapter 3 focuses on the spring and summer of 1967, a particularly appropriate period for study, because the commitment to South Vietnam had long since been made—U.S. troop levels were over 400,000. Protests against the war, though more frequent than in 1965, were less common than in later years. Military leaders asked Johnson to boost troop levels by either 89,000 or 200,000 men, depending (they said) on how quickly he wanted to win in Vietnam. Next, events in the winter and spring of 1968 during the Tet Offensive by the North Vietnamese and Vietcong are scrutinized in Chapter 4. At that time, the military again asked for a troop increase of 200,000.

The two final chapters summarize the evidence (much of it previously overlooked or unpublished), noting patterns over time in the American political environment, in Johnson's style of dealing with advice and advisers, and in the advisory system. I then assess the findings in these pages, offering explanations that are sharply at odds with much of the conventional wisdom regarding this complex president and the bewildering Vietnam War. Finally, I suggest a question that may be more worthy of future study than the old familiar one, How could Vietnam happen?

2 | 1965: "Our Last Clear Chance"

Vietnam and U.S. Presidents, 1950–1963

Lyndon Johnson's July 1965 decision to commit the United States to war in Vietnam is widely viewed as one of the most unfortunate episodes in American history. Flowing out of that decision were seven and a half years of active combat in South Vietnam, the deaths of over 50,000 Americans and hundreds of thousands of Vietnamese, and an intense polarization of U.S. society. Worst of all perhaps, the United States ultimately had little if anything to show for its venture in Indochina: In 1975, North Vietnam invaded the South, easily defeating the South Vietnamese military and chasing the few remaining Americans out of the country. With that, the late Ho Chi Minh's decades-old goal of uniting South and North Vietnam as an independent Marxist nation was achieved.

Many key developments in the administrations of his three predecessors set the stage for Johnson's choice to fight in Vietnam rather than withdraw U.S. forces. Following World War II, the nuclear arms rivalry between the United States and the Soviet Union (each with allies around the world) made conditions conducive for the American presidency to take on a new role in Harry Truman's administration as defender of the "free world," with Congress's and the Supreme Court's usual support. When communist North Korea invaded noncommunist South Korea in the summer of 1950, Truman sent U.S. troops to Asia without a congressional declaration of war. This was a key transition point in the history of executive-legislative relations in foreign affairs.[1] In Indochina, the United States backed the colonialist French against Ho Chi Minh's movement for independence. The "loss" of Indochina, coming so soon after China "fell" to Mao Tse-tung's revolution in 1949, would mean "the loss of freedom for millions of people, the loss of vital raw materials, the loss of points of critical strategic importance to the free world," said Truman. Therefore the United States spent over a billion dollars in 1951–52 alone on the French effort in Indochina. This was 40 percent of the total cost of the war for those years. A small U.S. military mission was also established in Saigon during the Truman years.

In 1954, President Eisenhower sent 200 advisers and 22 bombers to help the French. After France withdrew from Indochina, the United States began aiding and training the new South Vietnamese government of Ngo Dinh Diem. Said Eisenhower, "The loss of South Vietnam would set in motion a crumbling process that could, as it progressed, have grave consequences for us and for freedom."[2] As Leslie Gelb and Richard Betts have written, "the Saigon government was nearly totally dependent on Washington. American dollars underpinned the Saigon economy and underwrote most of the costs of the Saigon armed forces. American men trained and accompanied those forces. That dependence, plain for all to see, served both to heighten the American responsibility and to fashion an American-Vietnam tar baby."[3] Further, the Eisenhower administration oversaw the creation of the Southeast Asia Treaty Organization (SEATO), which pledged "mutual defense" cooperation between the United States and noncommunist countries of Southeast Asia.

John Kennedy came into office promising to "pay any price, bear any burden . . . to assure the survival and success of liberty." Vietnam was only one of the foreign policy dilemmas he faced that seemed linked to the Soviet Union's promise to support wars of "national liberation" around the world. The continuing insurgency of communist guerrillas in South Vietnam, with support from the North, prompted the United States to become a "limited [i.e., a greater] partner" in the war. There were fewer than 700 American advisers in Vietnam when Kennedy took office, but there were approximately 16,000 there when he died. The Kennedy administration also assented to, and covertly participated in, a coup that overthrew President Diem. In the process (though without Kennedy's approval), Diem and members of his family were assassinated. More than ever, with the blood of a South Vietnamese president on the hands of the United States, a full withdrawal from Indochina seemed almost unthinkable. There certainly was no backing off from what Kennedy told reporters in the fall of 1963: "What helps to win the war, we support; what interferes with the war effort we oppose. . . . But we are not there to see a war lost."[4] Lyndon Johnson fully supported most Truman, Eisenhower, and Kennedy policies in Indochina, but he thought that U.S. support of the coup against Diem was a horrible mistake.[5] Three weeks after Diem's assassination, Kennedy was also murdered. For almost two years afterward, a succession of unstable governments and coups followed in South Vietnam. Those in the Kennedy administration who had thought that getting rid of Diem would bring greater stability to South Vietnam were greatly mistaken.[6]

The Johnson Presidency and Vietnam, 1963–1964

Within hours of taking the oath of office, President Johnson pledged to carry out John Kennedy's policies, domestically and internationally, "from Berlin to South Vietnam." There were seven different governments of South Vietnam during 1964, prompting Johnson's remark that he was tired of "this coup shit."[7] One result of the governmental turmoil was a political vacuum in South Vietnam, prompting North Vietnam to take advantage of this instability and step up its support of the Vietcong. This would ultimately force Johnson to choose between two long-standing but increasingly contradictory goals: The United States could "limit" its role in Vietnam (but only by disengaging and allowing a process to unfold that would unify South Vietnam with the North) or it could honor its commitment to save the South (but only by taking on a direct military role in Indochina). Johnson was "the true believer who had to pay the full price for his thinking. Unlike his predecessors, he was confronted with the ultimate logic of U.S. objectives in Vietnam."[8]

For most of 1964, however, Vietnam was not yet a preoccupation of the president. The one time it had priority was in August, when North Vietnamese torpedo boats attacked a U.S. destroyer in the Gulf of Tonkin. The U.S. destroyer was vastly superior in firepower to what Johnson himself called "three little old PT boats," and the damage to the ship was slight, but the event caused a stir in Washington. When commanders of another American ship reported what they believed to be a second attack two nights later, Johnson consulted his advisers and authorized a retaliatory air raid on North Vietnam.[9] More importantly, consistent with his predecessors' approach to Congress during the Cold War, Johnson requested and received a congressional mandate to take whatever actions he believed necessary "to repel any armed attack against the forces of the United States and to prevent further aggression." Had he known what lay ahead in Vietnam, Johnson's friend Senator J. William Fulbright (D-Ark.) undoubtedly would have opposed the Tonkin Gulf Resolution. Instead, Fulbright floor managed the resolution during debate. Senator John Sherman Cooper (D-Ky.) asked Fulbright if it were true that "looking ahead, if the President decided that it was necessary to use such force as could lead into war, we will give that authority by this resolution?" Fulbright answered, "That is the way I would interpret it."[10]

For the rest of 1964, as the instability of South Vietnamese politics continued and the activity of Vietcong guerrillas and North Vietnamese troops increased, Johnson clung to the hope that major military intervention might be avoided, but he did not turn away from established U.S.

goals. The credibility of the United States was believed to be at stake.[11] Twice in the late months of 1964 the Vietcong attacked U.S. installations, causing loss of life. Both times Johnson resisted those urging retaliation. This distressed Secretary of Defense Robert McNamara and national security adviser McGeorge Bundy, who came to believe that hard decisions about the American role in Vietnam could no longer be put off by Johnson.[12]

Conflicting Interpretations of Early 1965 Decisions

From the afternoon of November 22, 1963, when Lyndon Johnson took the oath of office in an airplane at Dallas, Texas, to the morning of July 28, 1965, when he prepared at the White House for a midday announcement of an increased American role in Vietnam, there was no time when it would have been politically easy to announce a policy of disengagement from Indochina.[13] Richard Neustadt and Ernest May, in *Thinking in Time: The Uses of History for Decision Makers*, write of an enlightening experiment conducted in graduate seminars at Harvard: Students were challenged to imagine themselves working in the Johnson White House of 1965 and writing a speech in which the president would announce that the United States was getting out of Vietnam:

> The more often we review the case, the harder we find it to outline what LBJ could have said in 1965 to explain to the American people why he was dropping JFK's South Vietnamese allies or, alternatively, why he was beginning all-out war against Hanoi because of what impended in Saigon. Students, young and old, who try to outline the speech Johnson could have given over television, find the exercise distressing. They gravitate, as we do, toward the conclusion that LBJ's one real alternative . . . [was] another dose of 1963 medicine: engineering a change of regime in South Vietnam, but this time to bring a clique that would call for neutralization and American withdrawal.[14]

Yet most analysts have held in the intervening years that withdrawal is exactly the policy Johnson should have chosen: The United States could not save a government (or governments) that had so little legitimacy with the Vietnamese people; further (it is said), U.S. credibility with its allies would have survived if Johnson had withdrawn. Along with the prevailing view that the United States should have disengaged in 1965 comes a popular corollary: Johnson, at this utterly crucial juncture, did not want to consider that option. He "possessed substantial evidence that he was going to lose his war in Vietnam" but failed to make "careful, modest attempts to find a path away from such dangers." The matter of whether or not Johnson sought and listened to reasoned arguments against entry into the war is of real importance.[15]

Bombing the North to Save the South

In February 1965, the United States began bombing North Vietnam on a regular basis. The immediate provocation was another Vietcong attack against a U.S. installation—this time at Pleiku—with more loss of life. McGeorge Bundy was in South Vietnam at the time. Unlike Dean Rusk, who told Johnson early in the year that some alternative to those two awful options of withdrawal or escalation *must* be found, Bundy and Robert McNamara suggested a new, militarily stronger effort. Coming off the emotional experience of seeing the American victims at Pleiku, Bundy cabled Johnson, "Without new U.S. action defeat seems inevitable. . . . There is still time to turn it around, but not much."[16] Bundy envisioned sustained bombing as punishment of the North and hoped that, chastened by destruction in their country, the North Vietnamese leaders would stop or reduce shipments of equipment and men to the South. The bombing was also supposed to boost the morale of South Vietnam's leaders.

In the days after the Pleiku incident, Johnson huddled with advisers and posed the option of bombing. Most of his counselors were for it, but not all. *Senator Mike Mansfield* (D-Mont.) attended National Security Council (NSC) meetings on two consecutive days. Mansfield's views were important to Johnson for a number of reasons: His former majority whip in the Senate had also been a specialist in Far Eastern affairs since his days as a professor of history at Montana State University. Within months of the Kennedy assassination, Mansfield began warning Johnson in person and on paper (just as he had President Kennedy) that increasing the American role in Vietnam would be a major mistake. Mansfield's effort earned Johnson's full attention and that of Bundy, whom Johnson told to "keep up to date" in responding to Mansfield's memos. It was not an easy assignment for Bundy, as the memoranda sometimes came in more than once a week. These were in addition to frequent phone calls and personal encounters.[17] William Bundy—brother of McGeorge and an assistant secretary of state—recalls the atmosphere at one NSC meeting after the Pleiku bombing:

> Somebody was bringing messages . . . "Are they unanimous in Saigon?" "Yes," and so on. . . . Senator Mansfield was brought into

the meeting and sat right across from the President . . . and what
had happened [at Pleiku] was gone over, its background, the recommendations from the field, the whole thing. The President, in effect,
rehearsed all that he already knew for the benefit of Senator Mansfield. . . . I do recall very vividly . . . that Senator Mansfield said
to the President, "I would negotiate. I would not hit back. I would
get into negotiations." And it was dryly, but very feelingly put, and
the President was . . . unexpectedly brusque in dismissing it — "I
just don't think you can stand still and take this kind of thing. You
just can't do it." . . . knowing, as I had some reason to do, the close
personal relationship over the years between the President and
Senator Mansfield, I was a little taken aback that the President
should be as crisp as he was on that occasion. What I think it
reflected was that he'd gone through this in his mind 46 different
times; he tried that exit, and he didn't see anything but darkness
and gloom in it.[18]

Mansfield, though discouraged by Johnson's ultimate decision to
start regular bombing, continued to send long, detailed letters in the
days after the NSC meetings, outlining likely future problems:

Anticipate that the Communist defenses against air-attacks in the
North have been and will continue to be strengthened. . . . A closer
degree of cooperation by the Soviet Union and the Chinese will be
brought about . . . the prospect for enlargement now looms larger
and I think it is only fair that I give you my honest opinions, as
I did on Saturday and Sunday, because to do otherwise would be
a disservice to you and to the Nation. . . . What the answer to the
situation is at the moment I do not know nor does anyone else.
But I am persuaded that the trend toward enlargement of the conflict
and a continuous deepening of our military commitment on the
Asian mainland, despite your desire to the contrary, is not going
to provide one.[19]

Vice President *Hubert Humphrey* also opposed the new bombing
policy. His opposition in meetings with the president and other advisers
was "forceful and frank," according to Under Secretary of State George
Ball. Humphrey himself later wrote of a meeting that "went well into
the night. In addition to [Johnson's] regular advisers, George Ball, Adlai
Stevenson, and I participated. The three of us strongly opposed the
bombing of North Vietnam as a dangerous escalation. I was particularly
opposed because, for one reason, Alexei Kosygin of the Soviet Union
was in Hanoi at that moment."[20]

Like Mansfield, Humphrey did not give up after Johnson decided to start the bombing. In the interest of protecting his advisory relationship with the president, Humphrey probably should have altered his method of advice giving. Though the vice president was seemingly unaware of it, Johnson was irritated by the way Humphrey communicated with him, which Johnson thought was inappropriate for any vice president. Johnson's views on this were shaped by his own early experiences in the Kennedy administration: At an NSC meeting, Johnson asked what he later called "a leading question" of the Joint Chiefs of Staff. His distinct memory of that inquiry was that President Kennedy showed "some irritation" toward him. So Johnson, with Kennedy's approval, developed a new policy: "I . . . had a general policy of never speaking unless I was spoken to and never made a recommendation unless the President asked me, and never differing with him in public. Frequently, he and I would talk and I would say, 'We have this difference and here is my viewpoint.' But I never thought it would be appropriate or desirable to debate differences of opinion in open meetings with others."[21]

Others back up that recollection. William Bundy recalls, "I never heard him [Johnson] express his views." George Ball, who also served in the Kennedy administration, said of Johnson's participation in advisory meetings, "He said relatively little." With such experiences in mind, Johnson expected the same closemouthed restraint from his vice president. According to Ted Van Dyk, a top aide to Humphrey during his vice presidency: "Johnson had talked to him at great length before he took office, saying he didn't want Humphrey disagreeing with him at meetings, and that they should discuss their differences privately. And right at the start Humphrey breached this. I'm sure this angered the hell out of Johnson—maybe even more than the fact that Humphrey disagreed with him."[22]

Interestingly, however, Humphrey's memoirs make no mention of such a pact, nor of Johnson's strong desire for vice presidential reticence in White House meetings. Oblivious to Johnson's preferred approach, Humphrey kept at the president to act with restraint in Vietnam. After a thorough study of Vietnam cables and intelligence estimates following the Pleiku incident, Humphrey put his views on paper for the president, urging him to consider withdrawing U.S. forces from Vietnam:

> You know that I have nothing but sympathy for you and complete understanding for the burden and the anguish which surrounds such decisions. There is obviously no quick or easy solution, and no clear course of right or wrong. Whatever you decide, we will be taking big historic gambles, and we won't know for sure whether they were

right until months or perhaps years afterwards. The moral dilemmas are inescapable. . . . Some things are beyond our power to prevent. . . . It is always hard to cut losses. But the Johnson administration is in a stronger position to do so now than any administration in this century. . . . If . . . we find ourselves leading from frustration to escalation and end up short of a war with China but embroiled deeper in fighting in Vietnam over the next few months, political opposition will steadily mount.[23]

Humphrey's long letter was an eloquent, prescient document that will always be of interest to those who study the Washington end of the Vietnam War. Unfortunately, Johnson did not think much of Humphrey's committing his views to paper—they could be leaked! Johnson could picture the headlines, even if Humphrey could not, about a vice presidential suggestion that the United States set aside the commitments of three—and now, increasingly, four—presidents to stop communist expansion in Indochina.

Humphrey was slow to catch on to what was bothering Johnson. After another memo in March suggesting that Johnson seek "every indirect means of sounding out weaknesses on the other side that might lead to negotiations," the president told him, "We do not need all these memos! I don't think you should have them lying around your office."[24] Humphrey later wrote in his memoirs, "the President . . . apparently thought I had leaked something about the meetings. I had not, but that became irrelevant." But Johnson speechwriter John Roche recalls:

Johnson once said about ways of getting information around Washington: "Telephone, telegraph, or tell Hubert." . . . Johnson had the utmost regard for Humphrey, thought very highly of his wisdom and judgment, but didn't tell him things because Humphrey told his staff who leaked to the press. . . . I saw this happen five or six times, so that Humphrey really was, in effect, a security risk. . . . It wasn't that Johnson was mad at Humphrey for his views substantively, it was that Johnson had a passion for keeping things quiet.

Humphrey himself implied that he had a leakage problem in a memo to Bill Moyers later that year: "I see somebody's been talking, and this time it wasn't me."[25]

Later in the Johnson presidency, after Humphrey became a supporter of the war and subsequently, when he turned once more against certain administration policies, he gave Johnson advice in a manner that suited the president—in private. In 1968, for instance, he would attend many of the top war councils and say virtually nothing. Nor would he write long memos to Johnson on Vietnam. Privately he would tell Johnson to deescalate the U.S. role in Vietnam. But in February 1965, Johnson put the vice president in the doghouse over the issue.

Humphrey attended only occasional meetings on Vietnam over the next few months. The exclusions were frustrating, since Humphrey knew that Johnson respected his "ability to relate politics and policies" but obviously mistrusted him on Vietnam matters.[26] Unable in the short run to increase his influence on that issue, Humphrey turned his immense energies to promoting Johnson's domestic policy agenda.

The two men had been friends and allies in the Senate. Humphrey was, like Mansfield, a protégé of Johnson's, only closer. Just three weeks before the first Humphrey memo, Lady Bird Johnson reflected on a "delightful" dinner the Humphreys and Johnsons had late one night at the White House: "I have no illusions that a President and his Vice President can maintain unbroken, day after day, a completely *simpatico* relationship. But it is pleasant that we have it now." Similar spontaneous dinners continued over the ensuing months at the White House, with Humphrey providing good cheer, but the vice president was on the fringe—at best—of Vietnam decisionmaking.[27]

At the time, most Vietnam advisers did not agree with Mansfield and Humphrey on the bombing question. Even George Ball, who would energetically try to persuade Johnson to cut U.S. losses in Vietnam during the coming months, temporarily muted his opposition to bombing, in the aftermath of Pleiku. More common was the position of *McGeorge Bundy* that there was a "widespread belief" that the United States lacked the will and determination to do what was necessary in Vietnam. "The stakes in Vietnam are extremely high. The American investment is very large, and American responsibility is a fact of life," Bundy wrote to Johnson. Unless the United States acted soon, defeat was "inevitable" within the coming year or so.[28] These were strong words from a man of imposing intellect who had assisted John Kennedy during foreign policy crises for almost three years. It was Bundy who, in March 1964 (just months into Johnson's presidency) drew on his impressive background as a shaper of Kennedy's foreign policy to educate Johnson on "broad questions and answers on Vietnam." He reminded the president that it was Eisenhower who had "rightly decided to support the new government of South Vietnam and we have continued that support ever since in good times and in bad." This was no time to quit, he said, and "no time for discouragement." Back in 1963, Bundy and some other Kennedy administration officials had hoped that the U.S. role in Vietnam might be ended by 1965. Bundy assured Johnson, however, that "1965 has never been anything more for us than a target for the completion of certain specific forms of technical training and assistance. A struggle of this kind needs patience and determination. We and our friends in Vietnam entirely agree that as time goes on the responsibility for effective work in all fields should be carried more and more by the Vietnamese themselves." That would not come soon though.

Humphrey wrote of Bundy's message to Johnson after Pleiku:

> It may be that what Bundy cabled, moved Johnson more than would have been normal. Bundy was an impressive man. Ordinarily, he was factual, never tried to plead a personal point of view. He was not Secretary of Defense, he was not Secretary of State, and he never presumed to be either. He had clearly defined his role, and that was to present the President with a thoughtful analysis of options. At Pleiku, however, he became, for the moment, an advocate.

Bundy (a one-time Harvard dean) had, as a young man, helped former Secretary of War Henry Stimson write his memoirs. Despite Republican beginnings in Thomas Dewey's 1948 presidential campaign, Bundy later came to know and serve John Kennedy. Some thought that he was cold, smug, even arrogant, but Johnson kept Bundy on. He respected his national security adviser's mind and education and was perhaps a bit in awe of them. Certainly Bundy had a major advantage over other foreign policy advisers to the president—as national security adviser, his office was in the White House, not far from the Situation Room (which he and Kennedy had created in the aftermath of the Bay of Pigs disaster). It served as a round-the-clock nerve center for all of the nation's international activities. Bundy was arguably the most powerful national security adviser to date. The position had been less influential in the Truman and Eisenhower administrations, in part because those presidents had such confidence in their secretaries of state. John Kennedy, wanting to control foreign policy from the White House and perhaps having less faith in Secretary of State Rusk, had made the National Security Council bureaucracy into a "little State Department." Although Lyndon Johnson had a tremendous regard for Rusk, Bundy's influence largely survived the Kennedy assassination.

As Humphrey suggests, Bundy usually strove to bring a variety of viewpoints to Johnson's attention, and—unlike many others who filled his position in later administrations—he got along well with his president's other foreign policy advisers. Though not personal intimates and vastly different in personalities, Bundy and the president would sustain a working relationship through the entire Johnson presidency, even after Bundy left his White House post.[29]

Bundy's view on the necessity of bombing prevailed, with McNamara, Rusk, the military, and most other advisers concurring. The air war against North Vietnam was on. There was brief hope in top administration circles that it would strengthen the confidence and unity of the South Vietnamese government and limit or stop North Vietnam's support of the war in the South. The intelligence community, for instance, weighed in with the view that if the United States continued its air attacks, North Vietnam "might decide to intensify the struggle, but . . . it seems to us somewhat more likely that they would decide to make some effort to secure a respite from U.S. attack."[30] In short, they might stop their military attacks in the South, press for a negotiated cease-fire, and resolve to fight another day. Or they might not.

But it was a pitifully small air war—"token bombing"—in the view of *General William Westmoreland*, commander of American forces in South Vietnam. It may have boosted the morale of the South Vietnamese government, he thought, but "only" two to four attacks each week were "woefully weak to 'send a message' . . . to convince North Vietnamese leaders to desist. . . . Interference from Washington seriously hampered the campaign. . . . This or that target was not to be hit for this or that nebulous nonmilitary reason."[31] A native of South Carolina, a West Point graduate, and a World War II veteran, Westmoreland privately disdained many decisions by civilian leaders in Washington during his service in Saigon, which had begun in 1964 and would continue through most of the Johnson presidency. Despite a friendly enough working relationship with Johnson, there was an ineradicable tension between the two men stemming from their different positions on the war. As president, Johnson ultimately chose to do the minimum amount necessary to save South Vietnam, but no more. He had a Great Society to build—antipoverty, education, civil rights, and other bills to pass. Westmoreland understood all that and respected Johnson for his nonmilitary priorities, but his job as commanding general in Vietnam was to defeat the Vietcong and their North Vietnamese allies.[32] The beginning of regular bombing of North Vietnam was only the start of what Westmoreland saw as a long road ahead.

From the Bombing Decision to the Troop Decision

"Scowling clouds" (to use Lady Bird Johnson's words) hung over Lyndon Johnson from late 1964 through the first half of 1965, due to the looming possibility that South Vietnam might fall to the communist insurgency, provoking domestic and international repercussions. General Earle Wheeler later recalled the views of the U.S. military leadership: "In the summer of 1965 it became amply clear that it wasn't a matter of whether the North Vietnamese were going to win the war;

it was just a question of when they were going to win it."[33] Analysts laying out detailed accounts of the decisionmaking processes of those years can easily lose sight of this proverbial forest in studying the trees. Johnson had put off taking "decisive" actions urged on him by many advisers in the first year and a half of his presidency; had he been able to muddle through for *another* year and a half (or longer) in Vietnam and continue to give top priority to his domestic agenda, he would have done so.

Increasingly, however, a decision either to increase the American role in Vietnam or to disengage was becoming necessary, because the collapse of South Vietnam seemed imminent in the spring and summer of 1965 to most of those advising Johnson and to the president himself.[34] Westmoreland, for instance, warned in March that "we are headed toward a VC takeover of the country."[35] At the Pentagon, Assistant Secretary of Defense John McNaughton detailed the views of the civilian leadership in a March 24 memo to his boss Robert McNamara: "The situation in general is bad and deteriorating. . . . U.S. policy appears to be drifting. This because, while there is a near-consensus that [current] efforts inside SVN will probably fail to prevent collapse, *all three of the possible remedial courses of action have been rejected* for one reason or another: (a) Will-breaking [bombing] strike on DRV [North Vietnam]; (b) large troop deployments; (c) exit by negotiations" (emphasis added). McGeorge Bundy reported to Johnson on April 1, "The situation in many areas of the countryside continues to go in favor of the VC." Despite the U.S. bombing, the war was being lost, with the Vietcong seemingly attempting to cut South Vietnam in half as a prelude to ultimate victory. Increasingly, it looked to Lyndon Johnson like he was going to have to "either run or stand."[36]

The dilemma depressed Johnson enormously. A man who did not enjoy suppressing his emotions, he openly described his dilemma in many conversations. One reporter recalled Johnson seeming to think that doom awaited him, whatever he did. Johnson said that he was like a man standing on a newspaper in the middle of the ocean: " 'If I go this way,' he said, tilting his hand to the right, 'I'll topple over, and if I go this way,' tilting his hand to the left, 'I'll topple over, and if I stay where I am, the paper will be soaked up and I'll sink slowly to the bottom of the sea.' As he said this, he lowered his hand slowly to the floor."[37]

Joining the president at this crossroad, but decidedly less pessimistic, was the man widely perceived to be Johnson's most influential cabinet member, Secretary of Defense *Robert McNamara*. On Vietnam, McNamara was notably dominant among formal advisers in proposing policy. Dean Rusk's under secretary and alter ego George Ball was among those who thought that the secretary of state was too deferential to both

McNamara and the military. Johnson's congressional mentor Senator Richard Russell considered McNamara a man whose "enthusiasm clouds his judgment in the area of international relations." He also believed and regretted that McNamara "exercised some hypnotic influence" over Johnson. McNamara had become a legend during the Kennedy administration for his influence, his brains, his confident assertiveness, and his Johnson-like capacity for work. He was, said Johnson, the "smartest man" he had ever known, a man in whose presence you could "almost hear the computers clicking." Early in 1965, Johnson exclaimed about his secretary of defense, "The myth of McNamara is really true!" And, despite the fact that McNamara continued to be close to the Kennedy family, he was the administration official most frequently invited to join Johnson at Camp David.[38]

McNamara was a true believer in the righteousness, the feasibility, and the necessity of the growing American presence in Vietnam.[39] The bombing of North Vietnam after the Pleiku attack had been "exactly what I would do," he told friends. Publicly, he told the House Armed Services Committee, "The choice is not simply whether to continue our efforts to keep South Vietnam free and independent, but rather, whether to continue our struggle to halt communist expansion in Asia." Views to the contrary were not much welcomed by McNamara. George Ball authored an antiwar memo for Johnson in late 1964, one of many to come, and later recalled that McNamara "treated it like a poisonous snake." Humphrey felt slighted and even betrayed by McNamara in some of the Vietnam meetings where the vice president spoke dovishly.[40]

At every decision point in the first half of 1965, McNamara was the civilian adviser whose advice to Johnson was most consistently hawkish. In January he joined McGeorge Bundy in warning Johnson that continuation of "current policy can lead only to disastrous defeat." Both men "fully supported [Johnson's] unwillingness, in earlier months" to change direction in Vietnam, but the time had come for "harder choices."[41] McNamara and Bundy thought that the response to Pleiku was a step in the right direction, but it also created a new need—combat troops to protect the newly built U.S. installations. And those troops would need to be accompanied by support troops. (Historian and journalist Stanley Karnow makes two important points about the months between the Pleiku bombing decision and the decision five months later to provide General Westmoreland with whatever troops he needed: "Wars generate their own momentum," and "Americans never fight abroad without ample supplies of arms and ammunition, and vast quantities of beer, chocolate bars, shaving cream, and their favorite brands of cigarettes."[42])

Robert McNamara provided a kind of comfort to Lyndon Johnson in these months of momentum generated by the bombing decision, further attacks by the Vietcong, and requests by Westmoreland for troops to protect U.S. installations. Surely McNamara's appeal to Johnson was that he achieved results. If anyone could succeed in the treacherous terrain of Vietnam policymaking, McNamara could.

In late February and then in March and April, Johnson moved closer to the point of no return, granting Westmoreland's requests for marines to protect Da Nang airfield, then more troops to protect other bases, then 20,000 logistical support troops. The increase in numbers was considerable, yet there was no official announcement of a change in policy in Vietnam. *New York Times* columnist James Reston complained, "The time has come to call a spade a bloody shovel. This country is in an undeclared and unexplained war in Vietnam. Our masters have a lot of long and fancy names for it, like escalation and retaliation, but it is a war just the same."[43] Reston's complaint was justifiable, but the situation looked different to Johnson and most of his men, who did not want the South Vietnamese to construe recent actions as indicating a commitment to a ground combat role in the future. In a recently declassified memorandum of a conversation in the spring of 1965, Rusk told McGeorge Bundy, Maxwell Taylor, and William Bundy that the deployment of marines into defensive enclaves around two bases "should be treated in very low key and stated in very general terms with nothing that would lead the Vietnamese to begin to think in terms of deployment of U.S. divisions."[44] This was a time of experimentation with "limited" numbers of troops in South Vietnam and carefully chosen bombing runs over the North, all geared to force the communists to cease and desist or, failing that, to give Johnson time to make the ultimate choice—get in or get out.

Many of Johnson's advisers thought that it was time to get in, to grant Westmoreland's requests for troops and a free hand to use them in whatever way he deemed necessary—no more finely tuned, lengthy guidelines about when soldiers could or could not respond to or pursue Vietcong attackers.[45] The crunch came in June. On the fifth, Westmoreland and Ambassador Maxwell Taylor reported to Washington that if ongoing defeats of the South Vietnamese army continued, its "will to continue to fight" would collapse. "To ward against the possibility of such a collapse, it will probably be necessary to commit US ground forces to action," the cable added. Days later, Westmoreland requested 34 U.S. battalions, plus another 10 battalions from South Korea to be paid for by the United States. American troop levels would rise to 180,000 men, with more likely to be needed in 1966, Westmoreland said. Admiral U. S. Grant Sharp, commander of the air war from his base in Hawaii, agreed with Westmoreland's analysis: "We will lose by staying in enclaves defending coastal bases." The Joint Chiefs in Washington, headed by General

Earle Wheeler, quickly supported the request, reporting to McNamara that the "situation requires a substantial further build-up of US and Allied forces in RVN [Republic of South Vietnam], at the most rapid rate feasible on an orderly basis."[46]

Such analyses came at a time when the president and those few advisers who doubted that South Vietnam's army was on the ropes were pressed by battle reports from Vietnam. Two battles between army troops and communist forces began in late May and continued into the early weeks of June. "In a textbook display of tactical ineptitude, battalions of ARVN's [Army of the Republic of Vietnam] finest reserves were frittered away piecemeal during the fighting. The violence of the action at Dong Xoai and the level of RVNAF [Republic of Vietnam Air Force] casualties during the second week of June 1965 were both unprecedented," according to the Pentagon Papers. American troops were in the vicinity of both battles but did not assist the South Vietnamese, who suffered a demoralizing defeat.[47]

With those events unfolding on the ground in Southeast Asia, the definitive request—the one that previous events and decisions had perhaps made inevitable—was finally on the table in Washington. It stirred up a "veritable hornet's nest": "Up to that time, most of the Washington decision makers had been content to indulge in relatively low-key polemics about the enclave strategy and to advocate some experimentation with small numbers of U.S. troops in Vietnam. . . . Washington saw that it was Westmoreland's intention to aggressively take the war to the enemy with other than Vietnamese troops, and in such a move the specter of U.S. involvement in a major Asian ground war was there for all to see."[48]

Among Johnson's formal executive branch advisers on the war, Under Secretary of State *George Ball* saw the costs of such a war most clearly. Like Mike Mansfield, Ball discerned a momentum that had its roots in the pre-Johnson years but had become stronger during the Johnson administration—"there was an unmistakable smell of escalation in the air."[49] He thus gave spirited and prophetic warnings that the United States would be no more successful with its military intervention in Indochina than France had been over a decade earlier. Ball urged the president to assert his power in stopping the movement toward an open-ended commitment to save South Vietnam. "A review of the French experience more than a decade ago may be helpful," he wrote on June 18. "The French fought a war in Vietnam, and were finally defeated—after seven years of bloody struggle and when they still had 250,000 combat-hardened veterans in the field, supported by an army of 205,000 South Vietnamese." Well aware of Johnson's desire to be "in control" of events, he reminded the president of Emerson's saying,

" 'Things are in the saddle and ride mankind.' . . . Your most difficult continuing problem in South Vietnam is to prevent 'things' from getting into the saddle or, in other words, finding a way to keep control of policy and prevent the momentum of events from taking over." The more forces sent to Vietnam, he warned, the harder it would be to get out if things did not go well. This would be particularly true if the troops were given a full-fledged combat mandate to seek out and fight the communists, as Westmoreland wanted.[50]

Ball sent the memo to Johnson through *Bill Moyers*, the young presidential aide who had "built up his own kind of apparatus so he'd have information, intelligence . . . to keep abreast of things" in assisting Johnson.[51] The president had given Moyers a mandate in the early years of the administration: "Listen, read, tell me what you think. Don't worry if it's different from what a member of the Cabinet thinks." Patrick Anderson writes, "Johnson wanted ideas and information he might not have gotten through regular bureaucratic channels; it was to be a personal, informal arrangement." Moyers's success in this role is demonstrated not only by evidence of Johnson's confidence in him; the man who managed many of the "regular bureaucratic channels" — McGeorge Bundy — let Johnson know in early 1965 that he considered Moyers an ideal candidate for national security adviser, should Bundy ever depart the administration.

The president took the Ball memo with him for a weekend at Camp David and discussed it with Moyers.[52] Moyers reported back to Ball that Johnson agreed in substance with most of the memorandum and quoted the president: "I don't think I should go over 100,000 but I think I should go to that number and explain it. I want George to work for the next 90 days — to work up what is going to happen after the monsoon season. I am not worried about riding off in the wrong direction. I agree that it might build up bit by bit. I told McNamara that I would not make a decision on this and not to assume that I am willing to go overboard on this. I ain't."[53] McNamara thought that Ball's warning that the United States might ultimately send 250,000 to 500,000 soldiers to Vietnam, if Johnson followed McNamara's and Westmoreland's recommendations, was outrageous.[54]

Ball's position on the war at this time has been thoroughly documented and even celebrated for many years. But questions have been raised about his status as an adviser: Did he have access to Johnson? Did he get a serious hearing from the president, or was he merely a "domesticated dissenter" who alone advised Johnson to avoid a major war in Vietnam?[55] McGeorge Bundy apparently thought that Ball carried weight with Johnson. Either at the president's request or on his own initiative, Bundy reacted to Ball by writing to the president, "if and when we wish to shift our course and cut our losses in Vietnam we should do so because of a finding that the Vietnamese themselves are not meeting their obligations to themselves or us." Bundy also took the trouble to give Johnson a detailed memorandum denying that France's Vietnam experience foreshadowed what would happen to the United States.[56]

Johnson, Ball, and Rusk all later said that Ball was granted status and access allowing him to speak directly to Johnson about the movement toward war. On approaching the president, Ball recalls, "I was free to pick my timing. Dean Rusk had told me early in our relationship that the President was as entitled to my views as to his — a magnanimity that has haunted me ever since. . . . I am by no means sure that under similar circumstances I would have been so tolerant or generous."[57] Ball recalls that after Johnson received his first comprehensive memo on Vietnam:

> The President read it not once, but twice, so he told me, and he was very impressed, or shaken by it. So he insisted that we sit down and start arguments. Well, that was the beginning of a process I then employed, because then I wrote the President every few weeks . . . arguing that we were losing the war, that it was an unwinnable war, that we could commit any number of — 500,000 I think the figure I used at one point in a memorandum — and that we still would not win. . . . The President always read these things. And the reason I know he read them is because he always insisted on having a meeting then, and he would call on me to present my views, which I would do. The reason I know he read them was that he would sit there without looking at them and he'd say, "Now, George, you say on page nine so-and-so."
> [Interviewer:] He didn't block you out because he knew you were going to be unsympathetic?
> [Ball:] No. Let me say if I had found myself excluded from meetings . . . then I would probably have quit. But, on the contrary, I was always involved.[58]

After hearing the hopeful news that his June 18 memo had impressed Johnson, Ball presented a plan on June 28 for "Cutting Our Losses in South Vietnam," which had as its premise "we are losing the war." It laid out a sequence of events by which the United States could announce its intention to withdraw from Vietnam. Reacting to the latest change of governments in South Vietnam, Ball suggested that the United States put Marshal Nguyen Cao Ky and other South Vietnamese leaders on notice that the United States would give them precisely one month to put together a "government of national union under civilian leadership . . . what would be the effect of such a notice? Either it could induce the Ky government to adopt an extreme nationalist position and announce that it would go it alone without the United States' help or the Ky government would fall in favor of a government prepared to try to find a political solution with the Viet Cong." Going past the implication that the communists would ultimately take control, Ball focused on its meaning for the United States: "Our decision to force the issue of stability and responsibility was a mark of prudence and maturity." Most importantly, "The position taken in this memorandum does not suggest that the United States should abdicate leadership in the cold war. But any prudent military commander carefully selects the terrain on which to stand and fight." And, the core point: "South Vietnam is a country with an army and no government. Even if we were to commit five hundred thousand men to South Vietnam we would still lose."[59]

McGeorge Bundy sent a similar Ball memorandum, written on July 1, to Johnson along with ones from McNamara, Rusk, and Assistant Secretary of State William Bundy.[60] There were two "main alternatives," said the national security adviser: "George Ball's preference for a negotiated withdrawal, and Bob McNamara's recommendation of a substantial increase of military strength, with a call-up of reserves this summer."[61] The secretary of defense was strikingly more optimistic than Ball in his analysis. Although noting that "the VC are winning now," he presented a program of "expanded military moves . . . to prove to the VC that they cannot win and thus to turn the tide of the war." Endorsing the latest version of Westmoreland's 44-battalion request (34 U.S. battalions, nine from Korea, and one from Australia), an intensive bombing campaign, a call-up of the reserves, plus a worldwide diplomatic campaign to pressure Hanoi to give up its goal of taking South Vietnam, McNamara said that the American public "will support this course of action because it is a combined military-political program designed and likely to bring about a favorable solution to the Vietnam problem." The alternatives to military expansion, he told Johnson, were to "cut our losses and withdraw under the best conditions that can be arranged" or "continue at the present level, with US forces limited to say, 75,000 . . ., recognizing that our position will probably grow weaker." The latter two alternatives were not further addressed by McNamara.[62]

William Bundy found both Ball's and McNamara's prescriptions unattractive and posed a "middle way." Bundy had extensive experience in foreign policy bureaucracy circles, having served in the Defense Department in the Kennedy administration and in the CIA during the

Eisenhower years. Although he was no Johnson intimate nor at the very top of the State Department, he was on the fringes of the inner core of the president's formal foreign policy advisers. Occasionally, as in 1965, his ideas were at the center of deliberations.[63] Bundy proposed an increase of U.S. forces to just 85,000 men and advised Johnson to delay further deployment decisions while testing the ability of American troops already there to assist the South Vietnamese in preventing collapse. As the authors of the *Pentagon Papers* wrote, "This would allow for some experimentation without taking over the war effort—a familiar theme." Bundy's analysis was unusual for its assumption that collapse was not imminent in South Vietnam—the fight was not going "all that badly," he said.[64] His view on that was soon altered by events in South Vietnam.

Dean Rusk wrote relatively few memoranda to Johnson, saving most of his advice for personal sessions with the president. Uninterested in brawling with others in the administration, Rusk also found it unnecessary: He viewed himself "as a kind of personal counselor to the President," and Johnson was comfortable with that.[65] But on July 1, the secretary of state added his views in writing to those of Ball, McNamara, and William Bundy. While not going into specifics, Rusk said that there could be "no serious debate" over the U.S. commitment to assist South Vietnam: "The integrity of the U.S. commitment is the principal pillar of peace throughout the world. If that commitment becomes unreliable, the communist world would draw conclusions that would lead to our ruin and almost certainly to a catastrophic war." It might take a long time, he said, but the Vietcong could be denied victory. If they were not, then China, which Rusk saw as the chief supporter of Ho Chi Minh, would continue with what he believed were dangerous expansionist policies.[66]

Rusk's opinion counted heavily with the president. William Bundy, who saw Rusk and Johnson together frequently, thought that the president had greater doubts about escalation in Vietnam than either Rusk or McNamara. And though McNamara was more aggressive on Vietnam policymaking matters, it was the more restrained Rusk, thought Bundy, whose views were of "greater weight" with the president.[67] Johnson and Rusk came to understand each other's thinking almost by instinct. By all accounts, Johnson loved Rusk like a brother and accepted his secretary of state's familial way of calming him down. For example, in the spring, when a State Department spokesman described the role of American soldiers as having changed toward a less defensive posture, Johnson was furious. He wanted the press spokesman fired for his "leak." "He'll be giving his future briefings somewhere in Africa!" said the president. But Rusk went to Johnson and patiently explained, "A press secretary has a rough job. He has 100 times a day to stub his toe, and mistakes will happen. He's doing a good job."[68] Johnson's nerves were soothed and the press officer kept his job. Although he surely saw Johnson's occasional bursts of temper, Rusk insists that "a very marked personal characteristic" of Johnson's was his "great personal kindness and consideration." Their relationship had "ups and downs as far as policy matters were concerned," but the president knew he could talk "in the most intimate way, the most provisional way" without worrying about leaks from Rusk. And Rusk says, "I never let any blue sky show between his point of view and my point of view" in public settings.[69]

McGeorge Bundy weighed in with a summary of the four position papers and informed Johnson that "second-level men in both State and Defense are not optimistic about the future prospects in Vietnam." It might almost be expected that George Ball's position—get out of Vietnam—would be appealing, but it was not. The secondary figures "tend to cluster around the middle course suggested by my brother," said Bundy. The Joint Chiefs of Staff, however, "are strongly in favor of going in even further than McNamara." Then Bundy added,

> My hunch is that you will want to listen hard to George Ball and then reject his proposal. Discussion could then move to the narrower choice between my brother's course and McNamara's. . . . I think you may want to have pretty tight and hard analyses of some disputed questions like the following. . . . What are the chances of our getting into a white man's war with all the brown men against us or apathetic? . . . What is the upper limit of our liability if we now go to 44 battalions?[70]

Thus, within this group of formal foreign policy advisers to the president there was significant disagreement about both *what* the United States should do—save South Vietnam or not—and, if the military solution was attempted, *how* it might be done—send the troops Westmoreland wanted or try to get by with less. Judging by McGeorge Bundy's reading of the situation as well as Ball's, Johnson was leaning against following the Ball scenario. But he hadn't ruled it out and he wasn't hearing it from just George Ball: Lyndon Johnson was a complete extrovert as president, seeing more people than any one member of his staff or administration knew. William Bundy, for instance, ensconced in the upper bureaucracy of the State Department, had no idea who else was getting through to Lyndon Johnson on Vietnam. He was curious about it, but neither his position nor his limited personal relationship with

Johnson enabled him to know what else was being said to Johnson beyond what went through regular foreign policy advisory channels.[71]

One top informal Johnson adviser who shared all Ball's doubts was *Clark Clifford*, a former aide to Harry Truman, who joined Abe Fortas and New Dealer James Rowe in composing a "three man board" of informal but crucial advisers to Senate majority leader Johnson in the 1950s. The importance of the Clifford-Fortas-Rowe triumvirate was enhanced by Johnson's inability to function with a genuine chief of staff in charge of his Senate office—he had to do it himself, it seemed. Similarly, in the Johnson presidency, there was no White House chief of staff.[72] True, McGeorge Bundy functioned as a clearinghouse for most of the formal foreign policy advice, and Rusk and McNamara were top advisers in the one-on-one sense. But Johnson's system reached more widely than any formal chart could indicate. It included in its ranks a veteran Johnson adviser—Clifford—who feared that the United States was headed for disaster in Asia. While formal members of the Johnson advisory system—Westmoreland, Ball, McNamara, William Bundy, and others—were perfecting their arguments, Clifford gave his "one major point" to Johnson in a May 17 letter:

> I believe our ground forces in South Vietnam should be kept to a minimum, consistent with the protection of our installations and property in that country. My concern is that a substantial buildup of U.S. ground troops would be construed by the Communists, and by the world, as a determination on our part to win the war on the ground. This could be a quagmire. It could turn into an open end commitment on our part that would take more and more ground troops, without a realistic hope of ultimate victory. I do not think the situation is comparable to Korea. The political posture of the parties involved, and the physical conditions, including terrain, are entirely different.

Then, in an indication that this was not the first time he had raised the subject with Johnson, he added, "I continue to believe that the constant probing of every avenue leading to a possible settlement will ultimately be fruitful. It won't be what we want, but we can learn to live with it."[73]

Clifford's credentials with Johnson were of the highest order. Johnson used Clifford, as Kennedy had, on organizational matters and also appointed him chairman of his Foreign Intelligence Advisory Board, a part-time job. In that position, Clifford had access to information that many top leaders in Congress—Senate Foreign Relations Committee chairman Fulbright, for instance—did not have. In general, Clifford was what one writer of the time called an "extracurricular" player who was "faultlessly close-mouthed" as a Johnson insider.[74] Ball's doubts about escalation signaled a foreign policy professional's prophecy of doom in a Vietnam War, but those of Clifford were similar to Mansfield's and Humphrey's — cogently expressed analyses by political professionals that Johnson needed to halt the decade-long movement toward war in Indochina.

As with Johnson's other informal Vietnam advisers, the written record of Clifford's advice is limited. After all, part of the appeal to Johnson in spending time with such advisers was that their advice was off-the-record. They could have the most serious or frivolous discussions on any subject including Vietnam, and there was no chance that their views would show up in the newspapers. In some ways, this was much more to Johnson's taste than the normal bureaucratic process with all those memoranda that were so easily leaked. Clifford's advocacy on the war was not concluded in mid-May. Johnson did not reply in writing to Clifford's May letter, but the president would be summoning him to the White House later.

Another informal adviser whose sometimes daily talks with the president are only faintly reflected in the written remains of the Johnson administration was *Senator Richard Russell* (D-Ga.), chairman of the Armed Services Committee. During the holiday season at the end of 1964, Russell phoned a journalist friend from his Georgia home and said,

> I see you have just been in Vietnam, and I would like to get your impression of the situation out there. But first, let me tell you my impression which I am inclined to give my friend, who called me from the [LBJ] ranch this afternoon. He said they have just blown up the Brink's officers' quarters in Saigon, and on top of that the South Vietnamese government seems to be trying to declare Max Taylor persona non grata. I am inclined to tell the President when I call him back that if I were President I would sail the Seventh Fleet up the Saigon River, load those 23,000 Americans aboard and bring them home.[75]

It is not known what Russell said to Johnson when he returned the president's call. The senator and the president rarely communicated in writing about Vietnam, and most of their conversations were off-the-record, occurring at private White House dinners, during evening rides on the Potomac on the presidential yacht, or elsewhere. Many scholars have relied on official White House records of meetings and thus underrated Russell's importance and access as a counselor to Johnson on Vietnam in the first half of 1965. For instance, John Burke and Fred Greenstein's recent *How Presidents Test Reality: Decisions on Vietnam*,

1954 and 1965, relies on such records to assert that, between February 6 and July 28, 1965, "Johnson had little or no contact with a number of people on whom he might have been expected to rely—for example . . . his old friend and mentor Senator Richard Russell." Burke and Greenstein write that Johnson had *no* individual meetings with Russell but 17 telephone conversations during these five and a half months. Senator Russell's papers, though far from a systematic account, give a different picture. They show, for instance, numerous calls from the president or Mrs. Johnson inviting Russell to join them in the evening. This was part of a pattern that was established early in the Johnson administration and continued through the summer of 1968. Indeed, the invitations were so numerous that Russell did not always accept. Despite the obstacles in determining precisely what Russell said to Johnson and when he said it, evidence suggests that Dean Rusk's estimate that Johnson and Russell talked privately (by phone or in person) four or five times a week is probably accurate.[76] And, although Russell's views were not without ambiguity at times, the records show that Russell was a longtime opponent of involving American troops in Southeast Asia, well before Johnson committed to major combat in July 1965.

Ironically, Russell and his protégé Johnson worked together as senators in 1954 to fight U.S. intervention in Southeast Asia. In a confidential letter to a friend, Russell later described a showdown conference with pro-intervention Secretary of State John Foster Dulles and the chairman of the Joint Chiefs of Staff, Admiral Arthur Radford: "The first meeting held with the congressional leadership relative to our involvement in Vietnam was in 1954 about the time the French surrendered Dienbienphu. I opposed our involvement very vigorously because I have always been afraid of a conventional campaign on the land mass of Asia. . . . President Johnson was in this conference, he was then Majority Leader, and he supported me to the hilt. At that time, it was decided not to go into Vietnam." Russell enjoyed telling friends and constituents that he "managed to keep us out" of Vietnam until Eisenhower decided to give South Vietnam aid and advisers. During the Kennedy years, when some pushed for a greater American military role in Vietnam, Russell warned the young president in a phone call, "I hope you will take a long, hard look before you commit anybody over there. . . . It would be a festering sore. We'd be still sitting there three or four years from now."[77]

In June 1965, Russell made it clear in a letter that his views on U.S. intervention in Southeast Asia had not changed in the intervening years: "I have never seen where Vietnam has strategic, tactical, or economic value, and in addition to the billions we are spending there now, we lost three billion down the drain supporting the French in Dienbienphu."[78]

As Lyndon Johnson knew, Russell was a fervent anticommunist who nonetheless thought that the United States should choose its battle-grounds with communism carefully. "I am by instinct," he said, "an isolationist." Some months after the United States made its full-fledged commitment to South Vietnam in 1965, Russell wrote to a friend, "we have undoubtedly selected the worst possible place to fight them. . . . I earnestly and vigorously fought to kick communism, Castro, and the missiles out of Cuba instead of temporizing with the Russians. This was 90 miles from home, whereas Vietnam is about 9,000."[79]

Thus, to Russell, the very fact that the United States entered the Vietnam War represented a tactical victory for "communists [who] out-witted us in getting us pinned down in the most unfavorable place in Asia to fight a war, unless it be Afghanistan."[80] But despite this instinc-tive isolationism, Russell was a self-professed "American who supports the flag when it is committed to any danger or trouble."[81]

Consistent with his paradoxical views dating back through the Ken-nedy and Eisenhower administrations, Russell urged Lyndon Johnson in 1965 to find some way to avoid greater entanglement in Southeast Asia. One example comes from a detailed memo written by Mike Mans-field and addressed to Johnson, concerning a July meeting Mansfield had with Russell and four other senators who had doubts about escalation. Mansfield restated views that he and Russell had already expressed to the president and reported "full agreement" among the six senators that "in-sofar as Vietnam is concerned we are deeply enmeshed in a place where we ought not to be; that the situation is rapidly going out of control; and that every effort should be made to extricate ourselves." Further, there was "substantial agreement" among the senators that "even if you win, totally, you do not come out well. What have you achieved? It is by no means a 'vital' area of U.S. concern. . . . The country is backing the President on Vietnam primarily because he is President, not neces-sarily out of any understanding or sympathy with policies on Vietnam; beneath the support, there is deep concern and a great deal of confusion which could explode at any time." And, to cap it off, the senators sent word that the secretary of defense—the man they seemed to perceive pushing Johnson toward war—had been "a disappointment in his han-dling of this situation." Johnson passed on the senators' critiques—all but the final one—to McNamara, who gave a detailed response in favor of escalation.[82]

Russell, by numerous accounts, was the most influential and widely respected member of the Senate.[83] "Most influential," "completely dedi-cated," and "superior individual" were phrases that came to mind when, for example, J. William Fulbright was asked in later years to describe the Senator from Georgia. Russell and Johnson had a relationship that one White House aide described as "father/son, or elder brother and younger brother." Lady Bird Johnson says that her husband considered Russell "the one, the towering figure, the one that he respected most, admired most." Senator Sam Ervin, who served with both men in the Senate, said that Johnson "loved Dick Russell above any other member of the Senate or any other person in public life."[84] And Doris Kearns, who does not hesitate to chronicle the ways in which Johnson used people, writes that he shared with Russell "a genuine and consuming devotion to the Senate" and that Johnson "honestly respected and understood" Russell's fidelity to the institution. Certainly, Johnson never forgot that it was Russell who was chiefly responsible for the younger senator being chosen Democratic leader. But if President Johnson talked frequently with the senator, it wasn't just because of sentiment. Russell was not only chairman of the Armed Services Committee, with the power to make virtually unilateral decisions on certain military matters, he was also "de facto chairman" of the Appropriations Committee because its official chairman was the elderly and ill Carl Hayden (D-Ariz.).[85]

Johnson wasn't the only member of the administration who heard from Russell, of course. McNamara spoke frequently with Russell by phone and in the senator's office. Occasionally, the senator joined Johnson and his inner circle of formal advisers on foreign policy. Dean Rusk's distinct memory is that "Senator Russell's view all the way through was that we should not get into southeast Asia militarily."[86] This is consistent with notes in Russell's handwriting on White House stationery, undated but apparently written in 1965: "Westy wants 145,000 Americans. No Business there—cannot win if capture each + every Viet Cong."[87]

The regrettably scant archival record concerning Russell suggests the outlines of a deep personal and political relationship in which the man who had been Johnson's mentor in the Senate could not agree with his former protégé's decisions on Vietnam, as he could not agree with those of the presidents who preceded Johnson. As we will see, after Johnson announced his decision on troops in late July, Russell would jolt the president with a reminder that he had made choices that the senator would have avoided.

Meanwhile, the early days of July had their own surprises for Johnson. Vietcong successes "heralded the expected loss of the entire highlands area and the possible establishment there of a National Liberation Front government." The old enclave strategy set in force by Washington in the spring for American troops—a "masterpiece of ambiguity"—implied a commitment to fight on the part of the United States but simultaneously demonstrated in the placing of the troops with their backs to the sea a desire for rapid and early exit."[88] The strategy was overcome by events on the ground. As the South Vietnamese military's position weakened, the views of some of Johnson's advisers shifted — within two weeks after he proposed a "middle way" to Johnson, William Bundy came to believe that the only acceptable choice for Johnson was "to go hard and fast up" with the U.S. military role in Vietnam.[89]

One adviser whose views on the defensive enclave strategy were shaped by the ongoing battles was Ambassador *Maxwell Taylor*. A former general and chairman of the Joint Chiefs of Staff, a friend and adviser to President Kennedy, and a seasoned actor in the ways of Washington, D.C., Taylor was also a friend of Bobby Kennedy's. Not surprisingly, he was not personally close to Lyndon Johnson. Years after the Johnson presidency, Taylor recalled laughingly that, early in the war years, Senator Kennedy named one of his sons after him. Of that honor and its effect on Johnson, Taylor recalled, "every now and then he'd say, 'How is that Kennedy boy named after you?' [Laughter] I wasn't sure he was joking."[90] Still, the president had a high opinion of Taylor and would keep him on as a Vietnam adviser for the rest of his presidency, even after the ambassador completed his one-year tour of duty in Saigon.

Taylor had a unique, hawkish approach to the Vietnam dilemma. For most of the spring and early summer, he believed in taking the war to the North with bombing, punishing those that he thought were really responsible for the war in the South. Taylor's views on using ground troops, however, were ambiguous. He never favored U.S. withdrawal from Vietnam. There were "awfully good reasons not to do it," he later said, among them his belief that "we Americans had in large measure created or were responsible for the chaos by our action in the case of Diem." But at times, he almost sounded like George Ball. In February, he had "grave reservations" about bringing in more marines to protect Da Nang air base: "Such action would be a step in reversing the long standing policy of avoiding the commitment of ground combat forces in SVN. Once this policy is breached, it will be very difficult to hold the line. . . . The white-faced soldier armed, equipped and trained as he is, is not a suitable guerrilla fighter for the Asian forests and jungles." But, "in view of General Westmoreland's understandable concern for the safety of this important base, I would be willing to recommend placing in DaNang a marine battalion landing team." In late March, he told McNamara and the Joint Chiefs of Staff that the need for troops in Vietnam was not "manifest" and that the South Vietnamese would probably resent the arrival of American soldiers. And in April he did not fully share the fears of others that South Vietnam was about to fall. He was, in fact, remarkably optimistic, sending word to Johnson that although other advisers might believe it would take a year or two to achieve American goals in Vietnam, he thought that a "combination of continued air strikes and . . . the introduction of sufficent U.S. and third country forces" would bring about a solution in a matter of months.[91]

By June, when Taylor was in Washington and the South Vietnamese experienced another change in government while simultaneously losing a major military battle, the ambassador agreed that the situation was as bad as Westmoreland had been saying.[92] Taylor had frequently quarreled with particular estimates about the course of the war in early 1965 and thought that Johnson had not been aggressive enough in allowing the military to unleash a genuinely punishing air war against North Vietnam. He wanted "an inexorable continuity of attack repeated day after day without interruption."[93] But when push came to shove, he joined those recommending that troops take on a combat role in Vietnam. The man who had, at times, wondered about the feasibility of employing white-faced soldiers in a guerrilla war believed by early summer that "we would have to raise the level of our air effort over North Vietnam at the same time that we increased our strength on the ground. I had become convinced that we were going too slow in the application of military power, air and ground, to accomplish our intended purposes."[94]

At this stage of the Johnson presidency, a practice had developed of using groups of outsiders—elders from the political and foreign policy establishment—as consultants on Vietnam and other issues.[95] Now, at Johnson's behest, the President's Special Advisory Group on foreign policy, known as the "Wise Men," was called in to review his options in Vietnam. Included in the group were former Secretary of State Dean Acheson, former CIA Director John McCloy, World War II hero General Omar Bradley, and others. Considering the respect he had for these pillars of the establishment, Johnson was blunt and emotional in telling them of his unhappiness with the range of choices. One not very sympathetic description of Johnson comes from Acheson, secretary of state in the Truman administration. Acheson was not fond of Johnson, but later in the war he would play an important individual role among Johnson's advisers on Vietnam. In 1965, he was perhaps first among equals in the group advisory setting. On July 10, Acheson described the meeting with Johnson in a revealing, if self-serving, letter to Truman:

> We were all disturbed by a long complaint about how mean everything and everybody was to him—Fate, the Press, the Congress, the Intellectuals and so on. For a long time he fought the problem of Vietnam (every course of action was wrong; he had no support from anyone at home or abroad; it interfered with all his programs, etc., etc.). . . . I got thinking about you and General Marshall and how

we never wasted time "fighting the problem," or endlessly recon-sidering decisions, or feeling sorry for ourselves. Finally I blew my top and told him that he was wholly right in the Dominican Republic and Vietnam, that he had no choice except to press on, that explanations were not as important as successful action; and that the trouble in Europe (which was more important than either of the other spots) came about because under him and Kennedy there had been no American leadership at all. . . . With this lead my colleagues came thundering in like the charge of the Scots Grey at Waterloo. They were fine; old Bob Lovett, usually cautious, was all out, and, of course, Brad [General Bradley] left no doubt that he was with me all the way. I think LBJ's press conference of yester-day showed that we scored.

Johnson may have been unsure about U.S. goals in Indochina, but Acheson was not. He told a friend, "*what* needs to be done is not obscure. *How* to do it with the human material available, in the God-awful ter-rain given and against the foreign-directed and supplied obstacles is very hard indeed" (emphasis added).[96]

Similar confidence that military escalation in Vietnam was the only option for Johnson was reflected in a letter from former Kennedy ad-viser Roswell Gilpatric (a younger "wise man") to McGeorge Bundy after the Wise Men's meeting. He reiterated to Bundy the predominant view of the group:

The U.S. has a commitment in South Vietnam, non-fulfillment of which would have extremely grave consequences not only in Asia but in Europe . . . in order to hold on in South Vietnam, the U.S. faces a new role, that is, taking a major part in the combat itself. This means large additional forces and probably much heavier casualties. To carry out this role with some prospect of success calls for the application of whatever amounts of military power may be needed, perhaps as much as brought to bear in Korea fifteen years ago.[97]

Johnson paid special heed to another elder, former President *Dwight Eisenhower*. The two men saw each other during Eisenhower's occasional visits to Washington. They dined together twice in June and talked fre-quently on the phone.[98] The president assigned General A. J. Goodpaster from the office of the Joint Chiefs of Staff, and a former aide to Eisen-hower, as his emissary to the former president. Goodpaster took cable traffic concerning Vietnam to Eisenhower and returned with written summaries of Eisenhower's comments for Johnson. With Eisenhower,

President Johnson expressed doubts about Vietnam and about American critics of Johnson's policies. Goodpaster reported to the president Eisenhower's advice that Johnson "should not be too surprised or disturbed at the 'chatter' from certain quarters over the firm course the President is pursuing in Southeast Asia. . . . So long as the policies are right, as he believes they are, too much attention need not be given to these people."[99]

When Johnson sent his predecessor word of division among his advisers over how to respond to Westmoreland's needs, Goodpaster reported on June 16 that Eisenhower had "commented that we have now 'appealed to force' in South Vietnam, and therefore 'we have got to win.' For this purpose, simply holding on or sitting passively in static areas will not suffice . . . we should not only support Vietnamese forces in action, but should on occasion undertake offensive operations ourselves. After some further discussion he indicated that he believed General Westmoreland's recommendations should be supported."[100]

A few weeks later, when Westmoreland's request was the subject of almost daily debate in the administration, the two presidents talked over the telephone. Eisenhower thought that it was too late to consider anything other than deeper military commitment: "When you once appeal to force in an international situation involving military help for a nation, you have to go all out." The former president's secretary, taking notes on the conversation, wrote that Johnson "rather plaintively" asked, "Do you really think we can beat the Viet Cong?" It would depend, Eisenhower said, on factors including Vietcong force levels and infiltration from Vietnam. But he thought that Johnson should proceed with the military buildup as quickly as possible. When Johnson noted that U.S. escalation in Vietnam might not be supported by Britain and other allies, Eisenhower said, "We would still have the Australians and the Koreans, and our own convictions."[101]

In early July, Johnson sent his secretary of defense—the man with the most detailed plan for military escalation—to Saigon for a fact-finding visit to precede the submission of a revised version of his July 1 escalation proposal. McNamara left on July 14 and returned a week later. The circumstances of his return have shaped much of the literature on Johnson's policy of escalation in Vietnam as announced on July 28 and therefore deserve attention. The anonymous writers of the commentary in the *Pentagon Papers*, interpreting a July 17 cable from Washington to Saigon, report that when McNamara left Washington, the troop debate was unresolved but, "While he was in Saigon, he received a cable from Deputy Secretary of Defense Cyrus Vance informing him that the President had decided to go ahead with the plan to deploy all 34 U.S. battalions." The cable itself was not included by the authors in their history of the war. Elsewhere the *Papers* state, "Since Vance's cable to McNamara of the 17th of July indicated that the President had approved the 34 battalion deployment, it is probably reasonable to assume that the President spent much of the week assessing the political variables of the situation."[102]

The mildness with which the writers make these statements masks the implications of their claim. The significance lies in the fact that Lyndon Johnson held lengthy, in-depth discussions with advisers concerning his Vietnam options from July 21–27, the day before he announced his crucial decision to commit combat forces "as needed" to defeat the communist insurgency in South Vietnam. These discussions happened *after* Vance cabled McNamara in Saigon. The policy meetings involved the highest figures in government as well as outside advisory figures respected by Johnson as political and foreign policy consultants. In short, virtually all of the president's formal and informal advisers on Vietnam were called into the White House and/or Camp David to discuss the situation with Johnson and one another. Knowing well from their previous discussions with the president that he was generally leaning in the direction proposed by McNamara and Westmoreland, they understood him nonetheless to be exceedingly troubled by the implications of such a decision and uncommitted to a final choice. George Ball devotes some pages of his memoirs to describing the July 21–27 meetings as important decisionmaking sessions in which there was every indication of "the President's agonizing reluctance to go forward, his desire to explore every possible alternative, and, finally, his inability to reconcile his vaunted Texas 'can-do' spirit with the shocking reality that America had painted itself into a corner with no way out except at substantial costs in terms of pride and prestige."[103]

Despite the failure of the *Pentagon Papers'* editors to include the infamous Vance cable in their collection, some writers have accepted the *Papers'* understanding of the cable as proof that Johnson made up his mind on the troop question by July 17. Some accounts incorrectly describe McNamara, in effect, as dropping everything and returning immediately to Washington.[104] They then make a deduction consistent with the *Pentagon Papers'* account: that Johnson staged the tortuous discussions and debates of July 21–27 *not* to help him arrive at a decision but in order to fool the public, Congress, other government leaders and nongovernmental elites, and presumably history itself into believing that he had prudently engaged in wide-ranging discussions of his alternatives in Vietnam before making up his mind. Berman's *Planning a Tragedy* is the most prominent example of this school of thought. It holds that the "debate" over sending the troop battalions "never occurred," that the president had already decided that the troops "were needed to save South Vietnam—but he was unsure how to implement that decision."[105] This interpretation has flowed into many, though not all, recent published accounts dealing with Johnson and the war.[106]

The Vance cable was finally declassified in 1988. In it, the deputy secretary of defense told McNamara that he had seen Johnson three times on July 16 and summarized his understanding of the president's "current intention": to proceed with the 34-battalion plan.[107] Vance also told McNamara that the president was likely to call up the reserves and extend tours of duty for certain soldiers. What are analysts to make of the cable? The first, most obvious point is that the cable speaks of Johnson's "current" intentions. This ambiguity in the cable is not hinted at in the *Pentagon Papers* but is reflected in the July 28 outcome—Johnson did commit to "saving" South Vietnam and announced new troop levels, but without committing to the specific number of troops suggested by McNamara and Westmoreland. His other "current" intention, to call up the reserves, changed.

Since it was Vance's message that the *Pentagon Papers* authors relied on, his own understanding of the meaning of the cable is of interest. Asked in 1988 whether Johnson had given him and McNamara a "go-ahead" on the combat troop matter or whether "he meant to convey some uncertainty about what he would finally decide," Vance replied, "I believe it was the latter, namely that there was continuing uncertainty about his final decision, which would have to await Secretary McNamara's recommendation and the views of congressional leaders, particularly the view of Senator Russell." Like Dean Rusk, William Bundy, and most other foreign policy advisers to Johnson, Vance had a healthy respect for the importance of the Johnson-Russell relationship and its effect on the outcome of policy decisions. Vance's impression of Johnson's motives and actions is consistent with those of most others seeing and talking to the president, including Ball, Rusk, and Clifford.[108] It also reflects an understanding of a recurring pattern in the Johnson presidential style—keeping options open until the latest possible moment by shrouding advisory processes in secrecy, and reaching beyond formal advisory boundaries for diverse information and viewpoints.

Whatever the ultimate value of such an approach, Johnson's operational style was a fact of life for his counselors. Dean Acheson, for example, after working for months as an unpaid adviser to Johnson and Rusk on a NATO crisis involving President De Gaulle of France, wrote to Harry Truman that Johnson was "a worse postponer of decisions than FDR. The phrase for that now is 'to preserve all one's options.'" Acheson obviously disliked the advisory and policymaking processes of the Johnson administration—he thought that they led to "drift."[109] But his understanding of decisionmaking in the administration is consistent with the suggestion here that Lyndon Johnson simply leaned in favor of granting Westmoreland the troops he wanted at the time Vance sent his cable. As Richard Betts has said, Johnson "was hoping to avoid major troops commitment as long as there was some other possibility."[110]

During the weeks before Johnson's July 28 announcement, Vietnam was "a constant black background" for the president, according to his wife. He was "spending so many more hours of his day working on foreign affairs than on anything else." Among those he spent time with were critics of his policies to date in Vietnam. Senator Wayne Morse, a Johnson friend who had voted against the Gulf of Tonkin Resolution, rode with the Johnsons on Air Force I from Washington to New York on July 2. The conversation was "jocular" but otherwise unrecorded. It may well have dealt with the question of whether the United Nations could play a role in starting negotiations in Vietnam. Johnson had solicited Morse's views on the subject at the White House two weeks earlier. The president seemed to respect Morse's consistency on Vietnam, and the two men got along well.[111]

On July 16, Mrs. Johnson recorded in her diary, "I found Lyndon in the hall, deep in conversation with Bill Fulbright." The senator joined the Johnson family in riding to the funeral for Adlai Stevenson, the UN ambassador who had died suddenly in London.[112] The relationship between *J. William Fulbright* and Johnson and the advice the senator gave to the president in the first half of 1965 have been obscured by events before and after that crucial year. Fulbright is well known as a sponsor of the Tonkin Resolution in 1964 who later became a bitter critic of the war leadership of Lyndon Johnson. What has received less attention are the closeness of Johnson's relationship with Fulbright up until mid-1965 and the quiet but firm advice the chairman of the Foreign Relations Committee had for the president. The two men had both been southern senators who succeeded in rising above regional concerns to become national figures. Despite their different personalities, they became close friends. One Fulbright biographer wrote of the Johnson-Fulbright relationship, "Johnson seemed to see in Fulbright a shoot of his own life, an intellectual one that had never had a chance to grow."[113] Another set of biographers wrote that, in the first year of his presidency, Johnson brought Fulbright into his "closest confidences." The friendship extended to the wives of both men. In 1964, Lady Bird Johnson said of Bill and Betty Fulbright, "They are our best friends. We see them more than anyone else."[114]

After the escalation in Vietnam, the friendship died amidst mutual recriminations. In the first half of 1965, however, Fulbright tried earnestly to convince the president that a commitment to defend South Vietnam with combat troops would be a mistake. In essence, the senator believed that the United States could not "save" South Vietnam. The best and most realistic solution to the Vietnam problem from the U.S. vantage point would be the emergence of a "Titoist," independent, communist Vietnam. Such a nation, like Yugoslavia under Tito, would do the bidding of neither the Soviet Union nor China in international affairs.[115]

It is difficult to determine the exact number of meetings that Fulbright had with Johnson in the first half of 1965.[116] However, there is sufficient documentation to demonstrate that there were lengthy private visits by Fulbright to the president in February, June, and July.[117] Those meetings often focused on Vietnam. The senator had pondered possible troop commitments in an impossible situation, discussing his views with Richard Russell — the two men often had long, gloomy talks on the subject. Then Fulbright wrote to Johnson: "It would be a disaster for the United States to try to engage in a massive ground and air war in Southeast Asia. Not only would it be extremely costly, but it would also revive and intensify the Cold War which had begun to cool off following the missile crisis in Cuba, and it would lead to a revival of jingoism in the United States."[118] Well aware that simply pulling the United States out of Vietnam, without benefit of a diplomatic cover, could destroy Johnson politically, the senator suggested (like George Ball) that Johnson seek a negotiated settlement in order to secure an independent, albeit communist, Vietnam. A few days later, the president invited Fulbright to the White House where the two "conferred alone and at length."

Of his relationship with Johnson through the summer of 1965, Fulbright recalls, "I kept thinking that I could influence him privately. I saw him quite often." Fulbright avoided, for the time being, public criticisms of Johnson's Vietnam policy, knowing that if his questions were publicized, Johnson would be "off" him completely.[119] The senator told his friend David Lilienthal (former head of the Tennessee Valley Authority and the Atomic Energy Commission), "This President, he is a very remarkable man, no doubt about it. . . . When it comes to domestic things, he is a wizard, he works miracles. Hell, we have tried for twenty years to get an education bill through, and he gets it through just like that. . . . But he is in real trouble in Vietnam."[120]

Finally, in mid-June, the two men met for an hour and a half and Fulbright told Johnson that he would publicly oppose any escalation of the U.S. role in Vietnam. On the afternoon of June 15, after again sharing his views with the president, Fulbright rose on the Senate floor to say: "Escalation would invite the intervention or infiltration on a large scale of North Vietnamese troops . . . this in turn would probably draw the United States into a bloody and protracted jungle war in which the advantages would be with the other side."[121]

Fulbright was not "cut off" from Johnson during this key period of the war's incubation. Fulbright and his wife had dinner with the Johnsons and the McNamaras at the White House in February, he saw the president in various private settings, and on July 16 (when McNamara was in Saigon) he spent time in conversation with Johnson before joining the Johnsons in going to Stevenson's funeral.[122] Ultimately, of course, as Fulbright later put it, Johnson "was not persuaded."[123] Nonetheless, the president was fully aware that his friend and fellow southerner believed that Johnson would be choosing the wrong course by committing the United States to the defense of South Vietnam. A year later, when their friendship was effectively over, Johnson sent a note to Fulbright after encountering him briefly at a diplomatic reception: "I listen to everyone I can, but I must take the responsibility for deciding the policy—not my 'advisers'. . . . I have a fondness for you and Betty that is real."[124]

The Political Environment: Public Opinion and Congress

Later, public attitudes toward the war in Vietnam could be described with some precision. In 1965, however, the public's familiarity with the issues surrounding Vietnam changed noticeably, from general ignorance of specific events relating to the war early in the year to a much higher familiarity with Vietnam by midsummer.[125] In this section, I focus more on opinion in the early summer than that in previous months. But even when there was a low public awareness of the details of the Vietnam issue, the public displayed attitudes consistent with the bipartisan near consensus that the domino principle applied to Southeast Asia and that containment was the best solution for what was perceived as global communist aggression.

There was only limited polling in early 1965 dealing specifically with Johnson's handling of the Vietnam issue. The few surveys taken showed two-to-one approval of the president. Similarly, pollsters were only beginning to ask a question that would become a regular in later years: Had it been a mistake to become militarily involved in Vietnam? In January and May when this question was asked, respondents said no by similar two-to-one margins.[126] One question roughly reflecting the administration's options was: "Which of these three courses do you favor for the U.S. in Vietnam: carry the war into North Vietnam at the risk of bringing Red China into the war; negotiate a settlement with the Communists and get out now; continue to hold the line there to prevent the Communists from taking over South Vietnam?" In three polls

Table 2.1. Public Responses to the Question, Which Course Do You Favor in Vietnam? February–March 1965 (%)

	February	March	Late April
Negotiate/get out	23	35	28
Hold the line	40	46	43
Carry war to North	13	12	20
No opinion	24	7	9

Source: Polls conducted by the *Los Angeles Times,* cited in John E. Mueller, *War, Presidents, and Public Opinion* (New York: Wiley, 1973), pp. 82–83.

(Table 2.1), a distinct majority (growing from 53 percent in February to 63 percent in late April) preferred the United States to "hold the line" or "carry the war to the North." Those with no opinion were far fewer in the spring (9 percent) than in February (24 percent). Unfortunately, that precise question was not asked in the May–July period.

Two other questions—one asking for precise policy choices by respondents, the other posing stark either/or options in Vietnam— evoked answers that seem to summarize the public's view of the Vietnam dilemma. The latter question was, "Should the United States continue its present efforts in South Vietnam or should it pull our forces out?" Here again, a distinct majority favored continuation of policies consistent with the commitments voiced over the course of four administrations: Two-thirds of the respondents favored staying in Vietnam, and only one-fifth supported a pullout (Table 2.2).

Table 2.2. Public Responses to the Alternatives, Continue Present Efforts or Pull Out? March–June 1965 (%)

	March–April	June
Pull out	19	20
Continue efforts	66	66
No opinion	15	14

Source: American Institute of Public Opinion and the *Los Angeles Times,* cited in John E. Mueller, *War, Presidents, and Public Opinion* (New York: Wiley, 1973), pp. 83–84.

Another question pushed respondents to choose among more specific policy choices ranging from complete withdrawal to declaring war: "In your opinion, what would you like to see the United States do next about Vietnam?" Choices posed to respondents were withdraw completely, start negotiations and stop fighting, continue present policy, step up present efforts, go all out and declare war, other responses, and no opinion (Table 2.3). Although only a minority favored withdrawal and a plurality favored some version consistent with current and past policies, there was a rise in uncertainty from April to June. Apparently,

Table 2.3. Public Responses to the Question, What Would You Like the United States to Do in Vietnam? April–June 1965 (%)

	April	May	Early June	Late June
Withdraw	17	13	13	12
Negotiate, stop fighting	12	12	11	11
Continue present policy	14	13	16	20
Step up present efforts	12	8	6	4
Declare war	19	15	17	17
Other	5	6	4	5
No opinion	12	35	33	28

Source: Los Angeles Times and Gallup polls, cited in John E. Mueller, War, Presidents, and Public Opinion (New York: Wiley, 1973), pp. 83–84.

as the public became more familiar with Vietnam it also became less satisfied with the apparent options open to the United States.

In summary, polls of the time showed that a minority—albeit a healthy one ranging in size from 12 percent to 35 percent, depending on how the questions were worded—favored U.S. withdrawal from Vietnam. Support for withdrawal was highest—35 percent in March—when it was posed as a policy supposedly achievable through negotiations and lowest—12 percent to 20 percent—when it was portrayed as a unilateral pullout without benefit of diplomatic settlement. A plurality or majority favored the well-established American commitment to "protect" South Vietnam either by continuing current policies or by stepping up military efforts. Support was strongest when choices were posed most simply—an overwhelming majority chose continuing efforts over pulling out. This is significant, given the near consensus among both hawkish and dovish presidential advisers and the man they advised that he faced an either/or dilemma that his predecessors were spared: Either send combat troops to save Vietnam or pull out and lose it. When faced with relatively specific policy options such as declaring war or negotiating and stopping fighting, a plurality of the public favored some kind of war strategy, but almost a third of those polled could not choose a course of action. In short, most Americans supported the long-standing containment policies in Indochina and seemed to want to "save" South Vietnam but were uncertain over how to achieve that end.

In Congress, Vietnam was the focus of pointed debates in mid-May, when Johnson asked the legislature to authorize a $700 million expenditure on the existing U.S. mission in Vietnam. But Johnson wanted more than agreement to the appropriation. In fact, he told members of Congress and the press that he did not *need* congressional approval for the expenditure; legally, the money could be spent at his own direction.

Instead, the president wanted congressional approval of the thrust of administration policies up to that time. Johnson wrote to the members of Congress, "This is not a routine appropriation. For each member of Congress who supports this request is also voting to persist in our effort to halt Communist aggression in South Vietnam." To "persist," of course, was not necessarily to send hundreds of thousands of American troops. Johnson could have engineered a U.S. withdrawal under diplomatic cover (as George Ball and others advocated) while expressing "support" for South Vietnam and increasing aid. The near certain eventual takeover by North Vietnam would have made such a withdrawal very controversial, however.[127] The president's message was as ambiguous as most of the congressional speeches that were to accompany votes in favor of the resolution. He wrote, on the one hand, "the stakes are too high" for withdrawal or defeat; on the other hand, "in the long run, there can be no military solution to the problems of Vietnam."[128]

Johnson was addressing what has since become the historic Eighty-ninth Congress, the one that gave the United States the Great Society and Vietnam too. It was the most decidedly Democratic Congress since the Roosevelt era. All members of the House and a third of the Senate were elected at the same time as Johnson's landslide victory in November 1964. In the House there were 295 Democrats and 140 Republicans; the Senate had 68 Democrats and only 32 Republicans. As much as a Congress could "belong" to a president, this one was Johnson's, and he was determined to become a great president by persuading legislators to follow his lead.

On issues such as civil rights, he succeeded. When violence flared in Selma, Alabama, Johnson went before a televised joint session of Congress on March 15 to urge speedy passage of a tough voting rights act. The real hero in the turmoil of the day was the American Negro, he said: "Who among us can say that we would have made the same progress were it not for his persistent bravery, and his faith in American democracy." It was probably the best speech of Johnson's presidency, in which he adopted the language of the civil rights movement by saying, "We shall overcome." The speech also touched on Vietnam: "As we meet here in this peaceful historic chamber tonight, men from the South, some of whom were at Iwo Jima, men from the North who have carried Old Glory to far corners of the world and brought it back without a stain on it, men from the East and West are all fighting together without regard to religion, or color, or region, in Vietnam."[129]

That same spring, with little advance notice, he had congressional leaders put the Vietnam resolution before members of both houses for debate and a vote. In the Senate, Senator Albert Gore's (D-Tenn.) speech typified many others: "I support the pending appropriation, because wherever American soldiers are sent, they must be supplied with the necessary equipment and support." Yet Gore, unlike most others, also said that the United States "is tempting fate and is practicing brinkmanship with the greatest tragedy that might face the country." For Senator John Sherman Cooper (R-Ky.), it was "a solemn day and a solemn vote that we take. . . . We must recognize all the possibilities of an expanded war even though it is one we do not cause."[130] But Senator Wayne Morse (D-Ore.) thought that most of his fellow legislators were evading responsibility for what they were doing, as when they voted for the Tonkin Gulf Resolution the preceding August:

> The one painful fact about this joint resolution is that the President himself has stated its purpose: to obtain our endorsement of his policy in Asia. Senators can talk all they like about supplying our soldiers. But the President plainly and clearly stated . . . that the money is not needed. What *is* needed by the White House is another affirmation of our support. Last August, many Senators performed a rather pathetic exercise of explaining that their votes for the resolution should not be construed to support an expansion of the war. . . . This week we are hearing the "reservationists" saying now that their support for this appropriation should not be construed to be an endorsement . . . of the expansion by the President. Whom do they think they are kidding? . . . Let me say to the Senators who claim that they intend to be consulted again before there is another escalation of the war: You are being consulted right now. This is the President's consultation. When the President has this consultation under his belt, he is going to announce the landing of thousands more of American troops in Vietnam.[131]

Morse was in a tiny minority in the debate over the new resolution, joined by only two other senators—Ernest Gruening (D-Alaska) and Gaylord Nelson (D-Wis.). Said Nelson, in announcing his opposition, "The support in the Congress for this measure is clearly overwhelming. Obviously you need my vote less than I need my conscience." During the debate, none of the three senators explicitly called on Johnson to pull out the U.S. forces already in Vietnam, though that seemed to be their underlying logic. Significantly, Senator Mansfield reflected on the speeches of most dovish senators, pointing out and even emphasizing that no one "at any time during this debate . . . has advocated withdrawal."[132]

Senator Joseph Clark (D-Pa.) decried the Vietnam policies of the Eisenhower, Kennedy, and Johnson administrations but called them "past facts . . . the stakes are too high to back out now." Clark voted aye. Most senators unambiguously supported the resolution. Senator John Tower (R-Tex.) said, "For the sake of future peace, we resist tyranny today, and for the sake of future peace, I support our President in the actions he has thus far taken to thwart communism's advance." The final vote was 88 to 3. Those in favor included senators Church, Kennedy (Edward and Robert), McCarthy, and Mansfield. Richard Russell was ill on the day of the vote.[133]

In the House, the proportions were the same, with a vote of 418 in favor and 7 against. Representative John Conyers (D-Mich.) warned his colleagues:

> The President has stated he already has the funds available since he can reallocate current Defense Department funds to support the war in Vietnam. In fact, only $200 million of the total request of $700 million will even be spent during the remainder of this fiscal year. This resolution is not an emergency request for funds, but rather a way of securing a vote of confidence for our policy in Vietnam . . . as the President has stated, a "yes" vote means support of the Vietnam policy. I cannot vote "yes" because I cannot support that policy.

But Republican leader Gerald Ford (R-Mich.) was far more typical in urging that the resolution be "unanimously supported" and warning that dissent in Congress or outside could lead to "a miscalculation by the enemy of the firmness of our policy and the unanimity of our people."[134]

Clearly Congress was ready to spend the money necessary to continue U.S. military policies in Indochina, but there was more uncertainty than the vote totals indicate. Legislators such as Clark and Gore were not alone in their doubts about what the future course of American policy in Indochina should be. In this they were much like a majority of the public: They did not want South Vietnam to "fall" to communism but were not entirely comfortable with the idea of going to war.

The Final Deliberations

At 11:30 on the morning of Wednesday, July 21, Johnson met in the cabinet room of the White House with a set of advisers to hear McNamara's proposal for U.S. action in Vietnam. Among those present were Rusk, Ball, McGeorge Bundy, CIA Director Admiral Raborn, former Ambassador to South Vietnam Henry Cabot Lodge (who would soon return to that post), United States Information Agency Director Carl Rowan, and Chairman of the Joint Chiefs Earle Wheeler. The secretary of defense's proposal involved increasing American personnel in Vietnam to 175,000, which was 100,000 more than previously approved troop levels. McNamara also proposed a call-up of 235,000 men in the Army Reserve and National Guard.

Cautioning participants not to leak information or even speculate about the discussion, Johnson addressed McNamara and Wheeler (who joined in making the proposal). He said that when—not if—the time came for a reserves call-up, a full defense of the reasons demanding such action would be needed.[135] Then, attacking the McNamara report for giving "no sense of victory, but rather of continuing stalemate," Johnson asked why he should "select the recommended number of troops rather than more or fewer?"

Stressing Vietcong progress and South Vietnamese defeats, Wheeler and McNamara eventually came to a key response—the 75,000 already committed to Vietnam were "just enough to protect the bases—it will let us lose slowly instead of rapidly. The extra men will stabilize the situation and improve it. . . . There is no major risk of catastrophe."

"But you will lose greater numbers of men," rejoined Johnson.

Wheeler's response was, "The more men we have, the greater the likelihood of smaller losses."

But what, said Johnson, "makes you think if we put in 100,000 men, Ho Chi Minh won't put in another 100,000?"

"This means greater bodies of men," said Wheeler, "which will allow us to cream them."

With slight variations, all advisers at the meeting endorsed the McNamara-Wheeler-Westmoreland proposal, except George Ball. Johnson himself sent out conflicting signals, saying at one point, "I feel we have very little alternative to what we are doing." He clearly recognized that he was getting close to the point of no return, but he indicated that he wasn't there just yet: "I don't think we have made a full commitment." Another time, assuming temporarily that the United States would stay in Vietnam at *some* level, he voiced a priority that undoubtedly made Wheeler squirm: "Our mission should be as limited as we dare make it."

Seeking the group's consensus and finding Ball in opposition, Johnson listened to his most dovish formal foreign policy adviser warn him to take stiff medicine in the short run rather than worse medicine later. "Cutting our losses" and accepting the risk of a communist Southeast Asia was better than the "almost irresistible" movement toward a long, large, and probably unwinnable war. Johnson then offered the under secretary of state the chance to take the floor later that day.

In the meantime, McNamara resumed a defense of his proposal. Here the secretary of defense tried to be less ambiguous about the dilemma Johnson faced. He warned that the Vietcong had the "capability to push ARVN out of positions they now control with a consequent inevitable takeover of the government." He would not recommend that Johnson keep troop numbers at the then current level. Muddling through would no longer work. We have to "increase our forces or get out." Wheeler agreed, and then to make the picture more bleak, he warned Johnson that the 100,000 additional troops might not be sufficient to do the job. With those unappetizing conclusions, the meeting broke for lunch.[136]

An hour and forty-five minutes later, Ball took the floor for one of his last stands, warning Johnson and the others in the strongest possible language that increasing the U.S. military commitment would be disastrous. It would be long and protracted, he said, "because a great power cannot beat guerrillas." Knowing Johnson's fears well, Ball zeroed in on the president's reluctance to be held responsible for the fall of South Vietnam if he pulled out. "Every great captain in history is not afraid to make a tactical withdrawal if conditions are unfavorable to him." And conditions were just that. Sending in more troops would be "like giving cobalt treatments to a terminal cancer case." Ball then outlined his previously stated scenario for putting reformist proposals to the South Vietnamese government that it undoubtedly would reject. The result he suggested would be a South Vietnamese request for Americans to stop meddling in their affairs and get out. Here Ball did not engage in easy indifference about the fate of South Vietnam after a U.S. withdrawal: "I have no illusions that after we were asked to leave, South Vietnam would be under Hanoi's control." But under Johnson's questioning about the effect of withdrawal on the United States' credibility — "breaking the word of three presidents" — Ball insisted that the "worse blow would be that the mightiest power in the world is unable to defeat guerrillas."

Others rejoined the debate, attacking Ball's proposition. Said McGeorge Bundy, it "would be a radical switch without evidence that it should be done. It goes in the face of all we have said and done. . . . The world, the country, and the Vietnamese would have alarming reactions if we got out." Rusk added, "If the communist world finds out we will not pursue our commitment to the end, I don't know where they will stay their hand." And though Johnson had given indications that he shared Ball's worries about heavy American casualties, Rusk insisted, "We can't worry about massive casualties when we say we can't find the enemy. I don't see great casualties unless the Chinese come in." Henry Cabot Lodge added, "I can't be as pessimistic as Ball."[137]

That night, pondering what he had heard, Johnson read a memorandum from Horace Busby, a longtime personal aide who had joined the day's deliberations. Rusk had assessed "the stakes in Vietnam more precisely and convincingly than anyone I have heard," he told Johnson. But Ball was "impressively clear-headed . . . conscientious, not a critic . . . his argument is not the argument of the academic intellectuals—it is much more sane and sound, and merits respect as such." Although seeming to accept Rusk's logic, Busby cautioned Johnson: "What we are considering is not whether we continue a war—but whether we start (or have started) a new war. . . . This is no longer South Vietnam's war. We are no longer advisers. . . . The war is ours. We are the participants."[138]

The next day, July 22, Clark Clifford joined Johnson, McNamara, Vance, and McGeorge Bundy as the Joint Chiefs of Staff and the civilian heads of each branch of the military gave their views on escalation. Johnson opened the session by telling them that there were three options: (1) "leave the country—with as little loss as possible—the 'bugging out' approach," (2) "maintain present forces and lose slowly," and (3) "add 100,000 men, recognizing that they may not be enough, and adding more next year." There were disadvantages to the third approach, he said— "the risk of escalation, casualties will be high—[it] may be a long war without victory."

The response to Johnson by one admiral was typical of the group: "If we continue the way we are it will be a slow, sure victory for the other side. By putting more men in it will turn the tide and let us know what further we need to do. I wish we had done this long before."

"But you don't know if 100,000 will be enough," said Johnson. "What makes you conclude that if you don't know where we are going— and what will happen—we shouldn't pause and find this out?"

"Sooner or later, we'll force them to the conference table," said the admiral.

Secretary of the Navy Paul Nitze warned Johnson that "the shape of the world will change" if South Vietnam went to the communists. But when Johnson asked what were the chances of success, Nitze's answer was about 60/40.

Perhaps with Busby and Ball on his mind, Johnson asked the group, "Doesn't it really mean if we follow Westmoreland's requests, we are in a new war—this is going off the diving board?"

McNamara agreed that it would be a "major change in U.S. policy."

Then how about getting "out of there and mak[ing] our stand somewhere else?" said Johnson.

That would be the "least desirable alternative," said one general. The best option was to get in and get the job done.

"But I don't know how we are going to get that job done," said the president. "There are millions of Chinese. I think they are going to put their stack in. Is this the best place to do this? We don't have the allies we had in Korea." And so it went through the early afternoon hours.

One general was more pessimistic than others present about how long it would take to prevail militarily if there were no early peace agreement: "How long will it take? Five years, plus 500,000 troops. I think the American people will back you."

But the specter of China in the Korean War hung over Johnson, who reminded those present, "China has plenty of divisions to move in, don't they?"

"Yes, they do," said one of the generals.

"Then what would we do," said Johnson, cornering the general.

A long silence followed before the military leader responded, "If so, we have another ball game."

The president interrupted one speaker to warn those present, "Remember, they're going to write stories about this like they did the Bay of Pigs — and about my advisers." Asking McGeorge Bundy to summarize for the group the views he had been hearing from Ball, Mansfield, and other doves, Johnson prefaced the national security adviser's report with the comment, "Some congressmen and senators think we are going to be the most discredited people in the world. What Bundy will now tell you is not his opinion nor mine — I haven't taken a position yet — but what we hear." Once again, the antiescalation argument was heard: "For ten years every step we have taken has been based on a previous failure. All we have done has failed and caused us to take another step which failed."[139]

Later in the afternoon, meeting with another group that included McNamara, Clifford, Ball, Rusk, and nine others, Johnson sounded more like a president convinced that escalation was necessary. Perhaps the military leadership had impressed him, for Johnson spoke easily of a "basic objective . . . to preserve the independence and freedom of Vietnam." Yet later in the meeting he mulled over the three alternatives available to him again: "Sit and lose slowly, get out, put in what needs to go in." He seemed increasingly convinced that a middle road — applying military pressure (but less than the military leadership suggested) while pursuing a negotiated settlement (but more aggressively than in the past) — would work: "We have got to keep peace proposals going. It's like a prizefight. Our right is our military power, but our left must be our peace proposals. Every time you move troops forward, you move diplomats forward. I want this done. The generals want more and more, and go farther and farther. But State [Department] has to supply me with some, too."

But whatever confidence Johnson felt that afternoon did not last. Clifford had been with him for hours of discussion, keeping his opinions to himself in group settings. Now, with a predominantly civilian group of advisers present, Clifford spoke at Johnson's request. The occasion was recalled by Ball: "Presenting his argument with elegant precision and structure as though arguing a case before the Supreme Court, Clifford voiced strong opposition to the commitment of combat forces. He put forward the same arguments I had made the day before; in addition, he gave the President a more authoritative assessment of the probable domestic consequences."

Ball did not know then whether Johnson was surprised by Clifford's comments. (The president presumably was not, since he had seen Clifford's views on paper. Privately, Clifford told Johnson that day, "Some of what General Wheeler said today was ridiculous. . . . I am bearish about this whole exercise. I know what pressure you're under from McNamara and the military, but if you handle it carefully, you don't have to commit yourself and the nation."[140]) But Ball recognized a "formidable comrade on my side of the barricades" when he saw one:

> When the meeting was over, I asked Clifford to join me in the Fish Room. I told him that ever since the fall of 1961, I had been making the same arguments he now made so eloquently, and I gave him copies of the memoranda I had submitted to the President. The next day [July 23] Clifford told me that he had spent the previous evening until two in the morning carefully studying my memoranda. They were, he said, "impressive and persuasive." Throughout the last year he had come more and more to my opinion as he continued to receive reports of our deteriorating situation.
>
> I told Clark that judging from the meeting we had just had that day with the President, his intervention had had a salutary effect. Clifford replied that he had been told through "another source" that there would have to be a great effort made if we were to block this critical escalatory step that would change the character of the war. Though he hoped that through our combined exertions we could make progress, he was not optimistic.[141]

Clifford's pessimism that day was matched by Johnson's painful uncertainty. Coming out of one Vietnam meeting that day, the president complained to White House aide Jack Valenti, "All these recommendations seem to be built on a pretty soft bottom. Everything blurs when you get almost to the gate."[142]

On July 23, Mike Mansfield weighed in with another detailed memo to Johnson. Aware that the president might call up the reserves and ask Congress for a new Tonkin Gulf–style resolution, Mansfield warned him away from such a vote: "There will be more opposition than heretofore, more votes against such a resolution and more difficulty ahead. The divisiveness, moreover, is likely to affect other aspects of the Great

Society Program." And he warned Johnson that if American forces were increased, 200,000 to 300,000 would not be enough to do the job: "In my opinion, a figure of one million, if this situation continues to develop as it has, could be considered conservative."[143] As Jack Valenti wrote in a memo after these first couple of days of meetings, "the options are so narrow, and the choices are so barren."[144]

Despite a pessimism similar to Mansfield's about where U.S. policy was heading, Clark Clifford kept up his argument over the following weekend. At Camp David, with Johnson, the secretary of defense, and a few others present, he blasted the optimism of McNamara. Clifford recalls, "I put more passion into what I was saying than in any presentation I had ever made to a president." He said: "I don't believe we can win in South Vietnam. If we send in 100,000 more, the North Vietnamese will meet us. If the North Vietnamese run out of men, the Chinese will send in volunteers. Russia and China don't intend for us to win the war. If we don't win, it is a catastrophe. If we lose 50,000 plus [lives] it will ruin us. Five years, billions of dollars, 50,000 men, it is not for us." What was the alternative to that? Negotiate our way out, said one political pro to the other: "At the end of monsoon, quietly probe and search out with other countries — by moderating our position — to allow us to get out." Otherwise, warned Clifford, he could not see "anything but catastrophe for my country."[145] After the session, the usually extroverted Johnson was in an uncharacteristically introspective mood. Recalls Clifford, "He drove around the Camp David area alone for an hour; then, for another hour, also alone."[146]

Clifford captured Johnson's mood in a meeting the next day: "We are in a paradox. On one hand, we are ready to meet commitments, but we are really ready to get out." The comment reflected a hope that by going in with 100,000 troops, the United States could cause the North Vietnamese and Vietcong to stop fighting and come to the negotiation table ready to drop their goal of a unified Vietnam, thus allowing the United States to both "meet commitments" and "get out." But Clifford himself still belonged in the ranks of the doubters. He told Johnson and others present, "We cannot win the war in South Vietnam. China and Russia don't intend for us to win the war. They will match us in manpower. No matter how many men we send, they will match us."[147]

Noting Clifford's efforts plus those of Mansfield and Fulbright, George Ball had hope that week that their views might "turn the balance . . . [but] as the whole world now knows, we did not carry the day — neither Mansfield, Clifford, Fulbright, nor I — and the balloon went up farther and farther."[148]

When Johnson called in congressional leaders on July 27 to tell them of his decision, all spoke out in favor of it, with one exception. In the presence of his colleagues and Johnson, Mike Mansfield said that the president was making (and they were supporting) an ill-fated decision. "I would not be true to my conscience," he said, "to the people I represent or to my oath, if I did not, now, in the confidence of this room, make known to you my feelings on this matter. I would not want it said that the opportunity was offered and that it was met with silence on my part. This decision appears to have a certain inevitability in the light of other decisions going back months and years." But Mansfield then insisted, "We do not owe this present government in Saigon anything."[149]

The July 28 Announcement

Prophetic as the words of Ball, Clifford, Russell, Humphrey, Fulbright, Mansfield, and other less consistent doubters were, and despite their access to the president, they were still in the minority. The majority was represented by McNamara's scenario of falling dominoes if the United States got out of Vietnam: "Laos, Cambodia, Thailand, Burma . . . [it would] surely affect Malaysia. In two to three years Communist domination would stop there, but the ripple effect would be great — Japan, India. We would have to give up some bases. Ayub [Khan, President of Pakistan] would move closer to China. Greece, Turkey would move to a neutralist position. Communist agitation would increase in Africa."[150]

McNamara's words now seem anachronistic to some, but they were quite orthodox then. A sample of this orthodoxy comes from Henry Kissinger's account (for McGeorge Bundy) of a late June meeting with former West German Chancellor Adenauer. When Adenauer complained that Vietnam was a disaster because it turned the United States away from the "decisive area" of the world — Europe — Kissinger (then a Harvard professor and sometime foreign policy consultant) told Adenauer that "we were defending Europe in South East Asia."[151]

Not all arguments for or against U.S. escalation in Vietnam have been recited here. Others undoubtedly spoke impassioned words (not reflected by archival records) of advice to Johnson on Vietnam.[152] Still, the main currents of advice over the first half of 1965 have been traced. To those who have studied the July decision by looking primarily at Johnson's interactions with formal foreign policy advisers, the advisory system appears too narrow. Innumerable writers have described George Ball as the only adviser against escalation "used" or "domesticated" by Johnson. These assertions are untrue, and just as importantly, the assumption that Johnson's advisory system was confined to a small group of like-minded officials is mistaken. (Whether Johnson's war cabinet, the

Tuesday Lunch Group—not yet a regular institution in early 1965—was a small, like-minded group by 1967 is a question for the coming pages.)[153] This chapter's narrative of Johnson's interactions with over a dozen advisers describes a president who reached beyond the formal lines of his administration.

Procedurally, relations among Johnson's advisers were usually collegial, but despite the politeness, many meetings concerned absolutely fundamental disagreements over the administration's future goals in Indochina. Russell, Ball, and others thought that McNamara promoted dangerous policies and was downright hostile to their views. Said Mansfield to Johnson of McNamara and other pro-escalation advisers, "I think it is about time you got an accounting from those who have pressured you in the past to embark on this course and continue to pressure you to stay on it. It is time to ask . . . where does it lead in the end?" Ball thought that Johnson was probably too impressed with advisers like McNamara and McGeorge Bundy. Johnson, he adds, "didn't want to make this decision. He was always a very reluctant fellow, but he always got kind of dragged along, kicking and screaming. . . . The impetus toward escalation never came from Lyndon Johnson, I can assure you." McNamara and Rusk thought that Ball's views and those of other anti-escalation advisers needed to be kept secret—expressed only in small meetings—lest word get out that such views existed in the administration.[154] Meanwhile, Bill Moyers, sharing Johnson's fears and inclinations about Vietnam, funneled relatively dovish advice to Johnson. There were, in short, strong competitive elements in Johnson's Vietnam advisory system in the spring and summer of 1965.

On July 28, at midday, Johnson called a news conference to announce the decision coming out of his deliberations:

> I have asked the commanding general, General Westmoreland, what more he needs to meet this mounting aggression. He has told me. We will meet his needs. I have today ordered to Vietnam the Air Mobile Division and certain other forces which will raise our fighting strength from 75,000 to 125,000 men almost immediately. Additional forces will be needed later, and they will be sent as requested. . . . I do not find it easy to send the flower of our youth, our finest young men, into battle. . . . I think I know too how their mothers weep and how their families sorrow.[155]

Finally, Johnson decided against mobilizing the reserves, the supporting action toward which, according to the Vance cable and other sources, he had been leaning. It has been widely and plausibly reported that Johnson thought that mobilization or explicit predictions of the long-term costs of the war would divide Congress and public opinion at a time when he was trying to move major domestic reform legislation through the legislature.[156]

Johnson's decision was greeted mostly with acclaim. The prevailing reaction was that he had acted with moderation, sending in enough troops to keep South Vietnam alive but not putting the United States in a full-fledged war status.[157] Richard Russell, however, publicly parted company with Johnson in a television interview in Georgia three days after the president's troop announcement. South Vietnam, he said, had "no strategic value for the United States." He added that the United States would be right in pulling out of South Vietnam if its government did not want to fight and questioned whether the war would be worth the billions of dollars it would cost. Then Russell delivered what must have seemed to Johnson an almost heretical opinion: He said that if a plebiscite were held in South Vietnam to choose a leader, Ho Chi Minh would win "hands down."[158]

In criticizing Johnson, Russell was in the minority, of course. Some weeks later, when Republicans in Congress objected to the president's claim that his Vietnam policies were rooted in commitments made in the Eisenhower era, Eisenhower would not criticize Johnson. In an awkward phone conversation, House minority whip Gerald Ford pleaded with the former president not to "undercut" congressional Republicans, but Eisenhower told Ford and other Republicans on the line that he had always made it his business to "keep still while we are in a condition of crisis."[159]

Contrary to much that has been written in the intervening years, Johnson's "ego, stubbornness, and pride" did not prevent him from being attentive to those opposing escalation. A president who was sometimes convinced that he would "sink slowly to the bottom of the sea" whichever way he turned in Vietnam was not impervious to the arguments of Clifford, Russell, Ball, Mansfield, Humphrey, and the rest. George Ball says flatly, "I was listened to." Indeed, at times the president was taken with their arguments that escalation would lead to disaster. As William Bundy says, for Johnson and those advising him on Indochina, there was "a dark and lowering sky, and there was no pretense that it was otherwise."

There need be no mystery about *why* Johnson paid attention to the doves in his advisory system: They spoke to him about a crucial decision of his presidency, one that might determine his place in history. Unfortunately, for those who consider U.S. intervention in Indochina to have been a mistake, Johnson was also taken with and ultimately followed a logic that he shared (most of the time) with a majority of his advisers. It is there to see in *The Vantage Point*, where Johnson recites the premises and conclusions of a domino theory urged on him by McNamara, Rusk, Acheson, and many others. He then refers to the assault by antiescalation advisers on the "chain of conclusions" derived from the prevailing version of the domino theory. Of these latter men, Johnson wrote, none had given him "facts or arguments that broke or even weakened this chain of conclusions."[160] From this assessment of the arguments surrounding him ensued a tragedy of immense proportions for Southeast Asia and the United States.

3 | 1967: Waist Deep

FOR LYNDON JOHNSON, 1967 was a year of tumbling presidential approval ratings, riots in northern cities, increasingly frequent antiwar demonstrations, and widespread uncertainty about the war in Southeast Asia. Lady Bird Johnson recorded in her diary how a family dinner with some friends and three close White House aides present must have felt to her husband:

> It's strange. You feel soothed and happy by the companionship of your daughter and your son-in-law, and the fine young people who are their friends and the members of your staff. And the cool, brisk, shiny beauty of the day. But simultaneously, you are way down and grieved, emotionally wearied by the troubles that you must try to solve—the growing virus of the riots, the rising lists of Vietnam casualties, criticism from your own friends, or former friends, in Congress—and most of the complaining is coming from Democrats.[1]

For General Maxwell Taylor, a foreign policy consultant to the president, 1967 was a year in which "both sides slugged it out" in Vietnam, with "the enemy getting very much the worst of it." For lonely war critic Senator Wayne Morse, it was a time when "So many of my colleagues tell me, in the cloakroom and elsewhere, that they disagree with that [Vietnam] policy, yet they come on the floor and vote to carry on that policy."[2]

For many who have chronicled the American experience in Vietnam, 1967 is an "in between" year given little attention.[3] In part, that is because the U.S. war effort did not greatly change that year. The vast logistics of the U.S. military were in place, with 389,000 American troops in Vietnam when the year began and roughly 485,000 there at year's end. American casualties were growing (combat fatalities stood at 6,000 at the beginning of the year and were up to 15,000 by the end of 1967), but again there was a depressing sameness to that news.[4] The bombing of North Vietnam was heavy, but (to the distress of military leaders) it was an off and on affair. In short, 1967 lacked the sort of dramatic events that occurred in 1964 (the Gulf of Tonkin incident and

Resolution), 1965 (the massive escalation of troop levels and bombing campaigns), or 1968 (the Tet Offensive).

It may be that relatively little attention has been given to this part of the war because many documents written in 1967 are *still* classified by the federal government.[5] This may have steered analysts away from a period of passionate disagreement in the country and the Johnson administration over Vietnam. But one cannot understand the war or, more particularly, Johnson's Vietnam advisory system without understanding something of that period: A careful study of the opinions, analyses, and arguments in the White House and American society at that time reveals an important dimension in the history of the United States' attempt to secure an independent South Vietnam. Where 1965 saw an administration struggling over what its goal should be in Southeast Asia, and 1968 saw that goal's worthiness called into question, the goal was set and was relatively noncontroversial in 1967.[6] The deep controversy that year concerned the costly means to that end.

Conflicting published interpretations of the Johnson White House in 1967 serve as a useful reference point. Arthur Schlesinger writes of Lyndon Johnson that year that he was, "massive and immovable in the White House," joining the Joint Chiefs of Staff in pushing relentlessly "to escalate the war." Another interpreter, David Humphrey, describes Johnson seeking "advisory meetings that included individuals not present at the [Tuesday] luncheons."[7] This chapter will show that in the spring and summer of 1967, the Johnson White House was hostile to the idea of a quick withdrawal from Vietnam—like most of the country, most of Congress, and even most "doves" of the time. But Johnson was not sealed off from war dissenters or from evidence that his handling of the war inspired profound national uncertainty.

This chapter focuses on the controversy that swirled around a mid-March 1967 request by General Westmoreland for a significant increase in the number of troops in Vietnam. Because most advisers who staked out their positions on that request linked the issue to the bombing of North Vietnam, I examine that controversy as well. But first I turn to the United States' political environment at the time of Westmoreland's now mostly forgotten escalation proposal.

The Congress

The Ninetieth Congress was very Democratic, comprising 248 Democrats to 187 Republicans in the House and 64 Democrats to 36 Republicans in the Senate. But this Congress was not as responsive to Johnson as the Eighty-ninth had been, especially in domestic affairs. In foreign policy it was relatively cooperative, if grudgingly so. The legislature's most direct responsibility for the Vietnam War was in voting whether to fund it. In the weeks preceding General Westmoreland's request for up to 200,000 additional soldiers in Vietnam, Congress debated a bill appropriating over $12 billion to the Department of Defense for continued military operations in Vietnam. This was the third year in a row in which Congress was asked to provide supplemental monies for the war.

Many members of the House of Representatives had doubts about the war in early 1967, but these usually did not translate into votes against the war. Most doves did not favor American withdrawal from Vietnam. Instead they urged Johnson toward negotiations and generally distrusted administration claims that it *was* trying to arrange peace talks. These members typically saw a unilateral halt of U.S. bombing of North Vietnam as the key to a peace settlement. In retrospect, it is clear that neither the Americans nor the North Vietnamese were willing to trade away their goals for South Vietnam in negotiations.[8] Nor did bombing halts provide a quick path to peace. But these limited actions were the aims of most dovish legislators.

Members of Congress who considered voting against the Vietnam appropriation faced a tough political obstacle — the charge that such a vote would signify a lack of "support" for the soldiers in Vietnam. Among those facing this dilemma was Congressman Jonathan Bingham (D-N.Y.), who was convinced that Lyndon Johnson was a prisoner of hawkish advisers. The White House hawk of greatest notoriety, national security adviser Walt Rostow, helped arrange a meeting between Bingham and the president four days before the House vote and advised Johnson to stress his openness toward a negotiated settlement and to let Bingham talk. The result: Bingham expressed "respect" for those trying to stop funding of the war but voted for the appropriation "with grave reservations." He criticized Johnson's war policies before the House but added, "the intransigent nature of recent statements emanating from Hanoi, particularly Ho Chi Minh's reply to the Pope's appeal for peace, gives substance to the view that Hanoi is not interested in serious negotiations."[9]

But Congressman Donald Fraser (D-Minn.) voted against the appropriation because, he said, "The U.S. government is not dealing with the realities of Vietnam, but with self-manufactured myths." Another war critic, Congressman George Brown (D-Calif.) was the only House member to offer a floor amendment to the bill. It would have prohibited an invasion of North Vietnam with U.S. ground forces without a congressional declaration of war. The amendment would, he claimed, determine "if this Congress at long last is willing to take one responsible step in the direction of applying some sort of limit or guide on our involvement in Vietnam." The amendment lost by a vote of 123 to 2.

The appropriations bill was managed on the floor by Congressman George Mahon (D-Tex.), chairman of the Appropriations Committee. He spoke for the overwhelming majority of House members who supported the Johnson administration's stated goals in Vietnam. For these legislators there was no question of how they would vote, even if they had some misgivings about Johnson's conduct of the war. Mahon said that Brown's effort gave "aid and comfort to those in Hanoi who are holding out against settlement of the controversy at the peace table." The political logic of Mahon's argument was widely shared — to vote against the bill was tantamount to abandoning American boys in Vietnam. On March 16, the House passed HR 7123, 385 to 11. Of the House members voting to stop funding the war, one was a Republican, the rest Democrats.[10] All had previous credentials as antiwar members of Congress.

More complex maneuvers to influence the president's conduct of the war occurred in the Senate. Among its members were dozens of Johnson's former colleagues, some still friends, others his political enemies. Chief among the latter were Robert Kennedy, whom Johnson suspected would seek the Democratic presidential nomination in 1968, and J. William Fulbright, the one-time Johnson friend who now personified Senate opposition to Johnson war policies. Also in the Senate was Richard Russell (D-Ga.), who had become an important advocate of "unleashing" the military once Johnson sent combat soldiers to Southeast Asia in 1965. And there were a few unambiguous doves who challenged fellow legislators to stop appropriations for the conflict. Wayne Morse insisted, "Only when Congress begins to use its check of the purse strings on the President of the United States will we stop the killing of American boys in southeast Asia. . . . If I thought that a vote against this appropriation this afternoon would in any way jeopardize the security of a single American solder in Vietnam in the immediate future, I would vote for the appropriation."[11]

Although some who said "stop the war" meant just that, the position of most Senate war critics was ambiguous. Senator Joseph Clark (D-Pa.) spoke of an "obligation" to appropriate money to support the troops, even while "pointing out day after day and week after week . . . the folly of the escalation of the war in Vietnam." Clark's position put him uncomfortably close to the arguments of hawks such as Republican Senator John Tower of Texas, who cast his vote to support "the men who are risking their lives daily." Tower considered it "inadvisable" for the Senate to debate war policy when dealing with appropriations questions.[12]

Three Senators dominated the Senate's Vietnam debate in early 1967: J. William Fulbright, Mike Mansfield, and Richard Russell. It was widely perceived by those in and out of the Senate and in the White

House that Russell's support was particularly crucial to Johnson.[13] The White House worried and Senate doves hoped that Russell would become so fed up with the war that he would join those seeking a congressional end to the fighting. During debate in late February and into March, references to "the Senator from Georgia" were frequent and deferential as the Senate moved toward the war appropriation vote in March. Engaging Russell in a colloquy over the legal and constitutional basis of President Johnson's authority to wage war, Fulbright referred to Russell's reputation as a Senate authority on constitutional history and his leadership of Appropriations and Armed Services, the two committees most responsible for Vietnam funding: "If the Senator from Georgia could be persuaded to share my views, and so state them, this in itself could well bring about a change in the policy of this administration." Fulbright courted Russell during this time by telephone, by mail, and in private, suggesting that their mutual cooperation would "help the atmosphere here on the hill which gets pretty ugly at times." But Russell could see no practical alternative to military escalation to hasten the war's end.[14] It would be dishonorable and dangerous to the United States' world leadership simply to pull out of Vietnam, he believed, given the commitment made in 1965.

Russell's support of the war came in the ironic context of his having long lamented the "slow erosion of congressional power." But he taunted those who favored U.S. withdrawal from Vietnam with an option he would not support and they feared to choose—revoking the Tonkin Resolution. In 1966, he had said, "I cannot plead ignorance. I knew that the joint resolution conferred a vast grant of power upon the President. It is written in terms that are not capable of misinterpretation, and about which it is difficult to become confused." Responding to Fulbright and others, Russell added, "Personally, I would be ashamed to say that I did not realize what I was voting for when I voted for that joint resolution."[15]

In 1967 he again rebuked those who would limit the number of troops Johnson could commit to Southeast Asia and reminded them that they could take *real* action to stop the war, if they desired: "We can adopt a concurrent resolution terminating the authority in the previous [Tonkin] resolution." However, that was a step that war critics continued to reject. Fulbright considered such a step impractical. Thus, while he employed acid words to describe U.S. policy in Vietnam, Fulbright rejected Wayne Morse's plea that the Senate fulfill its constitutional responsibility by using "its check of the purse strings on the President of the United States [to] . . . stop the killing of American boys in southeast Asia." Instead, Fulbright answered Russell's call for senators to "provide the materiel and equipment needed by our gallant men who are doing the fighting and dying thousands of miles from home."[16]

Mike Mansfield also rejected Morse's approach. The Senate majority leader saw voting for Vietnam appropriations as a nonpolitical act, significant only in that it provided the materiel necessary to support troops already fighting a war. Distressed since before the Johnson presidency over U.S. policy in Southeast Asia, Mansfield nonetheless believed in presidential primacy in foreign affairs. Congress must be a discerning partner in foreign affairs, he said on March 13, but "it is the President . . . who makes the fundamental decisions of foreign policy."[17] As a "discerning partner," Mansfield proposed an amendment to the appropriations bill that declared the Senate's "firm intentions to provide all necessary support for members of the Armed Forces of the United States fighting in Vietnam"; "its support of efforts being made by the President of the United States and other men of good will throughout the world to prevent an expansion of the war in Vietnam"; and "its support of the Geneva accords of 1954 and 1962 and [urged] the convening of that Conference."

In defending the amendment, Mansfield was conciliatory toward the president. Johnson, he once noted, had examined all his proposals regarding Vietnam and had "listened to advice from many sources, including the Senate." Fulbright distrusted Mansfield's relationship with the president, who provided Mansfield with inside information on the war. Once, in early 1967, Johnson met with Mansfield and Senate minority leader Dirksen, showing them a cable concerning possible peace feelers from North Vietnam. He told the senators, "They want secrecy and I don't want anybody in our government to know about it, except the two [diplomats] that are doing it and you two. . . . I cannot tell Fulbright what is in this cable." Mansfield also gave Johnson information on activities within the Foreign Relations Committee. The net result, in Fulbright's view, was that Mansfield's war opposition was co-opted—he was "Johnson's alter ego."[18]

The debate on the Senate floor over the innocuous Mansfield amendment was confused and confusing. Its significance appears only in contrast to Senator Joe Clark's amendment, which would have required a formal declaration of war by Congress for the president to escalate troop levels beyond the 500,000 mark. Clark's amendment was withdrawn from consideration when its poor prospects set up the unattractive possibility that a decisive vote against it would appear to give unqualified support to Johnson's war policies. Senators of various stripes wanted to avoid that. Only senators Ernest Gruening (D-Alaska) and Gaylord Nelson (D-Wis.) supported Wayne Morse's view that voting for the appropriation signified voting "for an escalation of this war [which] is going to kill increasing numbers of American boys." The appropriations bill, Mansfield amendment intact, passed 77 to 3.[19] The amendment, later accepted in an overwhelming House vote, was the first official sense-of-Congress statement on the war since the Tonkin Resolution.

The other prominent Senate event in the weeks before the Westmoreland troop request was Senator Robert Kennedy's speech on March 2. Stop the bombing, said Kennedy, announce a readiness to negotiate, and halt further military escalations if the communists agree to do so as well. Although almost two dozen senators had previously urged a bombing halt, it was Kennedy whom Johnson most feared and whose plan to end the war gained the most press attention.[20] More than two weeks *before* the speech, the *New York Times* reported, "RFK Sets Major Speech on Bombing." Johnson anticipated Kennedy's proposal—Kennedy had given the president his ideas in early February. The meeting was not pleasant. Kennedy told his assistants that Johnson had been "abusive" toward him. *Time* magazine reported the unlikely story that Kennedy had called Johnson a "son of a bitch" to his face.[21]

The speech itself seems mild in retrospect. There was no call for unilateral withdrawal; in fact, Kennedy said that the United States should stay in Southeast Asia until its commitments were achieved.[22] But Johnson had Richard Russell called off the Senate floor to take his telephone call about the Kennedy speech. Russell made a note after the call, which he took in the Senate cloakroom: "Talked—Re Viet Nam Kennedy speech—wanted me to reply—I saw nothing new in the speech or worthy of my involvement." Another note, apparently made during the phone call itself, reads: "Wanted me to engage R. Kennedy in debate over V. N." Following cryptic summaries of Johnson's verbal list of all the things he had done to try to bring Ho Chi Minh to the peace table, Russell summarized the close of the phone conversation with, "on Kennedy suggestion, turned down."[23] That is, Russell declined the president's plea to confront Kennedy in the Senate.

Although Russell did not want to respond, others did for the president. Kennedy's old friend Senator Henry Jackson (D-Wash.) asserted that the speech put the United States in a weaker position. Republican leader Everett Dirksen said that it served to make the communists "think we don't mean it." Dean Rusk added his public reaction: "proposals substantially similar to those put forward by Senator Kennedy were explored prior, during, and since the [1967] Tet truce—all without result."[24] Privately, Johnson asked Rusk and McNamara to assess Kennedy's ideas. Rusk wrote to the president, "The main difficulty with the Kennedy proposals is that Hanoi has made it clear that they would strongly oppose every essential point in them. The Senator's problem, therefore, is not with us but with Hanoi." McNamara was in the ticklish position of evaluating his friend Kennedy's ideas for a president who disliked Kennedy. McNamara gave Johnson the painful assessment that "our" bombing of North Vietnam had reduced the political standing of "moderates" in Hanoi — hard-liners were thus in control of North Vietnam in 1967, and they "distrust both our statements and our motives." He suggested a unilateral suspension of the bombing of most of North Vietnam to see if that could lead to peace discussions.[25] The secretary of defense's position was almost the same as the senator's.

Johnson followed the House and Senate debates closely in his morning reading of the *Congressional Record* and in the coverage in newspapers and on the networks. If he had relied solely on vote totals and Mansfield's sense-of-Congress amendment, he might have told himself that the Senate and House were solidly behind U.S. policy in Vietnam. But neither these nor the debates that accompanied them were the only indicators of the mood of Congress on which Johnson relied. He met not just with prominent doves and hawks such as Kennedy, Morse, and Russell but with others not so powerful or well known. The president had long since laid down a crucial policy regarding Congress — an open-door policy for any member who wanted to see the president and a standard procedure of keeping any such meeting off-the-record unless other arrangements were made.[26] This was one part of the president's larger congressional liaison policy, which, according to top congressional assistant Lawrence O'Brien, meant that for the president, "Congress was a twenty-four hour a day obsession." White House aides acknowledged that meeting with war critics was not exactly fun for the president, but as one staffer wrote to another, it was important that such members of Congress "be impressed with the fact that the President is willing to listen to arguments from all sides." Therefore dovish members of Congress such as Senator Claiborne Pell (D-R.I.) and hawks including Congressman Jamie Whitten (D-Miss.) exercised their prerogative in 1967.[27]

The speeches on the floors of both houses, the votes, and the conflicting comments from hawks and doves reflected a deep congressional uncertainty about the means employed in Southeast Asia. But most members of Congress shared the administration's goal — to secure an independent, noncommunist South Vietnam.

Public Opinion

Public opinion about Vietnam, Johnson's handling of the war, and his general performance in office was mixed when 1967 began and generally became less favorable as the year went on. Richard Goodwin's impressionistic account of the year correctly describes opinion polls showing "that a majority of the country still 'supported' Johnson and the war. Yet behind the polls and precedents one could sense a growing discontent and frustration, a subtle but expanding change in the mood of the nation. Something was happening—not in Vietnam—but in America."[28]

In mid-1965, the public had approved of Johnson's handling of Vietnam by roughly a two-to-one margin. Those ratios declined appreciably during 1966. By January 1967, 43 percent disapproved of the president's management of the war, and only 38 percent approved (Table 3.1). There was a brief rise in public approval in May and June, but for the rest of the summer and fall there was another decline—from July onward slightly more than half of the public disapproved of Johnson on the Vietnam issue, and only a third approved of the president's war management.

As for his handling of the presidency itself, the verdict was more favorable, but the trends over time were not. In January, 47 percent of those surveyed approved of Lyndon Johnson's handling of his job; 37 percent did not. The president sustained roughly similar approval ratings through the first half of 1967—and even had a 52 percent approval rating after dealing with the Six Day War and meeting Soviet Premier Kosygin in June—but for most of the rest of the year his ratings slid. Disapproval outweighed approval by eight to twelve points.[29]

Table 3.1. Public Approval/Disapproval of Johnson's Handling of Vietnam in 1967 (%)

	Approve	Disapprove	No Opinion
January	38	43	19
February	39	44	17
March	37	49	14
April (early)	42	45	13
April (late)	39	45	16
May (early)	43	42	15
May (late)	38	47	15
June (early)	43	42	15
June (late)	43	43	14
July	33	52	15
August	33	54	13

Source: Gallup Opinion Index, April 1968, p. 3.

Another indicator was the "mistake" question. From August 1965 onward, the Gallup organization periodically asked respondents, "In view of the developments since we entered the fighting in Vietnam, do you think the U.S. made a mistake sending troops to fight in Vietnam?" All through 1966, a substantial majority or plurality of the American public believed that intervention in Indochina had been necessary. That view still prevailed in early 1967—in February, 52 percent thought that the United States had been correct to enter the war, and only 32 percent thought that it had been a mistake (Table 3.2).[30]

Table 3.2. Public Responses to the Question, Did the United States Make
a Mistake in Sending Troops to Vietnam? 1966–67 (%)

	Yes	No	Don't Know
November 1966	31	51	18
February 1967	32	52	16
May	37	50	13
July	41	48	11
October	46	44	10

Source: American Institute of Public Opinion, cited in John E. Mueller, *War, Presidents, and Public Opinion* (New York: Wiley, 1973), pp. 54–55.

Of course, dissatisfaction with the president's war leadership did not necessarily translate into "dovishness." In the spring of 1967, when respondents were presented with three possible options in Vietnam — continuing the present situation indefinitely, fighting a major war with thousands of American casualties, or a withdrawal of American troops leading to an eventual communist takeover in Vietnam — only 19 percent chose the withdrawal option, 39 percent thought that continuation of current policies was preferable, and 30 percent said that escalation to a "major" war was the best option. Thus 69 percent thought that the United States should secure its established goals in Southeast Asia, but there was a deep split over the means to achieve those goals.

The 19 percent of the public who thought that the United States should get out of Vietnam, even if that meant a communist takeover, had little representation in Congress or the news media. Expression of such sentiment came not from mainstream doves like Fulbright or critical news media outlets like the *New York Times* but from isolated legislators such as Morse, demonstrators, news media outlets with smaller circulations, and leftist political commentators such as Noam Chomsky. Chomsky wrote in 1967 that immediate withdrawal from Vietnam was the only "feasible" alternative and castigated those doves who criticized the war but favored a continued U.S. presence in Indochina. He could not understand how reporter Neil Sheehan of the *New York Times* could describe the U.S. strategy late in 1966 as "creating a killing machine" and then write, "Despite these misgivings, I do not see how we can do anything but continue to prosecute the war." Nor could Chomsky understand James Reston writing in 1967 that the United States was "fighting a war now on the principle that military power shall not compel South Vietnam to do what it does not want to do." And to Arthur Schlesinger's assertion that "we may all be saluting the wisdom and statesmanship of the American government" if the United States should win in Vietnam, Chomsky replied that it was "startling to see how easily the rhetoric of imperialism comes to American lips." In Chomsky's view the tragedy in Vietnam would end only when the Americans got out. Then, in his estimation, North Vietnam would probably "disengage" from South Vietnam.[31]

Lady Bird Johnson's diary, which sometimes treated the president's problems as her own, noted the restiveness evidenced in polls, Congress, and increasingly frequent demonstrations. In March, two youthful protesters threw themselves in front of the presidential car after Johnson gave a speech on Vietnam in Tennessee:

> It was all so fast we could hardly believe it. A youth broke from the thinning crowd and flung himself right in front of the car. The driver slammed on the brakes. Immediately there were officers at his side pulling him back, but suddenly a young girl threw herself more successfully flat to the ground, practically under the wheels. They were both picked up bodily and moved, and we drove on slowly. . . . I looked back and saw the young girl's naked legs—her dress around her hips, her feet held by one officer, her shoulders by another—being lifted from the road.[32]

Emissaries from Outside the White House

The president also heard from some he considered "natural leaders" of the country in the weeks preceding the Westmoreland request. The domestic controversy over U.S. bombing of North Vietnam troubled Johnson to the point that in early 1967 he directed his national security adviser to explore setting up a committee of outsiders to examine the effects and strategic value of the bombing. Probably with Johnson's blessing, Walt Rostow turned to *Clark Clifford* to discuss the idea. Still doing part-time work heading the president's Foreign Intelligence Advisory Board, Clifford's most important role was as a Democratic Party elder. Johnson respected his advice and liked to keep his advisory role out of the media spotlight. Meetings between Clifford and the president—with others present or not—were more frequent in 1967 than 1965, perhaps because, as Lady Bird Johnson wrote to Clifford, "the problems [are] more unrelenting here lately."[33]

Well aware that the bombing had taken on great symbolic importance in the national debate over Vietnam strategy, Clifford thought that setting up a formal committee would be a bad idea, impossible to keep secret, and indicate a lack of presidential confidence in regular advisers. Further, Clifford "strongly believed that this is not a subject on which a committee should make recommendations to the President. There is no substitute, in a matter of this kind, for the President's personal, lonely judgment." Instead, he recommended that Johnson have a small "non-committee committee" read cables from the bureaucracy but not file a written report to the president. They would "sit down with the President on a long evening and exchange impressions. If there were any leak, the President could then say truthfully: 'There was no committee. I talk to a great many people on a great many subjects.'" There is no record of such a noncommittee in the winter or spring of 1967, but the idea seems to have evolved into a "Wise Men's" meeting later in the year: Clifford and Rostow collaborated in the autumn, putting together a group of elders to "explore the problem of a pause" and related matters concerning Vietnam. The initiative was a response to what they understood to be a continuing desire on the part of Johnson to widen the advice he was hearing.[34]

McGeorge Bundy was another emissary from outside the White House who kept Johnson in touch with political currents. No longer serving as special assistant to the president for national security—having resigned in 1966—Bundy saw Johnson fairly often despite rumors that he had quit over disillusionment with the war. Whether or not Johnson believed such stories, he made the former national security adviser another "special consultant" for foreign affairs who occasionally attended Tuesday Lunch meetings.[35] Bundy was consulted particularly on matters relating to the Middle East, but his advisory contributions went beyond that. Before the military formally asked for troop increases and wider bombing of North Vietnam, Bundy learned of the forthcoming request and sent the president a long letter opposing both ideas as all too predictable. These proposals, he said "should be rejected and . . . as a matter of high national policy there should be a publicly stated ceiling to the level of American participation in Vietnam, as long as there is no further marked escalation on the enemy side." Bundy opposed a complete bombing halt—it would "give the Communists something for nothing"—but advised that bombing be limited to important military targets. Current bombing policies were dividing and distracting American society from "the real struggle in the South," he told Johnson. Admitting that "on the surface" it might seem cynically political, Bundy tied his arguments to the following year's presidential election campaign: "what we must plan to offer as a defense of Administration policy is not victory over Hanoi, but growing success—and self reliance—in the South . . . we can focus attention on the great and central achievement of these last two years: on the defeat we have prevented. The fact that South Vietnam has not been lost and is not going to be lost is a fact of truly massive importance in the history of Asia, the Pacific, and the U.S."[36] Johnson read the memo and passed it on to McNamara with instructions to share it with the military. General Wheeler, chairman of the Joint Chiefs, rejected Bundy's advice with language the *Pentagon Papers* called "terse and pointed."

Howard K. Smith, anchorman for ABC News, requested a meeting with Johnson for the purpose of urging him to improve the public's perception of the nation's Vietnam policies. Smith supported Johnson on Vietnam, but in a letter that preceded their meeting he told the president: "I have just returned from a lecture tour in which I devoted most of each talk to the case for Vietnam. Repeatedly at the end of a talk, people said to me, 'Why doesn't the Administration tell us that?' It does not help when I point out that in scattered statements and speeches over two years most of it has been said." In their meeting the next week, Johnson agreed that his administration had failed to reach the public, but lamented, "Nobody has tried as hard. I don't have an answer."[37]

Johnson's current and former staff members also warned him of his sinking reputation in early 1967. Speechwriter Harry McPherson told Johnson in March that his veil of secrecy around ongoing peace-seeking efforts led to a problem: "Unless we give some additional *outward* manifestations of searching for peace, we can very easily find ourselves identified along with Ky and the generals, as 'war-lovers.' . . . The impression of many people is that we are the intransigents." Jack Valenti, by then an outside adviser to Johnson, spoke of an "anti-Johnson" virus and offered the unoriginal observation, "What is needed now is to shore up contemporary public opinion so the President can have the kind of public support he needs to advance his cause."[38]

Two years after the 1965 troop decision, there were cracks in what had been solid support of Johnson's management of the war—doubts on the right and the left (and in the center) of the political spectrum. In that context, on March 20, Johnson traveled with an entourage to the island of Guam to meet with South Vietnamese leaders Thieu and Ky and his commander in Vietnam, General Westmoreland.

Westmoreland's Request

The ostensible purpose of the Guam conference was to introduce the Vietnamese to the new team Johnson had put together for the civilian side of the American effort in Vietnam. These included Ellsworth Bunker, the new ambassador to South Vietnam, and Robert Komer, new head of the high-priority "pacification" efforts in South Vietnam. David Lilienthal, the founding head of the TVA and the Atomic Energy Commission, had just been appointed by Johnson to advise South Vietnam's government on planning for postwar economic development.[39]

Johnson was proud to have Bunker, perhaps the most respected member of the diplomatic corps, and Lilienthal, an important figure in the Roosevelt and Truman administrations, on board. Besides his impressive record of service in and out of government and his impeccable humanitarian, liberal credentials, *David Lilienthal* had a rare ability to befriend people of diverse political persuasions. During the Vietnam War, he managed to retain friendships with Lyndon Johnson, J. William Fulbright, Robert Kennedy, and many others. Lilienthal took the job with mixed emotions after Johnson told him, "We have got to get this thing straightened out. It is ruining everything—NATO, everything." Lilienthal had seen presidents come and go, but he was virtually swept off his feet by Johnson at a February meeting:

> The hour and a half with President Johnson . . . resembled nothing I have ever been exposed to in as many sessions at the White House. The President's whirlwind manner I had seen before; still, I wasn't prepared at all for the tumultuous, almost visible emanations of vitality, exuberance, a sense of power . . . a flow of ideas, words, emotions, facial expressions that would tax an accomplished actor. . . . It was as prodigious an exhibition of energy and the pulling out of all the stops as I have ever seen, or expect to see.

In his journal, Lilienthal described his new position, which did not include giving military advice, as an "unappetizing job, with an absolute minimum of apparent prospects for doing something effective." But he added, "if in fact the hostilities may be within a year of ending, then a postwar planning job isn't entirely a public gesture, at this stage." Like some others in the Johnson administration, Lilienthal's work caused family problems: His son, a writer, told Lilienthal that Johnson and Rusk were overseeing an "evil" war.[40]

At Guam, the main base for the United States' B-52 bombers, the press was naturally curious to know whether an increase in troop levels was discussed. They were told little on the topic beyond a statement that military forces would be considered later, if necessary.[41] The veil of secrecy drawn by the Johnson administration around that aspect of the Guam conference has been broken at least once in General Bruce Palmer's *The Twenty-five Year War*, a careful book that is part memoir of the author's war experiences (as deputy commander of the U.S. Army in Vietnam) and part history of the conflict. His narrative reports an account of the Guam conference by Ellsworth Bunker:

> In January 1967, when President Johnson asked him to go to Saigon, the President said that Bunker's mission would be to wind up the

war for American troops as quickly as possible. The president apparently did not elaborate on what might constitute an acceptable South Vietnamese security posture which would allow U.S. troops to return home. It was a private conversation with only the two men present. Bunker's new assignment was announced just before the Guam conference. . . .

[At Guam] . . . the president clearly indicated his intentions: he would no longer go along with continuing escalation of the war by increasing U.S. troop commitments, or invading Laos or Cambodia to stop infiltration, or stepping up the bombing against North Vietnam; rather he intended to reduce the U.S. troop presence and shift the burden of the war to the South Vietnamese. According to Bunker, Westmoreland was aware of the president's intentions.[42]

Palmer adds, "Bunker's revelations to me in June 1981 threw quite a different light on the period and came as a distinct surprise."

There are other indications that Johnson was searching desperately for a way to gradually get out of Vietnam by turning over the military role to the Vietnamese. A briefing paper prepared for Johnson's use at Guam stated, "There does not appear to be any great return to be realized from further force increases," and mentioned the possibility of withdrawing 10,000 to 15,000 support personnel and up to 100,000 troops the following year if the war went well during the rest of 1967.[43] The idea of "Vietnamizing" the war had been presented to Johnson before: Prior to joining the administration full time with speechwriting and certain Vietnam-related duties, former Americans for Democratic Action (ADA) chairman *John Roche* went to Vietnam in 1966 to "sort of snoop around" on the president's behalf. Johnson told him, "I want to know, can they pull it off? What kind of options are there in the democratic development in Vietnam? . . . and I want it frankly. I want it with the bark off." Roche told him, among other things, that the U.S. presence was too large and unwieldy in South Vietnam: "It seemed to me that the only way we could do this thing in Vietnam was by getting the Viets into the action . . . the whole fundamental premise of the McNamara operation was to get the Viets off the street, run them in to sit in the balcony in box seats and watch us while we win this war."[44] Walt Rostow's memos to Johnson showed additional evidence that the president was thinking ahead and hoping for a diplomatic settlement of the war. In March 1967, the agenda for a Tuesday Lunch meeting included "the need for us to work systematically" to be prepared for cease-fire negotiations "should, by any small chance, the other side respond."[45]

While the president and some advisers had ideas on "Vietnamizing" the war, Westmoreland and his top military colleagues in Washington, the Pacific, and Saigon were dubious and dissatisfied with civilian decision-making. *William Westmoreland* confided to his diary, "There is an amazing lack of initiative in planning for the future by the higher echelons of government. There seems to be a tendency to recognize a problem and assume that it will be solved if let alone by it fading away . . . we are so sensitive about world opinion."[46] Now, at Guam, the general had his chance to insist face-to-face with the president and his men that greater Americanization was needed to win the war:

> As I see the situation, Mr. President, unless our military pressure causes the Viet Cong to crumble, or Hanoi withdraws her support, this war could go on indefinitely. It's a question of holding off the bullies from wrecking this structure that has been undermined over a period of years by the termites, and at the same time killing the termites. But we are making progress . . . we have found that we can fight the guerrilla. We can fight in the swamps. We can fight in the mountains. We can fight the Main Force. We can fight in the jungle. . . .
> [Johnson:] What signs do you see of the Viet Cong crumbling or the North Vietnamese indicating that they might not see this thing down the road for many years? Do you have any indication of either weakening?
> [Westmoreland:] Yes, sir. Well, there are several indications. First with respect to the VC, the defection rate is going up and up. But here again this is a function of military pressure.[47]

In his memoirs, Westmoreland writes,

> I provided the group with a frank review of the military situation, including my assessment of the advantage the enemy gained from pauses in the bombing of North Vietnam. Concluding my remarks, I said that if the Viet Cong organization failed to disintegrate, which I saw as unlikely, the war could go on indefinitely. As I sat down, my audience was painfully silent. On the faces of many of the Washington officials, who had obviously been hoping for some optimistic assessment, were looks of shock.[48]

Lilienthal recorded Westmoreland saying that the war could go on for 10 years without more troops and bombing. His journal caught the moment: "The look on the President's face! . . . Ten years, my god! . . . I imagined I could read the President's mind: think of the mothers of eight year old kids: could they possibly face up to that?" The president and the general seemed to be letting each other know that there were going to be hard choices in the future. Johnson took a sleeping pill that night.[49]

At the time of the Guam meeting, the military worked with a troop ceiling of 470,000 in Vietnam. Viewing that ceiling as inadequate, Westmoreland submitted two alternative troop plans to Washington:

> One plan was for what I called a "minimum essential" force; the other, for an "optimum" force. The minimum essential force, which I saw as necessary to continue and expand operations within South Vietnam . . . meant 80,500 additional troops, for a total of 550,500. The optimum force, which I saw as providing an even greater step-up of operations within South Vietnam plus an ability to take the war to the enemy in Laos and Cambodia . . . would entail an additional strength of approximately 200,000 men, for a total strength of about 670,000.[50]

For Secretary of Defense *Robert McNamara*, the Guam meeting meant that he faced another round of negotiations among military and civilian leaders in order to answer Westmoreland's proposal. By the early part of 1967, McNamara was despondent over the course of the war and the role he had played in it. He told David Lilienthal, "We have poured more bomb loads onto North Vietnam, than in the whole of World War II and yet we have no sign that it has shaken their will to resist, none." His wife was developing serious ulcers and the following summer would enter the hospital while McNamara was in Vietnam.[51] Reports of an ashen-faced secretary of defense abounded, and his public statements on the war lacked certainty. When he briefed the press after the Guam meeting, reporters weren't sure if they had heard McNamara correctly:

> In sum, the three individuals — Prime Minister Ky, General Vien, and General Westmoreland — agreed that the war could go on indefinitely unless the military pressure being imposed against the enemy forces breaks the will of the North and there is as yet no sign of that. . . .
> [Reporter:] Did you say it was agreed that the war could go on indefinitely unless military pressure breaks the will of the North, I have a feeling I missed one of your important points.
> [McNamara:] No, that is what they reported.
> [Reporter:] What does it mean? Are you going to put pressure on to break the will of the North?
> [McNamara:] I'm simply reporting to you what they said . . . the North is replacing those [its] losses and presumably will continue to replace them until they make a political decision to change their political objectives and modify their military program accordingly. . . . I didn't say we are going to increase pressure. . . .

[Reporter:] Did either you or General Westmoreland say that he believes the present level of pressure is sufficient to convince Hanoi they can't win?

[McNamara:] I don't think either of us did.[52]

Walt Rostow sent a copy of McNamara's briefing to the president, who read it and probably compared it to Rusk's more upbeat briefing: "We have had some pretty heavy fighting out there in the last few days. And I don't believe that these fellows can take, at a permanent rate, what is now happening in terms of casualties and desertions, prisoners, and shortages."

In his journal, David Lilienthal recorded, "The President understands the limitations of military action and . . . the Vietnamese across the oval table partly grasp it." He recorded no impression of Westmoreland's grasp but thought that Johnson performed magnificently, "a seasoned 'politician'—at his best, because he was functioning as a persuader."[53]

With the meeting at Guam over, the memos began to fly, and Johnson pondered his options. In a sense, the president's pressure on Westmoreland to deliver results in Vietnam had boomeranged. The general was saying that results could be achieved in two or three years *if* hundreds of thousands more soldiers were sent to Indochina.[54] Johnson, a sophisticated judge of "the art of the possible," understood the meaning of negative polls, a Congress fretting over unattractive options in Vietnam, and disapproving mail to the White House. He followed the latter by reading weekly reports from mail handlers. On March 31, flying with a number of diplomatic figures, the president startled a Latin American ambassador by showing him the latest unfavorable reflection on his leadership:

Memo to the President: Weekly Summary of the
President's mail on Vietnam—
letters—pro: 260, con: 467, comments: 152
cards—pro: 0, con: 10, comments: 0
telegrams—pro: 16, con: 30, comments: 14[55]

Johnson knew that although bombing North Vietnam might be palatable to the public, sending 200,000 more troops to Vietnam and calling up the necessary reserves would likely be a recipe for domestic political disaster. Westmoreland and other hawks would have a job on their hands trying to persuade Johnson.

Westmoreland Comes to Washington

Despite the seemingly innumerable approaches and opinions existing in U.S. government and society on the war, they all came down to a few basic options, outlined for the president by General Maxwell Taylor:

- "All out"—escalate American troop levels and bombing, call up the reserves, and refuse to soften previous negotiating stands—the option preferred by Westmoreland.
- "Stick it out"—pursue the same restricted bombing policy, keep troop levels at roughly the same or slightly higher numbers, and keep or only barely modify negotiating positions—unattractive as it was, a commonly held view in the administration and outside.
- "Pull back"—severely cut back or stop U.S. bombing of the North and develop a more conciliatory negotiating stance—the approach of Kennedy, Fulbright, McNamara, and most mainstream doves of the era.
- "Pull out"—withdraw American forces as promptly as could safely be done—advocated by staunch antiwar critics such as Morse in Congress and by some figures on the left such as Noam Chomsky.

In his memoirs, Taylor says of the pull-out option, "In 1967, there were few if any spokesmen for such a measure among men of substance in public life, and as I was unable to advance any arguments to support it, I did not include it among the alternatives worth considering."[56] But as Johnson knew, some in American society, among both the elite and the masses, advocated the pull-out position. Westmoreland traveled to Washington in April, just weeks after submitting his request, to meet Johnson, secretaries Rusk and McNamara, Walt Rostow, Senator Richard Russell, and other top officials in the capital. His visit was appropriate, given his status as chief strategist and tactician for the ground war effort.[57] But there was another reason for Westmoreland's presence—the president hoped that it would calm troubled waters at home. The general did not mind the invitation. He confidently told his diary, "Although not an expert in dealing with congressmen, I am not a neophyte."[58] Before a joint session of Congress, Westmoreland earned a standing ovation, saying, "Backed at home by resolve, confidence, patience, determination and continued support, we will prevail in Vietnam over the Communist aggressor." But the administration's motives for having Westmoreland speak to Congress and around the country came under fire. When the general said in New York that dissent in the United States gave the enemy "hope that he can win politically that which he cannot accomplish militarily," Senator George McGovern led an attack on Johnson: "In trying to imply that it is

American dissent which is causing the Vietnamese to continue the war, the administration is only confessing the weakness of its own case by trying to silence its critics and confuse the American people." Pro-Johnson senators returned fire.[59]

At a White House dinner in Westmoreland's honor, Johnson sat on one side of the general with Richard Russell on the other.[60] At another meeting, Westmoreland pushed for his "optimum" plan of adding 200,000 troops, knowing that it would require the president to do something he had resisted so far—use members of the military reserves in Vietnam. If there were no troop increases, "we would be setting up a meat grinder. We would do a little better than hold our own," he informed Johnson. Westmoreland told his diary, "The President has a very difficult decision to make as to whether or not he calls up the Reserves. I got the impression that he is in a mood to do so. However, I also got the impression that Secretary McNamara is somewhat reluctant on this score." Westmoreland later recalled how, in Johnson's presence, "McNamara wrung from me an estimate of how long it would take to 'wind down our involvement' under each of my two plans. Assuming that the air war against North Vietnam and in the Laotian panhandle would continue, I said finally: "With the optimum force, about three years; with the minimum force, at least five."[61] Westmoreland's prediction put considerable pressure on Johnson: If "only" 80,000 additional troops were sent to Vietnam, the war *might* come to a successful conclusion by 1972, the final year of Johnson's next term of office—*if* he sought reelection in 1968 and *if* he won and lived out the term. But Johnson was far from certain he would seek reelection, much less live until 1972.

General Earle Wheeler, chairman of the Joint Chiefs of Staff since 1965, supported Westmoreland's request at the White House meeting. Politically sophisticated and having Johnson's respect,[62] Wheeler watched the president interrogate Westmoreland: "When we add divisions can't the enemy add divisions? If so, where does it all end?" Westmoreland answered that the United States might have reached the "crossover point" (i.e., the point at which losses inflicted upon the communists could not be replaced by Hanoi or the Vietcong) in certain parts of South Vietnam. But when the president made what seems to be a reference to China's intervention in the Korean War—asking, "At what point does the enemy ask for volunteers?"—Wheeler must have winced, for Westmoreland's only answer was, "That is a good question."

Finally, the chairman spoke up. Supporting Westmoreland's maximum request, he urged Johnson to consider an invasion of Cambodia, Laos, and/or North Vietnam. Further, he suggested that port cities of North Vietnam be the next bombing targets. Reacting to those urging the president to stop the bombing of North Vietnam, Westmoreland then jumped in to tell Johnson that he was "dismayed at even the thought of stopping the bombing program." The president turned back to the troop request and questioned Wheeler about the minimal request: "What if we do not add the 2 and ⅓ divisions?" Wheeler predicted that the momentum gained in South Vietnam would die and that in some areas of the South the enemy would recapture the initiative. Echoing Westmoreland, he said that it would not mean military defeat for the United States, but rather a longer war. Giving no indication that he was inclined to follow the generals' advice, Johnson pressed them hard to "make certain we are getting value received from the South Vietnamese troops."[63]

Walt Rostow also joined the session, advocating a new strategy to achieve a breakthrough in Vietnam. He proposed that the United States "invade the southern part of North Vietnam in order to block infiltration routes and to hold the area hostage against North Vietnamese withdrawal from Laos and Cambodia as well as from South Vietnam."[64] Westmoreland confided to his diary that Rostow's suggestion led to awkward silences: "No one around the table, to include the President, expressed any great enthusiasm for the operation and the discussion died with only Rostow and me participating."[65]

Throughout the war Johnson feared intervention by China or the Soviet Union if he took the war into surrounding countries, so Rostow lost this round of advocacy and did not press the invasion plan again. In his view, "Johnson had an acute ear and a remarkable memory: repetition was not required." And despite his frustration with Johnson's approach to the war, Rostow rejected the idea of leaving the administration. In his view, "the positions of a President and an adviser are quite distinct. The best formulation of the problem was Rusk's. He used to say: 'If I urge a course of action on the President, he adopts it, and things go wrong, I can call up and say "Sorry, sir," resign, and disappear. The President must live with his decisions and their consequences.'" An economist and historian with prominent credentials in the academic world, Rostow had taken the job in 1966. David Lilienthal described Rostow as having a "disarmingly quick mind and imagination. . . . Walt shoots darts of ideas in all directions."[66] Rostow had not been close to Johnson before taking the national security job, having worked at less influential positions in the State Department and on the NSC staff. Now, despite whatever setbacks Rostow faced in his advocacy, he was in a position where his analyses for the president could be prefaced by the words, "I have spent some time reading literally hundreds of particular intelligence reports." As national security adviser, he actively promoted his own hawkish, optimistic views to the president but was an honest broker in routing various points of view to the president from the outside.[67]

Westmoreland also met with Dwight Eisenhower before returning to Vietnam. He recalls that "General Eisenhower told me more than once that he lamented the restrictions Washington was apparently imposing on the conduct of the war in Vietnam."[68] If Eisenhower did say this to Westmoreland, his public stance was different—he continued to refuse to criticize Johnson, even implicitly. Eisenhower told a friend that "it was clearly understood between the President and me that in domestic policies and programs, I was flatly opposed" to Johnson, but that "in all foreign problems, I was all ready to do the best I could." When, in 1966, some Republicans had urged Eisenhower to speak on war strategy, he instead called Johnson and complained, "They want me to say publicly how to win the war. I won't do it. I won't divide the United States when it needs unity. . . . I wish you to know how annoying all of this is to me." However, Eisenhower probably did prefer a more aggressive military strategy: In private he told Johnson that, once committed to war, it was "necessary to win it as quickly as possible."[69]

Another more controversial leader joined what turned out to be the largest antiwar demonstrations since the war began. With his antiwar stance newly announced, the Reverend Martin Luther King, Jr., spoke at a rally in New York in April that attracted somewhere between 100,000 and 400,000 people. On the same day, 50,000 showed up at a similar demonstration in San Francisco. And in the Senate, the Joint Economic Committee held public hearings that month, later unanimously reporting that the war was playing havoc with the economy.[70]

The Debate Continues

While diverse criticisms were aired on the outside, inside the administration there was a more focused debate centering on the troop request and bombing. One forum for debate was the Tuesday Lunch cabinet, in which Johnson and top advisers discussed not only Vietnam but other foreign and sometimes domestic policy problems.[71] Johnson aide Bromley Smith says that the Tuesday meetings were valuable because principal foreign policy advisers were present without their assistants. In this setting, he said,

> a principal can, without embarrassment, come off his position. If you have a meeting and advisers are right behind the principal passing him notes and saying, "Don't let them browbeat you on that, Mr. Secretary; here's the answer," et cetera, it makes compromises very difficult. But with a small group it is much easier for people to speak frankly. Even Secretary Rusk would speak frankly in those meetings. . . .

[Interviewer:] But all of this doesn't mean that Mr. Johnson was insisting on a sort of consensus among this very small number of people?
[Smith:] Not at all. What he was insisting upon, and what he got out of the Tuesday luncheon, was no public knowledge of the discussions and of the various positions taken.

Smith adds, "You knew that every single week Vietnam was going to be looked at by the President and the people who implemented that program — Defense, JCS, State, and to a lesser extent CIA . . . there was informal, intimate, off-the-record nonreportable conversation, and give-and-take exchange." Similarly, Dean Rusk says, "President Johnson discovered that at least that group knew how to keep their mouths shut."[72] When leaks about Vietnam policymaking occurred, Johnson assumed that lower-level officials — possibly assistants to the Tuesday Lunch participants — had talked to the press. He often spent time trying to pinpoint the offender. For example, when confidential information on bombing policies leaked in early 1967, Johnson had Rostow "ask Rusk to give me a written report on all in his department who knew of this."[73]

The Tuesday luncheon was not the exclusive Vietnam advisory body between mid-1965 and early 1967. David Humphrey describes one period when Johnson was alleged by critics to have cut himself off from those outside the Tuesday group: "During February and March 1966 Johnson periodically held lengthy sessions in the cabinet room with a 'Vietnam Group' which ranged in size from eight to seventeen advisers — this at a time when the President's circle of Vietnam advisers had supposedly narrowed to four or five principals."[74] Johnson relied on other often informal group sessions — smaller than the NSC but larger than the Tuesday Cabinet — plus innumerable one-on-one sessions. As one assistant said, "he had those damned telephones of his going all the time," talking to former colleagues in Congress such as Richard Russell, foreign policy establishment figures such as Dean Acheson, and venerable counselors like Abe Fortas, who now sat on the Supreme Court.[75]

Richard Helms recalls a few Tuesday meetings where it appeared that the president made a decision based on the group's deliberations. But more typically he noticed "that before [Johnson] made the major decisions he spent hours going over the facts and getting opinions and impressions and talking with all kinds of people that you never heard of and finally, in some strange way, coming to his decision. . . . I believe there were many people who influenced his decisions while he was in the White House that did not sit in the cabinet, that did not sit in the National Security Council, that did not attend the Tuesday Lunch."[76]

From early 1967 until almost the end of the Johnson presidency, Tuesday meetings were held on an average of four out of every five weeks. "This was the high tide of the weekly Tuesday Lunch, the period that most observers have in mind when they discuss the institution and whose characteristics they often ascribe to the earlier years," notes Humphrey.[77] Also, the Tuesday Lunch regulars often met with the president on occasions other than lunch, on days other than Tuesday. Although not technically "Tuesday luncheons," such meetings were obviously important. Because of this regularity of meetings in 1967 and the confidence Johnson had in its members, the Tuesday Lunch was decidedly more crucial as an advisory mechanism than it had been in 1965.

The Tuesday Lunch was also larger in 1967 than in previous years. CIA Director Helms and Chairman of the Joint Chiefs of Staff Wheeler were added to the roster of regulars that already included the secretaries of state and defense and the national security adviser. The press secretary (by then George Christian) also joined the group during 1967 in order to be current on policy decisions. Christian insisted on such access before accepting the job, but he offered relatively little to the substance of the discussions.[78] Thus the principal advisers within the Tuesday Cabinet in mid-1967 were Rusk, McNamara, Rostow, Wheeler, and Helms.

Doris Kearns has written that, as the United States' commitment to South Vietnam deepened, Johnson banished "doubters" from such meetings: "all who did not share Johnson's convictions ceased to attend the Tuesday lunches." In fact, other figures occasionally on hand included Vice President Humphrey, Under Secretary of State Nicholas Katzenbach, his predecessor George Ball, and former national security adviser McGeorge Bundy.[79] Ball and Bundy especially had public reputations as doubters by 1967, because they had left full-time positions in the Johnson administration.

One type of decision regularly made at Tuesday Lunches concerned bombing targets. The military leadership usually preferred more bombing to less, while Johnson, Rusk, and McNamara typically feared expanding target lists to include cities, ports, canals, and areas close to the Chinese border. So there was a procedure by which "the JCS made recommendations of what targets to hit. The recommendations would be discussed by General Wheeler with Secretary McNamara. They would agree or disagree or reserve their positions, and then go to the White House. Then the presentation would be made. Secretary McNamara would make his recommendation; Secretary Rusk would have his say, and the president would make his decision."[80]

Of those in the Tuesday group, none was more directly responsible for overseeing the U.S. war effort than Robert McNamara.[81] After the Westmoreland troop request came in with the endorsement of the Joint

Chiefs of Staff, McNamara and his associates at the Pentagon quickly opposed not only the optimum request of 200,000 troops but also the minimal request for over 80,000 military personnel.[82] McNamara presented a memorandum to the president on May 19: "Hanoi shows no signs of ending the large war and advising the VC to melt into the jungles. The North Vietnamese believe they are right; they consider the Ky regime to be puppets; they believe the world is with them and that the American public will not have staying power against them. . . . This memorandum is written at a time when there appears to be no attractive course of action." McNamara went on to suggest:

> Limit force increases to no more than 30,000; avoid extending the ground conflict beyond the borders of South Vietnam; and concentrate the bombing on the infiltration routes south of 20 degrees [i.e., the southern part of North Vietnam]. . . . We cannot ignore that a limitation on bombing will cause serious psychological problems among the men, officers, and commanders, who will not be able to understand why we should withhold punishment from the enemy. General Westmoreland said that he is "frankly dismayed at even the thought of stopping the bombing program." But . . . analysis shows that the actions may be counterproductive. It costs American lives; it creates a backfire of revulsion and opposition by killing civilians; it creates serious risks; it may harden the enemy. . . .
>
> The fact is that the trends in Asia today are running mostly for, not against, our interests. . . . To the extent that our original intervention and our existing actions in Vietnam were motivated by the perceived need to draw the line against Chinese expansionism in Asia, our objective has already been attained, and Course B [the McNamara stance] will suffice to consolidate it! . . . The time has come for us to eliminate the ambiguities from our minimum objectives — our commitments — in Vietnam. Specifically, two principles must be articulated, and policies and actions brought in line with them: (1) Our commitment is only to see that the people of South Vietnam are permitted to determine their own future. (2) This commitment ceases if the country ceases to help itself.[83]

As the *Pentagon Papers* authors later wrote, "these were radical positions for a senior U.S. policy official within the Johnson administration to take." His memorandum earned bitter condemnation by the Joint Chiefs of Staff, who responded to the memorandum by urging McNamara not to show it to the president. They did not know that Johnson had seen the memorandum 10 days earlier.[84]

A day later, the liberal Senator Edward Brooke (R-Mass.) wrote to Johnson, acknowledging, "I know that you are often overwhelmed by the volume of advice you receive from all quarters." He then detailed an approach to the war almost identical to that of McNamara. Though few outside the administration knew it, the secretary of defense was taking a stance inside the administration that was similar to the positions of Brooke, Kennedy, and Fulbright.[85]

The military's reaction did not surprise Johnson; both he and McNamara recognized that if the military leaders' ideas were accepted as policy, the United States would be expanding its commitment in South Vietnam not just quantitatively but qualitatively. In 1965, the American government had set the goal of defending South Vietnam while its people and government gained self-sufficiency. To add 200,000 troops; bomb Hanoi, Haiphong, and other civilian targets; and invade Laos or North Vietnam would have deemphasized the South Vietnamese military role, as any war critic would have suggested. But McNamara's qualms about plans for the war's expansion were similar in another respect to the suggestions of most doves, "radical" as his plan was, it did not extend to suggesting quick U.S. withdrawal from Vietnam.[86]

Dean Rusk's status as secretary of state and a personal intimate of the president's was unchanged in 1967, even though the two sometimes disagreed on policy. Rusk's restrained hawkishness had persisted in the months that had passed since 1965. He continued to believe that prospects for victory depended in large part on the success or failure of the South Vietnamese government in eradicating corruption, improving the less than stellar performance of its military, and pursuing "pacification" of the innumerable villages within its borders. Although he resolutely opposed U.S. withdrawal from Indochina, he also rejected the military's suggestions for extending the bombing of North Vietnam, invading Cambodia or Laos, and increasing troop levels by 200,000.[87] Knowing Johnson's thinking better than any other members of the Tuesday Group, Rusk was confident that Johnson would reject the military's optimum request: "It was clear to most of us in Washington that the increase of our forces by 200,000 in 1967 was simply not on." Rusk's answer to the military's request was derived from his one-time boss, Secretary of State George Marshall—"give a general one-half of the resources he asked for and double his mission."[88]

About the bombing part of the controversy, a biographer writes, "Rusk had never been a proponent of strategic bombing."[89] When Johnson delayed a decision in May on the McNamara proposal to limit bombing to the lower part of North Vietnam, Rusk waited until after a series of raids on Hanoi's thermal power plant and then offered McNamara's idea to the president again. But in the beginning of the summer of 1967, with the Six Day War in the Middle East and the visit of Soviet Premier Kosygin occupying his time, Johnson showed little interest in the proposal. Later in the summer, when the military wanted to bomb targets in and around civilian areas of Hanoi and Haiphong and others close to the Chinese border, Rusk joined McNamara (and opposed Rostow) in advising against such bombardments. He told Johnson at one meeting, "There appears to be no ascertainable connection between some of these targets and winning the war. . . . It's a question of what do you ask a man to die for. Some of these targets aren't worth the men lost."[90]

Presumably in response to McNamara's and Rusk's views, Johnson gave the army and air force chiefs of staff a chance to respond a week later. General John McConnell said that his air force pilots had a "growing frustration" about not knocking out bases for North Vietnam's MIG aircraft: "It hurts to see those planes on the runways and not be able to strike them, yet they appear shortly afterwards firing at our planes." McNamara admitted that senior military people were unanimously in favor of bombing the targets under consideration, and Johnson allowed that he was "inclined" to approve the request. Rusk, ever the Southern gentleman, was gentle but firm, however: "If you gentlemen will excuse my putting back on my uniform for a minute, it is my opinion that the military advantages do not outweigh the political disadvantages." Despite his instincts, Johnson sided for the time being with Rusk and McNamara against the two generals. Doing so, he complained, "You know I have great confidence in each of you. But you divide, 2-2, and throw it in my lap."[91]

Thus Rusk was no great hawk, opposing many of the military's troop and bombing proposals as well as Rostow's idea of invading North Vietnam. One author even claims that Rusk may have been more willing to support conciliatory offers toward the communists than the president was, but the evidence for this is lacking, and Rusk himself has never given any public hint of it.[92] On the contrary, in 1967 Rusk stood by his philosophy that "There ought not to be any blue sky showing between the President and a cabinet officer." Since then, he has declined opportunities to disassociate himself from major decisions of the two presidents he served.[93]

Richard Helms's advisory role was much more important in 1967 than it had been earlier.[94] During the months of decision in 1965, Helms was deputy director of central intelligence. In April 1966, Johnson made him director of the sprawling bureaucratic enterprise that provided what was supposed to be factual information to the president. Helms did not know Johnson well before his accession to the director's position. In the almost three years that Helms was in the Johnson administration, their relationship was not close in any personal sense but was characterized by directness and mutual respect. Helms recalls: "Whenever he asked me to do anything, he made it explicit what he wanted. When I had produced what he'd asked for, that was fine with him. I found that, in that sense, I was no exception in government; that he dealt through his cabinet officers, and he dealt through the heads of agencies; that he did not do what President Kennedy used to do, of going behind these people to lower down individuals whom he either knew or had some regard for."[95]

Johnson sometimes asked for detailed explanations of CIA figures and the reliability of the methodology used to put them together. In the winter of 1967, Johnson asked Helms for a report on bombing casualties in North Vietnam, further requesting "an analysis of the method used to estimate North Vietnamese casualties which gives us a certain confidence that we are in the right ball park in these estimates." In apparent response to public concerns, Johnson also requested a CIA analysis of innocent civilian deaths caused by U.S. bombing. Rostow later passed on the results (still classified decades later!), which attested, he said, to "the extraordinary care and accuracy of U.S. bombing of the North."[96] Helms says that Johnson "exhausted all the existing sources [of] information. . . . He never intimated to me by word, gesture, or deed that he wanted me to 'knuckle under.' . . . He wanted me to stand my ground and give him the best facts I had, and he made that clear."[97] Thomas Powers, a biographer of Helms, writes that the director of central intelligence was "part of the inner circle, one of the dozen top officials on whom the President genuinely depended," but says that Johnson did not turn to Helms for a personal viewpoint: "The opinions Helms carried in his briefcase were never his own: he knew what his Agency knew, and thought what his Agency thought."[98]

What the president heard from Helms in 1967 was not especially optimistic. The enemy in Vietnam was described as having an almost unlimited population base, a resolute determination to outlast the United States, and only modest needs to support its continuation of the war. In May, the CIA predicted that Hanoi would "continue the armed struggle vigorously in the next phase waiting for a better negotiating opportunity." Even with an intensified program of bombing military and industrial targets, "the minimum essential flow of supplies into the North and on to the South would continue."[99] If the United States chose to restrict its bombing to southern North Vietnam, the CIA anticipated two possible reactions from Hanoi: Either the communists would interpret the restrictions as a weakening of American will caused by international pressure or, if the United States increased troop levels and indicated that the change in the bombing campaign was designed to make infiltration more costly, Hanoi might see the Americans as reasserting their will to continue. As a picture of options in Vietnam it was not rosy, but neither was it a clear guide to what bombing policy Johnson should choose. The CIA, itself divided over "progress" in the war, rarely produced unambiguous reports on Vietnam.[100]

Others were considerably more optimistic. Though he lost in his attempt to interest Johnson in an invasion of the southern part of North Vietnam, Rostow continued through the spring to send Johnson optimistic memoranda and cover letters attached to the reports of others. Rostow believed that the United States was winning the war in Vietnam slowly but surely. One note in April reported defections by Vietcong fighters: "If that can be sustained for, say, 6 months, I find it hard to believe that the VC infrastructure can hold up."[101] The only real worry he mentioned to Johnson was that American public opinion might not support the war long enough to allow the American military and South Vietnamese government to secure victory.

Robert Komer was also unabashed in his optimism about Vietnam. Early in 1967, while serving as an aide to the president, he believed that the crossover point had been reached, with the United States "killing, defecting, or otherwise attriting more VC/NVA strength than the enemy could build up." He told the president, "By themselves, none of our Vietnam programs offer high confidence of a successful outcome (forcing the enemy either to fade away or to negotiate). Cumulatively, however, they *can* produce enough of a *bandwagon psychology* among the southerners to lead to such results by end-1967 or sometime in 1968."[102]

It was because the aggressive Komer believed that the so-called other war — winning the "hearts and minds" of the South Vietnamese — was most important that Johnson appointed his White House aide to a new job in Vietnam itself, with the personal rank of ambassador and the responsibility for overseeing pacification efforts. Komer gave Johnson hope that troops could start coming home within a year. He wrote to McNamara in April, "we should shoot for such concrete results in South Vietnam that it might permit us to start bringing a few troops home rather than sending ever more out. I confess here to a strong bias that we are already winning the war in the South."[103] To David Lilienthal, he said that spring, "We have won the war." About one of his own anti-escalation memoranda, Komer wrote to McNamara's assistant, John McNaughton, "I'd also see merit in *not* letting this get into the JCS stream, lest they get so eager as to rob us of flexibility."[104] To the president, Komer wrote that the Westmoreland troop request missed the point: "How much would we achieve from a major new US force commitment?" Not much, he thought. Instead, he proposed "jacking up the RVNAF [South Vietnamese armed forces] leadership at all levels," greatly expanding the American advisory structure, and expanding South Vietnamese forces "as a substitute for more US forces."[105]

Though Rusk was confident that Johnson would not send additional large numbers of soldiers to Vietnam, and most civilian advisers such as Komer were against such plans, General Westmoreland was apparently unaware at his outpost in Vietnam how steep the odds were against a major troop increase and a reserves call-up. In late May, Westmoreland pushed the South Vietnamese military to reorganize itself, hoping that then the United States could "afford to call up its reserves and effect partial mobilization in order to support the required level of troops in Vietnam."[106]

Walt Rostow was convinced that nothing shaped Johnson's perceptions of actual conditions in Vietnam more than *Ellsworth Bunker*'s weekly cables to the president.[107] The veteran diplomat understood Johnson to be anxious to end the U.S. role in Vietnam. In a typical weekly report, he therefore made it clear that he was pressing Thieu and Ky to work more on building a stable society and less on outdoing each other politically: "I am following the matter closely and do not propose to let it get out of hand." Perhaps because he was relatively new on the job, he did not take a prominent stance on the troops issue, but he supported the idea of South Vietnamese troops entering Laos to fight North Vietnamese regulars based there. He told McNamara that the Vietnamese armed forces were increasingly effective. And like the secretary of defense, Bunker pinned his hopes on an anti-infiltration barrier to do the job that the bombing had failed to do—"choke off infiltration." It meant much to Johnson when, some months after Bunker took over the ambassadorship, he cabled, "there may be some feeling at home that we have reached a stalemate out here . . . in my view and that of my chief advisers this is indeed not the case. On the contrary, I believe that we are making steady progress here."[108]

Hubert Humphrey wasn't so sure. Long since out of the doghouse with Johnson, the vice president attended NSC meetings and occasional Tuesday luncheons and saw the president frequently.[109] His feelings about the war were as mixed as anyone's in the administration. One biographer accurately describes a vice president who in 1965 opposed the president's war policy but later "persuaded himself that Johnson was right, and emerged as the leading spokesman for the president's course in Vietnam." Influencing Humphrey's thinking on Vietnam was a factor he found both curious and impressive: Leaders of Asian countries, even those publicly critical of the war, insisted that the United States' "excursion into Vietnam, bloody and expensive as it was, was indeed a responsible thing to do in defense of freedom of millions of people in

Asia."[110] Holding to this conviction in 1967, he lobbied members of Congress. In May he tried to stop Senator Vance Hartke (D-Ind.) from publishing a lengthy article in the *Saturday Evening Post* that criticized the war as too expensive. Humphrey tried but failed to buy Hartke off with promises of patronage. Afterwards, he wrote to Harry McPherson, "maybe we ought to try to do something with Hartke. I would welcome your advice. It would take more than Hubert Humphrey, however, to do the trick."[111]

By this time Humphrey had learned his lesson on advisory relations —he restricted his advice to Johnson primarily to private conversations.[112] Therefore, what Humphrey said to Johnson about possible troop increases in 1967 does not show up in declassified documentation. Certainly he had access to Johnson and foreign policy decision settings. The vice president sent Rostow a steady stream of memoranda on how to manage aspects of the war more effectively and on foreign policy matters in general. He attended all the important meetings at the White House during the Six Day War in June.

An indication that Humphrey was trying to push Johnson in a dovish direction came at an April meeting the vice president had with 10 longtime liberal leaders including John Kenneth Galbraith and Arthur Schlesinger. In an extended, heated conversation, his liberal friends tried to convince Humphrey that the administration's war policies were hopeless. When Humphrey polled them on whether the United States should halt all bombing of North Vietnam, the group said yes. The vice president responded quietly, "On balance, I think you are right. But the President's advisers don't agree."[113] That was as close as Humphrey came to public dissent from the war.

Mike Mansfield continued in 1967 to do what he had done in 1965 — urge the president away from military escalation. In one of his lengthy letters to the president (passed on by Johnson to Rusk, Rostow, and Katzenbach for reaction), Mansfield wrote:

> You may recall that when you were the Majority Leader and I was your Deputy sitting next to you, that on occasion I would lean over and tug at the back of your coat to signal that it was either time to close the debate or sit down. Most of the time but not all the time you would do what I was trying to suggest. Since you have been President I have been figuratively tugging at your coat, now and again, and the only purpose has been to be helpful and constructive. I am sure that every suggestion I have made has been given consideration by you and I appreciate their courteous consideration.[114]

Substantively, the senator suggested a bombing halt and erection of the barrier advocated by McNamara, Bunker, and others. The barrier would consist of "mined fields, electrical fences, and other devices for an increased concentration of men and materiel over the 175-mile to 200-mile strip." It would "confine the war to that country [South Vietnam] . . . whose integrity and stability we have been trying to maintain." But the idea, a brainchild of civilians in the Pentagon rather than military leaders, was ultimately deemed not feasible by the administration.[115]

Also in May, 16 dovish senatorial critics of the administration issued a surprising letter directed to Hanoi and, indirectly, voters back home. It said that the senators were "steadfastly opposed" to unilateral withdrawal of troops from Vietnam and that although many Americans were critical of the U.S. war effort, "many more" citizens either supported Johnson's war policies or thought that *greater* military force should be used in Indochina. Signers included Kennedy, Morse, Fulbright, and McGovern, the latter saying that the statement did not "signal the end of dissent" but would remove "the chief inhibition of dissent, which is the charge that our dissent might be misinterpreted in Hanoi."[116]

Senate Republicans also tried but largely failed to define a consistent stance on Vietnam. A report on Vietnam written by GOP staff members claimed that Presidents Kennedy and Johnson had diverged from Eisenhower policies in Southeast Asia: "Republicans for two decades have believed the United States must not become involved in a land war on the Asian continent. We are so involved today." But the report suggested no new policies and perplexed many GOP legislators. Everett Dirksen, although not explicitly rejecting the report, left his hospital bed to ask passionately for "foursquare" support of the president. House Republican leader Gerald Ford said that there was "overwhelming" support among House Republicans for fighting communism in Vietnam."[117]

As spring turned to summer, J. William Fulbright tried again to steer Johnson toward deescalation in Vietnam. It is hard to say which of the two men found the war more upsetting and which was more angry and distrustful of the other. When David Lilienthal called on Fulbright, the senator greeted the Johnson administration's new planner for postwar economic reconstruction:

"Dave," he said, with a slight croak of fatigue and hoarseness, "David, I'm so d-e-e-pressed by this whole war that it's no good talking to me; it might be contagious and I don't want to make you depressed about what you have to do." And he did seem terribly discouraged and down. "I think," he said sadly, "that right after [1967's] Tet (when there was a cease-fire for several days) the President decided there was nothing to do but win a military victory."[118]

Enmity between Johnson and Fulbright had been on public display since May 1966, when the president militantly defended his Vietnam policies before an audience including Fulbright and other Democratic leaders. Speechwriter Harry McPherson critiqued the speech for Johnson: "It was harsh, uncompromising, over-militant. It seemed you were trying to beat Fulbright's ears down before an audience of Democratic leaders who, I am told, had earlier applauded him strongly."[119]

Still, Johnson and Fulbright talked occasionally and traded letters in 1967. In June, Fulbright followed up conversations about the war with Johnson and Rusk with a letter to the president:

> As you know, I have thought for some time that it would be worthwhile to halt the bombing of North Vietnam for an indefinite period just to see what would happen. I understand your views to the contrary and the difficulty which Secretary Rusk has with Hanoi's demand for an "unconditional and definitive" cessation. I am not suggesting a public announcement of an "unconditional and definitive" cessation, and I am certainly not suggesting a promise never to bomb again, no matter what. . . . regardless of what is done about the bombing, I most strongly urge you to proceed with great caution in any significant increase in the number of American troops in Vietnam.[120]

In *The Arrogance of Power*, published at the end of 1966, Fulbright proposed inclusion of the Vietcong in peace negotiations, neutralization of Southeast Asia, an American pledge of eventual troop withdrawal from South Vietnam, and the termination of U.S. bombing of the North. He also proposed that if peace negotiations failed to end the war, "the United States should consolidate its forces in highly fortified defensible areas in South Vietnam and keep them there indefinitely." Why? "The United States, as the nation with principal, though not exclusive, responsibility for world peace and stability, cannot accept defeat or a disorderly withdrawal from South Vietnam." It might have surprised Fulbright to know that his views on the bombing were paralleled by White House speechwriter John Roche, who told Johnson in May, "In terms of the world opinion and all the rest of it and the way in which the bombing campaign has misled the American people as to what has to be done in terms of this war, I think it ought to be stopped." Thus, as a recent Fulbright biographer writes, Fulbright's dissent in this period was (like Roche's) rooted in tactical rather than strategic disagreement with U.S. policy.[121] That disagreement, however, would grow and become more bitter in the following months.

In the early summer, White House speechwriter *Harry McPherson* saw for the first time the war he had regularly defended in presidential speeches. McPherson's association with Johnson went back to his days as a congressional staffer in the 1950s. Like Bill Moyers, who left the Johnson White House in 1966, McPherson was an aide whose relationship with the president was close and sometimes tempestuous. Both Moyers and McPherson wanted to influence policy and occasionally told Johnson that he was simply wrong.[122] Sometimes this made the president "furious . . . obnoxious as hell." Other times Johnson took McPherson's critiques apologetically. On one such memo, there is a handwritten note: "Harry—I agree. I'm sorry I did it. I appreciate your honesty and forthrightness. LBJ."[123]

Just days before the Johnson presidency ended, McPherson recalled that in about 1966,

> I was in danger just like everyone around him of capitulating to what you might call the Valenti syndrome, which was to judge myself as a person by his judgment. . . . When I was in favor, I was on top of the world; when I was out of favor, I was in the dumps. And that struck me as ridiculous. I made a number of efforts to pull back . . . from a relationship, an intense relationship with him. It has saved my sanity and judgment . . . and made me a good deal more self-confident and steady in my relationship with him. . . . [I] feel easier about arguing with him and probably do a lot more arguing with him than anybody. I did more than Moyers did, for that matter, when he was here.[124]

Moyers has agreed that McPherson was an influential "steady hand" in the administration, without the notoriety that Moyers had sought and gained in his time.[125] Moyers's close relationship with the president ended in 1966 when he left his position as press secretary and all-around foreign and domestic policy adviser.[126] As Moyers became more and more a Washington celebrity with links to the president's political enemies, Johnson came to feel that Moyers had betrayed their friendship. (By the following year, the Moyers-Johnson relationship was over. Moyers's wife wrote to Lady Bird Johnson, asking her to try to bring about a reconciliation. The break between the two men was a personal disaster for her husband, she said, equal to that of the earlier suicide of Moyers's brother.[127])

McPherson joined the White House staff in the spring of 1965 but only later wrote Vietnam speeches. He believed in the goals of the war but had misgivings about its conduct and some of Johnson's seemingly unreflective war rhetoric. But he wrote later, "What I overlooked was that we were in a war. Ordinary citizens would have found it strange to hear their President, having just sent several hundred thousand Americans to Vietnam, wondering aloud whether [Walter] Lippmann was right and the whole affair a tragic mistake."[128]

In 1966, McPherson wrote his first war speech. The more he wrote the speeches, the more he interacted with Vietnam policymakers and became a part of Johnson's Vietnam advisory system. He was also a conduit for dovish advice from outside the White House to the president.[129] In late May 1967, McPherson finally saw the war he had been writing about: "I saw our limitless array of armaments in every region—thousands of choppers, tanks, APC's, jets, and the navy's 'riverine' assault boats, looking like relics of the Civil War. If anything had gone awry, it was not the American logistics system." After seeing a severely wounded soldier, "a wave of grief came over me. What if all we had tried to do was wrong. What if the stakes were not worth this suffering and waste, this effort to build a line of defense in a bog. God Almighty. I did not want to think about that."

While in South Vietnam, McPherson met its political leaders. Premier Nguyen Cao Ky, talking about the problem of corruption in the government, disarmingly admitted, "Most of the generals are corrupt. Most of the senior officials in the provinces are corrupt. But getting at corruption takes time. . . . You live with it in Chicago and New York."

Then, as planned, McPherson went to Israel—during the Six Day War, by chance. There he was an informal presidential envoy to Israeli leaders.[130]

After the trip, McPherson suggested (like McNamara and Rusk) that heavy bombing continue, but only in the area of North Vietnam and Laos close to South Vietnam, in order to limit infiltration. He wrote to the president, "After adopting this policy, I would renew the effort to talk, making it clear that as the infiltration diminished, so would the bombing." He added: "One thing you must always insist on is honest reporting by your own people. You must put a premium on candor, and a pox on what is only meant to make you, and other leaders at home, feel confident. . . . There is a natural tendency in the military to feel that things are going pretty well, and will go much better if we only have more bodies and bombs." And the speechwriter described to Johnson a wounded "young soldier—23, I would say," being lifted out of a rescue helicopter: "He had been hit in the stomach. Two big packs, soaked red, on his belly. He was pale, his eyes were opened wide, he was scared but holding on."[131]

Before McPherson went to Vietnam he had a worried conversation about the war with his friend *Senator Richard Russell*. Among the many things Russell shared with his former protégé Lyndon Johnson was a fondness for the much younger McPherson. Some months after the White House aide returned from Vietnam he heard about—and identified with—Russell's admission: "For the first time in my life, I don't have any idea what to recommend."[132] Despite the senator's perplexed comment, he was not without views, favoring virtually every military option except using atomic weapons, invading North Vietnam, or declaring war. Asked in Senate debate why he favored "further escalation and bombing of the north and further deployment of American troops in the south, with continuation of the costly search-and-destroy mission," he answered that those policies would end the war more quickly, "at a much lesser cost in American life."[133]

A measure of Russell's influence with Johnson appeared that summer when he advocated refitting an old World War II battleship and positioning it offshore of Vietnam to destroy facilities located near the sea, saving the lives of American aircraft pilots. McNamara opposed the idea, but Johnson invited Russell to argue his side in an evening meeting at the White House. Finally, Russell submitted victorious news to a scrap of paper: "Under Sec—Navy Baird—now have approval to activate New Jersey—Battleship—a long battle won." Russell wrote to a constituent, "this idea did not occur first to McNamara and his limited brain trust and I was compelled to keep hammering away until the President ordered him to start in this direction."[134]

In years past, Russell had corrected a Georgian journalist friend who, as the friend related it, "told him I liked Lyndon Johnson and felt he could have stepped out of any Georgia courthouse. Senator Russell agreed up to a point. He said that the difference was that Johnson was a lot smarter than anybody who ever stepped out of a Georgia courthouse and he understood the use of power better than anybody since Martin Van Buren."[135] Johnson still saw the senator frequently. Typically, a White House assistant would call to invite Russell to come over "in a car they would send to sit with him [Johnson] at supper." Russell's press secretary recalls that the senator used to say "that Johnson couldn't stand to be alone, and if he was in a situation where he was going to have to eat dinner by himself, frequently he would call Senator Russell and the two of them would have dinner together." As Sam Rayburn had been, Richard Russell was close to the Johnson family—"Uncle Dick" to both Johnson girls—and probably knew the president better than any other senators did, despite Johnson's domestic liberalism and Russell's conservatism.[136]

Throughout the years of the Johnson-Russell friendship, there was always an element of tugging back and forth. "When they were friendly, they just couldn't be on better terms, but when they were at odds, they virtually pouted in their relationship with each other," says a former

Russell aide. As with the Johnson-Rayburn relationship, neither man always did the bidding of the other. Perhaps to steel himself during Johnson's regular lobbying, the senator carried a sheet of paper in his wallet listing instances—from Johnson's election as vice president in 1960 to various bills passed during Johnson's presidency—when Russell had been crucial to Johnson's political success. It read on one side: "J's obligations to me." On the other side it read: "Carry in Wallet"—"Support in campaign Responsible for election (V-P 1960)"—"Farm Bill-Senate Public Works Senate Broke Approp. Impasse-1966."[137]

As in 1965, Russell left behind limited written evidence of what he advised Johnson on the troop level issue.[138] What is clear is that he favored increased military escalation in order to end the war quickly, that he was still at a peak of his power in Washington, D.C., and that he saw Lyndon Johnson frequently in formal and informal settings.

In contrast to Russell, Claiborne Pell was no Johnson intimate or close adviser, but he was a bellwether of dovish senators who wished to support Johnson when they could. In a June Senate speech, Pell advocated a complete halt of bombing of the North and no further U.S. troop escalations. Deeply troubled by the war, he talked with Walt Rostow, who reported to Johnson, "Claiborne Pell came in at 6:00 tonight with the attached letter and memorandum of conversation for you. We've known one another a long time, but he began by saying quite formally that, as a Senator, he would like to ask for an interview with you. He said he had only asked to see you three times. . . . Now he was asking to talk with you directly face to face on Viet Nam. I promised to deliver his message."[139]

The meeting (notes of which do not seem to exist) was not just about Pell's distancing himself from Johnson policies; the senator had also recently been an intermediary between a North Vietnamese representative in Paris and the White House. But Pell's departure from established policy on the Senate floor was a sign of the uncertainty in Congress over Johnson's war leadership.

Another such sign came that summer from an old Johnson friend, Leonard Marks, director of the United States Information Agency. Marks was not a regular adviser on Vietnam, but his job required him to know what the world press was saying. Marks decided that Senator George Aiken (R-Vt.) was right in advocating that the United States declare that it had achieved its objectives in Vietnam and withdraw:

One morning I was with the President in his family quarters, and he was getting dressed and looked at me—he had a wonderful way of reading your mind—and said, "Something is on your mind. What is it?" I said, "Mr. President, as your director of the United States

Information Agency, I get reports from all over the world on press reaction, on public reaction that's adverse. Senator Aiken made a suggestion I think is pretty good. The Vietnamese have just held a national election. They've elected a President. They've had a regional election and have elected their regional officials at local elections. Democracy seems to be thriving there. Why don't we say we've achieved that objective, provide equipment and take our troops out?" He looked at me — he had a way of staring at you — and finally I blinked. I said, "What do you think?" He said, "Get out of here." I picked up my papers and I left. That's the first and only time he'd ever been harsh with me.[140]

This was a rare case of a Johnson intimate telling the president in 1967 simply to get out of Vietnam. For a while, Marks was not invited to National Security Council and cabinet meetings. He was not a statutory member of either body, but Johnson normally invited him to attend anyway. Some weeks later, Mrs. Johnson invited Marks and his wife to a surprise birthday party for the president: "The President put his arms around me and started bragging about me, telling everybody what a wonderful job I had done, taking me around introducing me to anybody I didn't know." Years later, out of office and still confused and frustrated by the war, Johnson told Marks, "You and George Aiken were right."[141]

Abe Fortas was one of the president's oldest and closest advisers during the Johnson presidency. Although Fortas's only apparent role in July 1965 was helping with the press statement announcing troop escalations, his participation in formal Vietnam decisionmaking settings increased markedly in 1967.[142] With Johnson's 1965 announcement that he was sending thousands of combat troops to Vietnam came more news — Fortas would replace Supreme Court Justice Arthur Goldberg, who went to the United Nations. Johnson insisted that Fortas take the Supreme Court job, but Fortas resisted because he did not want to give up his friendship and advisory role with the president. The day after he accepted the job, he wrote to Johnson, "I only hope that you will continue to see me and to call upon me for anything I can do to help." A few months later, Fortas had a private, direct phone line established in his office and gave Johnson the number. More and more, the Supreme Court justice counseled the president on the "fantastically difficult decisions" about Vietnam.[143] Fortas's clerks remember that he took piles of work home with him, but after nights when he visited the White House, the Court homework was unfinished and the justice was "bleary-eyed." His role as an unofficial emissary to foreign leaders — dramatized by his role as a go-between during the Dominican crisis in 1965 — was evident again during the Six Day War in June 1967, when Fortas was a conduit to Johnson for the views of Israeli diplomats. Similarly, he was called to help Johnson at the White House that summer during massive riots in Detroit.[144]

Although Fortas was not seeing the president every day — the average was more like once a week — phone calls between them were numerous.[145] The justice also continued to be a confidant of Lady Bird Johnson, who felt that she and her husband could not "endure" another term in the presidency. She confided to her diary that "there is almost nobody in the world I can talk to. To Abe, I feel I can . . . he thought Lyndon had done enough — had worked enough in his life — so that about next March [1968] he could make that [retirement] announcement if the war situation had improved."[146]

There is as yet no firsthand evidence of how Fortas advised the president on Westmoreland's request for more troops. Undoubtedly they discussed the issue: Fortas was a true believer in the war effort to an extent that was rare even in the Johnson White House.[147] Unlike most Johnson advisers, the justice (unsuccessfully) urged the president to ignore opinion polls on the war. In the fall of 1967, he told Johnson to reject McNamara's continued suggestion that, since public tolerance of the war was wearing thin, Johnson should "stabilize" the U.S. role in Vietnam. Fortas wrote, "The analysis and recommendations are based, *almost entirely*, upon an assessment of U.S. public opinion and an *unspoken assumption* as to the effect that should be given to it. I am in *total disagreement*."[148]

Clark Clifford's role in Johnson's Vietnam advisory system was much the same in 1967 as two years earlier. After a conversation with Clifford, David Lilienthal wrote in his journal that Clifford projected "a sense of conviction when he said 'this President believes . . .' you would not doubt that not only was this true, but probably that this tall, wavy-haired, relaxed man had himself formulated for Johnson the things which Johnson believed."[149] What differed in 1967 was the substance of Clifford's advice. In contrast to his advocacy of a negotiated withdrawal from Vietnam up through July 1965, Clifford thereafter "accepted the judgment that such actions were necessary." Over the next two years he advised Johnson against every bombing halt the president made during that period. In Clifford's view at that time, such actions "could be construed by Hanoi as a sign of weakness." In general, he thought that the United States was "on the right road and that our military progress was bringing us closer to resolution of the conflict."[150]

In July, Clifford attended a meeting of the president and advisers at which McNamara reported on a trip to Vietnam to discuss troop levels with Westmoreland. Following three optimistic reports from McNamara,

Wheeler, and Komer, Clifford asked the sort of pointed question for which he would become well known a year later. Saying that "public sentiment in this country sometimes calls the Vietnam conflict 'the war that can't be won,'" he asked the secretary of defense, "Is that true?" Evasive at first, McNamara then predicted, "if we follow the same program we will win the war and end the fighting."[151]

Soon afterwards the president asked Clifford and special consultant Maxwell Taylor to travel to countries that were helping the American and South Vietnamese armies in Indochina to "see what additional assistance could be rendered." According to notes of a Johnson-Clifford meeting, the president "said he wanted the effort to be kept extremely quiet, that he wanted no advance publicity on the mission." He also coached Clifford to "get into the troop question slow" with the leaders he would meet. Clifford agreed, but said that he "did not want to leave the impression any firm commitments would be brought back."[152] Confirming those fears, the results of the trip were paltry in terms of allied troops added and disillusioning for Clifford: "When President Marcos got word that we were coming, he got a message to President Johnson saying he preferred that we not come at all."[153]

Clifford worried "that these countries were not looking at the Vietnamese problem in the same way we were," but he was still a "full supporter of our policy." Notes of Clifford and Taylor's meeting with Johnson in the family dining room of the White House show him pessimistic but hawkish, supporting an unspecified level of troop increase and more bombing: "Clifford said that if we continue at the same level of ground effort and bombing he is unable to see that this will bring us to the point we want to be. . . . We may be no closer a year from now than we are now. . . . Clifford suggested that the margins be moved closer to Red China and that additional targets be approved."[154]

When *Maxwell Taylor* left his job as U.S. ambassador to South Vietnam in the summer of 1965, he offered "to further the cause in any possible way when [he] became a private citizen." Taylor later said, "The President took me at my word . . . [he] had a new job awaiting me — special consultant to him on a part-time basis." Johnson gave Taylor an office in the Executive Office Building and a free-ranging mandate to keep abreast of all aspects of the war, call on any governmental agency for information, and make whatever recommendations he wished to the president. The retired general, who had worked closely with President Kennedy, took the job of consultant knowing that, "In official Washington such a man, particularly one who obviously has the President's ear, is generally unloved. He is viewed by officials on the job as an irresponsible rival who can peddle his advice in high places and then disappear before its flaws appear, whereas the full-time bureaucrat has to stay and live with the consequences of his own acts and with those of the consultant as well."[155]

Taylor strongly supported U.S. policy in Indochina. His only concern was a "burning national impatience for quick results." He was less dismayed than Clifford over the modest results of their Asian trip, noting later that allied troop levels increased by 20,000 during the two years after the summer of 1967. On the controversy over troop levels and bombing of the North, his views were the same during the entire course of 1967: "I recommended to the President that he continue his current strategy while making every effort to stiffen the backbone of the home front." He rejected the "all-out" views of the military leadership, as their course "would require more forces than we had available or could raise in short order and would be moderately risky in its foreign and domestic effects." The so-called pull-back option propounded by Fulbright, other critics, and (privately) McNamara "offered nothing beyond a temporary appeasement of some of our critics; it would . . . prolong rather than shorten the war."[156]

Late in July, Johnson met at the White House with the Senate's committee chairmen. It was there, as described in Chapter 1, that Senator Fulbright, in the presence of other legislators, confronted Johnson in an off-the-record meeting for at least the second time in 1967. The first encounter, in January, had been strained but civil: Johnson agreed with the senator that (in Fulbright's words) the president's first priority "must be the liquidation of the war—that the war poisons everything else." In return, Fulbright told Johnson that, other than the war, he had no "differences of substance with the President." Johnson had been "very generous" in talking with the senator over the months (Fulbright said), and the senator believed "every word that the President has said."

At the July meeting, neither man seemed to have it in him to understand the other. "The Vietnam War is a hopeless venture," Fulbright told the president. "I will not support it any longer." A longtime supporter of foreign aid as a tool of U.S. foreign policy, Fulbright added a potent legislative threat: "I expect that for the first time in twenty years I may vote against foreign assistance and may try to bottle the whole bill up in the Committee." Johnson, weary under the strain of ongoing racial riots in Detroit, fairly exploded: "If you want me to get out of Vietnam, then you . . . can repeal [the Gulf of Tonkin Resolution] tomorrow. You can tell the troops to come home. You can tell General Westmoreland that he doesn't know what he is doing!"[157] Unresolved, the discussion moved on to other matters up for consideration before the Senate.

Though it was not apparent to Fulbright—he no longer believed what the president or secretary of state told him about the war—such meetings, along with critical letters from citizens, seemed to affect Johnson's assessment of political support for the war.[158] The president told a group of advisers at a Tuesday Luncheon that same month that the public thought that his administration was "not doing all we should do to get the war over as quickly as it should be." At another July meeting (according to notes taken by a deputy press secretary), Johnson "read a letter to the group from a man in Arizona and quoted such in saying that U.S. people do not think the U.S. is sincere in its desire to end the war." Johnson described the letter as "symptomatic of what we will be facing on the Hill and around the country in coming months." Johnson's wife, meanwhile, recorded in her diary "a poll that showed a distinct downward trend in the number of people who approved Lyndon's handling of the war in Vietnam . . . it does seem the leaves of autumn are falling rather early, since there are eighteen months left of this term." And from the diary of David Lilienthal, who spent time with the Johnsons and Fulbright and worked part time in Vietnam: "I share with many of my fellow Americans some of their desperation, no, utter confusion about this inconclusive war."[159]

As summer progressed, advisers other than Wheeler and Westmoreland sensed that Johnson was leaning against major escalation of the war. Even Rostow joined McNamara in suggesting a limitation on bombing, restricting it to the so-called lower part of the funnel (i.e., the lower part of North Vietnam). But, in contrast to other civilian advisers Rostow also recommended a significant increase of troops — 100,000 plus a reserves call-up — in part to help persuade allied countries such as Korea and Australia to send more troops.[160] But after serving some months in Vietnam, Robert Komer still believed that major troop increases were unnecessary and reported personally to Johnson in July that he was "more encouraged than when he left." The war, he said, was becoming more of a "classical war" with the North fighting the South rather than southerners fighting each other.[161] As Johnson moved toward a decision on the Westmoreland request, he counted on Komer's analysis being correct.

The Decision

In mid-July the president tentatively decided that Westmoreland would receive troops approximating his "minimum" request for 80,000 new troops. He sent McNamara to Vietnam with directions to negotiate a troop increase in that range. When he returned, McNamara implied to the press that any addition would be minimal and added a comment that stung Westmoreland: "I am certain of one thing, that we must use more effectively the personnel that are presently there."[162] McNamara was more optimistic about the war at this time, for whatever reason. At a July 12 meeting with Johnson and 11 others, he said that for the first time he felt that if the United States stuck with its established approach in Vietnam it would win the war. He openly admitted to those present that he differed with military commanders over the efficacy of aerial bombing. The military thought that there had been "much more results since the Secretary's last trip." The secretary said that he did not agree. But he insisted bluntly, "There is not a military stalemate." This echoed Ambassador Bunker's recent report to Johnson, saying, "The military situation has greatly improved."[163]

Wheeler was disappointed that the president was not taking a bold new military approach in Vietnam.[164] Returning from Vietnam with McNamara, he confirmed to the president and the others "disagreement with Secretary McNamara" on bombing. But he agreed that there was "no military stalemate. There has been an unbroken series of military successes." These assessments and Johnson's acceptance of them strain the credulity of readers two and a half decades later, but William Bundy has said, from the perspective of a former policymaker who later wrote a history of Vietnam decisionmaking, "It was the honest conviction [of those in the administration in the summer of 1967] that we were making headway."[165]

General Westmoreland has subsequently complained about various military decisions made by Lyndon Johnson, but on July 13, 1967, he told the president that he was "delighted" with the troop decision. Indeed, Westmoreland confided in his diary, "I made the point that I fully appreciated his difficult position and had made every effort to ease his burden by my conduct and demands. . . . I have admiration for the President's broad-gauged judgment and high intelligence."[166]

After the preliminary July decision, the president held a press conference in Washington with McNamara, Wheeler, and Westmoreland (who was in the United States for his mother's funeral). In typical Johnsonian fashion, the president told the press, "We realize that some additional troops are going to be needed and are going to be supplied. The President, the Secretary, the Joint Chiefs, and General Westmoreland are in agreement on our needs. . . . We cannot, today, give you any specific figure. . . . We can foresee, at this time, no necessity to call up the Reserves." Here was Johnson's signal to the press, the public, and Congress that no short-term drastic changes were in store regarding U.S. policy in Vietnam.[167]

Negotiations continued between the Pentagon and Saigon before McNamara informed the Joint Chiefs of the final decision, which was made public on August 14: the addition of 47,296 troops. This number was close to the formula Rusk had borrowed from his mentor, General Marshall—that of giving a general half the troops he asked for and doubling his mission. The announcement evoked "in both the public press and in the public consciousness . . . a certain resignation which bordered on apathy." Johnson also decided not to halt the bombing of North Vietnam, despite the recommendations of many of his civilian advisers.[168]

The president essentially followed McNamara's advice on the troop question, but the relationship between the two men, although considerate and respectful, was awkward. Johnson thought that McNamara was too influenced by dovish civilian assistants in the Pentagon and by Bobby Kennedy: "Every day Bobby would call up McNamara telling him that the war was terrible and that he had to leave."[169] Johnson now prepared to consider McNamara's request to leave the administration to assume the presidency of the World Bank.

Disagreements over the progress of the war went on for the rest of the summer. During a visit by Army Chief of Staff Harold K. Johnson to Vietnam, the general said that there was a "smell of success in every major area of the war." But an August 7 article in the *New York Times* suggested that the war might be in a "stalemate."[170] The next day, Rostow and McNamara squared off in Johnson's presence at a Tuesday Lunch meeting. According to Tom Johnson's notes, there was "a discussion of the effects of bombing on infiltration. Mr. Rostow said *some reports* showed that as much as 50 percent of the infiltration was impeded by the bombing. Secretary McNamara disputed this. He said some reports showed only 1 percent of the infiltration was stopped by the bombing. He said much of the infiltration flow was cut down by diseases such as malaria—not by the bombing."[171]

By this time, public opinion polls were certainly negative. In July, 52 percent disapproved of Johnson's handling of the war and in August, after riots in a number of cities, only 39 percent approved of his overall performance as president.[172] Seeing Johnson at a White House dinner that month, David Lilienthal noted in his journal how the president "greeted a few friends, and then moved off and left for the family quarters. I have rarely seen anything so sad as the droop of his shoulders, the set of his back as he walked through a door and left." In September, pondering Johnson's declining popularity, Dwight Eisenhower told General Andrew Goodpaster, "Perhaps he tried too hard. It is too bad." In October, for the first time during the war, a plurality of Americans polled by Gallup thought that the original entrance into Vietnam had been wrong.[173]

After Johnson's decision, Walt Rostow asserted that the United States was "on a winning track," if it had "the capacity to sweat it out."[174]

And after a late summer visit to Vietnam, retired General Omar Bradley sent word to Johnson through Rostow that he was convinced that "we are well on the way to winning the war. The only serious problem, he said, was to keep a base of public support in the United States for the effort in Vietnam."[175] But Lady Bird Johnson recorded in mid-August: "Lyndon and I watched Senator John Tower for the Republicans and Senator Joe Clark for the Democrats on television—the *Today* show—talking about Vietnam. What a twist of fate it is to see the Administration—indeed us—being explained, backed—yes, even defended—by John Tower, while that red-hot Democrat Joe Clark slashes at the Administration's policy with rancor and emotion. The wheel does turn."

And on another day that month, she wrote: "I think the most frustrated I've been lately is reading a speech that Senator Fulbright made in which he indicated that the country is damned because we are spending so much in Vietnam instead of spending it here to take care of the poor and underprivileged—this from a man who has never voted for any Civil Rights measure and who even voted against Medicare in 1964. It will be sheer luxury someday to *talk* instead of to *act*." The days when Mrs. Johnson could sit on Fulbright's back porch and discuss his books were long gone.[176]

Johnson, the Political Environment, and His Advisory System

Regarding 1967, Admiral U. S. Grant Sharp, a key overseer of the U.S. bombing of North Vietnam, writes that Lyndon Johnson was a captive of dovish counselors. Arthur Schlesinger has vividly described Johnson teaming up with the military against civilian advisers such as McNamara who desired a negotiated solution to the war.[177] Johnson himself later wrote of the period when the troop request was under consideration: "The public was very much aware of the critical and well-publicized views of a few Senators and Congressmen regarding Vietnam. It was much less aware of the equally strong feelings of many other members of both Houses who believed that we should be taking stronger actions against the North and generally doing more bombing, not less."[178]

In retrospect, President Johnson's "moderate" decision on the war may have been greatly mistaken. But he seems to have been rational in his approach to the advisory system and its role of helping him assess his problems in Vietnam. The evidence shows that Johnson was not cut off from public opinion, congressional sentiment, journalistic assessments, and the views of elites—all part of the political environment. Here was a president with an open-door policy toward members of

Congress, a president who started each morning by devouring the previous day's *Congressional Record*.[179] With this knowledge base, the president could tell his Tuesday Lunch Group, "The major threat we have is from the doves," and a week later direct the Joint Chiefs to "search for imaginative ideas to put pressure to bring this war to a conclusion." He said that "he did not want them to just recommend more men or that we drop the atom bomb. The President said he could think of those ideas. . . . He pointed out that when this Congress comes back in January [1968] they will try to bring the war to a close, either by getting out or by escalating significantly."[180] Much like his critics, Johnson saw a reckoning on the way if success was not soon achieved in Southeast Asia.

Johnson was not personally isolated from those outside the administration — in the political environment — who opposed his policies.[181] This is an important point, for clearly the environment's collective evaluation of Johnson's handling of Vietnam was distinctly less favorable than it had been in 1965. Johnson's meetings with two critics whom he distrusted — Fulbright and Kennedy — were sometimes rancorous. But Johnson talked without acrimony to others who shared their views. Similarly, and equally distressing for Johnson, he talked to those on the outside who thought that his policies were too weak militarily. In doing so, and in interacting with his own close advisers, Johnson spoke both of a continuing need to widen his advisory circles and of the dissatisfaction of the public and Congress with his policies.

Certainly, Johnson understood that both the public and legislators were to be divided over the way in which he pursued a solution in Vietnam. One poll in the late summer showed that 32 percent of the public thought that he should start "to withdraw troops," 10 percent said that the United States "should carry on its present level of fighting," and 50 percent said that the United States "should increase the strength of its attacks on North Vietnam."[182] The poll suggests both frustration over a policy of more of the same and division over possible new approaches. Johnson found the more militant option unacceptable; it risked war with the Soviet Union or China, would harm the United States' alliance with Europe, and would cause a stronger antiwar movement to arise. And although some of his advisers told him that the time was nearing when the United States could begin disengaging slowly from Vietnam, he thought that the opportunity was not yet ripe.

Johnson's advisory system in 1967 was in one important respect narrower than in 1965 — relatively quick disengagement from Vietnam was not seriously discussed. Johnson convened no special meetings in 1967 — as he had in 1965 — for the sole purpose of having an adviser tell him and other advisers why he should get out of Indochina (though the question would be raised with the Wise Men the following November). Also, although Johnson continued to see and talk to more people about the war than any single aide could keep track of, his advisory system developed a regular focal point by 1967 — the Tuesday Lunch Group. It brought together men in whom the president had great faith and to whom he could say anything without fearing a leak to the press. But Johnson relied on no single individual or group for crucial advice. There was no Colonel House in the Johnson presidency because there were too many — with or without official standing — who had great influence with the president.

In summary, Johnson's Vietnam advisory system in 1967 was neither purely collegial (friendly and supportive on the inside, featuring orderly interactions and indifference to critical views in the environment) nor purely competitive (with numerous wide-ranging points of view being advocated by advisers competing with one another to win the president's agreement), but a hybrid with both characteristics.

As always, Lyndon Johnson shrouded the options being analyzed in secrecy until a decision was made. One observer of this was Robert Anderson, an influential former Eisenhower administration official who worked in 1967 as a special diplomat for Johnson. It is worth emphasizing that Anderson, privy to many of Eisenhower's secrets in the 1950s, was amazed at Johnson's efforts to keep advisory and decisionmaking processes secret. Anderson told his old boss, "This fellow is so afraid of having things disclosed before he makes an announcement."[183]

4 | 1968: Tet

January 30, 1968

January 30, 1968, was about as bad a day as Lyndon Johnson ever experienced in the White House. When Walt Rostow returned to a Tuesday Lunch meeting after taking a call from a National Security Council staffer, he told the president and those present, "We have just been informed we are being heavily mortared in Saigon. The Presidential Palace, our BOQ's, the Embassy, and the city itself have been hit." With that, Johnson knew that the Tet Offensive, only hours old, was going to be as difficult as he had feared in his gloomiest moments. "This could be very bad," he said. [1] Not that the offensive itself was a surprise—the military had told him to expect an enemy offensive around the time of Tet. It might begin just before or after, but *something* was coming. A week earlier, Earle Wheeler had told the Tuesday group that Westmoreland was about to have the most "vicious" battle of the war. [2] A month before that, Johnson had attended a memorial service in Australia for his friend Prime Minister Harold Holt, who had disappeared while swimming in the ocean. Holt had stood behind him in Vietnam, sending in troops from his own country. Johnson warned members of the Australian cabinet, who believed that communist forces were decreasing in strength, that the North Vietnamese and Vietcong would soon start using "Kamikaze attacks" in a desperate attempt to achieve "some tactical victory." [3] So he had expected an offensive, but not one like this, which would send guerrillas into the embassy compound and embarrass him with attacks against the Presidential Palace and cities all over South Vietnam.

While Johnson was learning of the attack on the embassy compound, Congress heard it too. Strom Thurmond took the Senate floor to announce, "Mr. President, I have just received information that our embassy in Saigon has been overrun. Our airstrips are under attack." [4] In fact, the embassy had not been "overrun." Its grounds had been broken into and a battle took place. The shock was palpable in Congress, but members were restrained in voicing their concerns on the floor over the coming week. Those who did speak up about international affairs that week focused mainly on the *Pueblo* affair. Just days before Tet, North Korea had seized an American naval ship and its crew, causing a furor in the United States. Members of Congress were as vocal on this as they were tight-lipped about the unfolding events in Vietnam, either commending Johnson for his restraint or condemning his "weakness" in relying on diplomacy to seek the return of captured American sailors.

Not wanting to create a new wave of opposition against the war, and not knowing for sure just how serious the offensive would be, Johnson had prepared neither Congress nor the public for what might come. He had thought about warning them in his State of the Union Address but decided against it.[5] Now it was too late; the news media portrayed a disaster in the works, and shock spread across the country. Militarily, Tet was not a disaster, as the coming weeks and months would show. The South Vietnamese military handled itself reasonably well, and the North Vietnamese and Vietcong suffered overwhelming casualties and gained no long-term military advantage in the South. But it seemed like a disaster to those covering the story in South Vietnam, and it was so reported in the United States.[6] Hence it was a disaster for Johnson. All the hopeful talk about Vietnam in speeches and press conferences in 1967 now seemed foolish.

The Johnson Administration from Tet to March 31

The two months between the Tet Offensive and Johnson's March 31 speech announcing his eventual political retirement and a change in war strategy have been the subject of much analysis. The dominant interpretation holds that a mostly insular advisory system was at work. Johnson, belligerent as ever, was "turned around" by his much-outnumbered new Secretary of Defense Clark Clifford, who brought in the so-called Wise Men to warn Johnson against further escalation of the U.S. role in Vietnam. This interpretation is most strongly advocated in Townsend Hoopes's *The Limits of Intervention*. Hoopes, under secretary of the air force in 1968, writes of the "enduring stupidity and the self-protecting tenacity of the inner circle" that surrounded Johnson, a circle where "never was heard a disparaging word." Only the heroic efforts of Clifford—knowing what the president did not know (that the Wise Men were backing off from support of the war)—led Johnson to meet the group and ultimately make the March 31 speech.[7] The villains in Hoopes's book include a hawkish Secretary of State Rusk and National Security Adviser Rostow, who shielded Johnson from unpleasant information. Hoopes's account has been tremendously influential with subsequent writers. Herbert Schandler's *Lyndon Johnson and Vietnam:*

The Unmaking of a President is more perceptive; the old view of Johnson as the bellicose president, craftily led by Clifford to reject escalation, is partially modified. Schandler writes that Johnson had important outside advisers, but he suggests that those who brought unpleasant information to the president were ostracized: "The advisers to whom he listened shared his view [of Vietnam] and reinforced his resolve. Out of a sense of awe, friendship, responsibility, hubris, and even fear, Johnson's advisers did not often cross him."[8]

Archival evidence demonstrates how widespread in Johnson's Vietnam advisory system in February and March 1968 was the view that further escalation would not work. Formal and informal counselors — Dean Rusk, Hubert Humphrey, McGeorge Bundy, and others — were in the White House urging Johnson to try a new approach. And although serious advisers, including Walt Rostow, General Earle Wheeler, and Abe Fortas, urged Johnson in the opposite direction, the president signaled key people prior to the Wise Men's sessions that he was likely to halt most of the bombing of North Vietnam and reject the military's request for 200,000 additional troops in Vietnam. More than Hoopes's or even Schandler's accounts suggest, the president sought out and listened to esteemed figures who told him that his Vietnam policies had failed. As a result of the sheer accumulation of such sentiment from advisers, the polls, the news media, and Congress — rather than the actions or words of any one adviser or group — Johnson turned toward deescalation in Indochina. He did so in secret. Johnson thought that this was his "prerogative as President," says George Christian; "he always wanted to keep his options open to the last possible minute."[9] That secrecy left almost everyone outside the administration (and many inside) ignorant of his emerging plans.

The Environment: Congress and Public Opinion

Even before the report of guerrillas in the embassy grounds, Johnson heard reactions that day to ominous early reports of the new offensive. Meeting with committee chairmen and leaders of both houses of Congress — all fellow Democrats and most former colleagues — the president listened to Russell Long complain that the United States was being soft in its initial responses to the offensive. Earlier that morning, Johnson had read the *Congressional Record*'s account of Long's lengthy and wandering attack the day before on the administration's handling of the *Pueblo* affair. The senator had declared his favored response to the Koreans: "Capture an equal number of seamen of North Korea. They have ships of their own on the high seas, and it would be quite a simple matter for the U.S. Navy to capture or sink as many of them as we felt like capturing or sinking." The chairman of the Senate Finance Committee continued, "If the Soviet Union wants to deal itself in on it, they can get in on it, too. We do not intend to be pushed around, bullied, or bluffed by small or great powers."[10] This was not the last time Long would push Johnson to be tougher; he would be the most vocal opponent among Senate hawks of Johnson's policies in Vietnam and on the *Pueblo* for the rest of that winter. Now Johnson shot back, "Russell, if you will just listen a minute, you will see that we are taking the action we believe to be right. There are 700 enemy dead now as a result of our actions in Vietnam. That is not 'soft'!"[11]

But Johnson was dealing with two different worlds at once. From Vietnam, Westmoreland sent word that the enemy had suffered "many casualties. . . . When the dust settles, there will probably be more. All my subordinate commanders report the situation well in hand." And from Johnson's trusted Ambassador Bunker, he heard a few days later, "The enemy has suffered a major military defeat."[12] But in Washington, it was different. Harry McPherson was in a unique position to view the conflicting worlds: "On several mornings I arrived at the White House filled with shock and foreboding over what I had seen [on television] the night before, and went to Rostow's office to read the cables from Saigon. They were invariably optimistic, full of stratospheric enemy body counts, inspiring stories of South Vietnamese resistance, and so forth." David Lilienthal also developed doubts about his project of planning for postwar economic reconstruction in South Vietnam: "It came over me that I ought seriously to consider whether I have any business in an enterprise based on so many assumptions of policy and of fact that, if not destroyed by the recent Tet Offensive, are crumbling."[13] McPherson's and Lilienthal's forebodings, fed by television news reports, were widely shared in Washington.

The response in Congress was mostly muted after Johnson asserted at a press conference that the communists' offensive had failed: "Communist leaders counted on popular support in the cities for their efforts. They found little or none." But one outspoken congressional response came from Senator Eugene McCarthy, Johnson's announced opponent for the 1968 Democratic nomination: "The administration claims that the enemy's military efforts this week were a complete failure. If taking over a section of the American embassy, a good part of Hue, Dalat, and major cities in the 4th Corps area constitutes failure, I suppose by this logic that if the Viet Cong captured the entire country, the administration would be claiming their total collapse."[14] Johnson could easily imagine what Long would say in the coming weeks, along with Bill Fulbright, Richard Russell, Bobby Kennedy, and the rest.

It was actually easier for Johnson to meet with Republican leaders that day, even with the worst of the news in. He, Everett Dirksen, and Gerald Ford sat for almost two hours that evening—longer than he had spent with his Democrats earlier. As messages came into the Situation Room in the White House basement they were sent up to Johnson, who read the latest on the attack on the embassy grounds out loud. All in all, Dirksen and Ford had been supportive on the war, Dirksen especially. The day before, Dirksen had told fellow senators that he did not want "the people of this country and the men in uniform abroad [to] get the idea that we are supine," but he expressed support for Johnson and had even altered his planned statement after talking to Johnson about it on the phone.[15] Ford occasionally criticized the Democratic president's war leadership, but his speeches were mild compared to some reviews from within Johnson's own party.

Ironically, on the same day that Senator Thurmond announced the "overrunning" of the U.S. embassy, a Democratic loyalist in the House heralded news of the latest Gallup poll: Lyndon Johnson had rebounded in a healthy fashion from the depths of unpopularity he had reached in the fall of 1967. Johnson's popularity was up 10 points from October, moving from a 38 percent approval rating to 48 percent. Gallup reported, "It was widely believed just three months ago that any of the leading Republican candidates could defeat the President in the coming election. . . . Today, however, the President leads each of these same men."[16] Though it would not hold steady over the coming two months, Johnson's rise in popularity was a respite from generally negative trends in public opinion. In the fall of 1967, the public had disapproved of his overall performance by a 10-point margin. Now his margin of approval was the same size.

Curiously, though his overall ratings were up until the Tet Offensive began, the public did not have much enthusiasm for his handling of Vietnam (Table 4.1): In January, 47 percent disapproved of Johnson's war management and only 39 percent approved. Three more Gallup polls would come out before Johnson's March 31 speech, showing a continual erosion of public support for his handling of the situation in Vietnam: By late March, 63 percent disapproved of his handling of the war, with only 26 percent approving. Similarly, his overall job rating as president turned negative again during the two months between the beginning of Tet and his March 31 speech: In late March, 52 percent disapproved of, and only 36 percent supported, Johnson's overall job performance. It was the highest negative rating he would ever earn in the Gallup poll.[17]

Gallup also reported early in the year that many Americans had come to view Johnson's 1965 decision to send troops into the war as a mistake. In contrast to most of 1967, when a plurality of those polled

Table 4.1. Public Opinion on Johnson's Handling of the Situation in Vietnam, December 1967–March 1968 (%)

	Approve	Disapprove	No Opinion
December 1967	40	48	12
January 1968	39	47	14
February	35	54	11
March (early)	32	57	11
March (late)	26	63	11

Source: *Gallup Opinion Index*, April 1968, p. 3.

Table 4.2. Mail Received in White House Mail Room

	Week Ending		
	1-18-68	2-15-68	3-21-68
Pro-escalation	79	319	330
Anti-escalation	115	537	642
Pro–U.S. Vietnam policy	155	243	517
Anti–U.S. Vietnam policy	527	1,135	2,537
Pro–greater peace efforts	1,424	276	300
Anti–greater peace efforts	0	6	0
Pro–nuclear weapons use	—	26	13
Anti–nuclear weapons use	—	182	67
Pro–200,000 more troops	NA*	NA*	14
Anti–200,000 more troops	NA*	NA*	144

Source: Mail Summaries, weeks ending January 18, February 15, and March 21, 1968, LBJ Library.
*Not applicable; the 200,000 troop option was not public knowledge in January or February.

said that it had been proper to enter the war, pluralities in early 1968 said that the original troop decision had been wrong.[18] Less scientific results from the White House mail room were no more approving (Table 4.2). The inveterate poll-reading, Congress-watching, mail-following president knew that Tet was more and more of a political rout for him as the days passed.

The First Phase: Emergency Reinforcements

Worrying that the United States and South Vietnam might suffer a military catastrophe, Johnson—not Westmoreland or Wheeler—was the first to raise the subject of more troops in Vietnam.[19] In the first week of February, Johnson pressed Wheeler on whether emergency troops should be deployed and implied that he was prepared to do anything necessary to stave off military disaster, particularly at the ongoing battle of Khe Sanh. Wheeler apparently gave the impression that there was no such emergency but passed on Johnson's question to Westmoreland in successive cables. On February 8, Wheeler virtually told Westmoreland what to do: "The United States government is not prepared to accept a defeat in South Vietnam . . . if you need more troops ask for them."[20]

Meanwhile, Wheeler pressed the president to allow the military to bomb closer to Hanoi and the harbor city of Haiphong. Aircraft had not been allowed to bomb any target closer than five miles to either city. When both Rusk and McNamara told Johnson that lifting such restrictions would cause significant civilian casualties, Wheeler exploded: "I am fed up to the teeth with the activities of the North Vietnamese and the Viet Cong. We apply rigid restrictions to ourselves and try to operate in a humanitarian manner with concern for civilians at all times. They apply a double standard. Look what they did in South Vietnam last week. In addition, they place their munitions inside of populated areas because they think they are safe there."[21] The president temporarily lifted the restrictions, allowing 14 targets to be hit, but held off from a permanent change in bombing policies.

On February 9, a worried Johnson told his civilian advisers, "I do not like what I am smelling from these cables from Vietnam and my discussions with outside advisers. We know the enemy is likely to hit the cities again. . . . I want you to lay out for me what we should do in the minimum time to meet a crisis request from Vietnam, if one comes." That same day, the president met with the joint chiefs of staff. General Wheeler told Johnson that Westmoreland would be cabling that he did need emergency troop reinforcements. Johnson was clearly of a mind to meet the request, but he shifted his tone, reminding Wheeler, "All last week I asked two questions. The first was 'Did Westmoreland have what he needed?' You answered 'yes.' The second question was 'Can Westmoreland take care of the situation with what he has there now?' The answer was 'yes.' Tell me what has happened to change the situation between then and now." Wheeler cited new intelligence reports of 15,000 additional North Vietnamese troops entering the South. The tone of the meeting was strained at times. When McNamara spoke of possibly sending U.S. troops with limited training to "rear areas" in Vietnam, Army Chief of Staff General Harold Johnson retorted, "Mr. Secretary, there are no rear areas in Vietnam anymore."[22]

Westmoreland's shift and Wheeler's lobbying caused confusion among the president's other advisers and set off renewed questions about how bad off the Americans and South Vietnamese really were. Rusk complained to the president and McNamara, "I can't find out where they say those 15,000 extra enemy troops came from." Two days later, Clifford told the Tuesday Lunch Group, "I believe our people were surprised by the 24 attacks on the cities last week. God knows the South

Vietnamese were surprised with half of their men on holiday." And the president wondered at one point, "What makes the North Vietnamese fight so well, with so much more determination than the South Vietnamese?"

Some expressed doubts that Westmoreland's cable actually expressed a need for emergency help. But *Maxwell Taylor*, who thought that Johnson should send 45,000 troops to Vietnam immediately, said, "I am out of tune with this meeting. . . . As I read it, Westmoreland's forces are tied down." If so, said Rusk, "he has a poor Colonel doing the drafting [of the cable] for him."[23] Johnson wanted more definite word from Westmoreland, who finally cabled, "I am expressing a firm request for troops, not because I fear defeat if I am not reinforced, but because I do not feel that I can fully grasp the initiative from the recently reinforced enemy without them." Westmoreland asked that the 525,000 troop level authorized the previous August be fulfilled as soon as possible and that an additional 10,000 soldiers be sent immediately. On February 12, there was continued confusion as to why Westmoreland now urgently requested troops but unanimous advice to Johnson from Rusk, McNamara, Wheeler, Rostow, Taylor, and Helms to send them. Said the CIA director, "This is an urgent situation." Johnson approved the proposal (in McNamara's words) "for the period of the emergency only, not [as] a permanent augmentation."[24] Whether others would be sent later or the reserves called up would be decided only after Wheeler visited Vietnam.

Johnson: Insulated from Dissent in the Early Weeks of Tet?

Given the nervousness in Washington and the nation over the Tet Offensive, sending quick reinforcements was a relatively easy decision for Johnson. It was made easier by the fact that no more than 10,000 troops could be sent without seriously depleting the United States' military resources in other parts of the world. Politically, though, it reinforced the impression that the Americans and the South Vietnamese were losing against the attacking Vietcong and North Vietnamese. In the coming weeks it would not be easy to decide on more drastic escalations of American involvement in Vietnam or to justify them to Congress or the public. For one thing, as the military began to formulate its proposals for the longer term, Johnson was hearing drastically different sentiments from varied sources: Military leaders were even considering whether tactical nuclear weapons should be employed if the battle at Khe Sanh turned in the communists' favor; McNamara, in his last weeks as secretary of defense, assured Johnson that a "true military defeat" was not about to happen.[25]

Also, it was an election year. Johnson told congressional leaders,

> I worked very long on the State of the Union and spent my Christmas on it, then I tuned in on the television one evening and I heard it discussed for an hour. When they got through I said, "The thing that amazes me, I had 4,000 words there and fifteen men couldn't find one good sentence. I just don't understand it. Am I that far off? Am I wrong? Has something happened to me?" My wife said, "I think so . . . you don't know what year you are living in— this is '68!"[26]

Johnson believed that statements on Vietnam by potential challengers in the Democratic and Republican parties were fueled largely by the nearness of presidential primaries. His would-be opponents' suspicions were mutual. Others, like Fulbright, believing that Johnson was determined to achieve military victory in Vietnam, thought that the president had "closed his mind to the consideration of any alternative, and his Rasputin—W. W. Rostow—seems able to isolate him from other views."[27]

Before sending the emergency troops, was Johnson closed to views that were different from Rostow's? Some Johnson administration figures—Rusk, Valenti, and Helms among them—were certain then and later that they did not know how many advised Johnson. A few—like Doris Kearns—thought that they understood the shape of Johnson's advisory system: It was narrow. What Kearns wrote could have been written by Fulbright: "Under siege . . . [Johnson's] operational style closed in and insulated him in the White House, where discussion was confined to those who offered no disagreement."[28] But Kearns's general assertion was mistaken, and Fulbright was wrong in particular about Rostow. The national security adviser was hawkish, raising with Johnson the options of extending the tours of duty of soldiers already in Vietnam and mobilizing the reserves in addition to sending in emergency reinforcements. But Rostow did not isolate Johnson, nor did the president wish to be isolated. Just before Tet, for example, Johnson directed Rostow to set up "a meeting with Congressional leaders in the field of foreign affairs on the Non-proliferation Treaty and possibly Vietnam."[29] After the offensive began, there was a succession of such meetings, though most were a response to the crisis at hand. A week after Tet started, and with the *Pueblo* affair still in the headlines, Russell Long confronted Johnson again face-to face: "How would the Soviets have reacted if Chiang-Kai-Shek seized a Soviet ship?" And Robert Byrd, while complimenting him on his handling of the *Pueblo*, reproached Johnson on Vietnam: "I am convinced that . . . we were not prepared for these attacks. We underestimated the morale and vitality of the Viet Cong. We overestimated the support of South Vietnam's government . . . something is wrong over there." (Byrd's language, only partially recorded in meeting notes, was so strong that he felt it necessary to call Johnson later in the day to apologize for his manner of speaking.)[30]

Others present defended Johnson and the leaders under his command in Vietnam, but the president scarcely concealed his beleaguered mood: "The popular thing now is to stress the 'mismanagement' in Vietnam. I think there has been very little." Then looking at Senator Mansfield, Johnson said, "I wish Mike would make a speech on Ho Chi Minh. Nothing is as dirty as to violate a truce during the holidays. But nobody says anything bad about Ho. They call me a murderer, but Ho has a great image." Finally pulling back from his self-pity, and probably in reference to the election year at hand, Johnson told his former colleagues, "Everybody should say and do what they want to." But he added a defense of those leading the war effort in Vietnam: "We have put our very best men that we have out there."[31]

That same day, Johnson met with his Tuesday Lunch Group, which dealt with the *Pueblo* affair and then somberly assessed Robert Byrd's critique. Johnson had an assistant recount Byrd's four main criticisms of the U.S. military command in Vietnam: "1. Poor intelligence. 2. Poor preparations for these recent attacks. 3. Underestimated Viet Cong morale and vitality. 4. Overestimated support of South Vietnamese people and army." Meeting notes report, "The President said he was alarmed at this and that the attitude expressed by Senator Byrd seemed to be reflected by much of the comment heard in Washington not only by politicians but by the press."[32]

Another meeting of top advisers in the early Tet period featured everything from a discussion between Johnson and Rusk about seeking a congressional declaration of war—Rusk advised against it—to some very pointed remarks from Clifford and Rusk that might have been made by dissenters in Congress or elsewhere. Rusk posed a question, the answer to which was not recorded: "In the past, we have said the problem really was finding the enemy. Now the enemy has come to us. I am sure many will ask why we aren't doing better under these circumstances, now that we know where they are." With the Joint Chiefs of Staff present, Clifford observed,

> There is a very strange contradiction in what we are saying and doing. On one hand, we are saying that we have known of this build up. . . . We have publicly told the American people that the

communist offensive was (a) not a victory, (b) produced no uprising among the Vietnamese in support of the enemy, and (c) cost
the enemy between 20,000 and 25,000 of his combat troops. Now
our reaction to all of that is to say that the situation is more
dangerous today than it was before all of this. We are saying that
we need more troops, that we need more ammunition and that we
need to call up the reserves.

Of course, with intelligence reports showing North Vietnam adding
15,000 men in the South, Johnson finally concluded "we must do
likewise"; but these and other meetings were anything but detached
from the reality of a political environment in turmoil, and they were
full of critical questions.[33]

Nor was Johnson's family shielded in early 1968 from the impact
of Vietnam on American society. In an incident that gained headlines
for days, entertainer Eartha Kitt challenged the war in a face-to-face
encounter with Lady Bird Johnson during a meeting of prominent
American women concerned about crime. Looking at Mrs. Johnson, an
angry Kitt denounced the government's allegedly stingy welfare policies,
its high taxes, and especially its war: "Boys I know across the nation
feel it doesn't pay to be a good guy. They figure with a [criminal] record
they don't have to go off to Vietnam. We send the best of this country
off to be shot and maimed. . . . I am a mother and I know the feeling
of having a baby come out of my guts. I have a baby and then you send
him off to a war. No wonder the kids rebel and take pot."[34]

Both Johnson daughters were about to see their husbands shipped
off to Vietnam. Lynda was bitter about the conflict and its casualties
but also toward its critics. In early February, she wanted to hold an unpublicized White House party for wounded, hospitalized soldiers back
from Vietnam. Lady Bird Johnson recorded in her diary that Lynda had
given her parents "the distinct feeling that they [the wounded soldiers]
are trotted out and put on review, and, in a way, used." So the party was
held, with Lynda and Mrs. Johnson as hostesses, and Carol Channing
providing entertainment. Lady Bird Johnson recalled:

So here I was, standing in the corridor that approaches the theater.
The hall was lined with shrubs, bright geraniums, and they came
down — about thirty servicemen, three or four in wheelchairs,
several on crutches; a pinned-up sleeve, an empty trouser leg. With
each new face, I felt uncertainty as to whether I should stick out
my hand or not. If you're new to crutches, can you take one hand
away with ease, to shake hands?

. . . I sat at a table about ten minutes and then moved on. It was not easy to make conversation. One opening always was, "Where are you from?" and the very first person I asked was from Austin! There were a lot of Southerners and three were West Virginians. The worst case of all was only half a man. He sat upright in his wheelchair, and his legs were amputated at the hips. He and two others were silent, unmoving, sort of stunned looking. Another was lively and smiled, and he and I talked animatedly but when I asked the others a question, they answered in monosyllables.[35]

Both Johnson and the First Lady were having nightmares. In the early weeks of the offensive, Mrs. Johnson had a recurring "long, long dream in which I'm lost and going from room to room and can't find my way." Her husband repeatedly dreamed that he was paralyzed, lying in a bed in the Red Room of the White House. His head and face were normal, but the rest of his body was thin and lifeless. The dreams reminded him of Woodrow Wilson and of his own grandmother who had suffered a stroke and lived in the Johnson home when Lyndon was a child.[36]

Two Hundred Thousand More Troops?

Once the Tet Offensive was under way, Johnson lived with the situation in Vietnam almost hour by hour. He wrote to McNamara, Rusk, and his director of the bureau of the budget,

I have been giving every moment, aside from time spent in meetings, to quiet thought about the crises which have blown up in the last week, particularly in Vietnam and Korea, but also some here at home . . . it appears to be the judgment of our enemies that we are sufficiently weak and uncertain at home, sufficiently stretched in our military dispositions abroad, and sufficiently anxious to end the war in Vietnam so that we are likely to accept, if not defeat, at least a degree of humiliation. . . . In one way or another in the days ahead, we have to rally our country so that the enemy comes to believe that we will insist on even-handed application of rules of international law.[37]

Johnson asked them "to put the ablest men who report to you at work to recommend action" on the problems at hand. This was the beginning of a process that would ultimately lead, through dozens of large and small meetings, to crucial decisions announced at the end of March.

One of the first decisions reached was to have Wheeler cable Westmoreland and Admiral Sharp: "The President desires that you make a brief personal comment to the press at least once each day . . . the purpose should be to convey to the American people your confidence in our capability to blunt the enemy moves."[38] Another, of course, was the decision to send the 10,000 troops as immediate reinforcements in Vietnam. This cleared the deck for longer-term matters. Westmoreland and Wheeler were pressing Johnson to mobilize the reserves, and they believed that his willingness to send emergency troops indicated his openness to sending more permanent, nonemergency military personnel to Vietnam.

Johnson liked to send one of his Washington advisers to Vietnam before making any major changes in war policy. In mid-February he directed *General Earle Wheeler* to make the rounds of consultations with Westmoreland, Bunker, and others "to find out what Westmoreland felt he had to have to meet present needs, and what he thought future needs would be for troops, equipment, or other support. Finally, [he] wanted Wheeler to find out how the South Vietnamese army was performing." Johnson did not want to send more troops beyond the emergency augmentation, but his attitude as he dispatched Wheeler was that if Westmoreland made a compelling case that "only a large number of reinforcements stood between his men and disaster, [he] would have managed to find them somewhere."[39]

While waiting for Wheeler's return, Johnson's advisers in Washington were looking ahead to a planned speech to the nation on Vietnam. Chief among them was *Clark Clifford*, who attended most meetings in January and February on Vietnam even though his appointment as secretary of defense would not take effect until March 1. Clifford was (in Wheeler's confidential description to Westmoreland) "very astute, intelligent and able . . . closely in touch with congressional leaders, the business community, and the heads of the news media . . . a man of stature and achievement, one whose views must be accorded weight." As secretary-designate, Clifford encountered a group of high-level civilian appointees in the Pentagon who shared and helped shape Robert McNamara's view that the United States needed to deescalate its involvement in Vietnam.[40] Though distrustful of Clifford as a Johnson crony, these men would begin to feel that they were having an impact on Clifford's thinking during his early weeks on the job. But in February, they were doubtful. One of them, Townsend Hoopes, nonetheless wrote to Clifford "with more candor than discretion," as he put it: "the idea of a US military victory in Vietnam is a dangerous illusion . . . if events in Vietnam are ever to take a turn toward settlement, definitive deescalation is a prerequisite."[41] Thus a longtime Johnson friend who had been consistently hawkish on Vietnam since late 1965 was about to take charge of the war effort at a time when some Pentagon civilians no longer supported the president's policies, a crisis was unfolding in South Vietnam, and controversy raged in the United States.

Assigning Wheeler to assess the situation in Vietnam relaxed some of the immediate pressure on Johnson for a week or so in February, allowing the White House to analyze the damage done to war support on the home front. Johnson had Rostow cable Bunker,

> We assume Embassy is now well protected against intrusion into compound or buildings. The earlier attack was blown out of proportion and was disproportionately damaging here. . . . It would help us greatly if Thieu, Ky, or both could somehow get to the U.S. press corps in Saigon with an account of: how the people behaved, how the ARVN fought, how recovery is going, how the constitutional machinery is working, how political groups are cooperating with the government.[42]

Also, at Johnson's direction, his Foreign Intelligence Advisory Board headed by Maxwell Taylor initiated the delicate task of investigating the adequacy of intelligence reporting overseen by another Johnson adviser, Richard Helms, prior to the first attacks of January 30.[43]

There were other, more personal chores. On February 17, Johnson visited troops in North Carolina and California who were bound for Southeast Asia as part of the emergency reinforcements. He met them, having read a captured document from those whom the young Americans were about to encounter—the Vietcong. Its assessment of the Tet Offensive so far spoke of failure, especially to inspire an uprising on the part of the people of South Vietnam.[44] But this provided little solace to Johnson as he met the American servicemen. By his account, the meetings were "among the most personally painful" of his presidency. He later told the Tuesday Group, "One soldier really melted me and brought me to my knees. I asked a boy from Ohio if he had been to Vietnam before. He said yes, he had been there four times. I asked him if he had a family. He said yes, sir, he had a little baby boy born yesterday. There wasn't a tear in his eye. No bitterness showed in his face. But I can assure you I sure stopped asking any men questions for awhile."[45]

On the carrier *Constellation*, Johnson also apparently overheard a meeting between his speechwriter Harry McPherson, White House aide Horace Busby, and a group of two dozen pilots recently returned from Vietnam. McPherson writes:

It began conversationally, with senior officers describing the excellent performance of pilots . . . and so on. There was a pause. A lieutenant with an Irish name broke in. "Permission to speak, sir." "Granted," said the commander. There followed a furious assault on the bombing program. Men were being asked to fly through the heaviest antiaircraft defenses ever seen, in order to bomb meaningless targets. "I've hit the same wooden bridge three times . . . for that I've flown through SAMs, flak, and automatic weapons fire. I've seen the god-damned Russian freighters sitting there, and the supplies stacked along the wharves. I can't hit them. 'It might start a wider war.' Well, the war is too wide for me right now. And it's stupid."[46]

On his way back to Washington, Johnson stopped for consultation and a golf game with Dwight Eisenhower at his winter home in Palm Desert, California. Johnson later told his advisers that Eisenhower "said it is a mistake to second guess the people who know the information. He spoke glowingly of General Wheeler and General Westmoreland." The weather was glorious as they played at the El Dorado Country Club, but afterwards Johnson wrote to Eisenhower, "The contrast between the beauties of El Dorado and the brutalities of Vietnam haunted me all day."[47]

In the days before Wheeler reported back from Vietnam, other opinions came in. Senator Richard Russell let it be known that he would oppose further "piecemeal escalation" of the war with additional troops unless Johnson was willing to take the war to the North with such initiatives as bombing the center of Hanoi, Haiphong, and rail lines from China into North Vietnam. Although Russell was still very much an intimate of the president and his family—having dinner at the White House and seeing top officials of the administration regularly—he sometimes sounded like Fulbright. Just a month before the Tet Offensive, Russell reacted to a military airlift to the Congo in Africa, authorized by Johnson in 1967 to support the government and protect (mostly European) lives: "While I'm happy over the safe return of our men and planes from this mission, I must regretfully advise that I still don't believe in the United States moving into situations of this kind unilaterally." Harry McPherson, meanwhile, urged Johnson to stop the bombing.[48] So did United Nations Secretary General U Thant, who, like some other sources, told Johnson that he had indications from unofficial sources that if the United States stopped the bombing, North Vietnam would be willing to start peace talks immediately. Johnson felt burned by previous U.S. bombing pauses that had led to nothing in the way of serious diplomacy, and he doubted that the latest indirect signs from

North Vietnam were significant. But the feelers made him start to think about including some sort of bombing halt in whatever speech he would eventually give to the nation on Vietnam.[49]

Johnson also had J. William Fulbright on his mind. Fulbright was pressing Dean Rusk to appear before the Senate Foreign Relations Committee for televised testimony. Johnson fretted and complained about Fulbright and had a gut desire to turn the senator's request down. He told his Tuesday Lunch Group for neither the first nor the last time, "Fulbright has an obsession on Vietnam."[50] Johnson wrote an angry letter to Fulbright on February 8, telling his one-time friend, "Think for a moment where we are right now. A half million American troops are engaged in an unresolved battle which could determine the outcome of the war in Vietnam." The letter rejected Fulbright's request but was never sent. Weeks later, after deciding to allow Rusk to give televised testimony over a period of days, Johnson told one of his secretaries not to file the letter: "Tear it up, flush it away! We didn't send it. I don't want a record of it."[51]

Meanwhile, in Vietnam, Wheeler and Westmoreland agreed on much. Both thought that the communists had failed to achieve their chief objectives in the Tet Offensive even though they had succeeded in taking certain parts of South Vietnam temporarily and in laying siege against American soldiers at Khe Sanh. Both generals thought that the time was ripe to persuade Johnson to mobilize the reserves and commit 200,000 more soldiers to Vietnam. But Wheeler was exhausted, depressed by the coverage of the war he had seen on American television. Westmoreland thought that Wheeler "mirrored the gloom that pervaded official circles in Washington." Westmoreland was politically naive compared to Wheeler and thus more optimistic about the number of troops he would get from Johnson. Westmoreland conferred with his superior "in the expectation that there was to be a reappraisal of American policy on conducting the war, presumably a new and broadened strategy. A change in strategy almost inevitably would involve a sizable call-up of National Guard and Reserves."[52] But it would be well justified in Westmoreland's view:

> I saw the possibility of destroying the enemy's will to continue the war. Indeed, a responsible member of the International Control Commission — the organization that had been created to police the Geneva Accords and was still around — had just returned from Hanoi and told me that the mood of the North Vietnamese leaders was one of dejection. The enemy, I theorized, had changed his strategy, gone all out, and his new strategy, like the old, had failed while generating — if we so acted — a new American strategy — a bold,

damaging reaction. If there was anything to the business of "sending a message" to Hanoi, surely that was a way.[53]

And so Wheeler, in transit from Vietnam back to Washington, cabled a report from Hawaii to the White House that proposed "a combat force structure of 133 US maneuver battalions, 37 free world military armed forces maneuver battalions, and 47 US TAC fighter squadrons. We estimate the US portion will require 200,000 additional US troops." Westmoreland did not know it, but Wheeler hoped to convince Johnson and his civilian advisers that so many troops were necessary by scaring them with a gloomy report that contrasted with more optimistic ones sent by Westmoreland and Bunker. Tet, said Wheeler, "was a very near thing." The enemy "displays a tenacity which we have not seen before . . . it is my belief he has forces available for a second round of attacks against selected urban areas, including Saigon. . . . Westy's forces are stretched too thin . . . we must reinforce him promptly and substantially."[54]

Johnson received a copy of the cable at his ranch in Texas. His immediate reaction—the details unrecorded for history—was strongly negative.[55] He missed seeing the adverse reaction Wheeler's cable garnered from many White House, Pentagon, and State Department people. A working luncheon in his absence on February 27 featured top State and Defense people (Rusk, McNamara, Clifford, Katzenbach, William Bundy), Rostow, speechwriter McPherson, and domestic assistant Joe Califano. Looking ahead to the president's upcoming speech on Vietnam, *Robert McNamara* outlined Wheeler's proposal and options before the president, noting that the military's plan would require "a sizeable reserve call-up—a minimum of 150,000—as well as an increased draft. In total, an increase in [worldwide American] uniformed strength of 400,000." This would require the president to ask that a surtax be imposed on the income tax rates of citizens, "plus additional taxes." The conversation took on a farfetched tone as McNamara posed the option of integrating such a military plan with "a new peace offensive." Rusk said that a bombing halt might be tried in conjunction with the troop increase, but McPherson was aghast at the possibility of a 200,000 troop increase. "Unbelievable and futile," he wrote to himself. Rusk and McNamara, veterans of discussions of many options that never had much chance of implementation, forged ahead, discussing the idea of reducing U.S. troop levels in Europe in order to add them in Vietnam. Rostow suggested that the enemy had taken such a beating that "he might be unable to mount heavy coordinated attacks on cities." If Westmoreland could get the troops he wanted "he should be able to handle the situation." But McNamara's language was skeptical: "Let's not delude ourselves."

The conversation turned almost surreal again when Clifford said, "Another possibility that should be considered—and I am not pushing it—is announcement that we intend to put in 500,000 to a million men."[56] Neither he nor McNamara favored such a drastic course, but as the latter said, "That has the virtue of clarity. Obviously, we would have decided to put in enough men to accomplish the job. . . . I do not understand what the strategy is in putting 205,000 men. It is neither enough to do the job, nor an indication that our role must change." Among the gloomiest at the meeting was William Bundy, who lamented, "South Vietnam is very weak. Our position may be truly untenable. Contingency planning should proceed toward the possibility that we will withdraw with the best possible face and defend the rest of Asia." This was heresy to Rostow and unacceptable to Rusk, but the advisers were neither required nor mandated to make a decision that day. On the contrary, their only agreement was that the president should not make a hasty decision. It was clear to all that a fork in the road had been reached, with no clear signal as to how to proceed. Clifford summarized part of the administration's problem: "Despite optimistic reports, our people and world opinion believe we have suffered a major setback. The problem is, how do we gain support for a major program—defense and economic—if we have told people things are going well? How do we avoid creating the feeling that we are pounding [sic] troops down a rathole? . . . Before any decision is made, we must re-evaluate our entire posture in South Vietnam." Unfortunately, Clifford said, the president was at the ranch with "hawks" whom he did not name.

When the meeting ended, *Harry McPherson* wrote, "General impression: prevailing uncertainty. Radically different proposals were offered and debated, none rejected out of hand. We are at a point of crisis." He added that the main question for him was whether the doubts expressed in the meeting would be presented to the president. Rostow immediately cabled a report of the meeting to Johnson at the ranch: "Although we had a fresh McPherson draft of a speech available, the lunch was taken up with an extended substantive discussion of the troop issue itself. . . . The only firm agreement . . . was this: the troop issue raises many questions to which you ought to have clear answers before making a final decision." Rostow, subsequently accused on occasion of biased reporting to the president, then recommended that Clark Clifford—who had already spoken in Rostow's presence of Vietnam as a "rathole"—chair a working group to sort out the alternatives and recommend a course of action to Johnson.[57]

Johnson was back in Washington at two in the morning on February 28. By coincidence, this was the day when the last of the emergency augmentation troops arrived in South Vietnam. At a 6:00 A.M. meeting, Johnson, Vice President Humphrey, and other leading advisers met the just-returned Wheeler to discuss substantial additions. Wheeler pressed his case, but Johnson asked what would happen if the troops were *not* sent. The United States should "be prepared to give up the two northern provinces of South Vietnam," Wheeler said. This would be politically hazardous and would, he believed, ultimately "cause the collapse" of South Vietnam's army. But even with 200,000 more troops there was no guarantee of prevailing if "the enemy ups the ante."

When Johnson brought McNamara into the discussion, the secretary of defense restated his views from the day before and specifically disagreed with Wheeler's estimate that not sending 205,000 troops would lead to a loss of northern South Vietnam. Instead, McNamara suggested a small call-up of reserves and a slight increase of troops in Vietnam, combined with new diplomatic efforts. Johnson finally turned to Clifford and, as Rostow had recommended, assigned him to head a group to consider the options and report back to Johnson in five days. "Give me the lesser of evils," he told his old friend.

After the meeting, Johnson sent Clifford, Rusk, and McNamara a directive to guide the working group: "I wish alternatives examined and, if possible, agreed recommendations to emerge which reconcile the military, diplomatic, economic, Congressional, and public opinion problems involved."[58] Consistent with the reference to economic problems, Johnson included Secretary of Treasury Henry "Joe" Fowler on the new task force. The United States had faced a balance-of-payments problem in recent months, which made it seem essential to pass a bill increasing taxes to cover the war's costs and other government ventures and, in turn (Johnson hoped), put a brake on growing inflation and stengthen the dollar internationally. Fowler thought that a military escalation, if it came, would be a "not unmixed evil": It might force Congress to pass the tax bill but also to cut Johnson's Great Society programs.[59] In the coming weeks, the financial crunch would worsen.

Later that busy day, a reception was held in the East Room of the White House for the retiring McNamara. It attracted a vast range of Washington officialdom from Bobby Kennedy to the most fervent congressional hawks. Johnson awarded his old comrade in arms, "this loyal, brilliant and good man," the Medal of Freedom. McNamara was considered by both friends and political foes — even those from the left or right who thought him responsible for the United States' military dilemmas — a decent man devoted to service. He was also exhausted by early 1968, and some feared that he might have a nervous breakdown or even commit suicide, as Harry Truman's Secretary of Defense James

Forrestal had years earlier. David Lilienthal wrote of McNamara near the end of his tenure, "I was appalled by his gaunt, worn appearance. The bones seemed to protrude from his face; his eyes were hollow."

When it came time for McNamara to respond to the president at the ceremony, the man with the computerlike brain and demeanor could not keep his composure. Several times he took a deep breath and tried to speak but could not get out the words he had planned to offer. Finally, he managed to utter, "Mr. President, I cannot find words to express what lies in my heart today. I think I had better respond on another occasion." Like Lyndon Johnson, McNamara had led a war but cared deeply about administration efforts toward domestic reform—offering a surprising number of ideas on the Great Society programs. Leaving office, he believed that the transformation of the United States into a great society had been substantially derailed, and he was haunted by his shared responsibility for tragedy in the United States and Vietnam.[60]

That night Johnson summoned former Secretary of State *Dean Acheson*, a man he greatly respected, to the White House. Acheson was a man of notable self-assurance and a venerable member of the Wise Men. An architect of the United States' containment policy and no particular fan of Johnson's, he spoke mockingly of the president to friends as "Our Hero" and a "real Centurion—part man, part horse's ass." When Johnson had met with Acheson and other elders of the foreign policy establishment three months before, Acheson and most of the others told the president that he was on the right track in Vietnam. The familiar exception at that November meeting had been George Ball, who thundered at Acheson and others after the session, "You're like a flock of buzzards sitting on a fence, sending the young men off to be killed. You ought to be ashamed of yourselves."[61] But Tet had affected Acheson in the same way it had millions of others. When he was called into Johnson's office, he encountered a blizzard of activity—aides coming and going, phones ringing, and a president in a bad mood. The intensity of activity and pressure on Johnson had resumed with Wheeler's report, and he was worried about the aftermath of an attempted assassination of the president of South Korea. The South Koreans blamed North Korea, and Cyrus Vance told Johnson that the picture in that region was "very dangerous." Furthermore, Johnson was still bothered by a conversation with retired *General Matthew Ridgway*, former army chief of staff who led U.S. forces in the Korean War after MacArthur's departure. Ridgway told Johnson that the United States' strategic reserve was depleted— the United States was "in no condition to react to any new crisis that might erupt in another part of the world." It was advice that made the idea of increasing the draft and calling up the reserves more compelling.

Johnson also received warning of a possible crisis in Berlin. The days of late February had "many sources of anxiety," he wrote.[62]

With Acheson, Johnson exuded anxiety. The generals wanted 200,000 more troops, he said, and the battle at Khe Sanh might turn out like the disastrous engagement that finished the French in Indochina in 1954: "I don't want no damn Dien Bien Phu's!" By Acheson's account, the president was doing too much talking and not enough listening. The former secretary of state at some point excused himself and walked back to his own office a block away. What happened next is disputed. Acheson claimed that Walt Rostow phoned immediately to ask why he had walked out and that he told Rostow, "You tell the President — and you tell him in precisely these words, that he can take Vietnam and stick it up his ass!" Rostow remembers no such colorful language, but Acheson's departure earned the president's full attention. Johnson got on the phone, asked Acheson to return, and they talked.

Picking up where Johnson had left off — the subject of the generals' advice — Acheson looked at the president, remembering as always the troubles President Truman had had with General Douglas MacArthur: "With all due respect, Mr. President, the Joint Chiefs of Staff don't know what they're talking about." That was a shocking thing to say, Johnson responded. "Then maybe you should be shocked."[63] Here the president persisted, saying that he wanted Acheson's considered judgment on choices in Vietnam. That would be possible, Acheson said, only if he could get beyond the "canned briefings" of Rostow, the CIA, and the Joint Chiefs of Staff. The two men agreed: Much like Maxwell Taylor, Acheson would have full access to information, cable traffic, and anything else he wanted from anyone in the foreign policy bureaucracy. Then, said Acheson, he would be able to advise Johnson on what needed to be done.[64]

For Clifford as well, the intensity of work increased dramatically on February 28. After the session with Johnson, Wheeler, and the civilian advisers, Clifford led the first meeting of his working group later that day. Present were Rusk, McNamara, Katzenbach, Nitze, Helms, Rostow, Taylor, Fowler, and others. The defense secretary-designate told the group that the real problem to be addressed wasn't whether to send 200,000 more troops. Instead, it was, "Should we follow the present course in South Vietnam? Could it ever prove successful even if vastly more than 200,000 troops were sent?"[65] There were five days for the members to wrestle with those questions before Johnson's March 4 deadline.

After the first task force meeting, *Dean Rusk* skipped the others. Years later he said, "Since I knew what the outcome was going to be, I had a representative [Nicholas Katzenbach] attend for me those other meetings." By now, Rusk and Johnson had an intimacy that did not exist between the president and any other cabinet member. "I love that Dean," Johnson would tell people, and Lady Bird told Rusk, "You are my hero." Rusk, in turn, told Johnson one Sunday morning, "Your courage keeps me going. These days are an exercise in sheer spirit." The secretary of state thought that there was virtually no chance of Johnson's approving the military's plan. Rusk was therefore formulating his own ideas about breaking out of the stalemate, ideas that had nothing to do with sending more soldiers to war. Devoted as Rusk was to Johnson, he shared with Clifford a Machiavellian appreciation of a strategic approach to the man being advised. That man being Lyndon Johnson, Rusk knew that floating new ideas in a large group that included second-level officials from State and Defense, especially Defense, would be foolish. In contrast to the protection offered by the near perfect confidentiality of the Tuesday Lunches, thinking out loud in the task force meetings would lead to stories on page one of the newspapers.[66]

The secretary of state had pondered the opinions of certain British figures that the United States needed to adopt the approach apparently chosen by the communists—fight and talk. Previously, the United States had made "peace moves" such as a bombing halt conditional on concurrent restraint by the communists. Now Rusk thought that the United States could afford some sort of bombing halt, keep its troop levels the same for the time being, and see whether serious negotiations resulted. His goal, therefore, was to convince an audience of one of the validity of the fight and talk strategy. Clifford, by contrast, was developing plans to persuade the administration and those outsiders whom Johnson respected—in the hope that they could in turn help Clifford convince Johnson—that greater militarization was futile. Rusk cared relatively little about the rest of the administration but very much about helping Johnson arrive at the right decision, one that would reject more troops, limit or halt the bombing, and try again for negotiations.[67]

Over the next few days, members of the Clifford working group debated their differences while the new secretary of defense did a lot of listening. His years as a lawyer were not irrelevant to the task of probing the Pentagon brass:

"Will 200,000 more men do the job?" I found no assurance that they would. "If not, how many more might be needed—and when?" There was no way of knowing. "What would be involved in committing 200,000 more men to Vietnam?" A reserve call-up of approximately 280,000, an increased draft call and an extension of tours of duty of most men then in service. "How long must we keep on sending our men and carrying the main burden of combat?" The South

Vietnamese were doing better, but they were not ready yet to replace our troops and we did not know when they would be. . . . I then asked, "What is the best estimate as to how long this course of action will take? Six months? One year? Two years?" There was no agreement on an answer.[68]

Clifford was rapidly moving toward a new sense of purpose — "to emphasize to my colleagues and to the President, that the United States had entered Vietnam with a limited aim — to prevent its subjugation by the North and to enable the people of South Vietnam to determine their own future. I also argued that we had largely accomplished that objective. Nothing required us to remain until the North had been ejected from the South, and the Saigon government had been established in complete military control of all South Vietnam."[69] But he found that Wheeler and others in the working group such as Taylor and Rostow believed that Tet gave the United States an opportunity to smash the communists, if only it had the courage to do so by increasing its strategic posture.[70] Katzenbach, Nitze, and Warnke argued the opposite, that neither side could win militarily. Although they did not talk of simply getting out of Vietnam, they did suggest a new strategy: Put a cap on the number of troops, pull back from remote areas like Khe Sanh and assume a defensive posture geared toward protecting already secure populated areas of South Vietnam, halt the bombing, and pursue peace talks aimed at a political settlement.[71]

Because members of the task force could not agree on a bold new approach, either hawkish or dovish, it could only compromise, recommending that Johnson send an additional 23,000 troops, call up 245,000 reserves, increase draft calls, and lengthen tours of duty of soldiers already in Vietnam. As to bombing, the group's differences were "profound": It was unable to agree on a recommendation. The report wasn't what Wheeler wanted, but he had already learned that the political establishment in Washington was wary of sending more troops and was especially reluctant to call up the reserves. On making the rounds of Congress, Wheeler discovered that (as Johnson knew), "The matter of the reserve call-up was very, very onerous for any of these gentlemen to accept." To Wheeler's dismay, his troop proposal was progressively "whittled down" in the ensuing weeks.[72]

The task force report was a far cry from what many other civilian advisers preferred — there was no proposal for a new peace initiative, noted some. Rostow thought that more military initiatives, such as mining the territorial waters off North Vietnam, were necessary.[73] Even Clifford didn't much like the report. He knew that he would have to do better than his own unwieldy working group had in persuading Johnson to act boldly in Indochina. He was also pessimistic at times that he could do so. He believed, mistakenly, that Rusk was whispering hawkish advice in Johnson's ears, and he was distressed by the militant language Johnson used in public speeches.

Johnson was at an air force base in Puerto Rico over the weekend that the task force completed its report. En route to the island, he spoke off-the-record about Vietnam to reporters: "I cannot say that I know or have ever had a satisfactory solution. . . . I take everything Mansfield and Fulbright and any others ever say into consideration."[74] He also had Walter Cronkite to think about: The popular television anchorman opined in a broadcast a few nights earlier that it was "more certain than ever that the bloody experience of Vietnam is to end in a stalemate." Former press secretary George Christian says that Johnson was "concerned about Cronkite coming home from Vietnam and portraying the 'cause is lost.' "[75] Arriving at Puerto Rico, Johnson visited his son-in-law Pat Nugent, who, like Chuck Robb, was bound for Vietnam. He also received a cable from Westmoreland saying, "Throughout the country, we are moving to a general offensive. I hope that the impact of these simultaneous major operations will convince the people in South Vietnam and in Washington that we are not waiting for either the VC to resume the initiative, or for someone to help us."[76]

Back in Washington on March 4, Johnson heard the Clifford group's report, with Vice President Humphrey and others present. "We recommend in this paper that you meet the requirements for only those forces that may be needed to deal with any exigencies of the next 3–4 months," reported Clifford. This would be 22,000 additional personnel. "This is as far as we are willing to go," he said, but then suggested a call-up of 262,000 members of the reserves in case there should be any further crises in Vietnam or elsewhere in the world. Clifford gave the report a modest endorsement, telling Johnson that sending the limited additional troops should be done "out of caution and for protection." But he warned, "We seem to be in a sinkhole. We put in more—they match it." Rusk spoke similarly, questioning whether substantial increases of the amount recommended by Westmoreland "would eventually increase or decrease South Vietnamese strength."

The hawks at the meeting were restrained in supporting the group's report. Maxwell Taylor supported it only because the United States lacked sufficient strategic reserves around the world to be able to send more than 22,000 men. Wheeler grudgingly agreed: "If we *could* provide Westy with the troops he wants I would recommend they be sent." Rostow thought that mining Haiphong Harbor needed a fresh look. In short, as Taylor told the president, "We are all for this recommendation tonight—but all for different reasons."

Johnson asked General Wheeler if he had told Westmoreland yet of the group's recommendation. No, he said, he had been waiting for the president's decision. Referring to what would have been the first stage of increased troops had the Wheeler-Westmoreland plan been approved, Johnson said, "Tell him to forget the 100,000. Tell him 22,000 is all we can give at the moment." Thus, for the time being at least, Johnson was not going to meet Westmoreland's request.

As important as that tentative decision was on March 4, something else was afoot. Speaking for his task force, Clifford told Johnson that "this is not the time to negotiate," but Rusk broached his idea of a bombing halt as part of a new "fighting and negotiating at the same time" strategy. He had prepared Johnson for the idea earlier in the day by sending him a memo written by his British friends Ambassador Patrick Dean and economist Barbara Ward, whose ideas on economic development of the third world had long impressed the president. Rusk rarely sent articles or memos by outsiders to the president, so Johnson suspected that Rusk had a new approach in mind. The memo read, "Is there an alternative? The Communists have invented one which America might adopt. It is called 'fighting and negotiating.' At some convenient point this spring, America should do two things simultaneously, stop the bombing of the North and mobilize more men for Vietnam. It should announce that it will talk at any time, appoint negotiators, appeal to world opinion, remind Hanoi of its offers to talk and conduct a major peace offensive."

Rusk had mentioned the possibility of halting the bombing over most of North Vietnam at the February 27 meeting of advisers while the president was away. Now, on March 4, having sent Johnson the memo, he raised the subject with both Johnson and other advisers present. As an attempt to get peace negotiations going, Rusk suggested that the United States "stop the bombing during the rainy period in the North." This would include the approaching spring months. Johnson told him, "Really get on your horses on that."[77]

The March 4 meeting was apparently a key one for Johnson. He told the Tuesday Group later on, "All of you moderated my judgment in that Monday meeting." Among other things, he said that the meeting persuaded him that a review of Westmoreland's "search and destroy" strategy was necessary. Johnson may have started considering promoting Westmoreland out of his command into another job as a relatively painless aid in instituting a new military strategy. If so, however, Johnson said nothing about it.[78]

On March 5, the president met again with his Tuesday Group and said to Rusk, "What about that suggestion of last night?" Putting the idea of a bombing halt in the context of an attempt to start negotiations,

Rusk replied, "There is one idea which would throw additional responsibility on Hanoi." The secretary of state then read a prepared statement that Johnson might use in his forthcoming (but still unscheduled) speech to the nation on Vietnam: "The President has directed that U.S. bombing attacks on North Vietnam be limited to those areas which are integrally related with the battlefield. No normal person could expect us to fail to provide maximum support for our men in combat. Whether this stage can be a step toward peace is for Hanoi to determine." Well aware of Johnson's fear of being burned by another bombing halt, Rusk added that it might be a very short one — "If there is no response from Hanoi, we could resume it."[79]

This sort of statement appealed to Johnson, who had heard with some skepticism the previous week that a North Vietnamese official had said, "Ho is waiting, but has insisted that the bombing be stopped first." The next day Rusk sent Johnson another secondhand report of the communists' attitude on negotiations, believing that it would support his suggestions of the previous two days. Other sources ranging from the French government to Supreme Court Justice William O. Douglas (relying on contacts from India) were sending word to Johnson that a cessation of U.S. bombing would be "necessary and sufficient" for the opening of peace talks.[80] Although Johnson had been skeptical of such peace feelers before, Rusk's gentle lobbying was working. The meetings of March 4 and 5 sparked the president's consideration of combining such a new "peace offensive" with an announcement that he would not seek reelection. Johnson also met with J. William Fulbright and three other senators for two and a half hours at the White House on the evening of March 6. Although no notes of the meeting are known to exist, what Johnson heard from them could not have been positive regarding the status quo in Vietnam.[81] He directed Rostow to give one written report of purported North Vietnamese peace feelers to Clifford and Rusk. On the memo he wrote, "Hurry!"[82]

The Second Phase:
Had a Decision Really Been Made?

Johnson may have decided against a major troop increase on March 4, but it was like many "decisions" of his presidency in that it was only tentatively final. He had Wheeler determine whether Westmoreland could live with only a minor troop increase, and he put off his speech to the nation. This left the decision on troops reasonably firm, giving Johnson time to confront other issues. Was the time right for a bombing halt? Should the speech emphasize standing firm in Vietnam or hint at a new, defensive strategy on the ground, one that was different from Westmoreland's old approach? At what all administration figures agreed was a critical juncture in the war, it was becoming increasingly apparent that a presidential speech could not be given without confronting the most basic questions about the U.S. commitment in Indochina. A decision to follow the task force report's recommendations was largely a decision of more of the same with one chief exception—the calling up of over 200,000 reservists. That was unsatisfactory to many in the administration, probably even to Johnson, and he was not going to address the country until he had settled more firmly in his mind what course he was going to take. Further, if a bombing limitation or halt were to be announced, indicating a turn toward deescalation, what should he say about his own political future? He therefore waited to see what others would say.

Plenty got said, but not always under a veil of secrecy. Under Secretary of the Air Force Townsend Hoopes, one of those meeting with Clifford at the Pentagon, confidentially told a *New York Times* reporter that a huge number of troops might be sent to Vietnam. On March 10, the *Times* reported that the administration was considering sending 206,000 troops to Vietnam and was deeply divided over the issue. It was just the sort of leak Johnson hated: the usual unnamed senior civilian in the Pentagon was quoted as saying that Johnson was "still intensely committed to a military solution." It "churned up the whole eastern establishment," thought Rostow. At a later Tuesday Lunch, Johnson learned that the leak to the *Times* had almost certainly come from the Pentagon. CIA Director Helms told Johnson of the secret memo from which the newspaper quoted: "All copies were passed out in Clark Clifford's office on March 2. No other copies were ever distributed." This could only have caused tension between the president and his old friend, the new secretary of defense.

The story would have been more accurate if it had not been outdated. Johnson was by now set against sending anywhere near that number of troops, but the story energized those in Congress, the news media, and elsewhere who were becoming fed up with the war. Fulbright warned Dean Rusk that Congress would have to be consulted before any such step was taken. Rusk also heard from his son Richard, then a college student: "I can remember calling up my dad and begging him for the first and only time in that war . . . 'Don't do it, Pop. You can't do this.' . . . I cried, I hung up the phone and just cried because here I am adding one more piece of a burden to the load he was carrying."[84] And Senator Richard Russell said that no such troop increase should be tried unless the military's air and sea power was unleashed against North Vietnam.[85]

The *Times* story reflected what Clifford's Pentagon subordinates thought was happening in the administration. At higher levels, the debate continued to move beyond the 200,000 troop question to consideration of what new steps the administration might take. No one much liked the report of the Clifford group, so its members lobbied the president individually. Clifford went to Johnson on March 8 and told him that the group's recommendations represented a course the president could take "if that is the way you wish to go." However, and this was the difficult part for Clifford, he told Johnson that he had "doubts" about the current ground and air strategies in Vietnam and about the efficacy of sending more troops. Knowing that he was implicitly telling Johnson that the president may have gone down the wrong road in recent years of Vietnam decisionmaking, Clifford stressed the tentativeness of his doubts and urged Johnson to take time before making final decisions and the speech. That last advice at least—taking his time—was palatable to the president.[86]

Another figure Johnson respected, this one from outside the administration, was former ambassador to South Vietnam *Henry Cabot Lodge*. Part of the Wise Men group, Lodge advised Johnson to direct Westmoreland to drop the aggressive "search and destroy" strategy in Vietnam, to avoid major troop increases, and to impose censorship on news coverage out of Vietnam. Johnson sent the Lodge idea to Wheeler, who was dubious: "In my view, it is not timely to consider fundamental changes in strategy when we are fully committed in what could be the decisive battles of the war."[87] He liked the idea of clamping down on the press though.

A few days later, Johnson summoned Dean Acheson back to the White House. The preeminent Wise Man had been briefed by foreign and defense policy bureaucrats and was ready to tell Johnson what he thought. Acheson later recalled that he wanted to banish any presidential hopes that significantly more soldiers would make a difference in Vietnam, saying, "Mr. President, you are being led down the garden path." But Acheson's version of the meeting may have become more colorful when talking to friends; in a memorandum written the day of the meeting, Acheson described a president very much in touch with reality. "He was quite aware of the serious knock that we have taken during the Tet offensive," Acheson recorded, adding that the time they spent together was "divided approximately equally between us, the President giving me a summary of the situation; I giving him the ideas I developed over the last couple of weeks." Then, most significantly, came a sentence that belies the myth of an outrageous president held in check by more rational advisers: "His report was substantially the same as what I had learned during my various briefings."[88]

Only such troops as needed for emergency purposes should be sent, Acheson said. But Johnson should appoint a panel of "the brightest and ablest civilians and military persons" to reexamine the United States' future in Indochina. The regular military leadership was not to be believed, he added, if only because its reports were a strange mixture of optimism and pessimism. He also threw cold water on Johnson's hopes that Hanoi might be ready to negotiate. The North Vietnamese leadership wanted control of South Vietnam, he contended bluntly. Still, the United States had wasted too much treasure and too many lives in Indochina, he thought. The president must focus on turning the war over to the South Vietnamese and start looking for a way to disengage the American military from the country. Acheson recalled having urged Johnson to listen more to "facts" and less to "uninformed opinion." It was a rare case of Johnson being talked to in a patronizing fashion. But Acheson then received a dose of his own medicine as Walt Rostow joined the two men. With Johnson about to leave temporarily for another crisis meeting, he asked Acheson to restate and summarize his views for the national security adviser. Acheson said that Rostow displayed "the bored patience of a visitor listening to a ten-year-old playing the piano."[89]

The following Sunday afternoon, Johnson brooded again about getting out of the presidency. First he called his wife in to go over the subject yet another time. Though she wanted him to announce his retirement from politics, she pushed him to explain his own reasoning of the subject—what could another man do in the office that he couldn't do? "He could unite the country and start getting some things done," he said. Then they talked to the Humphreys about politics. Hubert Humphrey said, "It's bad, and it's going to keep on being bad, through the primaries." Lady Bird thought that her husband was "serenely philosophic about politics. But about the war itself, he is deeply worried."[90]

Johnson assessed the advice he received in early March on Vietnam and his political future under the shadow of the approaching presidential primary in New Hampshire on March 12. Most political observers thought that McCarthy's was a hopeless cause, but the night before the primary, Johnson called speechwriter John Roche and said, " 'Well, what's Gene going to do?' I said, 'Well, his name is on the ballot, yours isn't. [Johnson was a write-in candidate.] I can't see how you can keep him under a third.' He said, 'No, he'll get 40 per cent, at least 40 per cent. Every son-of-a-bitch in New Hampshire who's mad at his wife or the postman or anybody is going to vote for Gene McCarthy.' " It wasn't a bad prediction—many dovish and hawkish voters, dissatisfied with Johnson's war leadership, voted for McCarthy. The senator came within a few votes of defeating Johnson in New Hampshire, the first such election of the year.[91]

McCarthy's showing made Johnson look vulnerable and changed Robert Kennedy's thinking. On January 30, Kennedy had ruled himself out of the presidential race "under any foreseeable circumstances." But after McCarthy's near victory, Kennedy told Clark Clifford that he would stay out of the race only if Johnson would appoint a public commission—made up of members suggested by Kennedy—to do a complete reevaluation of the war. Even Kennedy's own top advisers thought it a "curious idea" and found it "inconceivable that Johnson would surrender control over foreign policy to an outside group." Johnson discussed the Kennedy proposal with Humphrey, Fortas, and others. The idea of a *public* commission chosen by Kennedy was, of course, anathema to Johnson. He sent word to Kennedy (via an aide who contacted Kennedy adviser Theodore Sorensen) that he wanted "to consult with anyone—inside or outside of the government—who can provide good ideas or reasonable counsel on Vietnam. He carries on consultations all the time. But he is happy to continue and expand those consultations with persons like you, George Ball, both Senators Kennedy . . . Mac Bundy, and General Ridgway." But Johnson told Clifford to reject Kennedy's specific proposal. Within a few days, the family heir to the Kennedy legacy was challenging the man who had been its immediate political heir. Much of Kennedy's rhetoric in the opening weeks of his campaign dealt with the moral bankruptcy of U.S. policy in Vietnam: "Can we ordain to ourselves the awful majesty of God—to decide what cities and villages are to be destroyed, who will live and who will die, and who will join the refugees wandering in a desert of our own creation?"[92]

The pressure on Johnson grew. Although primaries determined the votes of only a minority of delegates for that year's convention and Johnson had reason to believe that he would be renominated, he also saw polls showing embarrassing primary defeats ahead. The prospect of renomination by a divided party was unappealing to him and his wife and reinforced their inclination to retire from politics at the end of the term. He told McPherson and Joseph Califano that he was thinking of getting out of politics. Not sure how seriously to take such talk, McPherson said, "Of course you must run."

"Why? Give me three good reasons why!"

"Well," said McPherson, "If I were you, I wouldn't run. It's a murderous job, and I see no way to change the things that make it so bad . . . but I'm not you. You have to run."

Johnson countered, "That's a conclusion, not a reason. What would be so bad about my not running? What would happen?"

McPherson answered, "For one thing, nobody else could get a program through the Congress. Nobody else knows how."

Johnson shook his head. "Wrong. Any one of them—Nixon, McCarthy, Kennedy—could get a program through next year better than I could. . . . Congress and I are like an old man and woman who've lived together for a hundred years. We know each other's faults and what little good there is in us. We're tired of each other."[93]

But the stepped-up public challenges to his Vietnam policies by Democrats led Johnson to give belligerent speeches on the war: "We must meet our commitments in the world and in Vietnam. We shall and we are going to win!" It was foolish language to use, since he had no desire to win the war in a conventional sense. Indeed, in his own speech he criticized those who "think that we ought to get it over with, with a much wider war." Advisers asked him to cool his rhetoric. Clifford urged "great caution about optimism" in public statements. McPherson reminded Johnson, "When you say 'stick with it in Vietnam' . . . you are saying stick with a rough situation that shows signs of growing worse." Such talk left Johnson a sitting target for criticism from other candidates for president, he added. "It seems to me that we are not going to win a military victory, in the ordinary meaning of that term, with forces we have there now, plus 25–30,000. Just saying we will won't make it so, and in the long run of 2-3 months it is a mistake to say it." McPherson told Johnson that he "prayed" that the course ahead would involve "de-escalating the fighting by changing our tactics, and ultimately even bringing a few Americans home."[94]

James Rowe, a Democratic party figure since the Roosevelt administration and another of Johnson's outside consultants, headed a group working for the president's reelection. His relationship with Johnson was similar to, if less influential than, those of Fortas and Clifford over the years. As Harry McPherson recalls, Rowe was the sort of adviser who could say to Johnson, "You're crazy as hell, Mr. President." On March 19, Rowe urged the president "with the frankness that, I think, has existed between us" to change his tactics "on the hard line. I am shocked by the number of calls I have received today in protest against your Minnesota speech [on Vietnam]." Tet had changed everything, he told Johnson: "It came as a great shock to the American people. . . . Since then the middle group, in which I count you, has dwindled alarmingly. There are more hawks and many more doves." Though discounting his own expertise on foreign policy, Rowe endorsed a bombing pause over North Vietnam and called any kind of troop escalation ("even 30,000") politically harmful.[95]

Johnson's rhetoric may have had its roots in the influence of *Abe Fortas*, a hawk who worried the deescalation proponents in the administration because of his closeness to the Johnsons. Fortas and Johnson usually talked rather than wrote to each other about the war. But in March, Fortas accepted Johnson's invitation to put his thoughts on Vietnam in writing. In doing so, Fortas showed himself to be as hawkish as anyone inside the administration at the time. He implied that Johnson had been irresolute in his war leadership—an all-out air offensive against North Vietnam should have been launched "right after the Tet atrocities." But it still made sense to "take the war to the North," to do everything short of invading North Vietnam with U.S. troops (South Vietnamese troops might try that) or using nuclear weapons. It was time to shelve "totally, for the time being, the 'what-can-we-do-to-get-them-to-negotiate' nonsense— regardless of provocation—and [carry] the war to North Vietnam—without explanation or apology." Further, "Unless we 'win' in Vietnam, our total national personality will, in my opinion, change—and for the worse. If we do not 'win' here, we will not participate elsewhere in the world on a substantial scale."[96]

Perhaps Fortas's hard-line sentiments were emotionally appealing to Johnson, but published claims that Fortas's views reflected Johnson's *real* sentiments are questionable at best.[97] The Lyndon Johnson of those accounts would not have sought Dean Acheson's lecture or Clark Clifford's elemental questions or spent time with innumerable other advisers. Nor would he have directed Rostow to have the State Department produce a massive compilation of current proposals on the war by a wide range of U.S. leaders. There Johnson read "Alternative Policies of Key U.S. Public Figures and Organizations," which outlined the plans of legislators such as Robert and Edward Kennedy, William Fulbright, and Wayne Morse; editorialists with *Time, Life,* and *Newsweek*; and a Republican proposal, among others. Many favored some sort of gradual disengagement from Indochina.[98] And if Johnson's mind was wholly in tune with Fortas, he would have already rejected Rusk's proposed new peace initiative with a bombing limitation or halt. And, most likely, he would not have spent an hour and 45 minutes on March 15 meeting with peace activist Norman Cousins, who lobbied Johnson on ways to reach out diplomatically to North Vietnam.[99]

Instead, Johnson considered such ideas in tandem with another dovish proposal that came in on March 16 from United Nations Ambassador *Arthur Goldberg.* Though he had never been a particularly important adviser to Johnson, Goldberg's proposal sparked major attention from Johnson, and it did not provoke major opposition from Rusk or Rostow. Goldberg reminded Johnson that "recent developments" had provoked deep concern on the part of the public that "our Vietnam policy is right or holds promise of results . . . if public support is permanently and substantially eroded, we will not be able to maintain let alone intensify the level of our military efforts in Vietnam." He suggested: " 'Stop' the aerial and naval bombardment of North Vietnam, for the limited time necessary to determine whether Hanoi will negotiate in good faith." In contrast to Fortas, Goldberg said, "No foreseeable time will be better for negotiations than the present and never has a serious move toward a political settlement been more necessary."[100]

Whatever the appeal of a Fortas-like view to Johnson, Goldberg's letter — not Fortas's — quickly entered the mainstream of the administration's debate. *Walt Rostow*, in forwarding the Goldberg idea to Johnson, cautioned only that "the right time" for such a halt would be "in a few months." Rostow's mildly positive reaction and suggestion of timing may well have been affected by a significant but possibly unpleasant task the president had given him: He was to follow up on Acheson's proposal (one of a few being discussed in the administration) for a new advisory body to do a full-scale review of Johnson's Vietnam policies and report to him by May. Thus, on the same day that Rostow was forwarding the Goldberg proposal, he informed Johnson, "I have translated the Acheson idea into [a] draft directive for the team leader." Rostow suggested that Cyrus Vance, Maxwell Taylor, or Acheson head the group, giving Johnson a range from hawkish (Taylor) to moderate (Vance) to newly dovish (Acheson).[101] Ultimately, Johnson would decide to accept Clifford's suggestion to call in the Wise Men who had met the preceding November as a quicker way of getting a review by outside elites. In mid-March, however, Rostow could not anticipate that, and he was busy serving a president who — by taking Acheson's idea seriously — gave indications that a change in Vietnam policy that Rostow would not like was coming. The national security adviser told Johnson that he was guiding speechwriter Harry McPherson to "put the South Vietnamese — their recruiting and modernization of equipment — front and center" in the draft of the president's upcoming speech. He added that *Ellsworth Bunker*, who was concerned about the war being further Americanized, "clearly leans that way."[102] Bunker, no dove, was well aware that public opinion in the United States would not support the war forever. Even before the Tet Offensive, he told David Lilienthal, "I have a brother-in-law who is quite a fellow: interested in business, in art, other things. I have a letter from him telling me how bad things are going with American public opinion. He ended his letter (at this Bunker smiled quizzically) by saying, 'Ellsworth, come home.' "[103]

At this time Johnson received a note from an old friend, the powerful Washington columnist, Drew Pearson. Fearing further escalation of the sort heralded by the *New York Times*, Pearson wrote that he was parting with Johnson on the war. Ironically, in light of all that Johnson was hearing, Pearson added: "I fear you have been led astray by such short-sighted advisers as Rostow and the military, while some of your other advisers have not spoken up."[104]

The same day that Rostow forwarded Goldberg's proposal to Johnson, Dean Rusk moved swiftly to get both Goldberg's and his own more moderate suggestion before Bunker in Saigon. Doubtful that any bombing halt would get Johnson's approval without Bunker's concurrence, Rusk sent the ambassador a "literally eyes only" message outlining the two approaches without identifying their authors.[105] Rusk had Bunker's answer four days later, on March 20, and passed it on to Johnson. Bunker cabled, "A premature move towards negotiations would unsettle the favorable trend of Vietnamese opinion and action at a critical moment . . . and undo much that we and the GVN have been trying to accomplish since the Tet attacks." Specifically regarding the two peace initiatives, he replied, "I recommend strongly that we not pursue" the complete bombing halt, which (as Bunker did not know) originated from Goldberg. About the other plan (Rusk's) to halt bombing over most of North Vietnam except the parts nearest to American soldiers in the South, Bunker was also critical — it "would have most of the negative effects" of the other plan. But perhaps sensing that a bombing halt and peace initiative were about to happen, he added that the latter plan would be easier to sell to the South Vietnamese. It was a grudging concession, however, in a long message full of foreboding about *any* peace initiative that involved a bombing limitation, unless it were held off for at least "a few more months."[106]

On that same day, Goldberg met with Johnson alone to press for the complete bombing halt as a path to negotiations. The meeting was "very pleasant," Goldberg later recalled. "The President indicated that he had read my memoranda thoughtfully, and that many aspects of it made sense." Johnson asked Goldberg to attend a Tuesday Group session that day and the Wise Men's meetings, which were scheduled for March 25 and 26. (The membership of the Tuesday Group was by now comparatively large: Those attending one or more March meetings included Secretary of the Treasury Fowler, Attorney General Clark, Justice Fortas, Assistant Secretary of State William Bundy, former National Security Adviser McGeorge Bundy, speechwriter McPherson, and Vice President Humphrey, in addition to the group's regular members.)

Goldberg's proposal was having a hard time winning approval in administration circles. Rusk obviously preferred his own proposal for a limited halt, and Clifford suspected that neither plan would bring Hanoi to the table and would quickly be followed by a resumption of the bombing. Goldberg's plan in particular was "fruitless," the secretary of defense said.[107] Clifford was interested in changing American strategy in the war and stopping troop escalations but was not presenting Johnson with a specific plan to make some kind of change in strategy.

Thus the focus of attention was on the Rusk and Goldberg approaches. Of the two, Johnson did not hide his preference for the more moderate one. According to one story, Johnson shouted in rage after seeing the Goldberg plan that he would *not* stop the bombing, but its anonymous and dubious lineage is contradicted by some who talked to Johnson and, more importantly, by the rapidity with which the Goldberg plan became a focus of analysis in subsequent days. Still, Rostow recalls that Johnson "looked at the proposal negatively" and "expressed himself vividly. The President was very worried about the area near the DMZ," where the North Vietnamese could enter South Vietnam and kill American soldiers.[108]

On the night of March 20, the Rusk and Goldberg proposals having circulated for days in the administration, Johnson met with his regular advisers as well as Humphrey, McGeorge Bundy, and Fortas. He heard lots of opinions, mostly conflicting. Goldberg pressed his unilateral bombing halt plan: "Our problem is profoundly serious. I am going to talk frankly. . . . Let's be realistic. The only thing Hanoi wants is a suspension of bombing. Where it will lead nobody knows. Hanoi sees it as a possibility for starting talks. I think we should do that." Both William and McGeorge Bundy supported Goldberg, but Fortas said, "I don't see it. That is a one horse–one rabbit deal." Clifford sounded surprisingly in tune with the Supreme Court justice: "I don't believe any approach to Hanoi at this time will be accepted." Rusk repeated his own more moderate bombing limitation idea but reported that Bunker was not in favor of either. Another problem, the advisers all agreed, was whether the president could offer a peace initiative and a troop escalation of any sort in the same speech. Much was left unresolved in the meeting itself, one in which Johnson exclaimed, "I want war like I want polio. What you want and what your image is are two different things."[109]

Johnson later wrote that, by the end of the meeting, he was impressed that Bunker, though dubious about both, found Rusk's limited bombing halt proposal preferable to Goldberg's. As for troops, negotiations between the Pentagon and Saigon had produced a plan to send only 13,500 more troops, which would reinforce the 10,000 emergency troops sent soon after Tet began. This, too, Johnson decided, looked like the best option. Still, there was a speech to be written and more consultations to be done with the Vietnamese and American leaderships in Saigon before the speech could be given. But Rusk was beginning to feel confident that he had the president on board.[110]

Clifford was not at all sure what Johnson was thinking and was still worried that the president would escalate the war.[111] Walt Rostow was by then convinced that Clifford was simply out of touch with what was really happening in Johnson's mind. He did not understand the president's thinking on the war: that a choice of limiting the bombing and making only token additions of troops would constitute a move toward peace, especially if combined with a retirement announcement. Rusk knew that retirement was on Johnson's mind, but Clifford did not believe it.[112] Clifford was greatly influenced by aides at the Pentagon who distrusted the Rusk bombing limitation idea and wanted the administration to make a more explicit commitment to deescalate the war. Thus, Clifford recalled, Rusk's "proposal seemed to be designed to provide the basis for greater pressure in the future. As far as I could tell, it did not constitute a good faith effort to get negotiations started." The secretary of defense told aides at the time that he felt outnumbered "seven or eight to one" by other advisers.[113]

Harry McPherson—by now a regular at Vietnam meetings—was an informal ally of Clifford's in the White House. Although Dean Rusk would not dream of calling up a White House aide, confiding in him his doubts about escalation proposals, and proposing an alliance, the secretary of defense did just that:

> Clifford called to ask what I really thought about the war. I told him. "Old boy . . . we have a lot of work to do together. And I think we are going to prevail." . . . His conclusion was that [the war] could not be won by the present level of effort, but only prolonged; and as escalation was inconceivable, we should have to "wind it down," beginning with an announcement that we would not commit substantial new forces. "Now you must tell me what you hear over there, and I will keep you advised of my activities."[114]

McPherson was impressed, even starry-eyed about Clifford's maneuvering, but later he would have doubts that the secretary's impact on Johnson was as critical as it first seemed. And he recalled, "Clifford spoke in a way that didn't seem to set us on a clear course, but at the same time doubted the course we were on."[115]

Johnson quickly accepted one idea first broached by Clifford and supported by other advisers—that of calling in the Senior Advisory Group, the Wise Men, to evaluate Johnson's options in Vietnam. Four months earlier, they were almost unanimous in support of the president's policies in Vietnam. Clifford knew that Dean Acheson and McGeorge Bundy were "in the process of reevaluation."[116] But this was no secret to Johnson, who had signs regarding the thinking of Acheson, Lodge, Goldberg, Bundy, and Ball—all increasingly dovish—and Taylor and Fortas, who were urging Johnson to stick with established policies. It was arranged that the men would meet on March 25 and 26; they would be briefed on the first day, have a discussion that night, meet with Johnson's formal foreign policy advisers the next day, and then with the president himself.

In the meantime, Johnson continued to wrestle with the war's dilemmas. On March 22, he met with essentially the same advisory group he had seen two days earlier. Most of those present wanted Johnson to take some kind of step toward deescalation, but pessimism abounded that a limited bombing halt of the sort Rusk proposed would bring Hanoi to the peace table. And the Goldberg proposal of a complete halt apparently earned little consideration. Yet Johnson felt pressured to do *something* — he told the group of his conviction that there had been "a dramatic shift in public opinion. . . . A lot of people are really ready to surrender," he complained, and then, showing a flash of paranoia, he added that such people were "following a party line" without knowing it. It was a gloomy meeting.[117]

The next day, March 23, McPherson suggested a sequence by which Johnson would announce a unilateral halt of bombing north of the 20th parallel — in other words, most of North Vietnam. Further, Johnson would challenge North Vietnam to stop pouring men and supplies down the Ho Chi Minh trail. McPherson wasn't optimistic that his approach — similar to Rusk's March 5 Tuesday Lunch proposal — would lead to talks, he told Johnson, but it would "show the American people that we are willing to do every reasonable thing to bring about talks." As a result of the previous day's unhappy meeting, McPherson also lacked a sense of where Johnson's thinking was heading, for or against a bombing halt. In its latest draft, the president's speech had no mention of a peace initiative. McPherson wondered whether Johnson could still be considering escalation, as Clifford feared.[118]

Within an hour of receiving McPherson's memo that Saturday afternoon, the president gave it to Rostow with a notation: "Walt — For Rostow, Rusk, Clifford comments at once. — L." And Johnson, unbeknownst to McPherson, discussed it with Rusk privately. Not until five days later would the speechwriter learn with certainty that it had been put before principals in the administration. It happened when Rusk casually mentioned to him, "We sent that idea out to Saigon. Bunker thinks the South Vietnamese can live with it."[119]

On Sunday, March 24, Wheeler met Westmoreland in the Philippines, staying up most of one night to talk about troops and a change in commanders. In Washington, Johnson set the stage for his upcoming speech by announcing the promotion (others said the kicking upstairs) of Westmoreland to army chief of staff, effective the summer of 1968. He was to be succeeded by General Creighton Abrams.[120] But more important than discussion of the change in command was Wheeler's mission to convey to Westmoreland what had been signaled to him earlier in the month by cable. Westmoreland recalls that Wheeler told him,

> "The President says very bluntly that he does not have the horses to change our strategy." By horses he meant votes among his advisers. Press and television reporting on the Tet Offensive had convinced many that the war was lost or could be brought to no satisfactory conclusion. The intelligence community and some who represented it in government were dead against the war and had no comprehension of the use of force. Under those circumstances, the President had asked Wheeler to tell me, making a major call-up of the Reserves and contesting the enemy's geographical widening of the war was politically infeasible.[121]

Wheeler also told Westmoreland that a chief factor in the president's decision on the troops had been congressional reaction. Even conservative southern senators John Stennis and Richard Russell had told Johnson that major troop increases were out of the question. Westmoreland wasn't happy, but he recognized the political division back home and agreed to change his "request" to 13,500 men so that, at the appropriate time, Johnson could describe his military and political advisers' "agreement" on troop needs in Vietnam.[122]

But uncertainty prevailed among most of official Washington as to Johnson's plans. Though he had informed the military and Rusk of his likely decision on troops, and the secretary of state knew Johnson's mind on the bombing, others like Clifford did not know which way Johnson was heading. The president could, if he wished, still change his mind about the troops. Similarly, he could decide against any sort of bombing halt (unlikely) or in favor of a complete halt (even more unlikely, given his concern that such a halt would endanger the lives of American troops). There were those who still pushed him to do the latter. *Hubert Humphrey* sat one evening with the president in his bedroom, discussing the war. It was a familiar setting for the vice president: "How well I recall President Johnson sitting night after night in his room, oftentimes just himself and myself and one or two of his military advisers. He would have a big map of Vietnam stretched out on the cabinet table. . . . He kept saying time after time, 'Any damn fool can get a bigger war. What I want is to end the war . . . to stop the shooting and get these people at the conference table so that we can settle this thing.' "[123]

Humphrey, a semiregular participant in Tuesday Lunch and other Vietnam meetings in early 1968, almost never spoke up, telling Johnson what he thought in private. In February and March, Johnson was "desperate for peace," Humphrey thought, and most of the president's nonmilitary advisers preferred some kind of deescalation. When told by the president that he was likely to stop most of the bombing, Humphrey responded, "Mr. President, stopping at the 19th parallel is not going to do much good. What you should do is stop it all."[124]

Even Lady Bird sounded fed up with the war. She was becoming attracted to isolationism and made what she later described as a "hotheaded" statement to her family "about when we got the Vietnam war finally settled, I didn't want to have another thing to do with any foreign country." And she told her diary, "I have a growing feeling of Prometheus Bound, just as though we were lying there on the rock, exposed to vultures, and restrained from fighting back."[125] White House aide Larry Temple saw how both Johnson and his wife were preoccupied with the speech. Temple worked an early morning shift, often seeing the president and Mrs. Johnson in bed. More than once in March he found Johnson handing a draft of the speech to his wife, saying, "Bird, what do you think about this?" But although Johnson told her what he was planning to do in Vietnam, Mrs. Johnson did not know for certain whether he would announce his political retirement or not. Neither did he. But he had set his deadline for both Vietnam and reelection decisions. The speech must be given by March 31, he concluded.[126]

When Wheeler returned with Abrams to the capital, they met alone with Johnson on March 26 for almost two hours, prior to the generals' meeting with the Wise Men. The president peppered them with questions—what about Howard Tuckner's report on NBC news that North Vietnam had 250,000 troops in reserve? Are we vulnerable at Hue? And he laid out for them his dilemma, much of it (he believed) economic:

> Our fiscal situation is abominable. We have a deficit running over 20 [billion dollars]. We are not getting the tax bill . . . the British pound may fall. The Canadian pound [sic] may fall. The dollar will be in danger. Unless we get a tax bill it will be unthinkable. They say to get $10 in taxes we must get $10 in reductions of appropriations. We have to take one half from non-Vietnam defense expenditures. That will cause hell with [Richard] Russell. If we don't do that we will have hell. What happens when you cut poverty, housing, education? This is complicated by the fact it is an election year. I don't give a damn about the election. . . . The leaks to the *New York Times* hurt us. The country is demoralized. You must know about it. It's tough you can't have communications. A worker writes a paper for the Clifford group and it's all over Georgetown.

Since early March there had been a renewed international economic crisis—a weakening of the dollar caused by another run on gold (which played a central role in the world's monetary system) in the international markets. On top of that, as Johnson suggested, it was far from certain that Congress would pass Johnson's tax increase bill. This had lessened Johnson's freedom of action, since increasing the U.S. presence in Vietnam would have had budgetary implications. Yet without the tax increases, the budget deficit would grow and inflation would likely increase, weakening the nation's international economic posture.

Speaking of possible peace plans, Johnson told the generals, "We must have something." The generals consoled him with word that Westmoreland would settle for 13,500 more troops plus some additional air force support. They also assured him that he had not overly restricted Westmoreland's military strategy in recent years, and that morale among American soldiers was "tops."[127]

This and other meetings indicated that, although there were still hawks in his administration (not to mention his party, the Congress, and the public), they were outnumbered and on the defensive. Rusk was certainly no longer one of the voices for simply "holding steady" in Vietnam. He told Johnson and Rostow that Harry McPherson's memo of the previous weekend essentially represented his line of thought, and he again presented proposed language for a bombing limitation announcement that he had read to Johnson weeks earlier.[128] Clifford, meanwhile, repeated sentiments he had offered three weeks earlier—"We seem to be in a sinkhole."

On the afternoon of March 26, generals Wheeler and Abrams joined Johnson in meeting the Wise Men. Wheeler told them that Westmoreland was on the offensive and added, "I see no reason for all the gloom and doom we see in the United States press." Abrams told them that South Vietnam's armed forces "performed well during the Tet Offensive. . . . I feel good about the way the thing is going." Assuring the group that he was "quite certain" South Vietnam would carry a larger part of the fighting in the future, he added, "I would have to quit if I didn't believe that."

But having told his military leaders that something new in the way of deescalation must be tried in Vietnam, Johnson saw how widespread that view was in the hours that followed. The Wise Men had been briefed the night before and talked among themselves the following morning prior to meeting with Johnson on March 26. In the meantime, Rostow had prepared Johnson for the meeting by suggesting a list of questions "as close to those of November 2 (the date of the previous meeting between Johnson and the Wise Men) so that you will be able to gauge the change of views between then and now."[129] But it was apparent to

Johnson that the group's views had shifted dramatically. Dismissing Rusk, Clifford, and most other formal advisers after an initial session, the president wanted to hear the elders' views directly, without any chance that the presence of his foreign policy managers would affect what the members of the group told him. Only Humphrey and Wheeler were allowed to stay.

McGeorge Bundy, Johnson's former national security adviser, spoke first. Bundy had been in the White House for days before the meeting and had told Johnson five days earlier that "a great many people — even very determined and loyal people — have begun to think that Vietnam really is a bottomless pit."[130] Now, with the president and the group of elders together, he summarized the views of the majority: U.S. goals, as previously outlined by the administration, could not be attained within reasonable time and with reasonable resources. Vietnam policies would have to be changed. After Bundy's characterization of the majority viewpoint, Johnson went from man to man, seeking each one's opinion, with Bundy answering first. The adviser who had urged Johnson to bomb North Vietnam in 1965 now explicitly reversed himself for all to see: It should be stopped completely, and no more troops should be sent to Vietnam. "I must tell you," he said in the eastern accent that Johnson knew so well, "what I thought I would never say, that I now agree with George Ball."[131] It was a significant, poignant statement, coming in the presence of the Wise Men. Bundy was implicitly admitting that he had been wrong, terribly wrong, in advising Johnson to go to war in 1965. Henry Cabot Lodge told the president to stop the "search and destroy" strategy employed by Westmoreland in Vietnam and shift to a defensive strategy geared toward protecting the South Vietnamese population. Douglas Dillon, a Republican who had served in the Kennedy and Johnson administrations, echoed Bundy — no more bombing, stop it all. And no more troops. When Johnson asked him what had changed his opinion on the war, Dillon cited the military and intelligence briefing the group had heard the night before.

Then Dean Acheson told Johnson that American interests "in southeast Asia, Europe, and in connection with the dollar crisis require a decision now to disengage within a limited time. . . . One thing seems sure — the old slogan that success is just around the corner won't work." Johnson then turned his gaze to former Under Secretary of State George Ball, who had left the administration in late 1966, unhappy about Vietnam but complimenting Johnson for his "insistence on full discussion and the unfettered expression of views" before making "hard choices." Ball had been silent when Bundy mentioned his name. Now he spoke: "I share Acheson's view. I have felt that way since 1961 — that our objectives are not attainable." All the bombing should be stopped, he said.

When he spoke of the political problems Johnson would face in turning toward deescalation, the president cut him off: "That's the last thing that would affect me." General Matthew Ridgway told Johnson that the South Vietnamese government should be informed that the United States would start withdrawing troops in two years. And Cyrus Vance, former deputy secretary of defense and decided Johnson loyalist, told the president, "I agree with George Ball." A way had to be found to get negotiations going.

Some disagreed. Abe Fortas, former Ambassador Robert Murphy, Maxwell Taylor, and retired General Omar Bradley more or less backed the old policies. Taylor said, "I am dismayed. The picture I get is a very different one from that you have. Let's not concede the home front, let's do something about it!" Fortas in particular argued against a new negotiating approach, and insisted that the United States "has never had in mind winning a military victory." He may have been correct, but the point irritated Dean Acheson, who exploded, "What in the name of God have we got 500,000 troops there for — chasing girls? You know damned well this is what we are trying to do — to force the enemy to sue for peace. It won't happen, at least not in any time the American people will permit."

Holding his baby grandson Lyn Nugent on his lap (the child had been brought to Johnson during the meeting) the president said to the group, "As I understand it, with the exception of Murphy, Bradley, Taylor, Fortas, and General Wheeler, all of you favor disengagement." Some quibbled about the word "disengagement" versus a more vague one, but the majority sentiment of the meeting was clear.[132] Johnson had opened the first session with the Wise Men hours earlier that day, telling them of his long-standing desire "to hear from people who are not regular advisers from time to time." Now, as they said good-bye and filed out, the president could easily "gauge the change" (Rostow's words) between the November 1967 meeting and that of March 1968.

The meeting was not quite the shock to Johnson that some writers have claimed: Johnson knew where Ball stood, and McGeorge Bundy had already told Johnson of his and Cyrus Vance's changes of heart. Dean Acheson's shift had been made clear earlier. And Henry Cabot Lodge had already pushed Johnson to initiate a new defensive strategy in Vietnam. But Johnson had not talked recently to others in the group such as Arthur Dean and Douglas Dillon and was probably surprised by Ridgway, who had only recently advised him to increase the military's manpower reserve but now opposed increasing combat troop levels in Vietnam itself.

Johnson grabbed George Ball on the way out. Relations between the two men were as comfortable as ever, but Johnson was suspicious about the cause of the shift of some of the foreign policy elders to Ball's camp. He complained, "Your whole group must have been brainwashed, and I'm going to find out what Habib [one of the briefers] and the others told you." Part of Johnson's immediate response probably resulted from Dillon's indication that his change of heart came out of those briefings. The next day, Johnson asked to hear the same briefings the group had heard, so two of the three briefers (Habib was out of town) were directed to repeat for Johnson what they had said to the Wise Men. One of the briefers was George Carver of the CIA. His review of the war had stressed (more strongly than CIA Director *Richard Helms* had) that "pacification" was not working in Vietnam, that the U.S. military had underestimated the number of enemy soldiers, and that it was nearly impossible to convince North Vietnam that the United States would stay in Indochina for decades. On March 27, in the cabinet room,

> Carver was invited to take the chair occupied by the Secretary of Defense during cabinet meetings. He laid out his sheets of yellow legal paper, covered with notes. Helms was there, of course, as well as Vice-President Hubert Humphrey, General Creighton Abrams (who was about to succeed General Westmoreland in Vietnam), General Wheeler from the JCS, and one young man in Army fatigues whom Carver had never seen before. He hesitated a moment; he was about to give out some highly classified information; who was this fellow? Then he figured: Well, if the President wants to declassify this stuff here and now, that's up to him — and he went ahead. Later he learned the fellow in fatigues was Johnson's son-in-law, Patrick Nugent.
>
> Carver's briefing lasted an hour and fifteen minutes, just about as long as he'd talked to the Wise Old Men. Johnson frequently interrupted him, squirmed in his chair, talked on the phone two or three times while Carver went on with his briefing, interrupted to ask another question or two, then asked, "Are you finished?" Not quite, said Carver, and proceeded. Again: "Are you finished yet?" No. Helms sat quietly throughout; Carver noticed a little smile playing across Helms' face; Johnson's restless irritation was amusing him. Finally Carver concluded and Johnson immediately jumped up and stalked from the room without a single word. But then, a moment later, he came back and pumped Carver's hand, before stalking out again, still without a word.[133]

Johnson ultimately concluded that the intelligence briefings, although too pessimistic, had not brainwashed the Wise Men. Reports by the news media (he later wrote) had affected them: "If they had been so deeply influenced by the reports of the Tet offensive, what must the average citizen in the country be thinking?"[134] The Wise Men's meeting was not so much revelation as important confirmation for the president that, as he had told Wheeler and Westmoreland days before, "something" different had to be done.

That evening, March 27, Johnson continued his whirlwind pace, bringing *Mike Mansfield* into the White House for three hours. Johnson's personal relationship with Mansfield (as with Ball) had endured without change. In the final year of his presidency, Johnson characteristically pushed Mansfield for support but, whether or not he got it, thanked the majority leader for his honesty. Now the president sought Mansfield's reaction to what, in a characteristically Johnsonian fashion, was the tentatively final decision to stop the bombing above the 20th parallel. Mansfield supported this decision and, perhaps in reaction to Johnson's reference to the military's request for troops, reiterated in person what he had written to Johnson 10 days before: "Our position for a negotiated settlement, it seems to me, will be no worse and it may well be better if we consolidate and concentrate rather than deepen and spread our involvement in South Vietnam with another great increment in men on the ground."[135]

Johnson also called in other former colleagues from the Congress, including *Richard Russell*, the man whose advice (according to Lady Bird Johnson) Johnson valued as much as that of Rusk, Clifford, McNamara, and Westmoreland. The president had stayed in touch with his former mentor throughout the month. Russell recorded in a personal datebook on March 13: "10 A.M. to W. H., 1 + 1/2 hr. w Pres. We discussed war + other difficulties." On March 24 he had breakfast with Johnson, only to return the next day for breakfast with the president and Mrs. Johnson.[136] Unlike Mansfield, though, Russell tried to talk Johnson out of a bombing halt. Returning to the White House on Friday morning, March 29, Russell saw a version of Johnson's upcoming speech that talked of bombing only in areas of North Vietnam where it was necessary to protect American lives (there was disagreement among Johnson advisers about which language would be more effective—specifying the 20th parallel or simply pledging to limit bombing to those areas where it would directly protect American lives). "I advised against any cessation of the bombing unless there was some indication of reciprocity on the part of the North Vietnamese," Russell told fellow senators a few days later. On this point he opposed Rusk, who for weeks had advised Johnson to stop the bombing without guarantee of a concurrent reciprocal action by the North Vietnamese. The point was to test the communists for a period of weeks *after* the halt began to see if they then altered their behavior. Russell lost on this point and complained defensively to his colleagues, "As has often been the case, the President did not take my advice or suggestions. . . . I want to be absolved of having anything to do with the . . . cessation or stopping of the bombing."[137]

But Johnson still had not confided in Clifford about the bombing halt. As late as March 20, Clifford (like Senator Russell) had advocated linking it to a reciprocal action on the part of the North Vietnamese.[138] Now Clifford (joining Rusk) favored a unilateral halt of most of the bombing. Disturbed by the belligerent language of some of Johnson's public speeches, he also fretted that the upcoming speech to the nation might lack pragmatic, conciliatory language. Johnson and Clifford no longer had the rapport of previous times. It was not the content of Clifford's advice as much as his way of presenting it that irked Johnson. And the president had a gut-level suspicion of anyone—even his old friend Clifford—who spent much of each working day with leaking "doves" in the Pentagon. Johnson thought (correctly) that the latter felt little loyalty to him. Obviously, however, a secretary of defense must spend time with his subordinates.

Those who have claimed that Clifford was the "good" dove, Rusk the "bad" hawk, and Johnson the paranoid president who wanted to hear only from Rusk are not supported by the notes of meetings. Although Clifford spoke colorfully of Vietnam as a "sinkhole" and of the need for the "beginnings of deescalation," Rusk spoke in tactful ways that were more likely to reach Johnson, the very president who had sent 500,000 troops to the sinkhole. But of the proposed bombing halt, Rusk told Johnson to say in his upcoming speech, "Whether or not Hanoi will take advantage of this, we don't know. But let's see." Only on March 22 had Clifford, under Rusk's prodding, agreed that a bombing halt need not be linked explicitly to a concurrent reciprocal action on the part of North Vietnam.[139] Neither the secretary of defense nor the secretary of state was radically hawkish or dovish during these days. Both wanted to move Johnson toward limited deescalation. Without realizing their common goals, they viewed Johnson in different ways, were suspicious of each other, and approached the president with different strategies.

The Final Days of Decision

Only on Thursday, March 28, was it becoming clear to all his advisers which way the president was going to go. A group of his top advisers met again to discuss the speech without the president there. Clifford was incensed that there was not yet a firm mention of a peace initiative in the latest draft of the speech he had seen. The speech as it stood was a disaster, Clifford said. "It offers nothing—neither hope nor a plan for either military victory or negotiated settlement." But what happened next startled the secretary of defense, because the secretary of state immediately said that of course the speech needed to sound more conciliatory.[140] Rusk then pulled out a slip of paper with the language from the March 5 meeting at which he had suggested a bombing limitation (similar to McPherson's later memo), and all now agreed that it should be incorporated into the new draft. Rostow called the president and asked him to meet with the group that night to discuss the new draft that McPherson was putting together that very moment. Johnson assented, and hours later he sat down with the group:

> I slowly read the key passage. "Beginning immediately, and without waiting for any signal from Hanoi, we will confine our air and naval attacks in North Vietnam to the military targets south of the 20th parallel. . . ." It was what I had decided needed to be done, but I felt I still should not say so flatly for fear of another damaging press leak. I indicated that I did not want to comment further at that time.[141]

Immediately after the meeting, Johnson and Rusk talked alone. Rusk showed the president a draft of a cable he had already written, telling Bunker in Saigon of the plan and asking him to secure the agreement, if possible, of the South Vietnamese government. Johnson approved the cable and out it went: "We are now thinking in terms of an early policy announcement that would have the following major elements." These included the bombing limitation, sending only 13,500 support forces to go along with the emergency troops sent in February, an emphasis on increasing the effectiveness of the South Vietnamese government and military, and a reduction of the U.S. budget deficit.[142] Perhaps to soften the blow to Bunker, Rusk added that there was a good chance that Hanoi would denounce the offer. If there was no discernible positive reaction from the communists in the following weeks, the bombing might be resumed.

But Johnson was more optimistic about the peace initiative than Rusk and his other advisers, in part because he had a surprise to sweeten the deal.[143] Just as he had kept his intentions regarding the military options in Vietnam a secret from many of his advisers until March 28 and 29, he now planned (tentatively, as always) to cap off the speech with an announcement that he would retire from politics at the end of his term. This, he thought, might convince Democrats, Republicans, the country at large, and maybe even Hanoi that he wanted to strike a deal to end the war. Congress might pass the painful but necessary tax increase to balance the budget. But he would not allow even the trusted

McPherson to write that part of the speech. He gave that task to Horace Busby, a Johnson aide for decades, known to the president and first lady simply as "Buzz."

There was no more debate about essentials of Vietnam policy, but much activity continued. Bunker's agreement and that of the South Vietnamese came in over the weekend. On March 30, Wheeler participated in the speech-drafting sessions. The speech, he noticed, still had no ending. Something was still bothering Johnson, he thought. The president "was in more of a swivet than I had ever seen him before in my life. He was really very much concerned about something; his manner was completely different than it usually was. He was obviously upset emotionally and, I would say, mentally. . . . I thought to myself at the time that he was just awfully tired."[144] Perhaps one thing bothering Johnson, even at this late stage in the speech's planning, was the incoherence of information coming in to the White House. A CIA memorandum written on March 28 and passed on to Johnson warned, "Signs are accumulating that a new Communist offensive may be imminent." It was reminiscent of the final days before the 1965 troop decision, when he told Jack Valenti, "Everything blurs when you get almost to the gate."[145]

Johnson fretted with Lady Bird over the speech. "I had spent a good part of Saturday and part of Friday making suggestions on it myself," she wrote. "I read it over again for what was the umpteenth time" on Sunday, March 31 — an unusually emotional day. It began early when Lynda Johnson Robb returned to the White House from California in tears, having seen her husband off to Vietnam. Why should he have to risk his life "for people who did not even want to be protected," she asked. His daughter was "lonely and bewildered," Johnson wrote. "I wanted to comfort her and could not."[146] In a few days, his other son-in-law would also leave for Vietnam.

Later that Sunday, Johnson told Humphrey and a few others what to expect in the speech, including the retirement. Some tried to talk him out of it, but none told him that he was wrong about changing course in the war.[147] Still, Johnson was acutely aware that some of his hawkish advisers — Fortas, Russell, Taylor, Wheeler, and Rostow among them — would have done things differently and that some doves might not be satisfied with the bombing limitation and the refusal to give the military 200,000 more troops. For three years he had listened to advisers pushing him in distinctly different directions. Usually, he had tried to reconcile their different points of view to achieve consensus among those he respected. It had achieved one substantive goal — South Vietnam had been "saved" for the time being at least — but it had gained Johnson little respect in Congress, among foreign policy elites, and with the public. Many thought that Johnson had been too weak; others thought him belligerent and militaristic.

That night he gave the speech without an ending that had been composed by McPherson. Its elements had been cleared with Bunker and rehearsed with select members of Congress. Then, pausing for just a second, he said what no one close to him, not even Lady Bird, was sure he would say until he spoke the words laid out in front of him, words implying failure on his part: "There is division in the American house now." Then, "I shall not seek, and will not accept, the nomination of my party for another term as your President."

A secretary jotted down what he said to his family and friends afterward: "I was never surer of any decision I ever made in my life. I have 525,000 men whose very lives depend on what I do, and I must not be worried about primaries."[148]

To the surprise of many — including Fulbright, who told the Senate, "I submit that this is not going to be a significant inducement to bring about a cease-fire and a conference" — Hanoi announced on April 3 its willingness to begin talks with the U.S. government. A tortuous and long road to settlement had its beginning.[149]

Thirty-six hours after the speech, congressional leaders uncharacteristically had to press Johnson to discuss the decision's political implications. He said that he was tired of "begging anyone for anything. . . . I've listened to all the people both for and against our foreign policy and have considered their suggestions carefully. . . . Last week we called fifteen men together including Matthew Ridgway, General Bradley, Maxwell Taylor, Arthur Dean, and Henry Cabot Lodge to hear their views, and as a result I made this speech proposal Sunday night."[150]

But as tempting as it is to treat that statement as "smoking gun" evidence of the roots of Johnson's decisionmaking, there was much more that created the decision than the Wise Men's meeting. Johnson's sentiments on the troops had been conveyed to Westmoreland on March 24 and on the bombing to Rusk in mid-March — all of this *before* the Wise Men spoke to Johnson. Besides the Wise Men, it was Clark Clifford and Dean Rusk — but especially the latter, thought Harry McPherson — whose interaction with Johnson had counted for much. After the March 28 meeting of the president's advisers, when it seemed to the secretary of defense that he had somehow *convinced* Rusk of the need for a peace initiative, it became clear to speechwriter McPherson that something besides Clifford's persuasiveness had gotten to Rusk and Johnson.[151] It was Rusk, he thought — the man who never clued others into what he said to Johnson in private — who had been most influential with the president. Richard Helms has also pondered claims about who influenced Johnson during this time:

> I have the greatest regard and respect for Clark Cliff
> [Townsend] Hoopes very much. I regard both of them
> Hoopes in his book makes the contention that it wa
> who was responsible for "turning President Johnson around,"
> Vietnamese war. . . . Hoopes asked me about this point before he ever wrote his book. I told him I did not believe this to be the case. I had never seen any evidence of it. I was in all the meetings.[152]

Helms thought that there was no single individual who set Johnson on a new course. McPherson and Wheeler thought that key members of Congress, men like Mansfield, Russell, Stennis, and Henry Jackson—whose advice conflicted—nevertheless helped convince Johnson that a new approach was necessary. More troops and bombing would not do, they said, even if Bunker, Taylor, Fortas, Westmoreland, and others thought otherwise. And Johnson's own assessment of opinion polls and news reports was that although he might win reelection after a bitter fight, he would never again have the confidence of the people or those elites whom he called the "natural leaders" of the country.

Moderating his stance in Vietnam and withdrawing from the election campaign provided a way to regain some control over events relating to the war, not to mention the economy. He might become, he hoped, a "non-political" president in the eyes of the public and Congress, one pursuing the national interest in his remaining months in office. And, as Kearns persuasively wrote, announcing his future retirement was a way to "retreat with honor" and lessen his own considerable pain. Part of the pain was over the deaths of so many people—soldiers and civilians—in Vietnam and the awful, nagging possibility that it was all for nothing. Harry McPherson, who believed that "all the conventional wisdom" had supported Johnson's escalation in 1965," once tried to conceive of that thought lurking around Johnson's mind: "Imagine! Christ, you put five hundred and fifty thousand Americans out there; you've lost twenty-five thousand of them dead! What if it's wrong? What if we've made an error?" Johnson later reflected privately on his withdrawal statement: "After 37 years of public service, I deserved something more than being left alone in the middle of the plain, chased by stampedes on every side." Everett Dirksen understood this: After Johnson's speech he exploded to reporters, "How long do you go on? After all, the President of the United States is a human being. You may laugh at this, and I don't give a damn, but Lyndon B. Johnson is one of the most sensitive men I ever knew."[153]

The speech was well received by a surprised public and most leaders around the country in the days that followed its delivery. It has been similarly regarded in subsequent years.

A Competitive Advisory System in Early 1968

Lyndon Johnson's advisory system became competitive, sometimes chaotic, in the two months preceding his crucial March 31 address. More so than in 1965 and 1967, his advisory system was open to outsiders. Arthur Goldberg, for instance, long a part of the administration but never an important adviser on the war, had significant status as an adviser for a brief period in March 1968, enjoying private access to Johnson, having his memoranda circulated widely in administration circles, and taking part in key meetings of presidential advisory groups. Members of the advisory system often disagreed with and distrusted or even resented one another. Westmoreland once complained to Wheeler of a burden he faced because of Johnson's use of informal advisers: "Special requirements for information are coming in from multiple sources . . . if this matter is not brought into hand soon, it will rapidly get out of hand."[154] Sometimes advisers did not even know they had the same goals. Despite the many published accounts that paint Clark Clifford as a dovish Lone Ranger among Johnson's advisers, other counselors shared or exceeded his hesitant, then growing attachment to the goal of turning away from further military escalation and toward a new peace initiative. Chief among these was Rusk, of course, but others included McGeorge Bundy, Hubert Humphrey, and Harry McPherson.

Other key participants with significant influence over Johnson but little or no formal foreign policy making status included Dean Acheson, Maxwell Taylor, Abe Fortas, Matthew Ridgway, Mike Mansfield, Richard Russell, and collectively, the Wise Men's group. Sessions with formal advisers were clearly still influential with the president, but there was no longer an orderly quality to their interactions with Johnson: In contrast to 1967, the Tuesday Lunch Group met so often that it was no longer a weekly forum for directing the war. Instead, the "Tuesday" meeting was sometimes nearly a daily occurrence, with a fluid membership.

Just as the range of advisers was broader in Johnson's White House during the Tet period, so was the range of advice. In 1967, the choices presented to Johnson ranged chiefly from serious escalation (what Maxwell Taylor labeled "all out") to a continuation of policies already in effect ("stick it out") to very moderate deescalation characterized by a bombing limitation ("pull back"). Most advisers favored the "stick it out" option. But in 1968, words were heard that had rarely been voiced in Johnson's presence since the first half of 1965—"disengagement," "deescalation," "withdrawal," "sinkhole." Many advisers urged Johnson to think of these short-term deescalatory policies as the beginning of the United States' disengagement from Indochina, which would take place over the coming year or two. Simultaneously, there were contrasting efforts to persuade the president to go "all out" with greater bombing campaigns, ground troop incursions into other parts of Indochina, and a public statement that there would be no more "groveling" for a peace agreement with Hanoi. Few advisers favored a policy of more of the same.

5 | The Evolution of Johnson's Vietnam Advisory System

ALTHOUGH LYNDON JOHNSON surely had an expansive, colorful, and complicated personality, he did not scare off dissent from the ranks of his Vietnam advisers. Instead, he usually sought a broad range of views from diverse and talented advisers and cloaked his advisory encounters in secrecy. Yet his advisory system *did* change over the course of three years—becoming sometimes more, sometimes less diverse and competitive. In this chapter, I address the question of how Johnson's Vietnam advisory system evolved in relation to changes in the political environment and spell out some of the implications of that evidence for the literature on Johnson and Vietnam.

1965, 1967, and 1968 Compared and Analyzed

The three periods focused on in the preceding chapters were characterized by one important similarity—the president faced proposals to increase the U.S. military commitment in South Vietnam. I now examine how the environmental conditions of each period shaped Johnson's advisory system, using the three propositions outlined in Chapter 1:

1. When certainty over a president's goals and the means to those goals is at its highest in the American political environment, collegiality and regularized decisionmaking will be at their highest in the advisory system. Such a collegial system is "clanlike"—friendly, cohesive, featuring orderly interactions between president and advisers—and is comparatively indifferent to the limited dissent in the environment.

2. By contrast, when the administration's goals and means are controversial or downright unpopular in the environment, the advisory system will be "marketlike"—competitive, less orderly, featuring procedural competition of advisers and substantive competition of divergent ideas. There will be greater openness to outside political currents, with an increasing number of advisers and advisory bodies constituting the advisory system.

3. Under environmental conditions of relatively high certainty over goals but low certainty over means, advice seeking and decisionmaking will take place in a hybrid system with mixed elements and moderate levels of collegiality and competitiveness.

With those propositions in mind, let us examine the essence of Johnson's advisory system and conditions in the political environment.

1965: "Some congressmen and senators think we are going to be the most discredited people in the world."
—Lyndon Johnson, July 22, 1965

During the first half of 1965, public and congressional opinion was substantially in agreement that "losing" South Vietnam to communism was unacceptable. In other words, the environment displayed a fairly high level of certainty that the *goal* of preventing the fall of South Vietnam was appropriate and even necessary, although some—a distinct minority—advocated that the United States abandon that goal and withdraw from Indochina. In contrast to this near consensus over goals, there was deep uncertainty in the political environment about *means*. This is not surprising, since early in the year the public was generally ignorant about events in Indochina. But even as public knowledge increased among elites and those in Congress, opinion was uncertain about the feasibility and desirability of various means of "saving" South Vietnam. As Dean Acheson wrote to a friend at the time, "*what* needs to be done is not obscure. How to do it with the human material available, in the God-awful terrain given and against the foreign-directed and supplied obstacles is very hard indeed."[1]

Contrary to many published accounts of Johnson's deliberations on Vietnam in 1965, Chapter 2 portrays a president who is painfully aware of the hazards of withdrawing *or* escalating—one who is genuinely, almost desperately, pondering the unattractive alternatives. These hazards existed both on the ground in Vietnam and in the political climate of the United States. A chronic measurer of public sentiment and congressional opinion, Johnson knew that a distinct majority favored the goal of preventing the fall of South Vietnam. He also knew that a minority favored cutting U.S. losses to avoid a land war in Asia against predominantly guerrilla forces. As he informed military and civilian Pentagon leaders in one meeting, some congressmen had warned him that escalation by the United States would cause Americans to become "the most discredited people in the world."[2]

By tracking polls and watching Congress, Johnson easily gauged the uncertainty in the American political environment over appropriate means to protect South Vietnam's independence. Further, he experienced that uncertainty firsthand. Advisers such as Taylor paralleled the views of some in Congress and elsewhere who thought American goals could be secured by "taking the war to the North," with a heavy bombing campaign. Others, such as Rusk and Humphrey, had less faith in bombing, reflecting the views of others in Congress.

By Johnson's choice, his Vietnam advisory system reflected prevailing and dissenting opinions existing in society and government. Advisers advocating escalation in Indochina, representing majority opinion in the country among the public, foreign policy elites, and Congress, obviously received Johnson's attention. He could easily have structured his advisory circles to exclude those who questioned plans for a greater American commitment to South Vietnam. Instead, he reached beyond interactions with mostly hawkish formal advisers to encounters with lower-level and informal counselors he respected, despite their views that the United States should make a drastic turn toward disengagement. Many of these advisers used blunt language: Clark Clifford, sitting across from the president and secretary of defense at Camp David, predicted years of failure, waste, and death if Johnson followed the advice of McNamara: "Five years, billions of dollars, 50,000 men, it is not for us."[3]

Consistent with proposition three, Johnson's advisory system of the spring and summer of 1965 did not display extreme levels of either collegiality or competitiveness. There were, however, elements of both of these characteristics: *Substantive* competitiveness—the competition of ideas—was high. Distinctly different proposals reached Johnson, ranging from U.S. withdrawal over a period of months to a call-up of the reserves and quicker and heavier ground troop commitments and bombing policies than those ultimately chosen by the president. *Procedural* competitiveness—tactical maneuvering to outdo those with competing ideas—was less evident. George Ball and Bill Moyers put some effort into mobilizing antiescalation sentiments within the administration to overcome the pro-escalation sentiments of powerful advisers such as McNamara and McGeorge Bundy; others such as McNamara occasionally maneuvered to limit the number of attendees at advisory meetings. But relations among advisers, even those with opposing views, were mostly collegial, as were relations between the president and advisers of varying types and views.

The president's advisory system of this period is therefore best characterized as moderately collegial or clanlike, with strong elements of substantive competitiveness and lesser elements of procedural competitiveness—a competitive-collegial hybrid. I place the word "competitive" first to give slightly more emphasis to that aspect of the advisory system.

1967: "There is an attitude in this country today that
we are not doing all we should do to get the war over
as quickly as it should be."
—*Lyndon Johnson, July 12, 1967*

In the spring and summer of 1967, when Johnson was considering proposals to increase troop levels "minimally" by 89,000 or "optimally" by 200,000, environmental conditions displayed high and almost unchanged certainty regarding the Johnson administration's major goal in Indochina but significant and growing uncertainty over means. Polling data suggest that the American public was almost as certain in 1967 as it had been in 1965 that the U.S. goal of securing an independent South Vietnam was correct. In both time periods, polls showed roughly two-thirds of the public supporting existing or increased military efforts to prevent the fall of South Vietnam. Signs of changing public attitudes about the legitimacy of the war's goal are found primarily in questions asking whether the government made a "mistake" in originally sending troops to fight in Vietnam. In the spring of 1967, about half of those polled denied that the troop decision had been a mistake; in the last half of 1965 (when pollsters began asking the question), 60 percent had said that the decision was not a mistake. Thus there was a limited decrease in certainty but still overwhelming support for achieving U.S. *goals* in Vietnam. As to the *means* employed by the government, there was significantly greater uncertainty in 1967 than in 1965: Late in the summer of 1965, citizens supported Johnson's management of the war by a two-to-one margin; two years later, a distinct plurality disapproved of the president's handling of Vietnam.

Congressional debates showed similar sentiment. Very few congressmen suggested abandoning the United States' goals in Vietnam, but many hawks and doves questioned the means (bombing and ground strategies) employed by the administration. Memoirs of such diverse figures as Maxwell Taylor and Arthur Schlesinger similarly characterize prevailing thought in American society about the war. Taylor wrote, "there were few if any spokesmen" favoring withdrawal among "men of substance in public life"; from Schlesinger: "Those of us who hoped for a negotiated peace believed that retention of American troops in defensive enclaves were [sic] essential to give the other side an incentive to negotiate."[4]

Johnson was very much in touch with public opinion and congressional sentiment during these months when the escalation proposal was on the table. He received weekly reports of public comments on the war in mail to the White House, continued to follow public opinion polls and the *Congressional Record*, and met with many congressmen.

He saw opinion in the environment as being against pulling out of Vietnam but dogged by an uncertainty that the war policies of his administration were working. At one July meeting, Johnson said that there was "an attitude in this country today that we are not doing all we should do to get the war over as quickly as it should be." That same month, his wife's diary recorded a poll showing a "distinct downward trend in the number of people who approved of Lyndon's handling of the war in Vietnam."[5]

Accompanying those trends was a growth in advisory bodies constituting the whole of Johnson's advisory system. He chose to have the Tuesday Lunch Group become the formal core of his advisory system. The group met almost weekly by 1967. It had become a war cabinet with an enlarged membership to oversee the administration's policies in Indochina, consider intelligence reports, and discuss political and public-relations problems having to do with the war. Not particularly a forum for discussing competing goals in Vietnam ("get in or get out") as in its irregular early 1965 meetings, the Tuesday Lunch Group focused primarily on effective means to win the war. As David Humphrey's history of the group says of the period from early 1967 onward, "This was the high tide of the weekly Tuesday Lunch, the period that most observers have in mind when they discuss the institution and whose characteristics they often ascribe to the earlier years." But most published accounts of the Johnson foreign policy process mistakenly "continue to single out the luncheons while disregarding the complex pattern of advisory meetings of which they were a part."[6]

That pattern included meetings and phone conversations with formal and informal advisers and advocates. Many were hawks, but others favored the sort of deescalation pressed by antiwar senators such as Robert Kennedy and J. William Fulbright. Although the president's meetings in 1967 with the latter two men were neither intimate nor particularly friendly, his meetings with others holding similar views were usually substantive and cordial. Such meetings with doves took place in both group and one-on-one settings. Chief among such figures was Defense Secretary McNamara, who advocated policy changes — especially a bombing limitation — that paralleled the views of Kennedy, Fulbright, and other critics.

Like most antiwar figures in American society at this time, McNamara, Kennedy, and Fulbright did not actually favor unilateral withdrawal from Vietnam. Certainly, almost no one advised Johnson simply to get out of Vietnam. One who did so, United States Information Agency Director and close Johnson friend Leonard Marks, met with a cold response from the president.[7] Thus the substantive range of views reaching Johnson *was* narrower in 1967 than it had been two years earlier. But by placing this narrowing of options in the context of the American political environment of the time, the substance of Johnson's discussions with advisers appears roughly reflective of the options discussed in the news media, in Congress, and by other elites and the public at large.

The president's interactions with advisers in 1967 were more orderly than in 1965. There was little procedural competition among advisers. Rostow and McNamara, for instance, treated each other's advocacy calmly, with a sense of fair play, despite their differences. The competition in 1967 was substantive, over ideas. Therefore, with high environmental certainty over *goals* and low environmental certainty over *means,* Johnson's advisory system in 1967 was as proposition three predicted, a hybrid of moderate collegiality and competition. Proposition two's prediction that new advisory bodies will make up the advisory system when environmental uncertainty increases also seems to have been borne out. I categorize the system as having been a collegial-competitive one in 1967, placing "collegial" first to reflect what seems to be a slightly greater collegiality than competitiveness in Johnson's advisory system during these months.

1968: "There has been a dramatic shift in public opinion.
—Lyndon Johnson, March 22, 1968

Disagreements over Johnson's handling of Vietnam were loudly and clearly voiced by members of Congress on the floors of both houses and in the White House as the shock of the 1968 Tet Offensive passed. As Senator Byrd told Johnson, "Something is wrong over there."[8] Meanwhile, the public had less and less faith in the president's management of war according to opinion polls, White House mail surveys, and news reports. In January, just before Tet, 47 percent of the public disapproved and 39 percent approved of the president's handling of Vietnam; in March, just before Johnson's speech, 63 percent of those polled disapproved and only 26 percent approved of his war leadership.[9] The legitimacy and importance of the goals of the war came under severe question in early 1968, as reflected in pollsters' continued use of the "mistake" question. Whereas a plurality of the public believed in the first half of 1967 that it had *not* been a mistake to enter the war, by March 1968 a 49 to 41 percent plurality thought that the United States should have stayed out of Vietnam.[10] This did not translate into majority sentiment that the United States should withdraw from Vietnam, but for the first time the American political environment displayed high uncertainty about not only the means the Johnson administration employed in Indochina but also the very goals and legitimacy of the war.

The proposition relevant to these environmental conditions appears to be number two, which suggests that an increase in environmental uncertainty leads the advisory system to expand and become more competitive and chaotic. Chapter 4 described a president who saw the environment as being in a near uproar and displaying increasingly less faith in his war leadership. In February, he told advisers, "The popular thing now is to stress the 'mismanagement' in Vietnam." In late March, he gloomily admitted to his Tuesday Lunch partners that there had been a "dramatic shift in public opinion."[11] In short, as in 1965 and 1967, Johnson understood prevailing opinion in the environment, but he continued to feel an enormous political and personal attachment to the commitments he and previous presidents had made in Vietnam. One might expect to find him as some critical writers have, "at bay . . . stubbornly determined to steer the ship his own way," surrounded by an inner circle of "enduring stupidity and . . . self protecting tenacity."[12] But the president, though under enormous stress and occasionally "exhaling frustration," possessed the requisite rationality to consult dozens of advisers reflecting the controversial disagreements being voiced in society and government in the first months of 1968. Chapter 4 showed a presidential advisory system exploding with information, formal and informal advisory meetings, new and changing advisory relations between the president and those with whom he counseled, a greater sense of competition between major advisers, and a widening range of policy options given serious attention.

During this time, members of the Tuesday Lunch Group met repeatedly with one another and with outsiders as the orderliness and regularity of top advisory meetings in 1967 were shattered by the demands of the military crisis in Southeast Asia and a public opinion crisis in the United States. Beyond President Johnson's normal habits of devouring news reports and the *Congressional Record* and using the telephone and other avenues to reach beyond his circle of formal advisers, he all the more insistently called in figures whom he and/or others respected as important opinion leaders for one-on-one sessions. These ranged from congressional leaders such as Mansfield and Russell to foreign policy elders such as Acheson and General Ridgway and those within his own administration such as Goldberg and McPherson. In group settings with nonadministration advisers, Johnson heard varying opinions expressed in blunt fashion by members of Congress and by the Wise Men.

These and other advisers evidenced a sharp division of opinion. Top military leaders and a few civilian counselors to the president believed that victory could be secured if the president went "all out" in Vietnam to take advantage of the communists' military failure. But the majority of his advisers—from Rusk, Clifford, and others inside the administration to McGeorge Bundy, Acheson, and others from outside—urged the president to eschew further escalation and move toward a hoped-for peace settlement.

More so than in the previous two periods under study, advisers to Johnson competed with and distrusted one another. The secretaries of state and defense used different tactics to try to move Johnson toward limiting the U.S. role in Vietnam. Neither Rusk nor Clifford understood or appreciated the other's stance. Many of his advisers seemed unhappy with group settings and sought out the president alone. Rusk, more inscrutable than ever to other advisers, leveled with Johnson in private about the war; Clifford believed that his own task force's report was inadequate and unreflective of his growing doubts about existing war policies and so informed Johnson in private. Others, including McGeorge Bundy and Henry Cabot Lodge, similarly lobbied Johnson confidentially, beyond their participation in group settings, presumably to enhance the impact of their advice.

The advisory system grew in 1968. Although the Tuesday Lunch continued to be important, its membership expanded and its meeting schedule accelerated notably, as did the range of substantive views expressed by participants. Johnson also called in the Wise Men to give him a face-to-face evaluation of his war leadership. This was in addition to the administration's ad hoc task force headed by Clifford, with Johnson's mandate: "I wish alternatives examined and, if possible, agreed recommendations to emerge which reconcile the military, diplomatic, economic, Congressional, and public opinion problems involved."[13]

Although the advisory system of early 1968 displayed some elements of collegiality—for the most part advisers treated one another respectfully—the system reached new levels of competition among advisers and over ideas, and is therefore properly characterized as a competitive, marketlike one.

THIS ANALYSIS SHOWS an evolution of Johnson's Vietnam advisory system that roughly corresponds to changes in the environment. In all three periods, Johnson displayed certain common traits—insistence on wrapping his advisory deliberations in a shroud of secrecy, for instance—but his advisory system was not static. And although it evolved largely in response to presidential preferences, those preferences were for points of view reflecting the diversity of opinion the president observed in the environment.

Among those confronting Johnson with hard realities were advisers without formal foreign policy advisory status. After his presidency,

Johnson told one confidant that, although he received a huge flow of official information, "the flow of unofficial information was greater and in many cases, more effective with me." It was undoubtedly hard for Johnson to listen to Dean Acheson's or Richard Russell's critiques of his war leadership, but judging by the archival records and the memories of most who saw Johnson, he listened to those and many others. In dramatic contrast to accounts of an isolated president "shutting out potential opposition" and advisers who "constantly tell him that he is right," the portrait here is of a chief executive painfully in touch with criticism in the political environment and shaping his own advisory system accordingly.[14]

Understanding the Johnson Administration, the Presidency, and Advisory Systems

Presidential advisory systems are often seen as reflections of personal factors, with presidential choices shaped by style and character.[15] To some extent they are: Lyndon Johnson *chose* to have Abe Fortas as a top adviser before and during the latter's tenure on the Supreme Court; Dwight Eisenhower *chose* to have Secretary of State John Foster Dulles as a foreign policy adviser of unequaled standing in his administration; Richard Nixon *decided* that National Security Adviser Henry Kissinger's advisory role would obliterate that of Secretary of State William Rogers. Political scientists Charles Walcott and Karen Hult, however, have justifiably criticized studies of "the organization surrounding the presidency" for relying on a "deeply embedded assumption of presidential control." As they suggest, organizational properties of administrations reflect structural factors (what they call "environmental demands"); they do not simply grow out of "presidential attributes or plans."[16]

In this study I demonstrate how one presidential advisory system evolved in response to environmental demands. But change in that system was not automatic. It occurred as the president—a prime mediator between the environment and the advisory system—chose to see more or fewer advisers with significant or no formal status and representing a narrower or wider range of opinion. These presidential choices were not made in a political or analytical vacuum—they were made largely in response to the president's assessment of political conditions in the environment. The case studies from 1965, 1967, and 1968 remind us that the presidency reflects both the personal attributes of its occupant and conditions in the political environment.

A second implication of this study concerns the assumptions—or what I call "implicit models" of presidential advisory systems—employed by political scientists analyzing presidential decisionmaking. The most common model includes formal foreign policy advisers — national security advisers, secretaries of state and defense, and others — and relies primarily on official records of the advice these figures give. Such models tend to exclude the political and personal intimates of a president — the Richard Russells, Clark Cliffords, and Abe Fortases — chosen by him as important counselors. The model of presidential advisory systems employed here relies not only on the official records of the formal advisers but also on the more elusive records of advice from informal advisers. The difficulty researchers face in obtaining evidence of informal advisory interactions should not obscure the importance of such encounters. As Dean Rusk said, "There was a lot of give and take there, in, behind, and around these memoranda."[17] Lady Bird Johnson said of Richard Russell what she might have said of others: Johnson "would value [his advice] . . . as indeed he would Rusk's and Westmoreland's . . . Lyndon would over and over call him and get him to come over to see him."[18]

Probably more than most presidents, Lyndon Johnson relied on a number of such unofficial advisers for crucial assistance in thinking through problems, but in this he was not alone. Andrew Jackson had his "kitchen cabinet." Chester Arthur had Daniel Rollins, district attorney in New York and an old friend who, without any official standing in the administration and in great secrecy, was Arthur's top assistant. Woodrow Wilson had Colonel Edward House, who, less secretly, was an intimate and influential adviser. And Franklin Roosevelt had Harry Hopkins as an important counselor, implementor, and personal representative, even though for a period of his crucial service Hopkins held no official position and literally had no office in which to work.[19] Thus scholars of the presidency need to beware of implicit models of advisory systems that portray formal charts of administration personnel as identical to presidents' actual advisory systems.

A third result of this study is a challenge to much of the literature on Vietnam, Lyndon Johnson, and his advisers. Most problematic is the school of thought that holds that Johnson's war advisory system was narrow, cohesive, and overwhelmingly hawkish. Whatever disagreements are found among their works, authors in this group agree that the president was not an honest and rational seeker of advice and information. For them, Johnson's pathological character and style combined to produce his flawed advisory system and war policies.[20]

Some published works using primary sources portray a president who sometimes reached beyond the boundaries of his formal advisory system to hear the views of outsiders.[21] Yet these authors seem wary of asserting that their research suggests a new understanding of the

Johnson presidency. They also repeat previously published stories of Johnson being sealed off from all but a few intimidated advisers.

A few authors hold that Johnson was a rational seeker of advice.[22] My analysis falls into this latter school of thought, and it is the most unambiguous interpretation to date in arguing that Lyndon Johnson had a voracious appetite for information and reached widely for diverse points of view. In choosing and overseeing the implementation of policies, Johnson occasionally indulged in what were (for him) emotionally satisfying displays of anger, sarcasm, hyperbole, and pointed humor. These personal traits, combined with his choice to cloak administration deliberations in secrecy, blinded many journalists, historians, and political scientists to the diversity and openness in the Johnson administration. Ironically, Johnson's success in protecting the confidentiality of his encounters with advisers contributed to the creation of the many critical but distorted portraits of his presidency. There is also the sense that some authors' anger over the sheer ugliness of the Vietnam War predisposed them to assume and assert that Johnson was an irrational advice seeker — indeed, some sort of American Caligula. But of Johnson and those who have written about him, one journalist put it best: "What is conspicuous and immediate and simple in a man, subject to our unrelenting stare, often outclamors what may be durable and longrange and complex."[23]

Unfortunately, skewed interpretations of Johnson's Vietnam deliberations regularly filter down to many widely used studies of the presidency. Students in college-level presidency courses a decade ago using Bruce Buchanan's *The Presidential Experience*, for instance, found Johnson to be the classic case of a president who used "his status to bludgeon the [advisory] group into rubberstamping his preformed decisions." Buchanan's treatment of Johnson was shaped by his reliance on the analyses of Janis in *Groupthink* and Barber in *The Presidential Character*.[24] In Frank Kessler's *The Dilemmas of Presidential Leadership*, students read in the 1980s that Johnson's immense ego "convinced him that the public was with him" on Vietnam and he "became a prisoner of his own delusions." Once again, Barber and Janis are prominent in the cited literature shaping this portrait of Johnson's interactions with Vietnam advisers. Students in the 1990s reading Barbara Kellerman and Ryan J. Barilleaux's *The President as World Leader* discover a president whose "stunning insecurity" led him to exclude advisers with critical views from his Vietnam meetings.[25]

Similar interpretations have appeared in prominent works on U.S. foreign policy. On the topic of Vietnam, Bernard Brodie's impressive *War and Politics* is, unfortunately, influenced by Hoopes's *The Limits of Intervention* and the *Pentagon Papers* in concluding that Johnson insisted "not only on the absolute rightness of the decisions he had made but also on having around him none who might cause him even a moment's self-doubt." With this understanding of Johnson's advisory system, Brodie largely "explains" American intervention and persistence in Vietnam, deeming it "next to impossible to imagine" that the same choices would have been made by the United States if John Kennedy had not been assassinated.[26] Such simplistic treatment of the Johnson administration steers students away from the complexity of presidential decisionmaking and the political environment in which it occurs. The early, influential analyses of authors such as Barber, Janis, Hoopes, and Kearns and the more recent accounts of Berman, Goodwin, and Reedy[27] do not give sufficiently accurate overviews of the Johnson administration's Vietnam deliberations to justify sole reliance on them as definitive treatments of Johnson and the war.

6 | Secrecy and Openness in the White House: An Interpretation of Johnson's Political Style

IF THE LYNDON JOHNSON I have portrayed here does not quite fit the conventional view of him and his Vietnam advisers, what might this mean for a broader understanding of his presidency? I offer here an interpretation of Johnson's overarching political style as president in dealing with foreign and domestic policies.

In essence my view is this: The interactions between President Lyndon Johnson and the people who assisted and advised him on policymaking were characterized by an unusual, uneasy, and ultimately misleading combination of Johnson's openness to wide-ranging information and advice and his extreme secrecy about the processes that brought those diverse views to the president.[1] This combination was unusual because openness and secrecy — especially when carried to extremes as in the Johnson presidency — do not easily coexist. It was therefore an uneasy combination for administration officials. White House secrecy also led some Johnson advisers and many subsequent analysts to miss the paradoxical essence of his advisory and policymaking processes.[2] These were not the only stylistic characteristics of this presidency, of course: Johnson was a master of crude, sometimes self-pitying or cruel, but often hilarious storytelling and mimicry; he preferred his advisers to reach a consensus after debating their views; and, Johnson's temper sometimes created difficulties for those who worked under him.

Lyndon Johnson's penchant for secrecy has often been attributed to traits in his character.[3] But it can also be attributed to his rational, even sophisticated understanding of how leaders might achieve political and policy goals in the American political system of the 1950s and 1960s.

Certainly, analysts writing before extensive archival records of the Johnson years became available deserve sympathy for their efforts to present the *real* Johnson White House: This president could be exceedingly generous yet callous toward those who worked for him; he could be deeply suspicious of some advisers yet place great faith in them.

In short, Johnson was sometimes difficult to work for and did not make it easy for those who would write about him in later years.

Perhaps only a theory of psychology can explain certain contradictions in Johnson's character, but a theory of strategic political leadership —Johnson's "theory"—can largely explain important sustained patterns of his advisory relations. Derived in part from Johnson's congressional career and his observations of Franklin Roosevelt, that theory of presidential power was utterly conventional in its time. Indeed, Johnson's views on the role of the presidency in the American political system were similar to those of pluralist theorists of the post–World War II era, who also appear to have been influenced by what seemed the nearly perfect bargaining presidency of Roosevelt.

An American Caligula or a Compassionate Samaritan?

An inescapable conclusion to be drawn from reading a few memoirs and many histories of the Johnson years is that, from November 1963 to January 1969, the White House resembled nothing so much as a tyrannical monarch's court. Patrick Anderson wrote of Johnson, "He has corrupted men and women who have worked for him." This can be called the "Caligula interpretation" of Johnson's White House.[4]

Former White House press secretary George Reedy's *Lyndon B. Johnson: A Memoir* says of Johnson: "As a human being, he was a miserable person—a bully, sadist, lout, and egotist." Writing of "the corrupting influence of the White House," Reedy says that when Johnson had been a senator, fellow legislators and his staff "minced no words in telling him bluntly that he had made a major boner. . . . [but] In the White House, neither his staff nor his colleagues could speak to him in the 'mother tongue.'"[5]

A former National Security Council (NSC) staff member, Chester Cooper, has written a widely repeated story of how an intimidating Johnson, after "bland and desultory" discussions at NSC sessions, would announce a decision,

> then poll everyone in the room—Council members, their assistants, and members of the White House and NSC staffs. "Mr. Secretary, do you agree with the decision?" "Yes, Mr. President." "Mr. X, do you agree?" "I agree, Mr. President." During the process I would frequently fall into a Walter Mitty–like fantasy: When my turn came I would rise to my feet slowly, look around the room and then directly at the President, and say very quietly and emphatically, "Mr. President, gentlemen, I most definitely do not agree." But I

was removed from my trance when I heard the President's voice saying, "Mr. Cooper, do you agree?" And out would come a "Yes, Mr. President, I agree."[6]

Other writings and recollections fit better into what I call the "Good Samaritan interpretation" of Lyndon Johnson's White House. Philip Rulon deals favorably with Johnson's life and presidency, even titling his book *The Compassionate Samaritan*. Former White House aide Jack Valenti writes of a president passionate about civil rights, poverty, education, and health care for the elderly. Johnson gathered around him "a talented and enormously gifted group . . . [who were] not at all reluctant to make their own views known to their boss."[7] Former Secretary of State Dean Rusk says, "The President never, never objected to people putting forward views that were contrary to his own inclinations in the course of making a decision." But "after the decision was made, the President expected his colleagues to support that decision."[8]

A reader might wonder whether these two sets of observers have described the same president and White House.[9] Some analysts try to bridge the gap between the two schools of thought. For example, Doris Kearns, who talked at length with Johnson during his retirement, writes in *Lyndon Johnson and the American Dream* that he would have preferred White House personnel of the highest intelligence and drive who would *also* bend to his will; recognizing the impossibility of this, Johnson hired smart, ambitious people. In the same account, however, Kearns writes that Johnson's personality "operated to distort the truth in much the same way an ideology works in a totalitarian society." She draws on Reedy and others to describe a White House resembling a king's court: "In this strange atmosphere, the men surrounding the President tend to become sycophants."[10]

Here I attempt to make sense of the Johnson White House's contradictions by pursuing my opening thesis: Johnson's political style in the White House, combining openness and secrecy, served serious purposes. The openness would bring him differing, even innovative, policy ideas and accurate information about conditions in the political environment; the secrecy would keep his political and policy options open until he made or announced his decision and improve the odds of persuading Congress and others to follow his lead.[11] Out of Johnson's fierce insistence on secrecy grew a number of written accounts of a White House with fearful, deferential advisers and a narrow, abusive president. Out of his desire for diverse information and innovative views grew other, less numerous accounts of a creative, open, even idealistic White House.

Johnson's "Theory" of Presidential Leadership

His obligations are heavy, but their effective discharge depends as much upon persuasion as upon force and legal authority. . . . Given the expectations that are focused upon the presidency, the indispensable qualification of a successful White House incumbent is that he be able to lead the Congress. . . . If the president does not capitalize on the opportunity offered by a legislative majority's procedural controls, it is not unlikely that these will be used against him. . . . One reason for the difficulty presidents have experienced in controlling their nominal subordinates is lack of information. . . . This ignorance may be made less serious if he has continuing facilities for aiding him both in securing such information and in acting upon it. [12]

In a relative but real sense one can say of a President what Eisenhower's first Secretary of Defense once said of General Motors: what is good for the country is good for the President and vice versa. [13]

Lyndon Johnson's beliefs (roughly constituting a theory) about presidential power and the American political system were conventional for their time and thus thoroughly steeped in a pluralist understanding of American politics. His beliefs did not emerge from reading the works of political scientists; although Johnson was a voracious reader of reports and memoranda, he read hardly any books at all. [14] Instead, they emerged from a long involvement in American politics.

Johnson's socialization in Congress, where he ultimately enjoyed tremendous success at acquiring and exercising leadership positions, probably had a substantial impact on his operating style in the White House. The early days of Johnson's congressional career were also a time when he enjoyed unusual access to President Franklin Roosevelt. Johnson befriended many of Roosevelt's White House aides and loved the president like a "Daddy." In this, Johnson followed a decades-long pattern of adopting successful older politicians as mentors. A confirmed New Dealer, Johnson was fascinated with Roosevelt's skillful use of information and power and the way he played one subordinate off against another. Though Roosevelt and his advisers were happy to have the up-and-coming congressman's support, they thought that his liberalism was pragmatic. [15] Had he lived long enough, it probably would not have surprised Roosevelt to see Johnson make a political shift to the right when he moved from representing a relatively liberal district in the House to representing a more conservative state in the Senate.

Johnson's pragmatism as Democratic leader in the Senate frustrated some liberals. He would not go out on a limb for their legislation, even if he personally supported it, if his extensive system of information gathering told him there was no chance of victory. Liberals such as Paul Douglas (D-Ill.) thought that it was preferable to put "progressive" legislation up for a vote even if defeat was inevitable. This approach was anathema to Johnson, who perfected an operating style as Senate majority leader described by Evans and Novak: "Johnson . . . slyly shielded his position on major issues, just as he had concealed his inner purpose on the censure of Joe McCarthy the previous year. He did not reveal— indeed, he did not fully determine in his own mind—what his position would be until the last possible moment, when the conditions of battle were fully known to him."[16]

Johnson's information gathering as a Senate leader—called the Johnson System by journalists of the time—was key to his operating style. As president he relied on the same approach of gathering knowledge widely but holding it closely. As one administration figure recalls, "He played the cards so *very* close to his chest."[17] McGeorge Bundy is characteristically unsentimental in asserting that, for Johnson, telling others the full truth about a situation "was kind of a waste of a very valuable substance unless you were careful about who you told. [It was] . . . something he would do only if he had to, so you could understand what the hell he wanted."[18] This frustrated advisers at times, but many understood that the secrecy was Johnson's response to the threat of leaks generated (according to General Earle Wheeler) "by people who are attempting to pre-empt the President and his decisions . . . this put Mr. Johnson under tremendous political pressure from various pressure groups." Of the array of political information circulating each day, Doris Kearns writes that Johnson "had to know these things himself . . . because only Johnson was in contact with all the varied groups and subgroups in both Congress and the administration. He alone could know the full implications and possible consequences of decisions in the conduct of relations with Congress."[19]

Johnson's political philosophy—New Deal liberalism[20]—thus affected his approach as senator and president, but in pursuing mostly liberal goals, Johnson never sought Pyrrhic victories. He bargained, persuaded, frequently hid his own personal preferences, and used information as a resource. "He wanted," Harry McPherson writes, "to be free of pressure—to fix the machine in his own time, without people standing in his light. That was his way in the Senate and he did not change in the White House."[21]

It is striking how closely Johnson's views on presidential power resembled orthodox American pluralist political thought of his time, and how his and their views were influenced by the presidency of Franklin Roosevelt. Political scientist David Truman's landmark *The*

Governmental Process suggested that U.S. presidents were only barely equipped by the Constitution to pursue policy goals. Truman saw interest-group leaders, members of Congress, and even those in a president's own cabinet (and the bureaucracies they headed) as naturally competitive with the president. Such actors pursued the interests of groups to which they were beholden or in agreement or that they led. Presidential success depended on aggressive acquisition of information, Truman wrote, on skillful bargaining and persuasion, and in particular on the adroit handling of congressional relations.[22]

Richard Neustadt's *Presidential Power* similarly reflects the era's conventional (if not unanimous) perceptions of Franklin Roosevelt's success as an active president, Harry Truman's attempts in those directions despite a recalcitrant Congress, and Dwight Eisenhower's fumbling approach to the presidency through the "tepid" 1950s. Because the Constitution creates a system in which the three branches of government share powers, the presidency is anything but too powerful. If forced to rely on his formal powers alone, a president would be little more than "an invaluable clerk," according to Neustadt, who quotes his one-time boss Harry Truman: "I sit here all day trying to persuade people to do the things they ought to have sense enough to do without my persuading them. . . . That's all the powers of the President amount to." Thus the skill of the person occupying the Oval Office in persuading and in gathering, protecting, and using power is crucial to his success and the nation's well-being.[23]

Like many political scientists of the 1950s and 1960s, Lyndon Johnson had a theory of presidential power. Like them, he would discover the potential for good and the possibilities of disaster inherent in a strong presidency. Here I explicate Johnson's view of presidential power by drawing primarily from his memoirs and secondarily from observations of those who interacted with him as president.[24]

On the *sources* of presidential power, Johnson found the formal powers of the Constitution inadequate to allow a president to lead the nation successfully: "Every President has to establish with the various sectors of the country what I call 'the right to govern.' Just being elected to the office does not guarantee him that right." Upon taking office, Johnson knew that he "had to secure the cooperation of the people who were natural leaders of the nation." These included cabinet members, congressional leaders, industrial leaders, labor chieftains, governmental workers, news commentators, religious leaders, and others. Persuasion of such leaders was necessary in order to build "a consensus throughout the country, so that we could stop bickering and quarreling and get on with the job at hand. . . . To me, consensus meant, first, deciding what needed to be done regardless of the political implications and, second, convincing a majority of the Congress and the American people of the necessity for doing those things."[25]

Thus Johnson joined many scholars (and most presidents since Theodore Roosevelt) in believing that a president's administration should be the center of the American political system, producing initiatives that would eventually attain the status of either law or established practice. In summary, the sources of such presidential power lay first, but inadequately, in the Constitution and second, but as importantly, in the array of interest groups that, when brought together, might constitute a rough consensus.

The *purpose* of presidential power was to pursue what Johnson called the "lasting good," the "interests of my country."[26] The crucial link between the sources of presidential power and its purpose is the drive and political skill of the man in office. Remembers Johnson, "I was President of the United States at a crucial point in its history, and if a President does not lead he is abandoning the prime and indispensable obligation of the Presidency."

"The indispensable qualification of a successful White House incumbent is that he be able to lead the Congress," wrote David Truman in 1951. "If the President does not capitalize on the opportunity offered by a legislative majority's procedural controls, it is not unlikely that these will be used against him."[27] Turning to the task of "trying to obtain . . . enactment into law" programs that were "acceptable to a majority of the people," Johnson saw a need to shepherd his administration's relations with Congress. He took pride in "accurate head counts" and wrote in his memoirs that his administration "made many mistakes, but failure to inform and brief the Congress was not one of them."[28] General Wheeler agrees, saying that Johnson "insisted that if we decided to take any action, political or military, that there should first be consultations with the congressional leadership."[29] Most administration officials understood and appreciated Johnson's insistence on this, but John Roche recalls a meeting in which the president had to educate HEW Secretary John Gardner on preparing for a crucial Senate hearing:

It was really obvious Gardner didn't know what the hell he was talking about. . . . So Johnson sort of explained to him patiently, he said, "Now, John, look here. You're going to go before the committee, and Senator So-and-So is on this Appropriations subcommittee. Now this particular provision here is something that he thought up. It's his bill. It goes back to 1956. When you come to that, you stop and say to him, 'Now, Senator, I hope you appreciate the extent to which we found your ideas valuable.' " Marvelous. Instructions that Gardner should have got there. He left and went back and started bitching at HEW that Johnson had been bullying him. Johnson turned to [Budget Director Charles] Schultze, and he said, "Charlie, will you please budget him a seeing-eye dog?"[30]

Joseph Califano has described what he sees as a typical case of Johnson's approach to the presidency. It also links and demonstrates (1) Johnson's understanding of the importance of interest groups as a source of presidential success, (2) his goal of implementing a bill that was in "the national interest," and (3) his instinctive pleasure in employing his political talents (what David Truman called "the personal characteristics of the president") as the connection between the sources and purposes of presidential power:

> Sitting in Johnson's small green hideaway adjoining the Oval Office one day, White House congressional lobbyist Larry O'Brien and Wilbur Cohen (later to become HEW Secretary) responded to Johnson's demand that they move the Medicare bill out of committee. "It'll cost a half-billion dollars to make the changes in reimbursement standards to get the bill out of the Senate finance committee," Cohen said.
>
> "Five hundred million. Is that all?" Johnson exclaimed with a wave of his big hand. "Do it. Move that damn bill out now, before we lose it."
>
> The opposition to Medicare by the health industry — insurance companies, hospitals, and particularly doctors — was so unyielding that we were concerned about whether the doctors would participate in sufficient numbers. LBJ decided to invite the American Medical Association leadership to the White House as the Medicare regulations were about to be issued and the program launched. Sitting on twin sofas under a portrait of Franklin D. Roosevelt in the Oval Office, the AMA officials waited politely for Johnson to say something as he settled into his rocking chair. The President took his time, assessing their cold stares. Then he talked not about Medicare, but of his need for physicians in Vietnam to help serve the civilian population. Would the AMA help? Could it get doctors to rotate in and out of Vietnam for a few months? "Your country needs your help. Your President needs your help," he said. He got the reply he expected. Of course, the AMA would start a program immediately, the doctors responded, almost in unison.
>
> "Get the press in here," Johnson told Bill Moyers, his press secretary, who was sitting with me off to the side of the office.
>
> The press tramped in, forming an uneven semicircle to Johnson's left. The President described the AMA Vietnam medical

program, heaping praise on the doctors present. But the reporters' first question was about Medicare. Would the doctors support the Medicare program?

Johnson acted annoyed at the question. "These men are going to get doctors to go to Vietnam where they might be killed," he said with quite apparent indignation. "Medicare is the law of the land. Of course, they'll support the law of the land."

LBJ turned abruptly to the head of the AMA delegation. "Tell him," he said. "You tell him."

"Of course, we will," the AMA official responded.

Johnson shook hands warmly with the delegation as the cameras clicked. We all breathed a little more easily.[31]

Though less nuanced, *The Vantage Point* agrees with *The Governmental Process* and *Presidential Power*: Having a skillful politician as president serves the public good.

Putting Theory into Practice: The Johnson White House Style

I now turn to two case studies by other scholars that examine Johnson's style of employing power and people in the pursuit of policy goals and thus presidential "success." These, along with the earlier chapters of this book, shed light on Johnson's operating style as president.

Case 1. The Domestic Policy Task Forces

First I examine Johnson's use of task forces made up largely of persons from outside the administration to develop reformist domestic policy ideas and programs. I draw in part from Norman Thomas and Harold Wolman's important article, "Policy Formulation in the Institutionalized Presidency: The Johnson Task Forces."[32] The authors describe a process of formulating domestic policy legislative proposals that constituted "a substantial departure from past practices," which usually involved consultation by a president and his staff with cabinet agency and other bureau leaders, after which the Bureau of Budget (or Office of Management and Budget in recent years) and the president's staff evaluated proposals from those sources.

The Kennedy administration had employed task forces to formulate policy goals, but their reports were published, giving the press, the public, and interest groups a yardstick by which to measure legislative proposals and achievements of the administration. Thomas and Wolman write: "In order to avoid the pitfalls encountered in the Kennedy task force operation . . . which forced the Administration to defend their reports even before they had become the basis for action, the Johnson task forces operated under a cloak of secrecy. The members agreed not to reveal their assignments to the press or to professional associates and not to disclose the substance of their deliberation or reports." This allowed the task force reports to play "a more significant role than any documents or proposals emanating from the [governmental] agencies."[33]

Significantly, Doris Kearns relates that, "Perhaps because their subject matter and memberships were kept secret from the public, Johnson managed to persuade selected Senators and Congressmen to serve on these task forces." The president created 40 outside task forces from 1964 to 1968, each with a mandate to examine a particular policy idea or problem, and each with "maximum freedom to come forth with ideas."[34] This was part of a larger process occurring each year in the administration that sought out "new ideas. Various officials who were regarded as 'idea men' were invited to submit proposals on any subject directly to the White House. This permitted them to by-pass normal bureaucratic channels and departmental and agency hierarchies. For example, according to one staff member, former Secretary of Defense McNamara submitted over 50 proposals on various domestic problems in one year".[35]

Johnson wanted the task forces' judgment on substance, not political feasibility. Those judgments would be his. Johnson told his cabinet in 1964 that the task forces "will operate without publicity. It is very important that this not become a public operation. The purpose of these task forces is to come up with ideas, not to sell those ideas to the public."[36] Unlike public study commissions (also appointed by Johnson and other twentieth-century presidents), the task forces were able to suggest controversial ideas to the president and his top aides without public controversy. After the administration examined the reports, the president decided which ideas were worth pursuing and spending his political capital on.[37]

The intra-administration process of reviewing task force reports involved White House staff, department and agency heads and their assistants, and representatives from the Bureau of the Budget and Council of Economic Advisers. Write Thomas and Wolman, "The participants received continuous direction from the President as to his priorities. After much discussion and bargaining, they developed a proposed legislative program which was presented to the President who then made *tentative final* decisions on it." The membership of task forces was not "balanced" in the way that public commissions were. There was a decided tilt in favor of academia, and "a conscious attempt was made to avoid overrepresentation of traditional clientele groups." Johnson did, however, want a minimal level of "representativeness" on the task forces: If a representative task force came up with a unanimous report, "a supporting coalition representing most of the major elements in American society would already have been constructed."[38]

Both secrecy and openness to diverse ideas were evident in Johnson's use of task forces for policy formulation. Thomas and Wolman describe secrecy as a "manifest characteristic" of the process and quote one task force staff member: "Our task force was a CIA-type operation. I felt very odd about it. We were not sure about what should be said and what shouldn't be said. There was no name on our door for the task force. The task force staff director simply had his name on the door. Papers were put under lock and key every evening."[39] But the president and his staff thought that such secrecy permitted openness — it allowed the administration to choose the best "idea people" without worrying about precise balancing of interest-group representatives. And they could adopt or reject the task forces' recommendations without paying costs of time, energy, and political capital. According to Thomas and Wolman, "The range of options was not only maximized, it was kept open for a longer period of time and at very little political cost. Thus, the secrecy of the reports prevented opposition from developing to task force proposals until a much later stage in the policy process."[40]

Some of those on the task forces, others in the administration, and some outside the administration objected to the secrecy surrounding task force operations. An Office of Education official complained of the assumption by the president and his people that task force reports were "correct." An interest-group representative saw the task forces as "the worst form of intellectual and educational elitism." But the impact of the task forces on policymaking was substantial: "In many cases the substance of President Johnson's legislative program was in large part shaped by task force recommendations. . . . They provided a means of maintaining a steady input of ideas new to the thought processes of high-level policy-makers."[41]

Case 2. Arms Control

The Johnson administration does not automatically come to mind when the topic is arms control. Still, as Glenn Seaborg's detailed history of arms control points out,

> the Johnson presidency was a period of great arms control ferment both within our own government and in international discussion. The period produced, moreover, two very significant results. First

of these was the signing in 1968 of the Nonproliferation Treaty, the most widely accepted among Americans of the arms control agreements thus far negotiated with the Soviet Union. Perhaps even more important to the world was the intellectual ground breaking by which President Johnson and his associates — principally Robert McNamara — persuaded the Soviet leadership to embrace the concept of a mutual limitation on strategic weapons, both offensive and defensive.

Seaborg concludes that the Strategic Arms Limitation Talks (SALT) would have begun in the Johnson administration had the Soviet Union not invaded Czechoslovakia in the summer of 1968, and that the Johnson presidency "deserves much more credit" for SALT than is generally recognized.[42]

The movement toward arms negotiations in the 1960s was complex, involving debates between and within many national governments. My interest here is not to recount that intricate history but to note advisory and decisionmaking patterns in the Johnson administration in this issue area.

At the end of 1963, Seaborg, chairman of the Atomic Energy Commission, told the new president that a proposal to halt production of all fissionable material for nuclear weapons was wise but politically dangerous: continued production would be a "prodigious waste of money," but regarding a curtailment, Seaborg "pointed out that the economic impact in terms of lost employment and income at the production sites could be severe, and that, consequently, President Kennedy had been inclined to postpone action until after the 1964 election."[43] Senator Henry Jackson (D-Wash.), whose home-state economy would be hurt by such cuts, warned Johnson of negative political fallout and suggested delaying action on the proposal. But the president "hadn't seemed very interested in approaching the problem this way," thought Jackson. It is prudent to be skeptical, however, about claims that Johnson did not care about the electoral consequences of presidential decisions. Surely the president took political factors into account and, as with domestic task force ideas, made judgments on political feasibility.[44]

A measure of Johnson's view of information as a resource is his resulting message to Congress and the nation on arms control (in his 1964 State of the Union Address), which mentioned only *limited* cutbacks in nuclear materials production. Johnson kept secret from all but a few his almost certain long-range plan for a massive production curtailment. Secrecy preserved future options, including "the President's desire to use the further cutbacks — the ones beyond those he had already announced — as a lure in arms control negotiations with the Soviet

Union." Thus Johnson secretly planned further cuts while engaging Premier Khrushchev in a dialogue on bilateral reductions of enriched uranium production. Soviet responses were not unpromising but were slow in coming. Doubtful that the major production cutback plans could be kept confidential indefinitely, Johnson informed Khrushchev that he would proceed with an announcement on April 20, 1964, of major unilateral U.S. cuts if he did not receive a Soviet pledge to make the cuts bilateral. Only a few officials in the administration knew of the ongoing exchanges of messages between Johnson and Khrushchev. Finally, as Johnson recounts,

> On April 20 I flew to New York City for the annual Associated Press luncheon . . . the text of my speech . . . contained the announcement that we were going to reduce further our production of fissionable material. I was disappointed that I could not say the Russians were taking similar action. Then, just before I was to speak, a courier brought me an urgent message that prompted me to pencil in a new paragraph. I had barely finished writing before the presiding officer completed his introduction and made room for me at the rostrum.
>
> Halfway through my speech I came to the key section, announcing the additional cutback in our production of enriched uranium. . . . Then I added what I had just written on a sheet of paper: "Simultaneously with my announcement now, Chairman Khrushchev is releasing a statement in Moscow, at two o'clock our time, in which he makes definite commitments to steps toward a more peaceful world. He agrees to discontinue the construction of two big new atomic reactors for the production of plutonium."[45]

The unfolding of events was not always so fortuitous. There is considerable evidence that Johnson would sometimes actually change intended personnel appointments or (at least temporarily) policy innovations if the press drew on leaks to report his plans.[46] Another example comes from Johnson's appointment of a prestigious panel of "wise men" to explore "the widest range of measures that the United States might undertake in conjunction with other governments or by itself" to stop the increasing spread of atomic weapons to new nations. In January 1965 the committee—including Dean Acheson, former NATO commander General Alfred Gruenther, and former Defense Secretary Robert Lovett—presented the president with its secret report (known as the Gilpatric Report) urging that nuclear nonproliferation become a top priority of the administration.[47] The report—which Dean Rusk called "explosive as a nuclear weapon" because of its potentially disruptive effect on the

NATO alliance—did not lead to an immediate formulation of a non-proliferation policy, in part because elements of the report began to leak soon after it was presented to Johnson. Johnson and McGeorge Bundy had warned the committee and top administration officials that no one was to see or know of the report outside of those in the room. As Seaborg recorded in his diary that day, "The President again reiterated the need to guard against newspaper leaks. He mentioned that he had FBI reports of government people talking to columnists under what appeared to be unauthorized circumstances. He said there would be a short release for the press but there must be no mention of the existence of a written report."

Despite the warnings, leaks occurred. Robert Kennedy's maiden speech in the Senate endorsed nonproliferation initiatives—his speech had recommendations that "were like those in the Gilpatric Committee Report in both substance and wording."[48] A week later, the *New York Times* announced, "A top-secret report to President Johnson is understood to have recommended that a treaty to halt the spread of nuclear weapons be given priority over the establishment of an Atlantic nuclear force." McGeorge Bundy believes that these events made Johnson feel that he was losing control over "what happened next."[49] As a result, Johnson put the report's recommendations on hold for over a year. Eventually, Seaborg writes, the president did make nuclear nonproliferation a high priority—one that was successfully pursued.[50]

Johnson's strategy of seeking diverse views while keeping the advisory and policymaking process secret did not extend to all aspects of his presidency. For instance, on the issue of civil rights, he showed only brief openness to conflicting views about whether he should press for passage of a civil rights act before the 1964 election.[51] Plenty of secret maneuvering of Congress occurred, however. Johnson lobbied the chairman of the House Rules Committee, "Judge" Howard Smith, to report the 1964 civil rights bill out of the committee for debate by the whole House. Later in the year, before Senate passage of the bill, Johnson had one senator's mistress contacted so that she might persuade her lover to vote in favor of breaking an anti–civil rights bill filibuster.[52]

Johnson's Temper and His Advisory System

Whatever else he is known for, Lyndon Johnson is generally remembered as a volatile president. Barbara Tuchman has, like many others, written of Johnson as "forceful and domineering" to the point of scaring off "outspoken or even unspoken" misgivings of others about his policies.[53] Did Johnson's temper prevent many advisers from leveling with him?

And did they infer that the president primarily wanted reinforcement of his own views?

There can be no doubt that Johnson unleashed his temper on some who assisted him. Former Speaker of the House "Tip" O'Neill recalls how he and others once spent "a very pleasant hour with the President," but

> before we left we saw another side of Lyndon Johnson. "I've got to show you the polls," he said. "Wait till you see them. I'm going to kill Goldwater. Where's Jack Valenti?" Valenti was Johnson's chief aide, but at that moment he wasn't around. "Where's Jack Valenti?" he screamed. Valenti came in a moment later. "Where the hell were you?" Lyndon roared. "I was getting a cup of coffee," said Jack. "You asshole!" said the President. "I told you never to leave my office!" And right there, in front of the Massachusetts delegation, Johnson proceeded to chastise and humiliate him.[54]

Nonetheless, it is significant that many of those advising Johnson rarely if ever encountered a temperamental, intimidating president. A few examples: General William Westmoreland has criticized Johnson's Vietnam decisions but says that there was no abusiveness on the part of the president: "I have never known a more considerate and thoughtful man than Lyndon Johnson." Dean Rusk recalls no outbursts from Johnson. Above all, "I never felt that I was inhibited in any way from going to the President and making to him any proposal that I had on my mind."[55] George Ball, Rusk's number two man in the State Department, recalls Johnson as consistently polite and considerate. Eugene Rostow, who also worked in the State Department, says,

> Everybody writes about his famous anger—I've only seen it once— we were sitting around in the Situation Room . . . it must have been May or June of '67. . . . An admiral in the Sixth Fleet said something in the presence of newspapermen which got into the papers, saying, "Oh, hell, we can take care of everything. We can bomb—." And at the end of a long meeting in which we disposed of a lot of business he said, "Now, I want to tell you fellows something. This admiral has made this statement. If the Johnson administration goes down next year. . . . I want it to go down on *my* words and *my* policies and not on what some goddamned admiral says.

Rostow says that Johnson did not "intimidate or coerce discussions— quite the contrary," but it was "absolutely inadmissible that they [advisers] go around town and leak."[56]

Vietnam critic and Republican Senator George Aiken, asked if Johnson gave an opportunity for those who disagreed with him to state their position adequately, answered, "Oh, yes indeed. I disagreed with him [in meetings between the president and small groups of members of Congress] and some of the other people who were present disagreed with him too. And he didn't appear to be resentful even though he didn't always take our advice." Senator Ernest Gruening, a critic of Johnson's Vietnam policies from the beginning, recalled that Johnson was always "kind and considerate" in meetings touching on Vietnam. Gruening had "no criticism whatsoever of Johnson's personal relations with me."[57]

Richard Helms, former director of central intelligence, was asked about Johnson "being volatile and . . . having tantrums when someone crosses him. Did you find this in your particular relationship to happen occasionally, or ever?" He responded, "No, I can't say that I ever did : . . he listened to what I had to say. . . . I must say that I felt rather keenly that he has been very unfairly criticized in his behavior as a human being."[58] William Bundy, former assistant secretary of state, attended many top-level meetings and does not recall any adviser who seemed to have "trimmed his sails because the President might not like something he said, or it might initially hit the President wrong." Pressed on whether dovish advisers were afraid to speak their mind on Vietnam, Bundy insisted, "I don't think that's true."[59]

Retired General Maxwell Taylor recalled that Johnson "had the reputation, as you know, of cracking whips over his subordinates. I never saw that. My relations with him were extremely pleasant."[60] And former press secretary George Christian, asked if Johnson raised his voice if an adviser or staff member differed with him, said:

> He tried to get everybody to speak his mind. I never saw him cut anybody down, particularly in a large group. He wouldn't embarrass someone by saying, "That's stupid," or something like that. . . . In a group of one or two he might do it. He would sometimes be irritated or something in a meeting, when you got the impression that he was sore at either somebody or a group of people, but it wasn't any table-pounding kind of thing. I never saw him do that in my life.[61]

Redford and McCulley, in *White House Operations*, depict the role of Johnson's temper in advisory relations as greatly overstated. They agree with Joseph Califano: "He thought Johnson gave vent to his anger only toward those who were in a sense 'his boys,' those who had grown up in his service."[62] Speechwriter John Roche, who became one of President Johnson's "boys", gives a similar interpretation:

He'd ask you what you thought about something, or yell. He would sometimes start to bellow. He used that horn on the desk, that microphone for his phone, so that by the time it came out of my phone it sounded like a riot on 14th street, as heard through the subway tunnel at 42nd. I couldn't understand half of what he was saying. I'd just hold the phone at arms' length and every so often say, "Yes, sir," and let it go at that, because he was just talking. So many people, again, have misunderstood him, it seems to me. They thought he was screaming at them; in fact he was screaming at the universe, and they were sort of witnesses to it.

I used to look up and see who was down there, who had been in on the off-the-record appointment list. Usually I'd discover that some guy had been in there that he wanted to kick the shit out of and he couldn't for political reasons, so when he got finished he'd hit some staff phone button and bitch about the world.[63]

Many character analyses have emphasized and repeated stories of Johnson's temper scaring off dissent in the White House. But as Califano, Roche, and others observe, when Johnson unleashed his temper it was usually with staffers who had worked for him for many years; and even those advisers characteristically leveled with the President.

Conclusion

The interpretation presented here, drawing on the works of others,[64] relies in part on a bold claim: As a matter of strategic political style, Johnson sought widely ranging points of view. The claim is bold not because there is a shortage of evidence but because of a long-standing, dominant interpretation of Johnson as "barricaded" against disagreement or criticism and because few have challenged this view head-on. But my thesis goes beyond that claim to suggest an elemental link between Johnson's openness to diverse ideas, information, and opinions and his insistence on secrecy about that very process. This desire for secrecy may have been rooted partially in Johnson's psyche, but it had distinctly rational political roots as well. Johnson saw the combination of openness and secrecy as an important means to the goal of good governance on issues as diverse as Vietnam, civil rights, and arms control. (It can almost go without saying that, in retrospect, not all the resulting government policies were "good.")

In terms of political theory, Johnson's was a conventional understanding of the role of the president in the 1960s: The occupant of the Oval Office had the special burden and opportunity to lead the U.S.

government toward fulfilling its missions in the world and at home. We can, of course, be critical of both Johnson's theory of presidential power and his energetic application of it. In being so, we are also necessarily critical of the prevailing views of post–World War II political scientists who—before Vietnam and Watergate—looked kindly and somewhat naively on the idea that the United States was in a "deadlock" without a strong president in charge and a Congress ready to follow his lead.

Afterword: On Rationality, Johnson's Worldview, and the War

THE EVIDENCE GATHERED in this study rather perplexingly suggests that the United States' immense Vietnam tragedy was, in part, the legacy of a political leadership that valued rationality. To this topic I now give final attention.

In *The Irony of Vietnam*, Leslie Gelb and Richard Betts write that for over two decades, the momentum of established doctrine, policies, and rhetoric from the Truman administration onward made it unlikely that any occupant of the White House in the 1950s and 1960s would choose to withdraw from Vietnam. It would have been difficult, but not impossible (they suggest), for a president to do so, because of the likely punishment from the domestic political arena.

The portrait offered here shows a president keenly aware of the constraints and imperatives of domestic politics. To that extent, the portrait of Johnson's advisory system is consistent with that part of the Gelb and Betts thesis. But the evidence suggests that domestic politics provided only partial motivations for his choice of committing American troops and prestige to a war in Indochina and persisting with that course. However wrong his Vietnam policies now appear to the majority of observers, Johnson believed that history would rightly condemn him had he pulled the United States out of Southeast Asia.[1] On this point, of course, he may have been right. The question remains, though, how an essentially rational advisory and decisionmaking process could produce such bad results. The Vietnam War, after all, is popularly regarded as one of the worst disasters in American history.

A distinction between wise *beliefs* (or theories) about foreign affairs, on the one hand, and rational foreign policy decisionmaking *processes*, on the other, helps in addressing the question. It is beyond the scope of this book to deal in depth with the debate over what the United States government *should* have done about the Vietnam situation. Some defend the idea that the United States had moral and legal responsibilities to defend South Vietnam against a communist takeover in the 1960s. Almost two decades after Johnson's 1965 decisions, Walt Rostow wrote,

"It was palpable to every Asian leader, as well as to Johnson, that if the United States permitted South Vietnam to be taken over, the whole of southeast Asia would be promptly endangered." Norman Podhoretz has written that by going to war in Southeast Asia, the United States engaged in "an act of imprudent idealism whose moral soundness has been so overwhelmingly vindicated by the hideous consequences of our defeat." And Guenter Lewy writes of "the moral impulse which played a significant part in the original decision to help protect the independence of South Vietnam" and notes the "sad fate of the people of Indochina" since U.S. withdrawal in 1975.[2] But much more common is the view of Henry Steele Commager and collaborators, who conclude that the United States met "unmitigated defeat" in Vietnam resulting in "incalculable damage to American society and to the effectiveness of the United States in world affairs." Even Philip Rulon, the most sympathetic of Johnson biographers, writes that history will assign him "some guilt for America's hasty entrance into this military conflict." And Dean Rusk, interviewed years after he left office, said, "There is nothing I can say now which can reduce in any way my share of responsibility in the events of those years. President Kennedy and President Johnson are not here to speak for themselves and I will just have to live with it."[3]

In addressing the rationality question, I assume that the conventional wisdom (to which I subscribe) is correct: The American intervention in Vietnam was misguided and ultimately a wasteful and tragic failure. Thus the stark question is posed: How could a rational advisory system produce such a "bad" war? The answer derives from the narrow meaning that must be ascribed to rationality if it is to be useful as a concept in political and historical analyses. If rationality is ill-advisedly equated with wisdom, which suggests "great understanding . . . of situations and unusual discernment and judgment in dealing with them,"[4] then the concept of rationality is dangerously broad: It can lead analysts to ascribe irrationality, after the fact, to any decisionmaking process that produced a bad outcome.

Rationality is better (and, in some scholarly fields,[5] more commonly) thought to imply "a latent or active power to make logical inferences and draw conclusions that enable one to understand the world about him and relate such knowledge to the attainment of ends." This process of building knowledge by making inferences, drawing conclusions, and relating means to ends stands in contrast to reaching conclusions by processes that are "emotional" or "animal."[6] Thus, analysts treating past decisionmaking processes need to look for patterns suggesting that means have been linked to ends, that a prudentially broad range of options has been considered, and that an openness to learning from new information has existed.

One political philosopher rightly suggests about rationality that the "whole subject, while of the greatest importance, remains shrouded in darkness."[7] Nonetheless, there are undeniably advisory and decision-making systems that, by the standards suggested here, are rational and others that are not. These standards for judging rationality versus irrationality are admittedly narrow, but usefully so. Although they do not settle important questions of moral philosophy, such standards allow us to make distinctions among advisory systems if we possess sufficient evidence.

Despite the continued classification of some archival records from the Johnson administration, there are sufficient resources available to draw conclusions about the manner in which decisions were pondered and reached by Johnson. Although it may strike an unsatisfactory chord with those who view the Vietnam War as an American-caused abomination, the evidence suggests that the advisory and decisionmaking process was, according to the definition laid out, rational in the three time periods studied. U.S. goals in Vietnam were discussed at length within the higher councils of the administration, as were potential means to those goals. Most of those who advised the president (including critics in the minority such as Ball, who advocated disengagement, and Helms, whose intelligence data were less optimistic than that provided by the military) found him generally open to diverse information and opinions.

A central truth about Lyndon Johnson and his advisers is that they were part of a larger society in which there were debates over the American role in world affairs, despite there also being dominant beliefs about the subject. In short, there were winning and losing sides to these debates. No less a figure than J. William Fulbright hinted at this in his 1964 book, *Old Myths and New Realities* — the very same book that Lady Bird Johnson discussed with Fulbright on his back porch during a barbecue the president and first lady attended. Fulbright described "an inevitable divergence, attributable to the imperfections of the human mind, between the world as it is and the world as men perceive it." It was necessary, he wrote, for "men in high office" to overcome the gap between the realities of international affairs and the "prevailing misconceptions" of the time. Those misconceptions grew out of ignorance about changing realities in world affairs, producing a tendency to relate the more unpleasant changes — such as "wars of liberation" — to the "Devil" in Moscow. But the "drawing back of the Soviet Union from extremely aggressive policies" was one aspect of a "complex and fluid world situation, and we are not adapting ourselves to it. We are clinging to old myths in the face of new realities."[8]

Judged in the context of its own times, Fulbright's analysis must be seen as the minority view in a debate among "realists" of the early

1960s over the application of containment doctrine policies. On Fulbright's side were those whose understanding of international affairs seems, in retrospect, sophisticated. These included men such as George Ball and Clark Clifford, who urged caution in the use of U.S. military power in the world. On the other side of the debate were those in the majority, such as Robert McNamara and Dean Rusk. Their beliefs seem (again, only in retrospect) a cruder view of international relations. They saw the application of U.S. military power in Vietnam as the logical (even moral) application of the United States' containment policy. No less an analyst of international relations than Henry Kissinger was on the dominant side of this debate among realists. Meeting with former Chancellor Adenauer of West Germany in June 1965, Kissinger told the skeptical leader that the United States was "defending Europe in South East Asia."[9]

Clearly Lyndon Johnson also accepted, for the most part, the orthodoxy of containment as represented by the domino theory.[10] In other words, his rational assessment of competing opinions and analyses regarding Vietnam was shaped by those beliefs — what others call ideology or worldview.

What is striking about Fulbright's 1964 analysis is that he has been joined in later years by such ideologically diverse authors as W. W. Rostow and Gabriel Kolko, whose structural analyses assert that the beliefs of American political leaders were crucial in shaping their foreign policies.[11] These and other authors disagree forcefully about the validity of the "theory" of international relations that guided Lyndon Johnson but agree that his understanding of world politics was important in influencing his choices about Vietnam. Their assertions are complex and more difficult to "prove" than personalistic ones that simplistically root U.S. intervention and persistence in Vietnam in the president's irrational advisory and deliberative processes — as Hannah Arendt put it, the American leadership's "willful, deliberate disregard of all facts."[12] If a rational president can enter a "bad" war, it suggests the need for further study of the influence of Johnson's (and other presidents') beliefs about international relations on decisionmaking during the Vietnam War and other major events in the history of U.S. foreign policy.

In conclusion, assertions that there must have been an irrational advisory process surrounding Johnson do not meet the test of evidence. This study finds a president who, as if schooled by pluralist theorists of presidential power, reached widely for advisory (and bargaining) encounters with diverse actors in the political system but shrouded that process in secrecy, always with an eye to preserving his options, marshalling his political forces, protecting his power, and acting at the strategically opportune moment in order to achieve what he, and those whom he viewed as enlightened, saw as good public policy. It finds as well that, as William Bundy has claimed, "the quality of men that President Johnson had around him and the way that he dealt with them, on the whole, created an atmosphere in which you did level."[13] But in dealing with Vietnam, the president ran head-on into what (retrospectively) is so widely seen as a reality of world politics that it now ranks as conventional wisdom: Guerrilla insurgencies with significant indigenous and external support are extremely difficult—indeed, nearly impossible—to defeat with conventional armaments and forces. In his own time, Johnson was a member (albeit sometimes a doubting one) of the majority side in the debate over the proper application of the United States' containment policies in the world—the side that believed that the United States could and should fight to preserve South Vietnam from communism. Lyndon Baines Johnson sought—sometimes secretly, sometimes more openly, and often urgently—diverse information and advice to help him make choices about Vietnam. But he made decisions that were shaped by his view of the United States' role in the world.

Properly understood, the Johnson administration's Vietnam deliberations dramatically illustrate how tragic consequences can flow from the actions of rational, well-intentioned leaders pursuing a vision of world order. In the late 1950s and early 1960s, a strong majority in American society, Congress, the foreign policy establishment, and the executive branch believed in what seems (retrospectively) a crude version of the containment doctrine. Given that, the best question is not How could Vietnam happen? but How could it not happen?

Appendix: Significant Advisers to Johnson on Vietnam — 1965, 1967, 1968

Formal Foreign Policy Advisers

Rusk, McNamara, Wheeler, Westmoreland, M. Bundy, W. Bundy, Taylor, Ball

Rusk, McNamara, Wheeler, Westmoreland, Bunker, Komer, Helms, Rostow

Rusk, McNamara, Clifford, Wheeler, Westmoreland, Bunker, Goldberg, Helms, Rostow

Informal Foreign Policy Advisers

1965

Russell, Mansfield, Fulbright, Clifford, Eisenhower, Wise Men, Humphrey, Moyers

1967

Mansfield, Fortas, Clifford, Taylor, M. Bundy, Russell, McPherson

1968

Mansfield, McPherson, Humphrey, Russell, Taylor, M. Bundy, Acheson, Wise Men, Rowe, Ridgway, Fortas, Lodge

Notes

Preface

1. Halberstam, *New York Times Book Review*, January 3, 1971, p. 1; Ellison, quoted in Jack Valenti, *A Very Human President* (New York: Pocket Books, 1977), p. 312; Bornet, *The Presidency of Lyndon B. Johnson* (Lawrence: University Press of Kansas, 1983), p. xv. John Schwarz, *America's Hidden Success* (New York: Norton, 1983), might lead Americans to reexamine current conventional wisdom about the "failure" of the programs and policies produced by 1960s liberalism.

2. Russell to constituent, January 26, 1966, Series F Dictation I J7, Russell Library.

Chapter 1. Lyndon Johnson, His Vietnam Advisers, and the American Political Environment

1. *New York Times*, July 24, 25, 26, 1967; *The Public Papers of the Presidents: Lyndon Baines Johnson, 1967* (Washington, D.C.: Government Printing Office, 1968), pp. 710, 711, 722; Lyndon Johnson, *The Vantage Point* (New York: Holt, Rinehart, and Winston, 1971), pp. 84, 85, 167–172.

2. "July 25, 1967 — Senate Committee Chairmen," Folder: July 1967–May 1968, Tom Johnson's notes of meetings, box 1, LBJ Library. Johnson, a former deputy press secretary (and no relation to the late president) retains copyright to the notes at the Johnson Library. (See Chapter 4, note 1, for more on these notes.) Notes of such meetings are sometimes sparsely punctuated; I have added what seems appropriate punctuation. There was a similar White House meeting on January 9, 1967, in which Fulbright spoke out against Johnson's war policies and Rusk's performance. Other senators expressed a range of opinions from "win or get out" (Russell) to "there's too much dissent" (Smathers). Hubert Humphrey, Memo for files, January 10, 1967, VP Notes, WH meetings, 1967, 24 F 8 2F, Minnesota Historical Society. That meeting apparently lacked the heated tempers of the July meeting. On LBJ's opinion of Fulbright as a racist, see David Halberstam, *The Best and the Brightest* (New York: Random House, 1972), p. 528; some former Johnson aides intimate this as well, off the record. On the previous Johnson-Fulbright friendship, see Tristram Coffin, *Senator Fulbright: Portrait of a Public Philosopher* (New York: E. P. Dutton, 1966), pp. 188–189, and Haynes Johnson and Bernard Gwertzman, *Fulbright: The Dissenter* (Garden City, N.Y.: Doubleday, 1968), pp. 6, 184.

3. John Stoessinger, *Why Nations Go to War*, 4th ed. (New York: St. Martin's Press, 1985), pp. 99, 102; Larry Berman, *Planning a Tragedy* (New York: Norton,

1982), p. 109; Barbara Tuchman, *The March of Folly* (New York: Knopf, 1984), p. 309.

4. Ball, oral interview, p. I, 18–20, LBJ Library; George M. Kahin, *Intervention* (New York: Knopf, 1986), pp. 348, 366. Emmette Redford and Richard McCulley, in *White House Operations: The Johnson Presidency* (Austin: University of Texas Press, 1986), say that the president's "direct and feverishly pursued contact with Cabinet and other executives, congressmen, trusted advisers, and numerous other persons supplemented the staff system and often left even the top staff assistants uncertain about the sources of his information" (p. 69).

5. Hannah Arendt, "Lying in Politics," in *Crises of the Republic* (New York: Harcourt Brace Jovanovich, 1972), p. 32. Patrick L. Hatcher, in *The Suicide of an Elite: American Internationalists and Vietnam* (Stanford, Calif.: Stanford University Press, 1990), says that Johnson "possessed substantial evidence" that "he was going to lose his war in Vietnam." Like John Kennedy, Johnson failed "to make careful, modest attempts to find a path away from the greatest dangers" in Vietnam (pp. 188, 288).

6. Mansfield to Johnson, June 5, 1965, NS file, Name file: Mansfield, box 6, LBJ Library.

7. Mansfield, quoted in Robert Byrd, *The Senate, 1789-1989: Addresses on the History of the United States Senate* (Washington, D.C.: Government Printing Office, 1988), p. 694. In a meeting on July 27, as Johnson prepared to announce the increased U.S. commitment to South Vietnam, Mansfield told Johnson and congressional leaders, "This decision appears to have a certain inevitability in the light of other decisions going back months and years." Yet Mansfield stunned them with a forceful criticism of Johnson's decision. Folder: "Mansfield, Mike, 1/1/65–7/30/65," File: Mansfield, Mike (Sen.), 1/1/65–7/30/65, LBJ Library. The letter quoted is Mansfield to Johnson, March 24, 1965, folder: M. Bundy, vol. 9, NS file: Memos to President from Bundy, box 3, LBJ Library.

8. In *Man, the State, and War* (New York: Columbia University Press, 1959), Kenneth Waltz divides explanations of the causes of all wars into three camps — those that see human nature, the nature of nation-states, or the anarchic international system as the main determinant.

9. I quote from Leslie Gelb and Richard Betts, *The Irony of Vietnam: The System Worked* (Washington, D.C.: Brookings, 1979), p. 13, an elaboration of "Vietnam: Some Hypotheses About Why and How," presented to a meeting of the American Political Science Association in 1970. Although seeing a certain narrowness to the advice and advisers surrounding presidents and accepting the conventional wisdom about Johnson's advisory relations, Gelb and Betts find this an unsatisfactory causal explanation.

10. James David Barber, *The Presidential Character: Predicting Performance in the White House* (Englewood Cliffs, N.J.: Prentice-Hall, 1972), p. 33.

11. Indeed, it is part of a larger debate over the causation behind political events. A recent study is in Bryan D. Jones, ed., *Leadership and Politics: New Perspectives in Political Science* (Lawrence: University Press of Kansas, 1989). Jones writes of two views of the role of leaders in shaping policy: "The biographical approach has pictured a political world that bends to the will of the dedicated leader, whatever that will may be. The more systematic approach tends to depict leaders as products of social, economic, or political forces or as responding rationally to institutionally structured incentives" (see pp. 3–16).

12. Irving Janis suggests the impact of groupthink—"a mode of thinking that people engage in when they are deeply involved in a cohesive in-group, when the members' strivings for unanimity override their motivation to realistically appraise alternative courses of action"—on Johnson. Janis, *Groupthink: Psychological Studies of Policy Decisions and Fiascoes*, 2d ed. (Boston: Houghton Mifflin, 1982), pp. 98, 130.

13. Berman, *Planning a Tragedy*, p. 146. Bruce Altschuler's *LBJ and the Polls* (Gainesville: University of Florida Press, 1990) describes an irrational president who, convinced that the public loved him and steeped in isolation, shut out critical advisers and ideas. See, for instance, pp. 49, 60, 101–102, 108. Altschuler relies on archival research but is clearly influenced by the analysis of Doris Kearns. Similarly, John Stoessinger draws on Kearns, David Halberstam, and James David Barber to write that Lyndon Johnson "led and dominated" his advisers and that, by late 1967, the "barriers separating irrational thought from delusion were fast crumbling." John Stoessinger, *Crusaders and Pragmatists: Movers of Modern American Foreign Policy* (New York: Norton, 1985), pp. 186, 193; David Halberstam, *The Best and the Brightest* (New York: Random House, 1972); Doris Kearns, *Lyndon Johnson and the American Dream* (New York: Harper and Row, 1976); J. Michael Quill, *Lyndon Johnson and the Southern Military Tradition* (Washington, D.C.: University Press of America, 1977), p. ii.

14. Hatcher, *Suicide of an Elite*. LBJ failed to make "careful, modest attempts" away from an unnecessary war. See pp. 12, 185–188, 286–288; John P. Burke and Fred I. Greenstein, with the collaboration of Larry Berman and Richard Immerman, *How Presidents Test Reality: Decisions on Vietnam, 1954 and 1965* (New York: Russell Sage Foundation, 1989), pp. 15, 17, 144, 149, 193–194, 248–249, 300. On the environment, Burke and Greenstein write of ealry 1965, "Johnson was not faced with the intractable political environment emphasized by Gelb and Betts." Brian VanDeMark's dispassionate *Into the Quagmire: Lyndon Johnson and the Escalation of the Vietnam War* (New York: Oxford University Press, 1991) states that the Johnson administration failed in the spring and summer of 1965 "ever to question whether it [escalation] could work—or at what ultimate price" (p. xvi). These three works offer structural and personalistic explanations of the war. Richard Goodwin, *Remembering America* (Boston: Little, Brown, 1988), p. 410.

15. Some analysts do not confront these causal controversies head on. Stanley Karnow's generally excellent *Vietnam: A History* (New York: Viking Press, 1983) presents an inconsistent view of Johnson's relations with advisers. George Herring's *America's Longest War* (New York: Wiley, 1979), also a good overview of the war, mostly avoids questions concerning Johnson's advisory system.

Most military historians reject personalistic explanations of the United States' entry into the war, seeing intervention as a rational, moral response to a crisis in the international political system—the attempt by North Vietnam to annex South Vietnam. They do, however, often explain the U.S. failure in Indochina by emphasizing Johnson's hesitance to secure military victory. Colonel Harry G. Summers writes, "The causes of U.S. failure . . . are complicated. And they start at the top. First of all, President Johnson made a conscious political decision not to mobilize the American people for war. This was a fundamental mistake." "Lessons: A Soldier's View," in Peter Braestrup (ed.), *Vietnam as History* (Washington, D.C.: University Press of America, 1984), p. 109. An exception is Bruce Palmer, a retired general, who shifts much of the blame for escalation and failure in Vietnam to military leaders: "Not once during the war did the JCS [Joint Chiefs of Staff] advise the Commander-in-Chief or the Secretary of Defense that the strategy being pursued most probably would fail and that the United States would be unable to achieve its objectives." General Harold Johnson, Army Chief of Staff during the war, was haunted by guilt feelings over this, and told Palmer, "For over five years after the war, I could not even bear to think about it." See Palmer, *The Twenty-five Year War* (Lexington: University of Kentucky Press, 1984), p. 46.

16. Gabriel Kolko, *Anatomy of a War* (New York: Pantheon, 1985), pp. 547, 168. Michael Hunt also questions the impact of leaders' personalities on U.S. foreign policy. See Hunt, *Ideology and U.S. Foreign Policy* (New Haven, Conn.: Yale University Press, 1987), p. 170 and, in general, chs. 2, 3, 4.

17. Giap, quoted in Stanley Karnow, "Giap Remembers," *New York Times Magazine*, June 24, 1990, p. 60. Ball, oral history, p. I, 14, LBJ Library. Walt W. Rostow, an economist and historian before and after his career as a foreign policy adviser in the Kennedy and Johnson administrations, agrees that ideas "matter because consciously or unconsciously they help determine the way the choices open to those making decisions are defined and the option actually chosen." Rostow, *The United States and the Regional Organization of Asia and the Pacific, 1965–1985* (Austin: University of Texas Press, 1986).

18. The *Pentagon Papers*, a huge collection of Vietnam-era policymaking documents, is sometimes treated as an unimpeachable mega-source for analyses of the Vietnam War. There are three different versions of the *Papers*: The *New York Times* edition, Neil Sheehan, ed. (New York: Quadrangle Books, 1971), is the briefest and combines documents and analysis produced by the Pentagon study with further documents and analysis provided by *Times* writers; the so-called Gravel edition (Boston: Beacon Press, 1971) includes more documentation, adding up to four volumes; the larger 12-volume *United States–Vietnam Relations, 1945–1967: A Study Prepared by the Department of Defense* (Washington, D.C.: Government Printing Office, 1971) nonetheless suffers from certain deletions. I use the Gravel edition.

Published in 1971, the *Papers'* impact on public and elite perceptions of the war's causes was undoubtedly significant. A typical reaction was Hannah Arendt's, who concluded in "Lying in Politics" that the U.S. leadership's "willful, deliberate disregard of all facts, historical, political, geographical, for more than twenty-five years" caused the disastrous intervention in Vietnam. See Arendt, *Crisis of the Republic* (New York: Harcourt Brace Jovanovich, 1972), p. 32; originally in *The New York Review of Books*, November 18, 1971, pp. 30–39.

There are glaring gaps in the *Pentagon Papers*, chiefly the sparse documentation shedding light on Johnson's thoughts or deliberations. Nor do the *Papers* indicate much of what Secretary of State Dean Rusk told the president. Readers learn more about the thoughts of McNamara and his subordinates in the Department of Defense, Rusk's assistants at State, those of the CIA and the military command at the Pentagon, in the Pacific, and in Saigon. The *Pentagon Papers* can mislead if not used carefully. See, for elaboration, George M. Kahin, "The Pentagon Papers: A Critical Evaluation," *American Political Science Review* 69 (June 1975): 676, and Herring, *America's Longest War*, p. 33.

19. Herbert Goldhamer, *The Adviser* (New York: Elsevier Press, 1978), p. 3.

20. This neglect in defining "adviser" happens in Cronin's essay, "Political Science and Executive Advisory Systems," in Thomas Cronin and Sanford Greenberg, *The Presidential Advisory System* (New York: Harper and Row, 1969). A

recent work on the Johnson cabinet is James Anderson's "President Johnson's Use of the Cabinet as an Instrument of Executive Action," *Journal of Politics* 48 (August 1986): 529–537.

21. Edward S. Corwin, *The President: Office and Powers, 1787–1957* (New York: New York University Press, 1957), p. 298. On the National Security Council and the Assistant to the President for National Security Affairs (known popularly as the "national security adviser"), see Joseph G. Bock, *The White House Staff and the National Security Assistant* (Westport, Conn.: Greenwood Press, 1987); Bradley H. Patterson, *The Ring of Power: The White House Staff and Its Expanding Role in Government* (New York: Basic Books, 1988), ch. 7; and The President's Special Review Board, *The Tower Commission Report* (New York: Bantam Books and Times Books, 1987), pt. 2.

22. Paul Kattenburg's *The Vietnam Trauma in American Foreign Policy, 1945–1975* (New Brunswick, N.J.: Transaction Books, 1980) describes Under Secretary of State George Ball as the only Johnson adviser opposing escalation in Vietnam in 1965, and later asks with frustration: "What keeps . . . any American President from asking the head of the AFL/CIO, the President of Yale, the head of General Motors, or the Chairman of any Senate committee . . . for key advice on an issue in foreign policy?" (p. 231). In fact, Johnson talked to just the sort of advisers Kattenburg suggests, but still escalated the U.S. military role in Vietnam.

23. A somewhat similar typology was offered by Sorensen, in Cronin and Greenberg, *Presidential Advisory System*, p. 9. There is occasionally some overlap in categorizing advisers: Richard Russell was both a member of Congress and Johnson's personal intimate.

24. For example, compare Clark Clifford's oral interview at the LBJ Library, recorded in 1969, with later publications based on documentary evidence. For the oral history, Clifford remembered being a hawkish supporter of the president's Vietnam policies from August 1965 through his accession to the office of Secretary of Defense in early 1968. He did not mention his opposition to committing ground troops in Indochina up through July 1965.

25. One example of this is the president's daily diary, which reflects his secretaries' (alas, imperfect) attempts to note every meeting in which the president participated and every phone call to and from him. If a researcher were to rely on the diary to determine how often Johnson saw Senators Richard Russell and J. William Fulbright in early 1965, he or she would underestimate the frequency of their meetings. Other archival materials, published diaries, and so on, give a fuller picture. These limitations of the diary have been confirmed in talks with an archivist at the Johnson Library. They are due primarily to the inability of secretaries in the Johnson White House to keep track of all the president's meetings and telephone conversations. See Chapter 3's treatment of Senator Russell and its comparisons with Burke and Greenstein's *How Presidents Test Reality*. James J. Best defends the diary's reliability in "Who Talked to the President When? A Study of Lyndon B. Johnson," *Political Science Quarterly* 103, 3 (Fall 1988): 531–546.

26. On organization theory, see Herbert Kaufman, "Organization Theory and Political Theory," *The American Political Science Review* 58, 1 (March 1964): 5–14; reprinted in Walter Hill and Douglas Egan, *Readings in Organization Theory* (Boston: Allyn and Bacon, 1967), pp. 633, 635, 638, 641. Carefully warning social scientists to define situations as they appear to the "rational actor" being studied, James March and Herbert Simon note the temptation of analysts

to describe conditions in the organization and in its environment with a false "objectivity" from their own privileged vantage points as outside observers. March and Simon, *Organizations* (New York: Wiley and Sons, 1958), pp. 11, 140–141, 150–152.

Stephen Hess, *Organizing the Presidency*, 2d ed. (Washington, D.C.: Brookings, 1988), ch. 1. Almost in passing, Hess correctly asserted in the first edition (published in 1976) that Lyndon Johnson was not cut off from competing, divergent views during the months in 1965 when important questions of escalation were being considered. See pp. 108–109.

27. Charles Walcott and Karen Hult, "Organizing the White House: Structure, Environment, and Organizational Governance," *The American Journal of Political Science* 31, 1 (February 1987): 110.

28. Jeffrey Pfeffer, *Organizations and Organization Theory* (Boston: Pitman, 1982), pp. 5, 8; and "Management as Symbolic Action: The Creation and Maintenance of Organizational Paradigms," in L. L. Cummings and Barry Stow (eds.), *Research in Organization Behavior*, vol. 3 (Greenwich, Conn.: JAI Press, 1981); Kaufman, "Organization Theory," in Hill and Egan, *Readings in Organization Theory*, pp. 633, 635. Pfeffer believes that leaders' more important roles are as affirmers of organizations' goals rather than as achievers of those goals. In this, his work resembles political scientist Murray Edelman's *The Symbolic Uses of Power* (Urbana: University of Illinois Press, 1967). In *The Domestic Presidency: Decision-making in the White House* (North Scituate, Mass.: Duxbury Press, 1975), John Kessel considers the influence of the political environment on one part of a president's advisory system — the Domestic Council in the Nixon administration.

29. Walcott and Hult (implying that a president is a rational actor) predict change in the structure of presidential staffs, based on changing conditions of certainty and uncertainty in the environment about goals of an administration and its means to achieve those goals. "Organizing the White House," p. 112. In a later work, *Governing Public Organizations: Politics, Structure, and Institutional Design* (Pacific Grove, Calif.: Brooks/Cole, 1990), Walcott and Hult take a "normative turn," prescribing what organizational changes a president should make under differing environmental conditions.

30. The rationality assumption concerns only a president's shaping of his advisory system, not larger, more controversial questions about the "rationality" of Vietnam or other wars. J. Glenn Gray's *The Warriors: Reflections on Men in Battle* (New York: Harcourt Brace, 1959) is an attempt by a philosopher and former combat soldier to make sense of the irrationality of war. See also the Afterword in this book for more on rationality.

A wholly deterministic situational theory assumes that a president's personal attributes are unimportant — changes in his advisory circle inevitably reflect changes in the environment (ideology, public opinion, and so forth). But I assume that change in a presidential advisory system is *not* automatic — a president is not a black box. He is the key mediator between the environment and the advisory system and has the power to make choices. A rational president, however — whatever his overarching style of operation — will pursue advice and information and structure his advisory circle in ways that reflect his understanding of environmental conditions. Advisers are also influenced by their understanding of the environment, which affects their interactions with the president and one another. Still, I assume that the president is by far the most important of those persons shaping the system.

31. Roger Scruton, *A Dictionary of Political Thought* (New York: Hill and Wang, 1982), p. 393.

32. I have drawn on Walcott and Hult, "Organizing the White House," in developing my propositions. In the language of political science, the advisory system is the dependent variable, the president is an intervening variable, and the environment is the independent variable. This, of course, contrasts with the many essentially personalistic accounts that treat the Johnson advisory system as an independent or crucial intervening variable that was responsible for ill-fated choices regarding Vietnam.

33. Fred Greenstein, *Personality and Politics: Problems of Evidence, Inference, and Conceptualization* (Princeton, N.J.: Princeton University Press, 1987).

34. Alexander George, "Case Studies and Theory Development: The Method of Structured, Focused Comparison," in Paul G. Laurens, ed., *Diplomacy: New Approaches in History, Theory, and Policy* (New York: Free Press, 1979), pp. 43-68; Harry Eckstein, "Case Study and Theory in Political Science," in Fred Greenstein and Nelson Polsby, eds., *The Handbook of Political Science: Vol. 7, Strategies of Inquiry* (Reading, Mass.: Addison-Wesley, 1975); Clifford Geertz, *The Interpretation of Cultures: Selected Essays* (New York: Basic Books, 1973); and Gordon S. Wood, "Intellectual History and the Social Sciences," in Paul Conkin and John Higham, eds., *New Directions in Intellectual History* (Baltimore: Johns Hopkins University Press, 1979), pp. 27-41. George calls his comparative case study approach "focused because it deals selectively with only certain aspects of the historical case . . . and structured because it employs general questions to guide the data collection and analysis in that historical case" (pp. 61-62). Wood writes that, in reconstructing the actions of individuals in the past, "we will have to know what structure of conventions existed, what choices of ideas were available to the historical participants, in order to know why they selected and used those they did" (p. 36). Thomas Cronin notes the difficulty in studying advisory processes, widely thought to depend on factors such as presidential character or style. He proposes comparative study as a way out of mere descriptive history of political leadership and decisionmaking. See Cronin and Greenberg, *Presidential Advisory System*, pp. 226, 322.

Chapter 2. 1965: "Our Last Chance"

1. See Raoul Berger's excellent *Executive Privilege: A Constitutional Myth* (New York: Bantam Books, 1975).

2. Leslie Gelb and Richard Betts, *The Irony of Vietnam: The System Worked* (Washington, D.C.: Brookings, 1979), pp. 45, 46, 56-57, 67. Eisenhower refused the advice of some, including Vice President Richard Nixon, to send U.S. troops to bolster the French position in the war. See Stanley Karnow, *Vietnam: A History* (New York: Viking Press, 1983), p. 197. Many analysts believe that the most significant outcome of Eisenhower's decisionmaking was that he did not send combat troops to Indochina. The most recent example is John P. Burke and Fred I. Greenstein, with the collaboration of Larry Berman and Richard Immerman, *How Presidents Test Reality: Decisions on Vietnam, 1954 and 1965* (New York: Russell Sage Foundation, 1989), which titles its section on Eisenhower, "Failure to Intervene in 1954." But Senator Richard Russell's analysis (similar to Gelb and Betts's and mine) was that what Eisenhower did not do

(go to war) was no more important than what he did—vastly increase U.S. aid to South Vietnam and send advisers. Burke and Greenstein applaud Eisenhower's systematic consultation with advisers and congressional leaders in deciding against going to war; but Russell wrote to a friend of the 1954 period, "it was decided not to go into Vietnam. Later, and after the adjournment of the Congress, Secretary Dulles prevailed on President Eisenhower to send a military mission and a great deal of equipment to Vietnam. I had been so vehement in my objection that the then Assistant Secretary of State Thruston Morton was sent down to Georgia to tell me what had been done (not ask or advise). . . . I told him then that I thought it was a mistake, that it would be a very costly adventure in blood and treasure." Russell to Wolfson, January 4, 1966, Gen. File, Inter. Series-Vietnam, Russell Library. Enigmatically, Russell also sent word to Eisenhower, as he would to subsequent presidents, that he would nonetheless "support the flag" wherever the United States made a commitment. Russell feared that the Soviet Union and China would mistake public dissent against presidential decisions in international affairs for weakness.

3. Gelb and Betts, *Irony*, p. 67. On this, see also James R. Arnold, *The First Domino: Eisenhower, the Military, and America's Intervention in Vietnam* (New York: William Morrow, 1991).

4. Gelb and Betts, *Irony*, pp. 75, 91. For a negative critique of Kennedy's Vietnam policies, see Lawrence J. Bassett and Stephen E. Pelz, "The Failed Search for Victory: Vietnam and the Politics of War," in Thomas G. Paterson (ed.), *Kennedy's Quest for Victory* (New York: Oxford University Press, 1989), pp. 223–252. A counterview, that Kennedy would have steered clear of large-scale war in Vietnam, is in John M. Newman's *JFK and Vietnam* (New York: Warner, 1992). After the war became unpopular, a few former advisers to Kennedy claimed that he planned to withdraw completely from Vietnam, but only after winning reelection in 1964. The evidence for this is skimpy. Kennedy had agreed to plans for a hoped-for partial withdrawal of American advisers, but this was to be dependent on further "progress" in South Vietnam. On this see McGeorge Bundy to Johnson, March 14, 1964, NS File, Memos to President, Bundy, box 1, LBJ Library.

5. Frederick Nolting, former ambassador to South Vietnam, took part in State Department and White House meetings concerning Diem, who was thought to be unpopular in his country. He writes of a State Department meeting at which Johnson was present: "He listened to the arguments and then made one remark. Otto Passman, he observed, has been a 'pain in the neck' to the Democrats in Congress for many years. (Passman was a Democratic Representative from Louisiana.) But do we try to throw him out? Do we try to undermine him with his own constituents? No, we try to get along with him as best we can. We should do the same with President Diem, he said." Nolting, *From Trust to Tragedy: The Political Memoirs of Frederick Nolting, Kennedy's Ambassador to Diem's Vietnam* (New York: Praeger, 1988), p. 127. See also Lyndon Johnson, *The Vantage Point: Perspectives of the Presidency* (New York: Holt, Rinehart, and Winston, 1971), pp. 45–46, 62.

6. Gelb and Betts, in *Irony*, write, "The coup marked a renewed and deeper assumption of responsibility by the United States. . . . A case could even be made that the train of events made direct U.S. intervention inevitable" (pp. 90–92). See also Maxwell Taylor oral history, p. II, 23, LBJ Library.

7. David Halberstam, *The Best and the Brightest* (New York: Random House, 1972), p. 352.

8. Gelb and Betts, *Irony*, pp. 111, 197. They write that opponents of U.S. intervention in Vietnam in 1965 rarely admitted that the price of their "preferred alternative was acceptance of the defeat of South Vietnam by the Communists." My "The Mythology Surrounding Lyndon Johnson, His Advisers, and the 1965 Decision to Escalate the War in Vietnam" suggests that some advisers admitted that letting South Vietnam become communist was an inevitable consequence of the disengagement they supported. See Barrett, *Political Science Quarterly* 103, 4 (Winter 1988-89): 657-658.

Walt Rostow says that Johnson's thinking about the U.S. role in the Pacific was heavily influenced by his travels to Asia and by the debates in the 1950s surrounding Hawaiian statehood. Johnson believed that the United States must support Asian nationalism and cooperative regionalism in that part of the world, Rostow says. Personal interview with Rostow, January 20, 1989, Austin, Texas.

9. Historians still struggle over the evidence from the Tonkin Gulf episode. The range of opinion varies: There are those who think that Johnson (and/or McNamara) simply lied about the second attack in order to persuade Congress to grant him wide war-making power in Indochina. Others claim that the commanders in Vietnam and the decisionmakers in Washington at least thought that there had been a second attack. Johnson himself came to doubt that there had been a second attack. Dean Rusk based his opinion regarding the alleged attack on his readings of intercepts of North Vietnamese communications. He says, "there is no question that in my mind at the time I had no doubt Hanoi thought a second attack was going on." Rusk, interviewed by Richard Rusk and William Bundy, tape NN, p. 26, Rusk Papers, Russell Library. General Andrew Goodpaster, who worked for the Joint Chiefs of Staff at the time, voices similar views about what military leaders at the Pentagon thought was happening. See his oral history, p. 23, LBJ Library. See also Gelb and Betts, *Irony*, pp. 100-105; George M. Kahin, *Intervention* (New York: Knopf, 1986), pp. 219-225; Karnow, *Vietnam*, pp. 369-374; Gabriel Kolko, *Anatomy of a War* (New York: Pantheon, 1985), pp. 122-125; Johnson, *Vantage Point*, pp. 112-115; Richard Goodwin, *Remembering America* (Boston: Little, Brown, 1988), pp. 359-361; George Ball, *The Past Has Another Pattern* (New York: Norton, 1982), pp. 379-380.

10. *Congressional Record*, August 6, 1964, p. 18409; August 7, 1964, p. 18471. On a similar, earlier resolution, see Howard Wiarda, *Foreign Policy Without Illusion* (Glenview, Ill.: Scott, Foresman, 1990), p. 289.

11. Gelb and Betts, *Irony*, pp. 105-106. The authors add, "The one disservice of the *New York Times* in its original expose of the Pentagon Papers was in implying that the decision to bomb North Vietnam [in early 1965] was made in September 1964 and concealed to avoid jeopardizing Johnson's reelection." Gelb was one of the compilers of the *Pentagon Papers*. See p. 108.

12. Gelb and Betts, *Irony*, p. 117.

13. For a directly contrary view, see George Reedy's *Lyndon B. Johnson: A Memoir* (New York: Andrews and McMeel, 1982), p. 146: "At the time he entered the White House, it would have been relatively simple to disengage from Vietnam." More nuanced is Burke and Greenstein, *How Presidents Test Reality*, p. 149.

14. Richard Neustadt and Ernest May, *Thinking in Time: The Uses of History for Decision Makers* (New York: Free Press, 1986), p. 88.

15. The quotations are from Patrick Hatcher, *The Suicide of an Elite: American Internationalists and Vietnam* (Stanford, Calif.: Stanford University Press, 1990), pp. 188, 288. I also believe that Johnson should have employed his outstanding

political skills to chart a course out of Vietnam. I think that the difficulty with which this could have been achieved is underrated by many authors, for example, Larry Berman, *Planning a Tragedy: The Americanization of the Vietnam War* (New York: Norton, 1982), p. 149, and Goodwin, *Remembering America*, pp. 384, 404. For an alternative view — that the pursuit of victory in Vietnam was an honorable, achievable course — see Guenter Lewy, *America in Vietnam* (New York: Oxford University Press, 1978); William Westmoreland, *A Soldier Reports* (Garden City, N.Y.: Doubleday, 1976); and Ulysses S. G. Sharp, *Strategy for Defeat* (San Rafael, Calif.: Presidio Press, 1978).

16. Bundy to Johnson on February 7, 1965, in *The Pentagon Papers: The Gravel Edition* (Boston: Beacon Press, 1971), vol. 3, p. 309, and NS File, Memos to President, box 2, LBJ Library.

17. M. Bundy to Johnson, February 11, 1965, NS file, Name file: Mansfield, box 6, LBJ Library. In late June, Bundy confessed to Mansfield, "I have been very slow in carrying out an instruction from the President to respond to your memoranda of June 5 and June 9. He has now passed me in addition of your memorandum of June 14. In hope you will forgive me if I comment on all three at once." Bundy to Mansfield, undated, but written in late June 1965, file: M. Bundy, vol. 11, 1965, NS file, Memos to the President from Bundy, box 3, LBJ Library. Regarding phone calls, see the reference in June 9, 1965, letter from Mansfield to Johnson, NS file, Memos to the President from M. Bundy file, vol. 11, box 3, LBJ Library.

18. W. Bundy oral interview, p. II, 12, LBJ Library. See also "Summary Notes" of NSC meetings, February 6 and 7, 1965, Meeting Notes file, box 1, LBJ Library.

19. Mansfield to Johnson, February 8 and 10, 1965, NS file, Name file: Mansfield, box 6, LBJ Library.

20. Albert Eisele, *Almost to the Presidency* (Blue Earth, Minn.: Piper Co., 1982), p. 233; Hubert Humphrey, *The Education of a Public Man* (Garden City, N.Y.: Doubleday, 1976), pp. 318–319. See also "Summary Record of NSC Meeting No. 548 . . . ," February 10, 1965, Meetings Notes file, box 1, LBJ Library. These notes show that when Johnson asked "whether all those present agreed we should launch a retaliatory strike," Humphrey said that he had "mixed feelings about whether we should retaliate as Secretary McNamara had recommended."

21. Johnson, oral interview conducted by William Jordan, p. I, 27, LBJ Library.

22. W. Bundy, oral interview, p. I, 27; George Ball, oral interview, pp. I, 3, LBJ Library; see also Nolting, *Trust to Tragedy*, p. 127. Van Dyk quoted in Eisele, *Almost to the Presidency*, p. 233; see also Carl Solberg, *Hubert Humphrey: A Biography* (New York: Norton, 1984), p. 271.

23. The memo is quoted in Humphrey, *Education*, pp. 320–324. A draft of the memo is in VP files, 1965–1968, Foreign Affairs, Vietnam, Minnesota Historical Society.

24. Humphrey to Johnson, March 31, 1965, Folder: Memos to LBJ from HHH — Vietnam, 1965, Humphrey Papers, Minnesota Historical Society; also, Solberg, *Humphrey*, p. 274. This memo shows Humphrey moderating his views somewhat; he now advocated keeping or even slightly increasing the U.S. military presence in Vietnam until a negotiated withdrawal or "de facto settlement" was achieved. Importantly, Humphrey saw the need to "put a cap on the Joint Chiefs" and to push the State Department to be more active in seeking a settlement.

25. See Humphrey, *Education*, p. 325. Roche oral interview, pp. 65–66, LBJ Library. Humphrey to Moyers, September 1, 1965, VP Memos, Personal HHH, Correspondence with WH staff, 1965, Minnesota Historical Society.

26. See NS file, NSC meetings, vol. 3, LBJ Library, showing Humphrey at the March 26 meeting of the National Security Council but not at meetings held in April and June. The words are from the first of the Humphrey memos to Johnson quoted.

27. Lady Bird Johnson, *A White House Diary* (New York: Holt, Rinehart, and Winston, 1970), p. 250. See pp. 260, 318, for similar references to Humphrey having dinner with the Johnsons.

28. *Pentagon Papers*, vol. 3, p. 311. This is an excerpt of M. Bundy to Johnson, "Re: The Situation in Vietnam," February 7, 1965, NS File, Memos to President, box 2, LBJ Library. Bundy also told Johnson that the struggle in Vietnam would be long and urged him to make this clear to the American public. On this, see also Bundy to Johnson, February 16, 1965, Reference file, box 2, LBJ Library, which refers to Johnson's reluctance to do so. Not all Johnson's advisers agreed that the war would last for a long time, of course. See note 91 below on Maxwell Taylor.

29. Bundy to Johnson, March 14, 1964, NS file, Memos to President, Bundy, box 1, LBJ Library; Humphrey, *Education*, p. 483; Bradley H. Patterson, *The Ring of Power: The White House Staff and Its Expanding Role in Government* (New York: Basic Books, 1988), pp. 62, 104, 119; Stephen Hess, *Organizing the Presidency*, 2d ed. (Washington, D.C.: Brookings, 1988), p. 81; Joseph G. Bock, *The White House Staff and the National Security Assistant: Friendship and Friction at the Water's Edge* (Westport, Conn.: Greenwood Press, 1987), pp. 45, 52–53. See also Chapter 4 of this book.

30. *Pentagon Papers*, vol. 3, pp. 269, 295.

31. Westmoreland, *Soldier Reports*, pp. 117–119.

32. See Westmoreland, *Soldier Reports*, pp. 233–234, 383–386, for his views of his personal relationship with Johnson. Westmoreland's personal respect for Johnson does not mask his memoirs' severe indictment of Johnson as commander-in-chief. Clark Clifford believes that Johnson had genuinely high personal and professional regard for Westmoreland and two other top military men—Earle Wheeler and Maxwell Taylor—but adds, "They did not control him; he controlled them." See Clifford's oral history, tape 5, p. 13, LBJ Library.

33. Johnson, *White House Diary*, p. 259; see also pp. 304, 312, 333. On expected reverberations following U.S. withdrawal, see Johnson, *Vantage Point*, pp. 151–152, and Gelb and Betts, *Irony*, pp. 128–130. Wheeler, oral history, pp. I, 17, LBJ Library.

34. *Pentagon Papers*, vol. 3, p. 337. There was a brief period in the spring when those in Saigon could report a "rise in Vietnamese morale occasioned by the air strikes against North Vietnam," as Ambassador Taylor did on March 11, 1965. See *Pentagon Papers*, vol. 3, p. 345.

35. Westmoreland, *Soldier Reports*, p. 122.

36. *Pentagon Papers*, vol. 3, pp. 694 (McNaughton), 346 (Bundy). Johnson oral interview by William Jorden, p. 11, LBJ Library.

37. Reporter David Wise, quoted in Karnow, *Vietnam*, p. 410.

38. Thomas Schoenbaum, *Waging Peace and War: Dean Rusk in the Truman, Kennedy, and Johnson Years* (New York: Simon and Schuster, 1988), p. 450. Russell to Louis E. Wolfson, January 4, 1966, and January 15, 1965, General file, Inter. Series-Vietnam, Russell Library. Similarly, former Johnson speechwriter

John Roche views McNamara as having been a "disaster for American policy" because Johnson was overreliant on him. For better or worse, Roche says that Johnson and McNamara were devoted and loyal to each other. Roche oral history, p. I, 12, LBJ Library. Charles Roberts, *LBJ's Inner Circle* (New York: Delacourt Press, 1965), p. 130; Halberstam, *Best and Brightest*, pp. 268, 376; Humphrey, *Education*, p. 289.

39. The portrait of McNamara here contrasts with that in the *Pentagon Papers*: "From the records, the Secretary [of Defense] comes out much more clearly for good management than he does for any particular strategy" (vol. 3, p. 473). This statement does not fit well with the evidence in this chapter. A revealing pair of documents are Mansfield to Johnson (reporting the views of six dovish or doubting senators) and McNamara to Johnson (responding to the senators' concerns), July 27 and 28, 1965, both in XVI Inter. B. Subject July '65 file, Russell Library. See also Henry Trewhitt, *McNamara* (New York: Harper and Row, 1971), pp. 197–198, 220–221; Kahin's overall portrait of McNamara in *Intervention*.

40. Trewhitt, *McNamara*, pp. 216–217, 220–221. Ball oral interview, p. I, 16, LBJ Library. Later, on July 1, 1965, McGeorge Bundy reported to Johnson that McNamara and Rusk felt that another "Ball paper should not be argued with you in front of any audience larger than yourself, Rusk, McNamara, and me. They feel it is exceedingly dangerous to have this possibility reported in a wider circle." M. Bundy to Johnson, July 1, 1965, NS file, M. Bundy, July 1965, vol. 12, box 4, LBJ Library. Solberg, *Humphrey*, pp. 271, 277.

41. Bundy to Johnson, conveying views of both aides, January 27, 1965, NS file, Memos to President, box 2, LBJ Library. The memo is also quoted in Johnson, *Vantage Point*, pp. 122–123.

42. Karnow, *Vietnam*, pp. 415, 417.

43. Quoted in Karnow, *Vietnam*, p. 414.

44. "Memorandum for the Record," April 3, 1965, Westmoreland Papers, #15 History Backup, box 5, LBJ Library.

45. See a June 3, 1965, memo from Westmoreland to Ambassador Taylor, in which the general tries to define his understanding of recent months' "mission" of U.S. forces in South Vietnam. There is an intricate description of "phases" and "concepts" of authority. Though he was probably wrong about it, Westmoreland concluded by telling Taylor, "I have the feeling that the general impression probably exists in Washington that these forces are already committed to combat and that the fine distinctions which we have drawn here between offensive operations on the one hand and reaction on the other may not be of great concern in Washington." Westmoreland Papers, #16 History Backup, May 10–June 30, 1965, box 6, LBJ Library.

46. Taylor to Rusk, concurred in by Westmoreland, June 5, 1965, p. 13, Westmoreland Papers, #16 History Backup, May 10–June 30, 1965, box 6, LBJ Library. *Pentagon Papers*, vol. 4, pp. 606–609, vol. 3, p. 468; Karnow, *Vietnam*, p. 422. Wheeler to McNamara, June 11, 1965, NS file, Country file: Vietnam, box 193, LBJ Library.

47. *Pentagon Papers*, vol. 3, pp. 392, 461.

48. *Pentagon Papers*, vol. 3, p. 462.

49. Ball, *The Past*, p. 383. Though Ball believes it would have been politically hard for Johnson to pull out of Vietnam in 1965, he also says of the early months of the Johnson presidency, "I think it would have been terribly difficult for him to have disengaged immediately, because it would look as though he were

repudiating the policy of Kennedy. . . . I just don't think he could have done it then, as far as the domestic political situation was concerned." See Ball's oral history, p. I, 14, LBJ Library.

50. Ball to Johnson, June 18, 1965, NS file, Deployment of Major U.S. Forces, box 42, LBJ Library. Days later, on June 30, McGeorge Bundy gave Johnson a memo entitled "France in Vietnam, and the U.S. in Vietnam, 1965 — A Useful Analogy?" Bundy's answer was no. See NS file, Memos to President, box 3, LBJ Library.

51. John Roche, oral history, p. I, 21, LBJ Library. Moyers recruited Roche, at Johnson's instigation, for the administration.

52. There is regrettably little evidence about what Moyers himself advised Johnson on Vietnam at this time. It appears that his views were close to Johnson's, in that Moyers's views were ambiguous. Patrick Anderson's account holds that, in the first half of 1965, Moyers came to believe that U.S. intervention was necessary to save the government of South Vietnam but that he was none-theless sympathetic to doves who argued otherwise. Thus, Anderson's *The Presidents' Men* (Garden City, N.Y.: Doubleday, 1969) contains a comment that Moyers was an "advocate of peace in Vietnam" and also states that "[Moyers] was convinced that the build-up was necessary to prevent the collapse of the U.S.-supported government in Saigon." See pp. 339–340, 341, 345. There are scraps of paper at the Johnson Library suggesting Moyers's access, such as a hand-written note Moyers passed to Johnson during a meeting on July 8, 1965, saying, "I appreciate the chance to sit in on this and other foreign policy meetings." Office of the President file, Moyers 1963–65, box 13, LBJ Library. On Moyers as a conduit of dovish advice to the president, see also Ball, *The Past*, pp. 392, 396. Goodwin's *Remembering America* portrays Moyers as having doubts about intervention but lacks specificity. Remarkably, the book says that Moyers, a close friend of Goodwin's at the time, was "ignorant of plans to escalate the war on the ground" (p. 385). Perhaps Goodwin was ignorant of such plans, as he claims, but Moyers was not. On Bundy's view of Moyers, see Bundy to Johnson, February 2, 1965, NS file, Memos to President, box 2, LBJ Library.

53. Ball, *The Past*, p. 396.

54. Benjamin Read, oral history, p. 9, LBJ Library. Ball says that McNamara "just regarded it as next to treason, that this [Ball's critique of escalation pro-posals] had been put down on paper." Other top Johnson advisers were "more tolerant." Ball oral history, p. I, 17, LBJ Library.

55. On Ball as a "domesticated dissenter," see James C. Thomson, Jr., who coined the term in "How Could Vietnam Happen?" *Atlantic*, April 1968, p. 49. See also Irving Janis, *Groupthink: Psychological Studies of Policy Decisions and Fiascoes*, 2d ed. (Boston: Houghton Mifflin, 1982), p. 120. So many works describe Ball as a lone, domesticated dissenter that it would be impossible to note them all. One recent example is Larry E. Cable's *Conflict of Myths: The Development of American Counterinsurgency Doctrine and the Vietnam War* (New York: New York University Press, 1986), pp. 269–270.

56. M. Bundy to Johnson, June 27, 1965, NS file, Troop Deployment History; on the French analogy, see NS file, Memos to President, box 3, LBJ Library.

57. Ball, *The Past*, p. 384. McGeorge Bundy was also "scrupulously fair" in getting Ball's memos to Johnson, says Ball. (Sometimes Ball sent his memo-randa to Johnson through Moyers, as noted earlier.) After leaving office, Johnson had occasion to compare Ball's status to that of Arthur Goldberg, U.S. ambas-sador to the UN. Ball was a "principal adviser, a strategic adviser," Goldberg was

not, said Johnson. Johnson oral interview with William Jorden, p. 18, LBJ Library. See also Schoenbaum, *Waging Peace*, pp. 279–280, which describes Ball as an alter ego of Rusk, with Ball taking care of most State Department business that Rusk could not deal with, due to the demands of the war. See also Benjamin Read (special assistant to Rusk) oral history, p. 34, LBJ Library.

58. Ball oral interview, p. I, 18, 20, LBJ Library. On another occasion, recalls Ball, "I wrote to President Johnson describing the escalatory steps which would follow one another until we got into deep trouble. . . . I sent this to the President and he called me and said come over. I went over with Mac Bundy. I think this was on a Saturday. We sat down and I went through it step-by-step and explained the logic of each step." See also p. I, 34.

59. Ball, *The Past*, pp. 396–397. Also Deployment of Major U.S. Forces, vol. 6, NS file, Troop Deployment History, box 43, LBJ Library.

60. Ball, *The Past*, p. 398.

61. Bundy to Johnson, July 1, 1965, NS file, M. Bundy, July 1965, vol. 12, box 4, LBJ Library.

62. McNamara to Johnson, July 1, 1965, NS file, Deployment of Major U.S. Forces, box 43, LBJ Library. For some reason, the complete version of this document is not in the *Pentagon Papers*, yet it is referred to and quoted; see vol. 4, p. 24. The authors, charged by McNamara to write the history, note unpersuasively, "It is difficult to be precise about the position of the Secretary of Defense during the build-up debate because there is so little of him in the files" (vol. 3, p. 473).

63. Ball says of William Bundy, "He was not in the top councils. He was an assistant secretary of state." George Ball oral interview, p. I, 21–22, LBJ Library. Nonetheless, during the months leading up to an "in or out" choice in Vietnam, Bundy was a key player in the deliberations.

64. *Pentagon Papers*, vol. 3, p. 475. William Bundy, "Holding on in South Vietnam," June 3, 1965, NS file, Deployment of Major U.S. Forces, box 43, LBJ Library.

65. The words are those of John Roche, a speechwriter involved in some Vietnam and other foreign policy sessions. See Roche's oral history, p. I, 12, LBJ Library. The sentiments are fully reflected in Dean Rusk's oral histories at the LBJ and Richard Russell libraries. McGeorge Bundy says that there was no "personal infighting" between Rusk and himself. Bundy, interviewed by Richard Rusk, tape CCC, p. 4, Rusk Papers, Russell Library. On Rusk's preference for oral rather than written communications with the president on matters of controversy, see Rusk, "A Modest Note to Future Archivists . . . ," January 13, 1975, NS file, Finding Aid, LBJ Library.

66. Rusk to Johnson, July 1, 1965, NS file, Deployment of Forces, box 43, LBJ Library. Schoenbaum, *Waging Peace*, p. 453.

67. Quoted in Schoenbaum, *Waging Peace*, p. 441.

68. Schoenbaum, *Waging Peace*, pp. 412, 440. The press spokesman was essentially correct in his statement, but the record clearly suggests that there was no widely shared understanding of the precise role of soldiers in Vietnam in the late spring. Cables went back and forth on the subject, as indicated elsewhere in this chapter. From Johnson's vantage point and certainly Westmoreland's, American soldiers were not yet mandated to take on full combat status. In late May and early June, at Ba Gia and Dong Xoai, the South Vietnamese army (RVNAF) was "desperately in need of assistance. Although U.S. troops were available in both instances, the Marines at Ba Gia and the 173rd at Dong Xoai,

they were not committed and the result in both cases was defeat for the RVNAF."
Pentagon Papers, vol. 3, p. 461.

69. Rusk oral interview, p. I, 9, 14, 15, 22, LBJ Library. Also, personal interview with author, 1989. Rusk's description of Johnson speaking intimately and provisionally without fearing leaks was specifically geared to the Tuesday lunch sessions, of which Rusk was a regular member.

70. M. Bundy to Johnson, July 1, 1965, NS file, Deployment of Major U.S. Forces, box 43, LBJ Library. In a June 30 memo to McNamara, Bundy also criticized the Secretary of Defense's first draft of his proposal as "rash to the point of folly." Bundy asked, "do we want to invest 200 thousand men to cover an eventual retreat?" NS file, Troop Deployment History, box 43, LBJ Library. Bundy's critique, of course, did not signify agreement with Ball.

71. William Bundy, correspondence with the author, March 12, 1989. On presidential advisers not knowing who else talked to Johnson, Jack Valenti once said, "White House staff members don't really know why a President came to a certain decision because they're not privy to all that was fed into his mind and heart before the decision was made." Valenti oral history, p. I, 27, LBJ Library.

72. Rowland Evans and Robert Novak, *Lyndon B. Johnson: The Exercise of Power* (New York: New American Library, 1966), p. 110. Clark Clifford with Richard Holbrooke, *Counsel to the President: A Memoir* (New York: Random House, 1991), p. 387. Walter Jenkins came closest to filling a chief of staff role before he left the administration in the summer of 1964.

73. Clifford to Johnson, May 17, 1965, NS file, Deployment of Major Troops, box 41, LBJ Library. Clifford, *Counsel to the President*, p. 410. Larry Berman's *Planning a Tragedy* suggests that Clifford's anti-escalation views were "heard but ignored" (see p. 121).

74. On a June 1, 1966, memo from national security adviser Walt Rostow to Johnson, in which Rostow referred to Fulbright as being "very unhappy that full information is given to Clark Clifford's committee and doesn't understand why his committee members should not be given the same treatment," Johnson scrawled, "Because they leak!" See file: CIA, vol. II, NS file, Agency file, box 8–10, LBJ Library. Roberts, *LBJ's Inner Circle*, pp. 174–175.

75. Eugene C. Patterson, "Sen. Richard Russell: A Study in Division," *Washington Post*, January 25, 1971, in U.S. Congress, *Richard Brevard Russell: Memorial Tributes in Congress* (Washington, D.C.: Government Printing Office, 1971), pp. 86–87.

76. Burke and Greenstein, *How Presidents Test Reality*, p. 140. On a little calendar used to track medical prescriptions, Russell wrote on June 4, "Pres. J called + asked to go down River. I declined—it was 7:30 PM. Had talked for 30 min. at about 3 PM." On June 5, he wrote: "Boating on River w/ Pres Johnson. McNamara, John [illegible] wife, 2 child. Valenti et al." On June 8: "Pres called at 7 PM invite to Boat + dinner. Begged excuses." Other notes made elsewhere by Russell that month give additional fragmentary sense of his involvement with the Johnsons and Vietnam discussions—June 19: "Admiral Mcdonald Report on Vietnam," also Russell requests economic and geographic information on North and South Vietnam from the Library of Congress; June 20: "to White House meeting," also "down river on boat," after Mrs. Johnson called; June 27: "talked to Fulbright"; June 28: at White House; June 29: talked to McNamara at White House; June 30: talked to McNamara; another undated June note: "Tue., Lady Bird called." Unfortunately, Russell made notes only sporadically in the little datebook calendars he had from 1964 to 1970 and on other calendars or scattered

bits of paper (e.g., the backs of envelopes). They are at the Russell Library. See also II Intra-Office Communications, and XVI International B Subject July '65, Russell Library. Mrs. Johnson recalls of Russell and her husband: "What brought them together time after time . . . was whenever any momentous decision was about to take place in regard to international affairs . . . Lyndon would over and over call him and get him to come over to see him, and a number of times, just the two of them . . . Lyndon always sought him out in times of crisis." Amazingly, President Johnson's daily diary shows Russell being alone with Johnson only twice from January to July 1965, which says more about the diary than it does about Russell and Johnson. The diary was kept by secretaries who monitored passage through one door to the Oval Office. Burke et al. describe the daily diary as "a seven-day-a-week, twenty-four-hour record of individuals with whom Johnson had telephone conversations and his meetings and other activities." In my view, based in part on a conversation with an archivist at the LBJ Library and in part on comparisons of other records with the diary, it is inadequate as a record of which people (especially informal advisers) Johnson was seeing. See also note 116 in this chapter. Dean Rusk, special oral interview conducted by Karen Kelly, p. 45, Richard Russell Library. Some notes on Johnson and Vietnam made by Russell are part of an unprocessed collection still unreleased by the senator's heirs.

77. Russell to Louis Wolfson, January 4, 1966, Gen. file, Inter. series-Vietnam; "Conversation between the President and Senator Russell on Nov. 9, 1961," Special presidential file, 1941–1967, Russell Library.

78. Russell, letter to constituents, January 6, 1966, and June 22, 1965, Series F-Dictation, Russell Library.

79. Russell to Wolfson, January 4, 1966, Gen. file, Inter. series-Vietnam, Russell Library.

80. Russell to constituent, January 26, 1966, Series F-Dictation, Russell Library.

81. Russell to constituent, February 23, 1966, Series F-Dictation, Russell Library.

82. Mansfield to Johnson, July 27, 1965, Inter. series-Vietnam, Subject file— July 23–31, 1965; McNamara to Johnson, July 28, 1965, Inter. series-Vietnam, Russell Library. The other senators present were Aiken, Cooper, Fulbright, and Sparkman. Russell lamented to friends that McNamara had made many mistakes in handling Vietnam, but seemed to "exercise some hypnotic influence over the President, just as he did over President Kennedy." See Russell to L. Wolfson, January 4, 1966, Gen. file, Inter. series-Vietnam, Russell Library.

83. See, for instance, Tristram Coffin, *Senator Fulbright: Portrait of a Public Philosopher* (New York: E. P. Dutton, 1966), p. 241, and Doris Kearns, *Lyndon Johnson and the American Dream* (New York: Harper and Row, 1976), p. 103.

84. Fulbright, Former Members of Congress oral history project, p. 23, Manuscript Division, Library of Congress. Harry McPherson, oral interview, p. I, 20, 31, LBJ Library. McPherson says of Johnson's other great mentor, Sam Rayburn, that Johnson was devoted to him "as perhaps he has never been devoted to any public figure, with the possible exception of Dick Russell." Lady Bird Johnson, oral interview, p. 8, Russell Library; Senator Sam Ervin, oral interview, p. 15, Russell Library.

85. Rusk oral interview, p. 10. Rusk recalls, "When the question came up as to whether this or that or the other country would be given an American destroyer, Richard Russell's view of that was absolutely final. There were no ifs,

ands, or buts about it. He decided that question." Russell also directed the Senate's oversight of intelligence agencies.

86. Rusk oral interview, p. 52, Russell Library. Former Assistant Secretary of State William Bundy, in an unpublished manuscript, writes of a meeting on June 10, 1965, among Johnson, most of his formal foreign policy advisers, and Russell. Bundy had the impression that Russell favored Westmoreland's troop request, that "driblets" of bombing or troops were not the answer. See ch. 26, p. 10, Bundy manuscript, LBJ Library. However, in personal correspondence with the author, Bundy seems to accept the broad picture of Russell as an anti-escalation figure as chronicled in my "The Mythology Surrounding Lyndon Johnson, His Advisers, and the 1965 Decision to Escalate the Vietnam War," *Political Science Quarterly* 103, 4 (Winter 1988-89). About his manuscript, Bundy requests those citing it to note his own comments about the manuscript: "It is not my final word, and has not been revised since it was written in 1969-72."

87. Special presidential file, 1941-1967, Russell Library.

88. *Pentagon Papers*, vol. 3, pp. 392, 395.

89. W. Bundy, oral history, p. 32, LBJ Library. Bundy notes that the Pentagon Papers "have made a good deal" of his July 1 memo but do not reflect his changed views of just days later.

90. Taylor, oral interview (1981), p. II, 37, LBJ Library. On Taylor and Vietnam, see Douglas Kinnard, *The Certain Trumpet: Maxwell Taylor and the American Experience in Vietnam* (New York: Brassey's, 1991).

91. Taylor oral history, p. II, 23; Taylor to Joint Chiefs of Staff, February 22, 1965, Westmoreland Papers, #13 History Backup, January 21-February 28, box 5; M. Bundy to Johnson, April 26, 1965, accompanied by McNamara to Johnson, April 21, 1965, with excerpts of Taylor cable to McNamara, April 24, 1965, NS files, Memos to President, box 3, LBJ Library. Bundy noted that Taylor's optimism was contingent on the introduction of "substantial" numbers of troops. See also *Pentagon Papers*, vol. 3, p. 407.

92. *Pentagon Papers*, vol. 3, pp. 449, 471. See also Taylor to Rusk, June 5, 1965, Westmoreland Papers, #16 History Backup, May 10-June 30, box 6, LBJ Library.

93. Taylor oral history (1969), p. 15; (1981), pp. III, 2-3, 8-9, LBJ Library. Maxwell Taylor, *Swords and Plowshares* (New York: Norton, 1972), p. 347.

94. Taylor, *Swords and Plowshares*, p. 347.

95. See Glenn T. Seaborg and Benjamin S. Loeb, *Stemming the Tide: Arms Control in the Johnson Years* (Lexington, Mass.: Lexington Books, 1987), pp. 136-149, for an account of a Wise Men-style group for arms control matters.

96. Acheson to Truman, July 10, 1965, and Acheson to Erik Boheman, July 7, 1965, in David McClellan and David Acheson (eds.), *Among Friends: Personal Letters of Dean Acheson* (New York: Dodd, Mead, 1980), pp. 272-273. Emphasis added.

97. Gilpatric to M. Bundy, July 9, 1965, file: "President's consultants," NS file, Files of M. Bundy, box 18 & 19, LBJ Library. There was one dissenter in the group of Wise Men: Arthur Larson, an Eisenhower administration figure, believed that the United States should rely on the United Nations or other negotiating forums to take care of the problem of Vietnam. According to William Bundy, who was present at the meetings, the rest of the group was agreed that "Thailand could not be held if South Vietnam were taken over, and they thought that the effects on Japan and India could be most serious. They particularly felt

that the effect in Europe might also be most serious . . . the group generally felt that there should be no question of making whatever combat force increases were required." Bundy, "Report on Meeting with Foreign Affairs Consultants," July 22, 1965, NS file, Deployment of Troops, LBJ Library.

98. See file: Calls and Appointments 1965 (2), DDE Post-Presidency, Appointment Book series, box 2, Eisenhower Library. For an overview on Johnson, Eisenhower, and Vietnam, see Henry W. Brands, "Johnson and Eisenhower: The President, the Former President, and the War in Vietnam," *Presidential Studies Quarterly* 15, 3 (Summer 1985): 589–601.

99. Goodpaster, Memo for the Record, May 13, 1965, Post-Presidency, Gettysburg-Indio Collection, box 2, Eisenhower Library. Notes of a Johnson-Eisenhower meeting on February 17, 1965, are in Meeting Notes file, box 1, LBJ Library.

100. Goodpaster to Johnson, June 16, 1965, Name file: Pres. Eisenhower, NS Name file, box 3, LBJ Library.

101. Memorandum of telephone conversation: 10:55 A.M., July 2, 1965, File: President Johnson-1965 (2), Eisenhower Library. Notes taken by Lillian H. Brown, corrected by Eisenhower. This conversation indicates how decisions were never final with Johnson until they were actually announced. In this conversation, Johnson sounded as if he would likely send some unspecified amount of troops *and* call up the reserves. He did the first but not the latter.

102. *Pentagon Papers*, vol. 3, p. 475; vol. 4, p. 299. Sometimes there are references to 44 battalions, which would include troops from other friendly countries such as South Korea.

103. Ball, *The Past*, pp. 399–403. See also Ball, oral history, p. I, 31, LBJ Library; Earle Wheeler, oral history, p. I, 18, LBJ Library; W. Bundy oral history, p. 42, LBJ Library; and Bromley Smith (executive secretary of the National Security Council), oral history, p. I, 25–26, LBJ Library. See also Kahin, *Intervention*, p. 527.

104. Karnow, *Vietnam*, p. 425. McNamara left Washington on July 14 and returned on July 20. His time in Saigon was shorter than originally planned, but his departure was not as hasty as implied by Karnow's account. See Berman, *Planning a Tragedy*, pp. 98–105, and Kahin, *Intervention*, pp. 361–365.

105. Berman, *Planning a Tragedy*, pp. 99–100. On p. 106, he writes that the president's questions to George Ball during this period appear to have been staged for the purpose of consensus building: "Johnson already had the answers and the policy." Berman cites with emphasis a remark by William Bundy that a July 21 meeting in which Ball vigorously challenged escalation plans was "a bit of a set piece . . . you felt it had been scripted to a degree." However, in the oral interview, Bundy quickly pointed out that the meeting in question was not like many National Security Council meetings, where views put forth "were really simply recitals, quite frankly." Instead, the July 21 meeting "was all the senior advisers; it was a major meeting . . . a real meat and potatoes meeting . . . a nitty-gritty meeting." Bundy's "set piece" comment was intended to reflect not on the seriousness with which Ball's views were considered but rather Bundy's feeling "that the President had already started to formulate [a decision]." Bundy describes Ball's advice as "real strategic dissent" and attacks the notion that there was a "sort of 'kept voice' of dissent." W. Bundy, oral interview, p. 42, LBJ Library. See also Berman's comments in Peter Braestrup (ed.), *Vietnam as History* (Washington, D.C.: University Press of America, 1984), p. 16. In light of the declassification of the Vance cable and correspondence with Vance himself

as to the meaning of the cable, the claim is softened: "Johnson was leaning so strongly toward approving the troop request that he had begun to stipulate what else he would or would not do in the way of mobilizing the American people and their resources for the military effort in Vietnam." Burke and Greenstein, *How Presidents Test Reality*, p. 215. The thesis in the *Pentagon Papers* and *Planning a Tragedy* is rejected in Kahin's *Intervention* ("It is clear . . . that the President had not yet made a decision . . . until five or six days after McNamara returned"), pp. 362, 527. William Bundy formerly was of the opinion that Johnson had made up his mind before the July 21–27 period, but he now believes that the president was still considering alternative plans during that period. See Kahin, *Intervention*, p. 527. Dean Rusk says that, over a period of months preceding the decision, Johnson moved slowly toward his choice. Asked if he believes that Johnson had made up his mind by July 21 and was "using" advisers such as Clifford and Ball during the final week, Rusk says, "Not at all." Personal interview with the author, June 9, 1989.

106. See, for example, Kinnard, *Certain Trumpet*, p. 158. Chester Cooper made the same point less elaborately in *The Lost Crusade: America in Vietnam* (New York: Dodd, Mead, 1970), pp. 284–285. A dramatic example is in Charles O. Jones's *Introduction to the Study of Public Policy*, 3d ed. (Monterey, Calif.: Brooks/Cole Publishing, 1984), pp. 1–2; see also Karnow, *Vietnam*, p. 425. Though it is inconsistent with his larger and prudentially sympathetic portrait of Johnson, Karnow deduces from the *Pentagon Papers* and Berman's account that Johnson "went through the motion" of probing his advisers for their views during the July 21–27 period. Also see John P. Burke, "Responsibilities of Presidents and Advisers: A Theory and Case Study of Vietnam Decision Making," *Journal of Politics* 46, 3 (August 1984): 818–845. My response is in Barrett, "The Mythology Surrounding Lyndon Johnson," pp. 659–660. Burke drew on Berman, who had drawn on the *Pentagon Papers*.

107. Vance to McNamara, July 17, 1965, Reference file: Vietnam, box 2, LBJ Library.

108. Correspondence between Fred I. Greenstein and Vance, March 10, 1988, cited in Burke and Greenstein, *How Presidents Test Reality*, p. 215, n. 30; Rusk oral history, pp. 30–32, LBJ Library; William Bundy, correspondence with the author, March 12, 1989. See also Jack Valenti, *A Very Human President* (New York: Pocket Books, 1977), p. 271.

109. Acheson to Harry Truman, October 3, 1966, in McClellan and Acheson, *Among Friends*, p. 281.

110. Betts, in Braestrup, *Vietnam as History*, pp. 46, 47. Betts compares his view of Johnson as hoping that some alternative to escalation "might turn up" between the 1964 election and the July 1965 decision with what he sees as Berman's view of Johnson as "the cynical manipulator of the advisory process."

111. Johnson, *White House Diary*, pp. 312, 321. On Johnson and Morse, also see Melvin Small, *Johnson, Nixon, and the Doves* (New Brunswick, N.J.: Rutgers University Press, , 1988), p. 78. Of interest is Morse's memorandum of the conversation with Johnson on June 17, 1965, during which the president solicited Morse's views on the UN and Vietnam. The memorandum is in an untitled folder, "C. M. chrons '65" box, Carl Marcy Papers, National Archives, Washington, D.C.

112. Johnson, *White House Diary*, p. 325. The meeting is not recorded in the daily diary.

113. Coffin, *Senator Fulbright*, pp. 188–189.

114. Haynes Johnson and Bernard Gwertzman, *Fulbright: The Dissenter* (Garden City, N.Y.: Doubleday, 1968), pp. 6, 184.

115. Coffin, *Senator Fulbright*, p. 191.

116. A researcher naturally longs for definitive information on such matters. Using the president's daily diary at the LBJ Library, James Best indicates that the two men saw each other privately only three times from January to July 1965. Author's correspondence with James J. Best, who also wrote "Who Talked to the President When? A Study of Lyndon B. Johnson," *Political Science Quarterly* 103, 3 (Fall 1988): 531–546. However, other sources such as Mrs. Johnson's diary indicate additional contacts, including the July 16 conversation. In talking with an archivist at the Johnson Library, I indicated my intention to rely on the diary for making comparisons of the numbers of times Johnson saw various advisers as well as comparisons of how frequently Johnson saw particular advisers at different stages of his presidency. The archivist cautioned me against assuming that the diary's data were accurate for such purposes. Problems with the diary resulted because there was a second door into the Oval Office that was not fully monitored, and secretaries charged with noting those Johnson met with were sometimes busy with other duties, according to the archivist. Also, it appears that record keeping was more efficient late in the administration, compared to earlier years. I use the daily diary for supplementary purposes, but do not put its data at the heart of my analysis.

117. In addition, there were other more public contacts between the two, such as at meals with others present and at public functions. See "Contacts between the President and Sen. Fulbright," undated, Name file: Fulbright, LBJ Library.

118. Coffin, *Senator Fulbright*, p. 243.

119. On what the consequences would be for Johnson if he simply pulled the United States out (without diplomatic cover), Fulbright's close aide Carl Marcy confided to Hubert Humphrey that "Fulbright knows . . . that no U.S. government could survive and pull out." Marcy to Humphrey, May 7, 1965, "C. M. chrons '65" box, Marcy Papers, National Archives. According to biographers Haynes Johnson and Bernard Gwertzman, Fulbright was hopeful in January 1965 "and for months to come . . . that he would be able to persuade the President. He was still seeing the President often, and he was expressing himself." Johnson and Gwertzman, *Dissenter*, pp. 202, 205; Coffin, *Senator Fulbright*, p. 253; J. W. Fulbright oral history interview, p. 20, Former Members of Congress project, Manuscript Division, Library of Congress, Washington, D.C. The strain in the Fulbright-Johnson relationship obviously developed over time; in February, Johnson described Fulbright as a "cry baby" to an aide. See Douglass Cater to Johnson, February 8, 1965, Reference file — Vietnam, box 1, LBJ Library.

120. David Lilienthal, *The Journals of David Lilienthal, vol. 6: Creativity and Conflict, 1964–1967* (New York: Harper and Row, 1976), p. 132. I take Fulbright to mean that Johnson would be "off" him if there was a public difference between the senator and the president, though Fulbright does not specify his meaning in the comment to Lilienthal. Clearly, Fulbright *was* criticizing proposed Vietnam escalation policies in Johnson's presence at the time.

121. Quoted in Coffin, *Senator Fulbright*, p. 254.

122. Johnson, *White House Diary*, pp. 265, 325.

123. Coffin, *Senator Fulbright*, p. 244. Eventually, Fulbright came to believe that Johnson had never really listened to him. In an oral interview in the Russell

Library collection, Fulbright says that Johnson "rarely consulted in the sense of seeking advice and certainly being influenced by it." William Berman's *William Fulbright and the Vietnam War* (Kent, Ohio: Kent State University Press, 1988) follows Fulbright's views of recent years; the two older Fulbright biographies seem to reflect the way Fulbright felt about his relationship with Johnson well before the administration came to an end.

124. Confidential name file: J. W. Fulbright, May 27, 1966, LBJ Library.

125. John E. Mueller says in his *War, Presidents, and Public Opinion* (New York: Wiley, 1973), "For the purpose of public opinion analysis . . . it seems sensible to take mid-1965 as the starting point. Before that, Americans were strikingly ignorant of the war" (p. 35). Nonetheless, for our purposes it is worthwhile to consider the limited evidence on public opinion and Vietnam earlier in 1965 as well.

126. Mueller, *War, Presidents*, p. 54; *The Gallup Opinion Index*, April 1968, p. 3.

127. Quoted in *Congressional Record*, May 5, 1965, p. 9502.

128. *Congressional Record*, May 5, 1965, p. 9473.

129. *Congressional Record*, March 19, 1965, pp. 445–447.

130. *Congressional Record*, May 5, 1965, pp. 9497, 9498.

131. *Congressional Record*, May 6, 1965, p. 9763. General Earle Wheeler, chairman of the Joint Chiefs of Staff, shared Morse's (and Senator Richard Russell's) understanding. Recalled Wheeler, "The Tonkin Gulf Resolution, which was passed by Congress, told the President to . . . use that force that was necessary to protect the freedom of South Vietnam . . . [it] put the executive branch and the congressional branch in the same bed." Wheeler oral history, p. I, 28, LBJ Library.

132. *Congressional Record*, May 5 and 6, 1965, pp. 9498, 9772.

133. *Congressional Record*, May 6, 1965, pp. 9754, 9769, 9772. Russell's close friend, Senator John Stennis (D-Miss.), said that Russell would have voted for the appropriation despite his misgivings about the United States' long-standing Vietnam policies. See p. 9771. Senator Fulbright did not vote.

134. *Congressional Record*, May 5, 1965, pp. 9531, 9537. The vote was on May 5, 1965.

135. For Wheeler's reasoning on the reserves, see his oral history, p. I, 19–20, LBJ Library.

136. "Meetings on Vietnam, July 21, 1965" (summarizes views of participants), file: July 21, 1965, meeting, and "Cabinet Room . . ." (transcript of dialogue), file: July 21–27, 1965, meetings on Vietnam, both in Meeting Notes, box 1, LBJ Library.

137. Ibid. Clark Clifford's *Counsel to the President* also describes Ball's presentation and the other advisers' responses on pp. 412–413.

138. "Impressions, Vietnam Discussions," July 21, 1965, Office of files of H. Busby, box 3, LBJ Library. Busby was also close to Mrs. Johnson.

139. "Cabinet Room, July 22, 1965," July 21–27 Meetings on Vietnam, Meeting Notes, box 1, LBJ Library.

140. Clifford, *Counsel*, p. 415. Clifford's and Ball's memoirs do not agree on the sequence of Clifford's spoken participation in meetings, but they agree on the substance of his comments.

141. Ball, *The Past*, pp. 402–403. I have accepted Ball's placement of this meeting on July 22. Declassified notes of this meeting show that both Ball and Clifford were there, but they do not reflect the comments of either man. Such

notes are, of course, always fragmentary. It is possible that Ball's account has the date wrong, but this seems unlikely, since he remembers Clifford speaking out at this particular session, which followed Johnson's meeting with the military leadership.

142. Valenti, *A Very Human President*, p. 271.

143. Mansfield to Johnson, July 23, 1965, NS file, Name file: Mansfield, box 6, LBJ Library. In a June 9, 1965 memo (from the same file), Mansfield had been more specifically against such a new resolution and vote. He told Johnson, "A request at this time could set off a wave of criticism and of demands for inquiries which, in the end, even though a resolution were overwhelmingly approved, would not in any way strengthen your hand, render your task easier or make your burden of responsibility lighter."

144. Valenti's was a long, pessimistic memo, both hawkish and dovish, which had an ending only Valenti could write: "I *do* sleep more confidently because you are President, and I thank the dear God for that." For whatever reason, Valenti did not share this particular memo with Johnson for another six months. July 22, 1965, Office Files of W. House Aides: Valenti, 1965–66, LBJ Library. (Indications that the memo was not sent until January 31, 1966, come from the cover note to the Valenti to Johnson memo, January 31, 1966, Office of the President file: Valenti, LBJ Library.) Other Valenti memos on Vietnam were sent to Johnson during the summer of 1965 and through 1966 and are available in this file. On April 3, 1966, he wrote to Johnson, "We need to find some way out of Vietnam."

145. "Camp David Meeting," Meeting notes file (July 21–27), box 1, and "Views of Clark Clifford" (notes taken by Valenti), July 25, 1965, Misc. Vietnam Documents, Reference file, LBJ Library. See also Clifford, *Counsel*, pp. 419–420.

146. Clifford, *Counsel*, p. 421. Clifford "assumes" that Johnson made up his mind during this time alone.

147. "Cabinet Room NSC Meet," July 26, 1965, Meeting notes file (July 21–27), box 1, LBJ Library. Clifford's comments were made during a meeting that preceded a larger NSC meeting that same day.

148. Ball, *The Past*, p. 403.

149. Mansfield statement, the title of which is partially obscured by handwritten notation, "This appears to be Mike Mansfield's statement." File: Mansfield, Mike (Sen.), 1-1-65-7-30-65, LBJ Library.

150. Minutes of July 22, 1965 meeting, file: July 21–27, 1965, Meetings on Vietnam, Meeting notes, box 1, LBJ Library.

151. Henry Kissinger, "Conversation with former Chancellor Adenauer, June 22, 1965," NS file, Files of M. Bundy, box 15, LBJ Library.

152. Others with some level of access to the president who told him not to get into full-fledged combat included Senator Wayne Morse and influential journalist Walter Lippmann. See Morse to Johnson, June 21, 1965, NS file, NSC history, Deployment of Major Forces, box 42, LBJ Library, and various memos, M. Bundy to Johnson on Lippmann and Morse, in M. Bundy, vols. 10, 11, NS file, Memos to President from Bundy, box 3, LBJ Library. It may well be that Abe Fortas, Johnson's friend and longtime counselor, was advising Johnson in favor of escalation, but the written record does not exist for such a conclusion. See Bruce A. Murphy's *Fortas: The Rise and Ruin of a Supreme Court Justice* (New York: Morrow, 1988), ch. 10. Fortas's nomination for the Supreme Court was announced at the same press conference where Johnson announced that he was sending combat troops to Vietnam.

153. Assertions that Ball was Johnson's only dovish major adviser in 1965 are so widespread that they hardly need citation. One recent example is John M. Blum's *Years of Discord: American Politics and Society, 1961-1974* (New York: Norton, 1991), pp. 234, 240. Chapter 3 will examine the existence of the Tuesday Lunch Group, which was meeting almost weekly by 1967, as a kind of inner directorate of the war. Contrary to some accounts, the Tuesday Lunch Group met sporadically (although not infrequently) during the first two years of the Johnson presidency and dealt with Vietnam and other foreign policy issues. David Humphrey, "Tuesday Lunch at the White House: A Preliminary Assessment," *Diplomatic History* 8, 4 (1984): 81-101.

154. Mansfield to Johnson, June 5, 1965, NS file, Name file: Mansfield, box 6, LBJ Library. Ball, in T. George Harris, "A Policy-Maker's View: Experience vs. Character," *Psychology Today*, March 1975, p. 39; and Ball oral interview, pp. I-26, 34, LBJ Library. M. Bundy to Johnson, July 1, 1965, NS file: M. Bundy, July 1965, vol. 12, box 4, LBJ Library.

155. Johnson, *Vantage Point*, p. 153. In *Remembering America*, Goodwin claims that Johnson said in this announcement that he "intended to send only 50,000 men to Vietnam" and labels this a lie (p. 383).

156. Berman's *Planning a Tragedy* is chief among those accounts that focus on domestic political implications as a reason for Johnson's not calling up the reserves. A memo written on November 2, 1968, by McGeorge Bundy, reporting on a July 27, 1965, meeting on Vietnam, also implies this. It can be found in Reference file, box 2; see also Bundy to Johnson, July 21, 1965 (on likely costs of the war if Johnson chose escalation), both LBJ Library.

157. *Pentagon Papers*, vol. 4, p. 299; Kahin, *Intervention*, p. 398.

158. Coffin, *Senator Fulbright*, p. 261.

159. The phone call occurred on August 24, 1965. See "Calls and Appointments 1965 (2)," DDE Appointment book series, box 2, Eisenhower Library.

160. George Ball, oral history, p. I, 31; William Bundy, oral history, p. 42, LBJ Library. Johnson, *Vantage Point*, p. 365. Contrary to the interpretation presented here is George Reedy's in *Lyndon B. Johnson*: "The few dissenters who could reach him made absolutely no impression" (p. 148).

Chapter 3. 1967: Waist Deep

1. Lady Bird Johnson, *A White House Diary* (New York: Holt, Rinehart, and Winston, 1970), p. 555.

2. Maxwell Taylor, *Swords and Plowshares* (New York: Norton, 1972), p. 382. General William Westmoreland began the year with a private speech predicting that 1967 would be "the year during which it will become evident that the communists cannot win." Westmoreland Papers, "Baguio Speech," #13 History file, box 10, LBJ Library. *Congressional Record*, March 20, 1967, p. 7193.

3. Exceptions to this are Larry Berman, *Lyndon Johnson's War: The Road to Stalemate in Vietnam* (New York: Norton, 1989), and Larry E. Cable, *Unholy Grail: The U.S. and the Wars in Vietnam, 1965-8* (New York: Routledge, 1991). Leslie Gelb and Richard Betts's *The Irony of Vietnam: The System Worked* (Washington, D.C.: Brookings, 1979) analyzes this "in between" period in part of its fifth chapter. Though its focus is on a figure who was not a presidential adviser, Neil Sheehan's *A Bright Shining Lie: John Paul Vann and America in Vietnam* (New York: Random House, 1988) describes the debate surrounding Westmoreland's troop request on pp. 683-684.

4. Department of Defense, cited in *Congressional Quarterly Almanac*, 1967, p. 923. Casualty figures are from Stanley Karnow, *Vietnam: A History* (New York: Viking Press, 1983), pp. 502, 512, and from the Department of Defense, cited in *CQ Almanac*, 1967, p. 923.

5. See Vaughan Davis Bornet, *The Presidency of Lyndon B. Johnson* (Lawrence: University of Kansas Press, 1983), p. 386, for his protest of this in a historiographical essay on Johnson.

6. Thomas Powers, *The War at Home* (New York: Grossman Publishers, 1973) gives an extremely critical account of the Johnson administration's response to the peace movement, yet he writes of the spring of 1967 as a time when unilateral withdrawal "was considered to be unthinkable" (see p. 199). See also note 22 below.

7. Arthur Schlesinger, *Robert Kennedy and His Times* (Boston: Houghton Mifflin, 1978), p. 883; David Humphrey, "Tuesday Lunch at the White House: A Preliminary Assessment," *Diplomatic History* 8, 4 (Winter 1984): 99. In *The Suicide of an Elite: American Internationalists and Vietnam* (Stanford, Calif.: Stanford University Press, 1990), Patrick Hatcher writes that Johnson was "desperate to raise more troop units in order to support the military's insatiable appetite" (p. 293). There is little commentary on advisory relations in the Johnson administration in George Herring's generally sound *America's Longest War* (New York: Wiley, 1979); however, Herring writes that it is a "fact" that Johnson did not listen to critics in 1967 and that his "pride" kept him in the war (see pp. 180–181). Berman, in *Lyndon Johnson's War*, says that Johnson's reasoning in dealing with the Westmoreland request "bordered on the outer limits of logic" and implies that many of Johnson's advisers told him what he wanted to hear rather than what he needed to hear during this period (see pp. 37, 56).

8. Paul Conkin, *Big Daddy from the Pedernales* (Boston: Twayne Publishing, 1986), p. 275; Karnow, *Vietnam*, p. 421.

9. Rostow to Johnson, March 10, 1967, Diary Backup, box 57, LBJ Library; *Congressional Record*, March 16, 1967, p. 6885.

10. *Congressional Record*, March 16, 1967, p. 6885. *Congressional Quarterly Almanac*, 1967, p. 211. House members voting against HR 7123 were Brown, Burton, Conyers, Dow, Edwards, Fraser, Kastenmeier, Mosher, Reuss, Rosenthal, and Ryan.

11. *Congressional Record*, March 20, 1967, pp. 7193–7195.

12. *CQ Almanac*, 1967, p. 211; *Congressional Record*, March 1, 1967, p. 4947.

13. Caroline Ziemke, "Senator Richard B. Russell and the 'Lost Cause' in Vietnam, 1954–1968," *Georgia Historical Quarterly* 72, 1 (Spring 1988): 30–70; Rusk oral interview, Russell Library, p. 38; William Berman, *William Fulbright and the Vietnam War* (Kent, Ohio: Kent State University Press, 1988), p. 136; *CQ Almanac*, 1967, pp. 220–221, 945.

14. *Congressional Record*, February 28, 1967, p. 4723. Fulbright to Russell, IVI Inter., Vietnam file, May 19 to 31, 1967, and, in general, II Intra-office communications, April 7 to May 18, 1967, Russell Library. However, Russell still toyed with the idea that an election should be held in South Vietnam, with Ho Chi Minh's name on the ballot. He thought that it was a real possibility that Ho would win. Letter to constituent, May 8, 1967, Series F Dictation, box I J7, Russell Library.

15. *Congressional Record*, March 1, 1966, p. 4370.

16. *Congressional Record*, February 28, 1967, p. 4723; March 20, 1967,

pp. 7193, 7189. Some accounts have erroneously described Russell as proposing revocation of the Gulf of Tonkin Resolution in early 1967. See Ziemke, "Senator Russell," p. 52, which appears to be guided by the similarly mistaken Karnow, *Vietnam*, p. 490. On Russell and Tonkin, see David M. Barrett, "Communications: Sen. Russell and the Tonkin Resolution," *Georgia Historical Quarterly* 73, 3 (Fall 1989): 698–699.

17. University of North Carolina address, March 13, 1967, quoted in Louis Baldwin, *Hon. Politician: Mike Mansfield of Montana* (Missoula, Mont.: Mountain Press, 1979), p. 173.

18. Baldwin, *Hon. Politician*, pp. 172–173; "Meeting with the President in His Bedroom," January 17, 1967, Schoenbaum files, Rusk Papers, box 45, Russell Library. National security adviser Rostow and note taker Marvin Watson were also present. Johnson wanted Mansfield and Dirksen to lobby Fulbright to delay Vietnam-related hearings because of the peace feeler from North Vietnam (he said). Johnson agreed at the end of the meeting to see both senators plus Fulbright the next day, but he may have told Fulbright less than he did Mansfield and Dirksen. Berman, *Fulbright*, pp. 79–80.

19. *Congressional Record*, March 1, 1967, p. 4948; March 20, 1967, pp. 7189, 7193, 7212; Berman, *Fulbright*, pp. 79–80.

20. Schlesinger, *Robert Kennedy*, p. 830; *CQ Almanac*, 1967, pp. 927–928.

21. Schlesinger, *Robert Kennedy*, p. 828. Neither Johnson nor his aides Rostow and Katzenbach wrote about the incident.

22. Kennedy biographer Arthur Schlesinger explains that in 1967 all but those in the New Left still believed that withdrawal would lead to a communist Vietnam: "Those of us who hoped for a negotiated peace believed that retention of American troops in defensive enclaves were [sic] essential to give the other side an incentive to negotiate." Schlesinger, *Robert Kennedy*, p. 833.

23. II. 6 Intra-office communications, March 2, 1967, Russell Library.

24. *CQ Almanac*, 1967, p. 927. The word "Tet" conjures up the year 1968 in the minds of many Americans, but of course Tet is a yearly holiday in Vietnam.

25. Rusk to Johnson, March 10, 1967, and McNamara to Johnson, March 9, 1967, NS file: Vietnam, boxes 211–212, LBJ Library.

26. Emmette Redford and Richard McCulley, *White House Operations: The Johnson Presidency* (Austin: University of Texas Press, 1986), pp. 158–162. The policy was not perfectly upheld; I have come across one case in 1967 in which Johnson declined to see Congressman Ogden Reid, who already had an appointment to see national security adviser Walt Rostow; Rostow to Johnson, June 20, 1967, Rostow Memos, NS name file: Rostow, LBJ Library. But quite typical in the archives are indications such as a May 2, 1967, breakfast Johnson had with Morse and Mansfield to discuss Vietnam and the United Nations. NS file: Name file: Mansfield, box 6, LBJ Library.

27. Henry Wilson to Marvin Watson, March 11, 1967, Diary backup, box 57, LBJ Library. Whitten told the president on March 14 that the United States should announce, "We expect to pursue present policies for [unspecified number of] days without letup. If at the end of that time the North Vietnamese haven't taken official actions toward a just settlement, we will take it that present efforts aren't sufficient and the Joint Chiefs of Staff shall be directed to 'win the war,' after which we can discuss an honorable relationship." Notes by Whitten found in the president's pocket March 14, 1967, Diary backup, March 10, 1967, box 57, LBJ Library. Pell's meeting with Johnson is treated later in this chapter.

28. Richard Goodwin, *Remembering America* (Boston: Little, Brown, 1988), p. 472.

29. Data are taken from the *Gallup Opinion Index*, December 1968, p. 2, which shows public opinion trends on Johnson's "handling of his job as president" from April 1966 to November 1968, and April 1968, p. 3, which gives trends of public opinion on his "handling the situation in Vietnam" from July 1965 to April 1968.

30. These figures from the American Institute of Public Opinion are from John Mueller's important *War, Presidents, and Public Opinion* (New York: Wiley, 1973), pp. 54-55.

31. Noam Chomsky, "The Logic of Withdrawal," originally written in July 1967, published in *Ramparts*, September 1967, and revised and reprinted in *American Power and the New Mandarins* (New York: Pantheon, 1969), pp. 246-269. Chomsky cites Neil Sheehan, "Not a Dove, But No Longer a Hawk," *New York Times Magazine*, October 9, 1966, and Arthur Schlesinger, *The Bitter Heritage* (Boston: Houghton Mifflin, 1967), p. 34.

32. Johnson, *White House Diary*, pp. 501-502. Melvin Small's *Johnson, Nixon, and the Doves* (New Brunswick, N.J.: Rutgers University Press, 1988), an analysis of the impact of the peace movement on the Johnson and Nixon administrations, describes 1967 as the worst year of the Johnson presidency, one in which "protestors and riots dominated much of the news" (see pp. 92, 110).

33. See Valenti memo, December 29, 1966, saying that the *Newsweek* article of January 2, 1967, on Clifford was full of errors, as in its claim that Clifford saw Johnson three times a week. Perhaps because of Johnson's view that secrecy kept his options open, the president did not like the article, which stressed Clifford's influence. Office of the President file: Clifford; also, Clifford oral interview, tape 1, p. 29; and Lady Bird Johnson to Clifford, January 12, 1967, Office of the President file: Clifford, all LBJ Library.

34. Rostow to Johnson, January 19, 1967, NS file, Memos to the President: Rostow, vol. 18, DSDUF, box 2; Rostow to Johnson, October 20, 1967, NS file, Memos to the President: Rostow, vol. 47, box 24, DSDUF, box 2, LBJ Library.

35. Since he brought him into confidential sessions, Johnson obviously trusted Bundy to keep secrets and to offer his best judgment on Vietnam matters, whatever doubts the former national security adviser had come to have. Former speechwriter John Roche, no fan of Bundy's, says, "I have no reason to believe that Bundy was not totally loyal to Johnson. I think he felt that perhaps Johnson should have listened to him more than he did, because after all, he, Bundy, knew a great deal more about things than Johnson did, which is a doubtful proposition." Roche oral history, p. I, 13, LBJ Library.

36. *Pentagon Papers: The Gravel Edition* (Boston: Beacon Press, 1971), vol. 4, pp. 157-169.

37. Smith to Johnson, March 23, 1967; memoranda of Smith's meeting with Johnson, March 31, 1967, Diary backup, box 59, LBJ Library.

38. McPherson to Johnson, March 7, 1967 (emphasis added), Vietnam-1967 (part 1) folder, Office files of McPherson, box 28; Valenti to Johnson, January 30, 1967, Office files, White House aides, LBJ Library.

39. W. W. Rostow, *The Diffusion of Power: An Essay in Recent History* (New York: Macmillan, 1972), pp. 509-510.

40. David Lilienthal, *The Journals of David Lilienthal, vol. 6: Creativity and Conflict, 1964-1967* (New York: Harper and Row, 1976), pp. 286, 297, 402, 404, 410.

41. *Pentagon Papers*, vol. 4, p. 424.

42. General Bruce Palmer, Jr., *The Twenty-five Year War: America's Military Role in Vietnam* (Lexington: University Press of Kentucky, 1984), pp. 48-49. In contrast to a number of histories or memoirs by military figures who were involved in the Vietnam War, Palmer's is notable because he describes what he sees as the failure of the military command to tell political leaders in Washington that "the strategy being pursued most probably would fail and that the United States would be unable to achieve its objectives" (p. 46).

43. *Pentagon Papers*, vol. 4, pp. 425-426.

44. Roche oral history, p. I, 18-20. Roche was hired despite the fact that he had publicly criticized U.S. bombing of North Vietnam and was against the U.S. invasion of the Dominican Republic in 1965: "President Johnson knew that. Walt [Rostow] knew it . . . the ground rules were simply that as far as I was concerned, I was not going to undercut the President in public. I didn't talk to newspapers" (see p. I, 45-46). Former press secretary George Christian says that Roche was an important adviser—"Johnson's thinker"—by virtue of Johnson's respect for Roche. Personal interview with the author, January 1989.

45. The agenda was for March 29, 1967. See NS files, Files of Rostow, box 15, LBJ Library.

46. Westmoreland Papers, folder #3 History briefing, January 27-March 25, 1967, box 10, Johnson Library. See also box 6, April 8, 1967, memo for the record by Westmoreland, in which he tells how he informed military colleagues in Vietnam that he planned to "press for authority to conduct air strikes against enemy facilities and activities in Cambodia."

47. Presidential trip to Guam (Conference), March 1967 (I), NS file: International Meetings and Travel, box 12-13, LBJ Library. See also "Gen. Westmoreland's Historical Briefing, 25 Mar 67," p. 21, #13 History file, Westmoreland Papers, LBJ Library.

48. William Westmoreland, *A Soldier Reports* (Garden City, N.Y.: Doubleday, 1976), p. 214. There has been a lawsuit and continuing controversy about the accuracy of Westmoreland's estimates to Washington decisionmakers of enemy troop strengths. Some, including CBS News, have claimed that there was outright deception on Westmoreland's part. I do not detail the complexities of the controversy here, but my reading of the evidence is that differences among military and intelligence officials over enemy troop strengths were instances of bureaucratic infighting and substantive disagreements rather than overt dishonesty. What is crystal clear is that Lyndon Johnson was no unwitting tool of any single set of analyses on such questions—his sources of information were too numerous for that. Among those treating the topic is Berman's *Lyndon Johnson's War*, pp. 27-31, 38-39, 49-51, 73-76, 81-83, 109-113. In *A Matter of Honor* (New York: Macmillan, 1984), Don Kowet writes that Johnson was aware of a debate between military and civilian intelligence agencies over enemy trooop strength, and that Helms, Rostow, McNamara, Rusk, Wheeler, and at least three others in the administration knew of "the general debate" as well. There is evidence enough in the LBJ archives to show that Johnson knew of the controversy. See, for example, Robert Ginsburgh to Rostow, August 18, 1967, NS file, DSDUF, box 2 (Vietnam); Rostow to Johnson, November 15, 1967, and Helms to Johnson, November 15, 1967, both NS Country file: Vietnam, boxes 81-84, all LBJ Library. The case for a conspiracy by Westmoreland to conceal information is made in Bruce E. Jones, *War without Windows* (New York: Vanguard Press, 1987). For an in-house critique of CBS's controversial reporting

on the alleged Westmoreland conspiracy, see Burton Benjamin, *The CBS Benjamin Report* (Washington, D.C.: Media Institute, 1984).

49. Lilienthal, *Journals*, vol. 6, pp. 418, 420. The *Pentagon Papers* claim that Westmoreland's report was "basically optimistic," but the transcripts show otherwise. See vol. 4, pp. 424–425.

50. Westmoreland, *Soldier Reports*, p. 227.

51. Townsend Hoopes, *The Limits of Intervention* (New York: McKay, 1969), p. 50; Lilienthal, *Journals*, vol. 6, p. 418. On McNamara's doubts about the war, see Henry Trewhitt, *McNamara* (New York: Harper and Row, 1971), ch. 9.

52. Sec. McNamara backgrounder briefing, March 22, 1967, pp. 3, 6, 8, 16, Presidential Trip to Guam file [II], NS file: Inter. Meetings and Travel, box 12/13, LBJ Library.

53. Lilienthal, *Journals*, vol. 6, p. 415.

54. Dean Rusk believes that the troop request resulted from Johnson's pressure on Westmoreland to produce results in Vietnam; Rusk, correspondence with the author, November 4, 1988; interview with the author, June 9, 1989.

55. Diary backup, March 31, 1967, box 57, LBJ Library.

56. Taylor, *Swords and Plowshares*, p. 379. The labels of the options are Taylor's, but the descriptions of each option are mine and are slightly different from Taylor's. The general formulated the list late in 1967, after the period under study in this chapter. However, Taylor says (and all evidence suggests) that the four basic alternatives existed throughout the year. Note the similarity of views held by Taylor, a hawk, and Arthur Schlesinger, a dove, as to what options existed for the U.S. government in 1967 and the extent to which the pullout option was not seriously considered even by leading war critics. See note 22 above.

57. Johnson and other civilian advisers were very much involved in passing judgment on potential aerial bombing targets, as is well known; on ground strategy, however, Westmoreland says, "the President never tried to tell me how to run the war. The tactics and battlefield strategy of running the war were mine." Of course, Westmoreland's military decisions were made after Johnson set national policy on issues such as whether or not to invade North Vietnam. See Westmoreland oral history, p. I, 12, 13, LBJ Library.

58. Westmoreland Papers, folder #15 History file, March 27–April 30, 1967, box 11, LBJ Library.

59. *CQ Almanac*, 1967, p. 926.

60. "Letters to Save" file: 1966–1967, XV Gen. EE Red Line file, box 5, Russell Library.

61. Westmoreland Papers, folder #15 History file, March 27–April 30, 1967, box 11, LBJ Library; Westmoreland, *Soldier Reports*, pp. 227–228. Another account of the meeting is "Notes on Discussions with the President, 27 April 1967," from the papers of Paul Warnke, and found in Reference file-Vietnam, box 1, LBJ Library. Here Westmoreland is described as saying that the war might go on as long as *three* more years with only the minimum troop package.

62. Palmer, *The Twenty-five Year War*, p. 90.

63. *Pentagon Papers*, vol. 4, pp. 441–443.

64. Rostow, *Diffusion of Power*, p. 513.

65. Westmoreland Papers, folder #15 History file, March 27–April 30, 1967, box 11, LBJ Library.

66. Rostow, *Diffusion of Power*, pp. xvii, 513, and personal interview with the author, January 20, 1989. Lilienthal, *Journals*, vol. 6, p. 174.

67. Rostow to Johnson, July 22, 1967, NS file, Aides memos to the President: Rostow, vol. 35, DSDUF, box 3, LBJ Library. On Rostow, see Joseph G. Bock, *The White House Staff and the National Security Assistant: Friendship and Friction at the Water's Edge* (Westport, Conn.: Greenwood Press, 1987), pp. 69–70. "There is no tangible proof that Rostow ever withheld from the President information on the war which challenged Rostow's views," writes David K. Hall in "The National Security Assistant as Policy Spokesman, 1947–1981," a paper presented at the 1981 meeting of the American Political Science Association, p. 53, and cited in Bock, p. 80. See also Richard Helms's agreement in his oral interview, pp. 29–30; Dean Rusk's oral interview, pp. I, 26–28; John Roche's oral history interview, p. I, 45–46; and Bromley Smith's oral interview, p. I, 31, 35, all LBJ Library. Also Redford and McCulley, *White House Operations*, p. 111. These views challenge earlier accusations against Rostow typified by Louis W. Koenig, "The Invisible Presidency," in Sidney Wise and Richard F. Schier (eds.), *The Presidential Office* (New York: Thomas Crowell, 1968), p. 36; Hoopes, *Limits of Intervention*, pp. 59–61; and Doris Kearns, *Lyndon Johnson and the American Dream* (New York: Harper and Row, 1976), p. 335, among others.

68. Westmoreland, *Soldier Reports*, p. 230.

69. Eisenhower, Memo for the Record, November 23, 1966, and "RLS notes taken in presence of DDE telephone conversation to the President," October 3, 1966, File: President Johnson—1966, Eisenhower Library.

70. Differences over the size of the New York crowd are unresolved. Thomas Powers, in *The War at Home*, insists that "it was by far the largest demonstration in American history up until that time" (see pp. 181–183). *CQ Almanac*, 1967, p. 931. The economic report was released in July.

71. Humphrey, "Tuesday Lunch," p. 91. On November 4, 1967, Tom Johnson recorded, "The President then asked Sec. McNamara what can he do to solve crime in the District of Columbia. The President said he asked Wirtz the same thing. 'Crime will be the principal problem [the President said], even more so than Vietnam. We've got to show some progress and action.'" Meeting notes file, box 2, LBJ Library. For typical Tuesday Lunch agendas, see NS Name file: Rostow Memos, LBJ Library.

72. Smith was Executive Secretary of the National Security Council, 1961–1969. See his oral history, pp. I, 26, 27, and II, 2, 3, LBJ Library. Rusk, oral history, p. I, 22, LBJ Library. Clark Clifford recalls that the Tuesday Cabinet "never had a leak." Clifford, oral history, tape 5, p. 19, LBJ Library. See also Benjamin Read's oral history, pp. 8–10, LBJ Library. Read, special assistant to Rusk, views the Tuesday Lunch forum as having developed because "ad hoc meetings and NSC discussions weren't suitable" to all of Johnson's needs. "[U]sually a day before a Tuesday lunch, I will be in touch by phone with the President's Special Assistant and we'll swap ideas of what might go on the agenda and start the list and add to it in that manner. Before the day is out, I've usually checked with the Secretary—if Walt Rostow or Mac Bundy haven't directly, I have—to determine his wishes, both taking things off the list and putting them on again. It's a constant interchange and we supplement this process by a procedure in State in which the Secretariat officers contact each of the bureaus, maybe two days in advance or a day or so in advance at least, to get their ideas of what is of sufficient importance and timeliness to put on the luncheon platter. So it's not as unstructured as some of the recent newspaper accounts . . . would have you believe. . . . After the lunch, Walt Rostow has been scrupulous in

calling me to run down the list of items, item by item, to relay any action instructions which may flow from the discussion at the meal." See also Lyndon Johnson, *The Vantage Point: Perspectives of the Presidency* (New York: Holt, Rinehart, and Winston, 1971), p. 370; and David M. Barrett, "Doing 'Tuesday Lunch' at Lyndon Johnson's White House: New Archival Evidence on Vietnam Decisionmaking," *P. S.: Political Science and Politics* 24, 4 (1991): 676–679.

73. Johnson to Rostow, January 6, 1967, NS file, Agency file: Defense, vol. 4, box 12, LBJ Library.

74. Humphrey, "Tuesday Lunch," pp. 82, 99–100. See also Redford and McCulley, *White House Operations*, p. 111.

75. John Roche oral interview, p. I, 63, LBJ Library. President Johnson claimed that "the Tuesday meeting was patterned after meetings that President Eisenhower told me he had with Prime Minister Churchill during the war, that he would have a luncheon meeting and an evening meeting, and they were regular. And they were quiet and free from publicity." Johnson oral interview with Elspeth Rostow, p. II, 10, LBJ Library.

76. Richard Helms, oral interview, p. I, 30, 32–33, LBJ Library; similar views are expressed in Redford and McCulley, *White House Operations*, p. 42; also Rusk oral interview, p. I, 31–32, LBJ Library. To an interviewer who said that such informal advisers were not reading "the traffic [i.e., interagency memoranda] in foreign affairs," Rusk said, "Well, they may have good ideas even though they don't read the traffic. I never had any problem about that myself."

77. Humphrey, "Tuesday Lunch," p. 89.

78. Assistant press secretary Tom Johnson sat in as well to take notes for the sake of history and to help the president keep track of the twists and turns of developing policymaking in Vietnam. See Humphrey, "Tuesday Lunch," pp. 88–90. Christian also had presidential permission to enter Johnson's office at any time. See Christian oral interview, p. I, 9, LBJ Library.

79. Kearns, *Lyndon Johnson*, p. 320. Among other places, see Tom Johnson's notes of meetings, CBS subpoena releases, box 3, LBJ Library. After Robert McNamara left the administration, he too attended at least one more Tuesday Lunch on May 28, 1968.

80. Bromley Smith, oral history, p. II, 4, LBJ Library. Benjamin Read, special assistant to Rusk, recalls, "I used to load the Secretary down on these Tuesday lunches with very detailed memoranda of the volatile in-close targets with a discussion of pro and con of what the problems might be if they were struck and not struck precisely, as my Air Force friends always try to convince us will happen." Read oral history, p. 16, LBJ Library.

81. John McNaughton, assistant secretary of defense, was influential with McNamara and in the foreign policy bureaucracy, though not with Johnson himself. McNaughton's views were so close to McNamara's that memos from the Defense Department seem to reflect the collective thoughts of the two men. See Hoopes, *Limits of Intervention*, pp. 50–51. He wrote to McNamara on May 6 that the war was polarizing American society, noting, "A feeling is widely and strongly held that 'the Establishment' is out of its mind. The feeling is that we are trying to impose some US image on distant peoples we cannot understand (anymore than we can the younger generation here at home), and that we are carrying the things to absurd lengths." See *Pentagon Papers*, vol. 4, pp. 478–479. As noted earlier, McNaughton died in the summer of 1967.

82. This request is frequently referred to in various histories as a 100,000

troop request. The *Pentagon Papers*, other histories, and some policymakers simply rounded the approximate 80,000 number up to 100,000.

83. *Pentagon Papers*, vol. 4, pp. 169–175. John McNaughton drafted the original version of this statement for McNamara's use.

84. *Pentagon Papers*, vol. 4, p. 175. Ulysses S. G. Sharp, *Strategy for Defeat* (San Rafael, Calif.: Presidio Press, 1978), p. 175.

85. Brooke to Johnson, May 19, 1967, folder: Dept. of Defense, vol. iv, NS Agency file, box 12, LBJ Library. McNamara's views on the bombing of North Vietnam were informed by innumerable written analyses. One recently declassified Pentagon report, though written just after McNamara's memo to Johnson, is in generally the same spirit: It told McNamara that the bombing had successfully sustained "the morale of the South Vietnamese" and made North Vietnam's "support of insurgency in SVN as costly and difficult as possible," but that influencing Hanoi toward a negotiated settlement was "difficult to measure." The report somberly added that "there is no evidence that the bombing has weakened the will of the leadership to continue the war." "Bombing North Vietnam," prepared by Office of the Assistant Secretary of Defense (OASD), International Security Agency (ISA), and Program Analysis and Evaluation Office (EAPR), June 2, 1967, declassified by Office of the Assistant Secretary of Defense.

86. Press secretary George Christian later said that he could not recall the "dovishness" that came to be associated with McNamara. This shows the problem with that label, for Christian goes on to say that McNamara was against bombing in 1967 and 1968 Tuesday Lunch meetings but did not question the U.S. "commitment of being there." Christian oral history, p. II, 35, LBJ Library.

87. Warren Cohen, *Dean Rusk* (Totowa, N.J.: Cooper Square Press, 1980), pp. 271–273, 316–317; Thomas Schoenbaum, *Waging Peace and War: Dean Rusk in the Truman, Kennedy, and Johnson Years* (New York: Simon and Schuster, 1988), p. 461. Though Rusk did not believe it, journalist Harrison Salisbury (after visiting North Vietnam) told the secretary of state in January 1967 that his impression of North Vietnam's leaders "confirm the possibility—if not the probability—that they're looking for a way out" of the war. Rusk sent Johnson a copy of Salisbury's report. Amazingly, at about the same time, Walt Rostow wrote to Johnson that it was conceivable or probable that "they're trying to get out of the war, but don't know how." DSDUF, NS file, Memos to President, box 12, vol. 19, and Rostow to Johnson, DSDUF, box 3, LBJ Library.

88. Rusk, correspondence with the author, November 4, 1988.

89. Cohen, *Rusk*, pp. 271, 276, 277. Cohen's portrait of Rusk throughout Chapter 14 is of a steady advocate of "progress" in the South without great escalations of bombing or troop levels.

90. Cohen, *Rusk*, p. 227. Tom Johnson's notes, August 7 and 16, 1967, box 2 and box 1, LBJ Library. Rusk was not at the first of these Tuesday Lunch meetings but sent his evaluation of the bombing request through McNamara. Regrettably, notes of many earlier 1967 meetings do not exist or have not been released or discovered.

91. Tom Johnson's notes, August 24, 1967, box 1, LBJ Library.

92. Cohen's *Rusk* sees Rusk this way; see Schoenbaum, *Waging Peace*, p. 458. As for a bombing halt, Johnson seems slightly more flexible than Rusk in a transcript of the September 5, 1967, Tuesday Lunch meeting. See Jim Jones to the president, September 5, 1967, p. 7, Diary backup, box 75, LBJ Library.

93. Rusk, oral history interview, p. I, 25, LBJ Library. In an inteview conducted by his son, Richard, Dean Rusk comments, "To say that I disagreed with

President Kennedy or President Johnson on major decisions would be wrong." Richard Rusk: "You think so?" Dean Rusk: "Yes." Richard Rusk: "When Lyndon Johnson decided to land Marines, for example, in February (1965) to protect the bases . . ." Dean Rusk: "I was in favor of that." Richard Rusk: "You were in favor of that?" Dean Rusk: "Yes." Richard Rusk: "What about the introduction of more combat forces?" Dean Rusk: "Yes, I was in favor of that." Richard Rusk: "And the bombing of North Vietnam?" Dean Rusk: "I had some misgivings about that and expressed them at those Tuesday luncheon sessions from time to time." Rusk oral history PP, pp. 10–11, Rusk Papers, Russell Library.

William P. Bundy, assistant secretary of state for East Asian and Pacific affairs since 1964, and Nicholas Katzenbach, under secretary of state since 1966, were prominent within the State Department but were nonetheless a bureaucratic level away from top presidential advisory roles on Vietnam. Nor were they close to Johnson personally. Katzenbach, for years thought by Johnson to be a "Bobby Kennedy man," seems not to have had the same status vis-à-vis the president as his predecessor George Ball. But undoubtedly, as Chapter 2 indicated, Bundy and Katzenbach had influence with Johnson and within the foreign policymaking bureaucracies. At the end of May 1967, Bundy wrote a memo circulated at the State and Defense departments that said, "If we can get a reasonably solid GVN [Government of South Vietnam] political structure and GVN performance at all levels, favorable trends could become really marked over the next 18 months, the war will be won for practical purposes at some point, and the resulting peace will be secure." He opposed troop increases of the level requested by Westmoreland and favored only restricted bombing of the North. See *Pentagon Papers*, vol. 4, pp. 181, 445. Katzenbach favored adding 30,000 troops over the coming year and a half, limiting bombing of North Vietnam to known infiltration routes, and informing South Vietnam that U.S. withdrawal of troops would begin by the end of 1968, leaving further "progress" up to them. See *Pentagon Papers*, vol. 4, pp. 507–508.

94. Humphrey, "Tuesday Lunch," p. 90.

95. Much of Johnson's regard for Helms appeared to result from the CIA's performance during the Six Day War in the Middle East, when the Agency correctly — but controversially — predicted that Israel would win the war within a week. See Thomas Powers's excellent *The Man Who Kept the Secrets* (New York: Knopf, 1979), p. 202. Helms oral interview, pp. 5–6, LBJ Library.

96. Rostow to Johnson, January 16, 1967, NS file: Vietnam, box 40, in DSFUF Collection, box 2, LBJ Library.

97. Helms oral interview, p. 31, LBJ Library. Helms considers himself to have been an adviser whom Johnson asked about "facts in the case, what was happening in the overseas areas under consideration, what I thought the opposition might do" but not an adviser who advised the president on major war strategy or administration policy (see pp. 6–7). Notes of Tuesday Lunches show Helms somewhat more active as an adviser than Helms's memory suggests.

98. Powers, *Man Who Kept Secrets*, p. 203. See also Palmer, *The Twenty-five Year War*, p. 166, and Henry Kissinger, *The White House Years* (Boston: Little, Brown, 1979), pp. 36–38, 319–320, 491–497, 995–1001.

99. *Pentagon Papers*, vol. 4, p. 155.

100. *Pentagon Papers*, vol. 4, pp. 180–181. Like some others, Hatcher's *Suicide of an Elite* claims that CIA officials "repeatedly warned both presidents [Kennedy and Johnson] of an impending disaster in Vietnam" (p. 176), but Johnson administration archives show otherwise: Intelligence agencies tended to

produce sober, "balanced" analyses describing both problems and opportunities in Vietnam. For example, a January 1967 Office of National Estimates report for Helms reported that in "the past year and a half the chances that the Communists would win South Vietnam by military victory have vanished." But, it said, "There is no evident diminution of the Communist capability to continue the struggle." Then it said, "the strains upon the Communist side are great and increasing." See NS file, DSDUF, box 2 (Vietnam), LBJ Library. A December 1967 CIA report read by Johnson said, "the situation in Vietnam has developed unevenly . . . no early turning point appears likely." But it added, "In the political realm, the South Vietnamese have made considerable strides in establishing the framework for developing national political institutions." See NS Country file: Vietnam, folder: Vietnam 2 C (2) Gen. military activity, box 69, LBJ Library. In *Counsel to the President* (New York: Random House, 1991), Clark Clifford writes that nothing in CIA "analyses suggested that the basic American objective was unattainable" (see p. 425).

101. Rostow to the president, April 6, 1967, NS file: Vietnam, NODIS V. (a), box 47, DSDUF, box 4, LBJ Library.

102. *Pentagon Papers*, vol. 4, pp. 390–391; emphasis in the original.

103. "National Security Action Memorandum No. 362," written by the president and addressed to Rusk and McNamara, May 9, 1967. NS Name file: Rostow memos, LBJ Library. Robert W. Komer, *Bureaucracy at War: U.S. Performance in the Vietnam Conflict* (Boulder, Colo.: Westview Press, 1986). Komer to McNamara and Vance, April 24, 1967, folder: N. Katzenbach, files of Komer, box 5, LBJ Library.

104. Lilienthal, *Journals*, vol. 6, p. 350; Komer to McNaughton, April 8, 1967, folder: McNamara, Vance, McNaughton, files of Komer, box 5, LBJ Library; emphasis in the original.

105. *Pentagon Papers*, vol. 4, pp. 440–441.

106. Westmoreland Papers, folder #18 History file, May 23–May 31, 1967, box 12, LBJ Library.

107. Rostow, personal interview, January 20, 1989. Although previous ambassadors Lodge and Taylor had their critics, it is hard to find criticism of Bunker's performance in Saigon during the latter part of the Johnson administration. Westmoreland says, "Lodge was a poor organizer; he was superb on political matters. . . . Taylor was the reverse; he was not an accomplished diplomat. . . . Bunker was a combination of the two, a statesman, a diplomat, and an organizer, a man of tremendous depth." Westmoreland oral history, p. II, 3, LBJ Library. Elsewhere, Westmoreland said of Bunker, "He was on-the-scene boss. . . . I never talked to [Johnson] a single time between Washington and Saigon, not once. My chain of command was to the Ambassador, who had responsibilities for all activities in Vietnam" (quoted in Benjamin, *The CBS Benjamin Report*, p. 38. David Lilienthal thought that Bunker was "easily the strongest man in the Foreign Service, perhaps in the whole government except the President" (*Journals*, vol. 6, p. 424). See also Palmer, *The Twenty-five Year War*, p. 47.

108. Bunker to Johnson, May 25, 1967, NS Aides file: Rostow, vol. 29, DSDUF, box 3, LBJ Library. *Pentagon Papers*, vol. 4, pp. 192, 195, 517; Bunker to Johnson, July 6, 1967, NS file: Vietnam, boxes 104–106, LBJ Library.

109. Carl Solberg, *Hubert Humphrey: A Biography* (New York: Norton, 1984), p. 292.

110. Solberg, *Humphrey*, pp. 285, 333.

111. Senator Vance Hartke, "Vietnam Costs More Than You Think," *Saturday Evening Post*, April 22, 1967, pp. 10, 11. Humphrey to McPherson, May 17, 1967, Vietnam-1967 (part 1) folder, Office files of McPherson, box 28, LBJ Library.

112. According to John Roche, one continuing problem from Johnson's vantage point was that "Humphrey would go out and make a speech, come out for a domestic Marshall plan or something like that . . . Johnson would call up Califano and say, 'Goddamn that Hubert, can't you tell him something?' So Joe would call up Hubert: 'Mr. Vice President, you simply can't say that sort of thing,' and so on. . . . Hubert at this point would blow his stack. . . . The President would then call me and say, 'I understand that Hubert has got his feathers ruffled. Now I didn't mean for Joe to put it to him quite that hard. . . . But somebody tell him. Somebody tell him. I don't want to read the speeches, but somebody tell him.' So I took the cue. I'd call up Hubert and tell him the President loved him, and there was just a little misunderstanding." Roche oral history, p. I, 46–47, LBJ Library.

113. Solberg, *Humphrey*, p. 307.

114. Mansfield to Johnson, May 29, 1967, NS Name file: Mansfield, box 6, LBJ Library.

115. On Mansfield and Johnson, also see Memos: Rostow to Johnson, May 30, 1967, reporting Rusk's and his responses to Mansfield's letter of May 29, 1967, and Rostow to Johnson, August 7, 1967, NS Name file: Mansfield, box 6, in DSDUF, box 4; also, a draft of a "Dear Mike" letter to Mansfield, January 19, 1967, written by Rusk and Rostow, in NS file, Memos to President: Rostow, vol. 18, DSDUF, box, 2, all LBJ Library. On the barrier, see Karnow, *Vietnam*, p. 500.

116. *CQ Almanac*, 1967, p. 928.

117. *CQ Almanac*, 1967, pp. 939–940; Terry Dietz, *Republicans and Vietnam, 1961–1968* (Westport, Conn.: Greenwood Press, 1986), pp. 119–120.

118. Lilienthal, *Journals*, vol. 6, p. 433.

119. McPherson to Johnson, May 13, 1966, Office files, White House Aides: McPherson, LBJ Library.

120. Fulbright to Johnson, June 30, 1967, NS Name file: Fulbright, box 3, LBJ Library. The two men had a friendly talk and other communication about the possibility of Johnson's meeting with Soviet Premier Kosygin; see Fulbright to Johnson, June 19, 1967, NS file: files of Rostow, folder: Fulbright, LBJ Library.

121. William Fulbright, *The Arrogance of Power* (New York: Vintage Books, 1966), pp. 188–197. Berman, *Fulbright*, pp. 78, 92. Roche, oral history, p. I, 72–73, LBJ Library. Roche remembers the memo being called the "pneumonia memorandum" because Roche said that the military reminded him of physicians who had a cure for pneumonia but not for the common cold, so they had a vested interest in the patient with the cold getting pneumonia. For whatever reason, it was not well received, he says, by McNamara, but Johnson did not object to Roche's advocacy.

122. On McPherson and other speechwriters, see Redford and McCulley, *White House Operations*, pp. 166–167. McPherson says that he and a number of other staffers had "complete access to the President on any subject." See his oral history, p. III, 35, LBJ Library. George Christian says that McPherson had more influence, year in and year out, on Vietnam and other foreign policy issues than any other White House staffer who was not formally assigned to foreign policy. Personal interview with the author, January 1989.

123. McPherson oral interview, pp. 3, 31; McPherson to the president, June 18, 1965, Office files of White House Aides: McPherson, LBJ Library. The handwritten notation may be McPherson's account of Johnson's spoken response.

124. Harry McPherson oral interview, tape 4, pp. 2–3, LBJ Library.

125. Quoted in McPherson oral interview, tape 4, p. 6. The point is made in Redford and McCulley, *White House Operations*, p. 72, quoting another former Johnson adviser: "[John] Roche was emphatic—McPherson had 'tremendous integrity,' 'a guy who used to lay into Johnson, too. I mean he used to really sock it to him.' "

126. The archival record at the Johnson Library suggests that Moyers kept in touch with Johnson, but that the president did not respond. In July 1967, Moyers wrote to the president to let him know of the latest Vietnam-related gossip: a campaign by Arthur Schlesinger and others to persuade McNamara to resign "as a moral protest to the Vietnam War," deep division in the *New York Times* editorial board over the war, and a stout defense of Johnson as president by Averell Harriman in "the drawing rooms of New York." Moyers to Johnson, July 18, 1967, file: Moyers (1966 and 1967), Office of the President file, LBJ Library.

127. Mrs. Moyers to Mrs. Johnson, May 6, 1968, Office files of the President, File: Moyers, LBJ Library.

128. Harry McPherson, *A Political Education* (Boston: Little, Brown, 1972), pp. 391, 395.

129. Redford and McCulley, *White House Operations*, p. 68; Office files, White House Aides: McPherson, LBJ Library. Douglass Cater, who advised Johnson mostly on domestic matters, also played such a conduit role after Moyers's and George Ball's departures, with Johnson's approval. As Cater wrote to Johnson, Rostow was "widely recognized as a leading architect of policies in Vietnam"; therefore, some people might "prefer to communicate with you via another route." See Cater to Johnson, January 12, 1967, Reference file, Vietnam, box 1, LBJ Library.

130. McPherson, *Political Education*, pp. 404, 412. McPherson to Johnson, June 13, 1967, Reference file, Vietnam, box 1, LBJ Library. There was an irony about the Six Day War best captured by David Lilienthal some days before the war started: "Writes the gifted historian Barbara Tuchman, in a passionate letter to the *Times* the other day: If the U.S. doesn't act, right now, unilaterally, to kill the Arabs, our moral foundations are gone. And the *Times* editorial writers have had to do a big flip. . . . Art Buchwald, the nutty humorist, is the only pundit capable of handling this flip—and he did it in a funny way tonight. 'But I thought, Mr. Dunkleberry, that you are a dove, not a hawk.' 'I'm a dove that has lost its temper.' " Lilienthal, *Journals*, vol. 6, p. 449.

131. McPherson, *Political Education*, pp. 401, 412–413; the full memo to Johnson, dated May 15, 1967, is in Reference file, Vietnam, box 1, LBJ Library.

132. McPherson, *Political Education*, p. 420.

133. *Congressional Record*, March 1, 1967, p. 4723. At a White House meeting of the president with Senate chairmen on January 9, 1967, Russell told Johnson, "win or get out," according to notes taken by Hubert Humphrey. See memo for files, January 10, 1967, VP Notes, WH Meetings, 1967, 24 F 8 2F, Minnesota Historical Society.

134. Powell Moore oral history, p. I, 7, LBJ Library; II, 4, Intra-office communications; and Series I, letter to constituent, June 26, 1967, Russell Library. The battleship idea was dropped by the Nixon administration.

135. Jack Spalding, *Atlanta Journal*, January 26, 1971, reprinted in U.S. Congress, *Richard Brevard Russell: Memorial Tributes* (Washington, D.C.: Government Printing Office, 1971), p. 139.

136. See, for instance, II, 5 Intra-office communications, Russell Library. Powell Moore oral history, p. I, 6, 12, LBJ Library. Moore says that he sensed tension between Johnson and Russell by early 1967 but that the "real strain" between the two came later. See Russell's 1968 Datebook, April 3, 1968, Russell Library, for an indication that the Johnson-Russell closeness continued beyond 1967.

137. Rowland Evans and Robert Novak, *Lyndon B. Johnson: The Exercise of Power* (New York: New American Library, 1966), pp. 11-13. The aide quoted is Powell Moore, oral history, p. I, 10, LBJ Library. Note found with Datebooks, 1964-1970, Russell Library.

138. Some notes by Russell on conversations with Johnson have not yet been released by the senator's heirs.

139. Rostow to Johnson, June 20, 1967, NS file: Vietnam, Memos to the President, vol. 1, DSDUF, box 2, LBJ Library.

140. Leonard Marks, "Johnson and Leadership," in Kenneth W. Thompson (ed.), *The Johnson Presidency: Twenty Intimate Perspectives of Lyndon B. Johnson* (Lanham, Md.: University Press of America, 1986), pp. 285-286. It takes some construction to place this incident in time; like many oral histories, Marks's captures the spirit of an event but is imprecise on its date. He refers to Aiken's position—first advocated by the senator in October 1966—but also to national elections in Vietnam and the approach of Johnson's next birthday, which was in August 1967. It seems likely, therefore, that Marks's exchange with Johnson occurred in June or early July, when the administration was struggling with the troop decision.

141. After the party, Marks continued to be invited to NSC and Cabinet meetings thereafter. On Johnson's comment, he says, "Several years after he left the White House I was invited to spend a weekend at the ranch. We were by ourselves. It was on my conscience and I said, 'Mr. President, I have to ask you something. In all the years we've been together, only once did you act in a way that I could really complain,' and I recalled this experience. Why did you do it? He looked at me and said, 'Because you and George Aiken were right.' I tell you that story because it shows the torment of a man who had to make enormously important decisions and perhaps was carried away by the force of circumstance so that he couldn't control those decisions. When he lashed out in anger, he did it emotionally, but intellectually he realized it was the wrong thing and he did apologize" (Marks, "Johnson and Leadership," p. 286). The importance of Johnson's statement should not be exaggerated—Johnson said various, sometimes conflicting, things about the war to many people after he left office. For instance, he told Elspeth Rostow that General Earle Wheeler and retired General Maxwell Taylor gave him advice that was "better than anybody else's." Wheeler and Taylor, of course, gave advice conflicting with that of Marks and Aiken. Johnson oral history, p. 23, LBJ Library.

142. Bruce A. Murphy, *Fortas: The Rise and Ruin of a Supreme Court Justice* (New York: Morrow, 1988), p. 238.

143. Fortas to Johnson, July 29 and October 7, 1965, Folder: Fortas, A. (1964-1967), "Files pertaining to A. Fortas and H. Thornberry," box 1, LBJ Library; Robert Shogan, *A Question of Judgment: The Fortas Case and the Struggle for the Supreme Court* (Indianapolis: Bobbs-Merrill, 1972), pp. 165-166.

144. Shogan, *Question of Judgment*, pp. 134–135, 139. Joseph Califano to Johnson, passing on Fortas's advice, June 6, 1967, NS file, Name file: Califano Memos, box 1, LBJ Library. Typically, Fortas called Califano with specific advice on the Middle East, freeing Johnson to return calls as necessary. See also Murphy, *Fortas*, pp. 236–237. Redford and McCulley, *White House Operations*, pp. 129–130. Fortas's views prevailed over those of others on how to announce federal action to quell the unrest.

145. Usually Johnson called Fortas rather than the reverse. Fortas oral interview, p. 22, LBJ Library.

146. Johnson, *White House Diary*, pp. 518–519.

147. Contrary to the overall picture of this chapter's account, Murphy's *Fortas* treats the president as an "unregenerate hawk" (see p. 241 and ch. 10 in general).

148. Fortas to Johnson, November 5, 1967, File: "Vietnam, Mar. 19, 1970," Decision to Halt Bombing, NS file, Country file: Vietnam, box 127, LBJ Library; emphasis in the original. Fortas wrote, "Our duty is to do what we consider right," but added that the public did "not want us to achieve less than our objectives—namely to prevent North Vietnam domination of South Vietnam by military force or subversion." See also Johnson, *Vantage Point*, pp. 372–378, 600–601, for a fuller description of McNamara's memo, which Johnson passed on to Fortas, Rusk, Rostow, Taylor, Clifford, Westmoreland, and Bunker. McGeorge Bundy and Katzenbach also responded to the McNamara stance, though not specifically his memo.

149. Lilienthal, *Journals*, vol. 6, p. 351.

150. Clark Clifford, "A Viet Nam Reappraisal: The Personal History of One Man's View and How It Evolved," *Foreign Affairs* 47, 4 (July 1969): 605–606. On Clifford and Vietnam in 1967, see his *Counsel to the President*, pp. 425, 447–452.

151. Quoted in Tom Johnson to the president, July 12, 1967, Tom Johnson's notes of meetings, Feb. 1967 to Feb. 1968 folder, box 3, LBJ Library.

152. Tom Johnson's notes, July 12, 1967, box 3, LBJ Library.

153. Clifford oral interview, tape 3, p. 6, LBJ Library.

154. Notes of the president's meeting with Clifford and Taylor, August 5, 1967, Tom Johnson's notes, Feb. 1967 to Feb. 1968 folder, box 3, LBJ Library.

155. Taylor, *Swords and Plowshares*, pp. 358–359. On Kennedy and Taylor, see pp. 178–303. Out of Taylor's subsequent review of insurgency "on the Vietnam model," he advocated and saw enacted a new government apparatus linking ambassadors overseas to regional assistant secretaries of state and the secretary himself. Taylor notes, "in an odd way, the quest for a way to deal with subversive insurgency led to the adoption of a whole new organization for dealing with foreign affairs in general" (*Swords and Plowshares*, pp. 360–361).

156. See Taylor, *Swords and Plowshares*, pp. 379–380, for Taylor's end-of-the-year review; compare January 1967 views, pp. 374–375. Troops in South Vietnam from other countries allied with the United States rose from 50,000 to 70,000 by 1969.

157. "July 25, 1967—Senate Committee Chairmen," Folder: July 1967–May 1968, Tom Johnson's notes, box 1, LBJ Library. See the opening of Chapter 1 of this book for a fuller account. At the White House meeting on January 9, 1967, Fulbright spoke out against Johnson's war policies and Rusk's performance. Other senators expressed a range of opinions from "win or get out" (Russell) to "there's too much dissent" (Smathers). "Meeting in Cabinet Room with

Senators," Misc. Vietnam documents, Reference file-Vietnam, box 1, LBJ Library; Hubert Humphrey, memo for files, January 10, 1967, VP Notes, WH meetings, 1967, 24 F 8 2F, Minnesota Historical Society.

158. For Fulbright's thoughts at the time, see the New York newspaper *Newsday*, May 4, 1967, based on a reporter's conversation with the senator, which Fulbright believed to be "off the record." A clear example of the impact of a legislator's criticisms comes from a meeting between Johnson and legislators in January 1968. See Chapter 4 of this book.

159. Tom Johnson's notes of meetings, July 12 and 18, 1967, box 3, LBJ Library; Johnson, *White House Diary*, p. 550; Lilienthal, *Journals*, vol. 6, p. 461.

160. He also assured the president that construction of the barrier across the north of South Vietnam could begin in a matter of months. As noted previously, the project was dropped. *Pentagon Papers*, vol. 4, pp. 188, 470. Also see Rostow to the president: "Response to Sen. Mansfield," August 7, 1967, NS file: Vietnam, Memos to the President, vol. 1, box 56, DSDUF, box 4, LBJ Library.

161. Memo to president from Tom Johnson, July 12, 1967, Meetings from Feb. '67 to Feb. '68 folder, Tom Johnson's notes, box 3, LBJ Library.

162. *Pentagon Papers*, vol. 4, p. 514; see also Johnson, *Vantage Point*, p. 370, and Trewhitt, *McNamara*, p. 239. In a meeting with both men on July 13 (the day after McNamara's remark), Johnson told McNamara that Westmoreland had been upset by press reports of the remark. He added that he had assured the general that "he has never heard anybody who has ever been critical of General Westmoreland in any way." Tom Johnson's notes of president's meeting with McNamara, Westmoreland, Wheeler . . . ," July 13, 1967, box 1, LBJ Library.

163. Tom Johnson's notes of meetings, July 12, 1967, box 3, LBJ Library. On this brief period of McNamara's relative optimism about the war, see also Westmoreland's comments on July 8, 1967, in his Historical Notes, July 6–August 3, box 12, LBJ Library, and notes by Humphrey of a July 21 meeting: "McNamara gave us review of Vietnam, military situation better—no stalemate." See file: VP Notes, WH meetings, 1967, box 412, VP WH papers, Humphrey Papers, Minnesota Historical Society. See also Lilienthal, *Journals*, vol. 6, p. 474. Bunker to Johnson, June 28, 1967, folder: Vietnam 8 B (1) [A] 6/67–11/67, NS file: Vietnam, boxes 104–106, LBJ Library. Bunker's weekly cable to Johnson on July 12, 1967, was important: "Bob McNamara, Nick Katzenbach, and my senior colleagues and I have come to a meeting of the minds on how we ought to proceed in reinforcing the success we already have had here . . . we should provide Gen. Westmoreland the number of maneuver battalions available without calling up the reserves . . . maintain our bombing of North Vietnam through the remaining months of good weather. We can then decide whether to cut back to the 20th parallel." NS file, Bunker cables, boxes 104–106, LBJ Library.

164. Wheeler's recommendations were heartily supported by Admiral U. S. Grant Sharp who, from his post in Hawaii as Commander in Chief, Pacific (CINCPAC), directed the air war against North Vietnam. Technically Sharp was Westmoreland's superior, but he was not always treated as such by McNamara. See Sharp's memoir, *Strategy for Defeat*, especially p. 184. Sharp blames civilian leaders, especially Johnson, for the U.S. defeat in Vietnam, citing what he believes were excessive restrictions placed on the military.

165. Wheeler's comments are in Memo to the President from Tom Johnson, July 12, 1967, Tom Johnson's notes, box 3, LBJ Library. This meeting is also

reported in Johnson, *Vantage Point*, p. 262. Bundy, in an inteview of Dean Rusk by Bundy and Richard Rusk, tape 00.1, p. 15, Rusk Papers, Russell Library.

166. Tom Johnson's notes of the president's meeting with McNamara, Wheeler, Westmoreland, Christian, July 13, 1967, box 2; Westmoreland Historical Notes, July 12, 1967, p. 5, box 12, LBJ Library. For evidence of how Westmoreland now says that he felt then, see *A Soldier Reports*, p. 230.

167. The President's News Conference of July 13, 1967, *The Public Papers of Lyndon B. Johnson, 1967*, vol. 2, pp. 690–691.

168. *Pentagon Papers*, vol. 4, p. 527; Johnson, *Vantage Point*, pp. 368–369.

169. Kearns, *Lyndon Johnson*, pp. 320–321; Karnow, *Vietnam*, p. 511; Hoopes, *Intervention*, pp. 90–91; Conkin, *Big Daddy*, p. 281; George Christian oral interview, p. II, 33, LBJ Library.

170. *Pentagon Papers*, vol. 4, p. 527.

171. Tom Johnson's notes, August 8, 1967, box 3, LBJ Library; emphasis in the original. In an earlier meeting, McNamara told Johnson that military commanders in Vietnam were interested in "free bombing." Of 129 targets recommended for bombing, McNamara supported bombing 17; some of the others, he said, were "not worth the loss of a single U.S. plane or pilot." Tom Johnson's notes, July 18, 1967, box 1, LBJ Library.

172. *Gallup Opinion Index*, April 1968, p. 3, and December 1968, p. 2.

173. Lilienthal, *Journals*, vol. 6, p. 484; Eisenhower and Goodpaster, September 1, 1967, file: Calls and appointments, 1967, DDE post-presidency, appointment book series, box 3, Eisenhower Library. Forty-six percent considered intervention to have been a mistake, and 44 percent thought it had been proper. See Mueller, *War, Presidents*, pp. 54–55.

174. Rostow to Johnson, August 1, 1967, NS file: Vietnam, Memos to President, vol. 1, box 56, DSDUF, box 2, LBJ Library.

175. Rostow to Johnson, memo of conversation, September 9, 1967, Vietnam 7 F (1), 1/66–11/67, Congressional attitudes, NS file: Vietnam, box 102, LBJ Library.

176. Johnson, *White House Diary*, pp. 185, 549, 556; emphasis in the original.

177. Sharp, *Strategy for Defeat*, pp. 225–226, 239–240. Schlesinger, *Robert Kennedy*, pp. 883–884.

178. Johnson, *Vantage Point*, p. 368.

179. On Johnson and the *Congressional Record*, see Redford and McCulley, *White House Operations*, p. 66; George Christian recalls, "He read religiously the *Congressional Record* every morning and had it brought to his room about six o'clock or seven o'clock in the morning and he read all the available daily papers very early in the morning before anybody else even got to stirring and he watched the network morning shows." See special oral history by David Culbertson, p. 6, LBJ Library.

180. Notes by Jim Jones, September 5 and 12, 1967, Appointment file, Diary backup, box 75, LBJ Library.

181. Later in the year, on November 24, Johnson met with 11 people in one Vietnam session during a visit to Washington by Westmoreland, Komer, and Bunker. Johnson displayed sensitivity to charges that the military's system for counting bodies of enemy troops killed in action needed reform. The president said, against the opinions of Westmoreland, Wheeler, and McNamara, that the body count system needed to be changed. (McNamara agreed with Johnson that the press believed that the administration was lying about body counts.)

Johnson told the group, "No matter what others may believe, this is an issue in this country and we need a committee to investigate the system." Finally, Johnson suggested that Westmoreland appoint a committee of news correspondents to investigate the system. "Meetings — Feb. 67 to Feb. '68," Tom Johnson's notes, CBS subpoena releases, box 3, LBJ Library.

182. Mueller, *War, Presidents*, p. 88.

183. Anderson and Eisenhower, July 21, 1967, file: Calls and appointments, 1967 (4), DDE post-presidency, appointment book series, box 3, Eisenhower Library. When Johnson took office, Eisenhower urged him to make use of Anderson, whom Ike considered extremely talented, even worthy of the presidency. Johnson used Anderson to oversee negotiations concerning the Panama Canal. Anderson died in disgrace and relative obscurity after being convicted of financial misdealings in the 1980s.

Chapter 4. 1968: Tet

1. "BOQs" are bachelor officers' quarters. Tom Johnson's notes of meetings, January 30, 1968, box 3, LBJ Library. In December 1990, Tom Johnson, former deputy press secretary in the Johnson administration (and no relation to the late president) granted me permission to see all his declassified notes of meetings he had attended. A few notes are still classified by the government. Although the notes are now open to researchers at the LBJ Library, Mr. Johnson retains literary ownership of them. In a telephone conversation with me, he said that he used a kind of speedwriting to take the notes. He says that although "they are not perfect," they represent his effort to create an accurate record of deliberations in Tuesday Lunch and other meetings. He says that President Johnson never asked him to alter the content of the notes. The notes were to have two purposes — that of serving history, and, prior to that, providing President Johnson with a reliable record of the evolution of Vietnam decisionmaking. During his presidency, access to the notes was limited to the president.

2. Tom Johnson notes, January 25, 1968, box 3, LBJ Library. On January 15, 1968, Westmoreland met Thieu and expressed concerns about an impending offensive: "I speculated that this might be the largest enemy campaign in the history of the war." Memo for the record, January 16, 1968, Westmoreland's Historical Papers, December 27, 1967–January 31, 1968, box 15, LBJ Library.

3. The characterization of Johnson's friendship with Holt is widely shared but comes from an interview with Walt Rostow, Johnson's former national security adviser, January 1989, Austin, Texas. December 21, 1967, meeting with Australian Cabinet, Meeting Notes file, box 2, LBJ Library.

4. *Congressional Record*, January 30, 1968, p. 1397.

5. Lyndon Johnson, *The Vantage Point: Perspectives of the Presidency* (New York: Holt, Rinehart, and Winston, 1971), p. 380; Harry McPherson, *A Political Education* (Boston: Little, Brown, 1972), p. 423.

6. The claim that the Tet Offensive was not a military disaster was controversial in 1968 but is now widely accepted by analysts across the political spectrum. See Peter Braestrup, *Big Story: How the American Press and Television Reported and Interpreted the Crises of Tet* (Boulder, Colo.: Westview, 1977), for a lengthy critical treatment of the news media's coverage of Tet in 1968.

7. Townsend Hoopes, *The Limits of Intervention* (New York: McKay, 1969), pp. 59–61, 150, 181, 185, 207, 218. Clifford cooperated with Hoopes when the

book was being written and obviously influenced its contents. Clifford's memoirs, *Counsel to the President* (coauthored by Richard Holbrooke) (New York: Random House, 1991), are certainly more nuanced but stress that Clifford had only a few allies in a "war" for the president's mind. John M. Blum's *Years of Discord: American Politics and Society, 1961-1974* (New York: Norton, 1991) fully accepts Hoopes's view of Clifford as the dovish hero of this period. See pp. 296-298 and Blum's acknowledgment of his reliance on Hoopes, pp. 495-496. See also Richard Goodwin's *Remembering America* (Boston: Little, Brown, 1988), p. 486: "Leadership [in early 1968] was in the hands of a man I knew had an uncertain, intermittent grip on reality."

8. Herbert Schandler, *Lyndon Johnson and Vietnam: The Unmaking of a President* (Princeton, N.J.: Princeton University Press, 1983), pp. 256-259, 326-327, 330, 338. Unlike Schandler's generally sound account, this chapter focuses on the advocacy of certain advisers without formal foreign policy advisory status — Hubert Humphrey, McGeorge Bundy, and Abe Fortas. Schandler deals with Bundy and Fortas only as part of the Wise Men's group. Melvin Small's *Johnson, Nixon, and the Doves* (New Brunswick, N.J.: Rutgers University Press, 1988) is an important account that accepts the old view of Clark Clifford "turning around" an escalation-minded Lyndon Johnson just before his March 13 speech (see pp. 142-148). Larry Berman's *Lyndon Johnson's War: The Road to Stalemate in Vietnam* (New York: Norton, 1989) curiously reverts to Hoopes's interpretation of the period: "It was left to Clark Clifford as secretary of defense to convince Johnson that Vietnam had become a sinkhole" (p. 203; see also pp. 189, 191, 199-200). Dean Rusk virtually fades from view in the climactic March 1968 period in Berman's account. As much or more than Hoopes, Berman lays the blame for U.S. failure in Vietnam squarely on Johnson. See his conclusion on p. 203.

9. Christian, oral history, p. III, 24, LBJ Library.

10. *Congressional Record*, January 29, 1968, p. III, 24, LBJ Library.

11. January 30, 1968, the president's meeting with Democratic leadership, 8:30-10:00 A.M., Tom Johnson's notes, box 2, LBJ Library.

12. Westmoreland to Wheeler and Sharp, January 30, 1968, folder 28, History file, Westmoreland Papers, box 15; Bunker to Johnson, February 8, 1968, folder: Vietnam 8 B (1) [A], NS Country file: Vietnam, boxes 104-106, LBJ Library. Bunker advised Johnson that it was necessary for the United States and South Vietnamese to "take the initiative" and go on the offensive against the Vietcong. This, he said, would probably take some additional U.S. troops.

13. McPherson, *Political Education*, p. 423; David Lilienthal, *The Journals of David Lilienthal, vol. 7: Unfinished Business, 1968-1981* (New York: Harper and Row, 1983), p. 28.

14. *Congressional Quarterly Weekly Report*, February 9, 1968, pp. 229, 246.

15. January 30, 1968, president's meeting with Dirksen and Ford, 6:04-7:55 P.M., Tom Johnson's notes, box 2, LBJ Library; *Congressional Record*, January 29, 1968, p. 1234.

16. Quoted in *Congressional Record*, January 30, 1968, p. 1473.

17. In the fall of 1967, the Gallup poll showed 52 percent disapproving of his handling of Vietnam, with only 35 percent approving. All figures are taken from the *Gallup Opinion Index*, April 1968, p. 3, and December 1968, p. 2.

18. John E. Mueller, *War, Presidents, and Public Opinion* (New York: Wiley, 1973), pp. 54-55.

19. Special file: CBS Interviews, "Why I Chose Not to Run," folder: Transcript-original, p. 89, LBJ Library.
20. Schandler, *Unmaking*, pp. 92, 95.
21. Tom Johnson's notes, February 6, 1968, box 1, LBJ Library.
22. Tom Johnson's notes, February 9, 1968, box 2, and February 10, 1968, box 3, LBJ Library.
23. Taylor to Johnson, February 10, 1968, NS file, NS history, March 31 speech, box 49, LBJ Library; Maxwell Taylor, *Swords and Plowshares* (New York: Norton, 1972), pp. 388–389, shows Taylor's views slightly later on. Tom Johnson's notes, February 10 and 11, 1968, box 3, LBJ Library.
24. See Wheeler to Westmoreland, February 13, 1968, Westmoreland Papers, box 16, LBJ Library. Westmoreland's second cable is quoted in Schandler, *Unmaking*, pp. 98–99; reaction to it is in Tom Johnson's notes, February 12, 1968, box 2, LBJ Library.
25. Wheeler to Sharp and Westmoreland, February 1, 1968, March 31 speech, vol. 1, NS file, NSC history, box 48; NSC meeting, February 7, 1968, Tom Johnson's notes, box 2, LBJ Library.
26. Folder: "Jan. 31, 1968 [Cong. leaders]," p. 35, Meeting notes file, box 2, LBJ Library. I have added what seems appropriate punctuation.
27. William Berman, *William Fulbright and the Vietnam War* (Kent, Ohio: Kent State University Press, 1988), p. 93. Fulbright was responsible in part for bringing Rostow into government circles. Nancy Dickerson, an NBC reporter who once worked for the Foreign Relations Committee, recalls Rostow being given a job in the 1950s by the committee, with Fulbright's help. See her *Among Those Present* (New York: Ballantine Books, 1977), p. 161.
28. Rusk, personal interview; Doris Kearns, *Lyndon Johnson and the American Dream* (New York: Harper and Row, 1976), p. 318. Valenti, of course, was by then an outside adviser to Johnson.
29. "The Mar. 31 Speech," summary account by Robert Ginsburgh, file: Mar. 31 speech, vol. 1; Rostow to Johnson, January 22, 1968, folder: Rostow memos, NS file, Name file, box 6, LBJ Library.
30. Tom Johnson's notes, February 6, 1968, box 1, LBJ Library.
31. Notes of meeting with Democratic congressional leadership, February 6, 1968, Tom Johnson's notes, box 2, LBJ Library. I have placed quotation marks around "mismanagement" because President Johnson thought that the charge was wrong.
32. Tom Johnson's notes, February 6, 1968, box 1, LBJ Library.
33. Tom Johnson's notes, February 9, 1968, pp. 13, 14, box 2, LBJ Library.
34. Lady Bird Johnson, *A White House Diary* (New York: Holt, Rinehart, and Winston, 1970), p. 685.
35. Johnson, *White House Diary*, pp. 690–691.
36. Johnson, *White House Diary*, pp. 692–693; Kearns, *Lyndon Johnson*, p. 342.
37. Johnson to Secretary of State, Secretary of Defense, and Director of Bureau of Budget, January 31, 1968, file: March 31 speech, vol. 1, NS file, NSC history, box 48, LBJ Library.
38. Wheeler to Westmoreland and Sharp, January 31, 1968, Westmoreland Papers, folder #28, box 15, LBJ Library.
39. On possible emissaries, see Robert Ginsburgh to Rostow, November 8, 1968, file: March 31 speech, vol. 1, NS file, NSC history, box 48, LBJ Library; Johnson, *Vantage Point*, pp. 389, 415.

40. Wheeler to Westmoreland and Admiral Sharp, March 8, 1968, Westmoreland Papers, box 16, LBJ Library. Congressman F. Edward Hebert, who was influential on defense matters, compared Clifford and McNamara. The latter was "just a computer," but Clifford was the "greatest pitchman I ever met . . . a real con artist. And you loved it, and you knew it was happening to you." Hebert, oral history, p. I, 43–44, LBJ Library. Among the civilian Pentagon leaders were Paul Warnke, assistant secretary of defense for international security affairs; Paul Nitze, deputy secretary of defense; and Phil Goulding, deputy secretary of defense for public affairs. See Schandler, *Unmaking*, p. 124; Phil Goulding, *Confirm or Deny* (New York: Harper and Row, 1970), ch. 10.

41. Hoopes to Clifford, February 13, 1968, Vietnam 3G 5/67–8/68, NSF Country file: Vietnam, boxes 81–84, LBJ Library; also quoted in Hoopes, *Intervention*, pp. 151–155. Typical of reactions to Clifford's appointment was that of David Lilienthal: "The President picked this way of telling the world that, come what may, he is going to continue his commitment to a military road to some kind of settlement in Vietnam. Those of us who hoped that a new 'fresh' mind would tackle this intractable and tragic stalemate won't get much comfort from this nomination." Lilienthal, *Journals*, vol. 7, p. 8.

42. Rostow to Bunker, February 27, 1968, file: March 31 speech, vol. 1, NS file, NS history, box 48, LBJ Library.

43. Maxwell Taylor to Richard Helms, February 23, 1968, file: March 31 speech, vol. 4, NS file, NSC history, box 48, LBJ Library. Taylor later wrote, "After going over the available documentary evidence and talking to many officials, we concluded that there was nothing to indicate that a lack of information had caused any American unit to fail to carry out its assigned mission at the time of the enemy attack. That did not mean, of course, that our commanders knew in advance the time, place, and intensity of every attack made. Intelligence is rarely that explicit" (*Swords and Plowshares*, p. 383).

44. Sent to Johnson by Rostow with accompanying summary, February 16, 1968, file: March 31 speech, vol. 1, NS file, NSC history, box 48, LBJ Library. Helms also confirmed this to Johnson: "They thought a political uprising would take place. They did not get it." See Tom Johnson's notes, February 20, 1968, box 2, LBJ Library.

45. Tom Johnson's notes, February 20, 1968, box 2, LBJ Library.

46. McPherson, *Political Education*, p. 426. I have put quotation marks around "It might start a wider war" because clearly the pilot was sarcastically enunciating the views of others. McPherson believes that Johnson, in an adjoining stateroom, heard part of the conversation. The president did report such sentiments of the sailors at his subsequent Tuesday meeting.

47. Tom Johnson's notes, February 20, 1968, box 2, LBJ Library; Johnson to Eisenhower, February 22, 1968, file: President Lyndon B. Johnson, 1968, Postpresidency, Gettysburg-Indio Collection, box 2, Eisenhower Library. Johnson and Eisenhower traded many letters for the rest of the year.

48. Russell to Johnson, December 21, 1967, Series I J 7, Famous people file, 1967–69, Russell Library. On the Congo airlift, see W. W. Rostow, *The Diffusion of Power: An Essay in Recent History* (New York: Macmillan, 1972), pp. 405, 411. On Russell's contacts with Johnson and other top officials of the administration, see Series II-4 files of January through March, Russell Library. Russell occasionally spent time with Lynda Bird Johnson, as indicated in the Series II-4 files and Series XV Gen. EE Red Line file, box 5, Russell Library. Judging by notes scrawled by Russell on the back of an envelope, the senator questioned

sending the emergency troops to Vietnam in early February. The envelope is in Series XV, Gen. Red Line (Winder), Russell Library.

49. Johnson, *Vantage Point*, pp. 395–396.

50. "Notes of President's Meeting with Senior Foreign Policy Advisers," February 9, 1968, file: March 31 speech, vol. 7, NS file, NS history, box 49.

51. Johnson to Fulbright, February 8, 1968, with cover memo indicating Johnson's comment on the letter, February 21, 1968, Office of the President file: Fulbright, box 4, LBJ Library. The secretary (who, like many Johnson aides, perhaps knew when Johnson preferred them to ignore his temper) saved the letter and noted Johnson's comment. Johnson may have approved of Rusk's testimony in order to save a foreign aid bill under consideration by Fulbright's committee; see Berman, *Fulbright*, p. 96. The President's daily diary at the LBJ Library shows five occasions when Fulbright was in group meetings with Johnson in the January–March period. They talked by phone once in January and again on April 1, the day after Johnson's retirement speech. On May 1, they met one-on-one for 11 minutes.

52. William Westmoreland, *A Soldier Reports* (Garden City, N.Y.: Doubleday, 1976), p. 354.

53. Westmoreland, *A Soldier Reports*, p. 355.

54. Rostow to Johnson (passing on Wheeler's cable), February 25, 1968, March 31 speech, vol. 1, NS file, NSC history, box 48, LBJ Library.

55. NSC aide Robert Ginsburgh wrote to Walt Rostow on November 18, 1968: "What were the reasons for the President's being initially upset by General Westmoreland's troops recommendations? Unexpected size of the requirements? Manner of presentation? Defense opposition? Leaks?" Ginsburgh was preparing an NSC history of the March 31, 1968, speech for Rostow and the president. See Ginsburgh to Rostow, March 31 speech, vol. 1, NS file, NS history, box 48, LBJ Library.

56. Author David Halberstam (who wrote a colorful, critical account of Johnson in *The Best and the Brightest* [New York: Random House, 1972]) criticized Johnson for portraying Clifford in a misleading fashion in *The Vantage Point* by using quotations selectively. (See the *New York Times* book review section, October 31, 1971, pp. 1, 10, 12, 14, 16.) The Clifford quotation comes from Meeting notes, February 27, 1968, box 2, LBJ Library. In describing this meeting on p. 484, Clifford's *Counsel to the President* does not mention his remarks.

57. Meeting notes file, February 27, 1968, box 2; Rostow to Johnson, February 27, 1968, March 31 speech, vol. 1, NS file, NSC history, box 48, LBJ Library.

58. Tom Johnson's notes, February 28, 1968, box 2, LBJ Library; Wheeler to Johnson, "Military Situation . . . ," February 17, 1968, NS Country file: Vietnam, box 127, LBJ Library; also Johnson, *Vantage Point*, pp. 390–393.

59. Rostow to Johnson (reporting on the first task force meeting), February 28, 1968, NS Country file: Vietnam, box 127, LBJ Library.

60. Hoopes, *Intervention*, pp. 165, 167; Lilienthal, *Journals*, vol. 6, p. 529. His description of McNamara is from another meeting from the same period. Norman C. Thomas and Harold Wolman, "Policy Formulation in the Institutionalized Presidency: The Johnson Task Forces," in Thomas Cronin and Sanford Greenberg (eds.), *The Presidential Advisory System* (New York: Harper and Row, 1969), p. 127; Henry Trewhitt, *McNamara* (New York: Harper and Row, 1971), ch. 11.

61. David McClellan and Dean Acheson (eds.), *Among Friends: Personal Letters of Dean Acheson* (New York: Dodd, Mead, 1980), p. 297; Walter Isaacson and Evan Thomas, *The Wise Men* (New York: Simon and Schuster, 1986), p. 680. The authors, perhaps following Hoopes's *Limits of Intervention*, place the Johnson-Acheson meeting on February 27, but Johnson was in Texas that day. It presumably occurred the next night.

62. Johnson, *Vantage Point*, pp. 388–389.

63. Isaacson and Thomas, *Wise Men*, p. 686.

64. Hoopes, *Intervention*, pp. 204–205.

65. Johnson, *Vantage Point*, p. 394.

66. Johnson, *White House Diary*, pp. 701, 703; Thomas Schoenbaum, *Waging Peace and War: Dean Rusk in the Truman, Kennedy, and Johnson Years* (New York: Simon and Schuster, 1988), pp. 469–471; and Rusk oral interview II, tape 2, p. 11, LBJ Library. It was not just supposed doves in the administration, such as Clifford, who were unaware of Rusk's evolution of thought; Maxwell Taylor was surprised by Rusk's advocacy of a bombing halt in the March meetings he attended that led up to the president's March 31 speech. He wrote that Rusk's "change on this point should have alerted me to the probability that something unusual was up" (see *Swords and Plowshares*, p. 391).

67. Accounts such as Hoopes's *Intervention* suggesting that Rusk favored troop increases (p. 175) are incorrect. They seemingly grew out of the assumption of Clifford and others that Rusk felt as Wheeler and Rostow did. These assumptions were passed on to various authors and journalists in the late 1960s and 1970s. See the Rusk oral interview II, tape 2, p. 14, LBJ Library, plus transcripts of meetings cited in this chapter, none of which shows Rusk favoring serious troop increases.

68. Clark Clifford, "A Viet Nam Reappraisal: The Personal History of One Man's View and How It Evolved," *Foreign Affairs* 47, 4 (July 1969): 610–611.

69. Clifford, "Viet Nam Reappraisal," p. 613.

70. This did not necessarily mean giving Westmoreland 200,000 troops. Taylor had favored sending limited emergency reinforcements, putting on hold a decision about further troops for Vietnam, and calling up the reserves in order to strengthen the United States' strategic position worldwide. Like many doves, Taylor thought that Westmoreland should assume a more defensive position with his soldiers in Vietnam. See Taylor, *Swords and Plowshares*, pp. 388–389.

71. Hoopes, *Intervention*, pp. 173–175; Schandler, *Unmaking*, pp. 143–156, 173.

72. Johnson, *Vantage Point*, p. 397. Rostow to Johnson, March 4, 1968, DSDUF, box 4; "Draft memorandum for the President," (summarizing the task force report), March 4, 1968, NS Country file: Vietnam, box 127; Wheeler, oral history, p. II, 8, LBJ Library.

73. Rostow to Johnson, March 6, 1968, folder: Vietnam, March 19, 1970, Decision to Halt Bombing, 1967, 1968; NS file, Country file: Vietnam, box 127, LBJ Library. Blum's *Years of Discord* misleadingly says that the report "granted substantially everything the military had asked for" (see p. 296).

74. "The President with the Press Aboard Air Force I Enroute to Puerto Rico," March 2, 1968, Tom Johnson's notes, box 1, LBJ Library.

75. Cronkite, quoted in Kathleen Turner, *Lyndon Johnson's Dual War: Vietnam and the Press* (Chicago: University of Chicago Press, 1985), p. 231. Another broadcast journalist, Frank McGee, said 10 days later, "the time is at hand when we must decide whether it is futile to destroy Vietnam in order to

save it" (ibid.). On Johnson's reaction to Cronkite, see George Christian, special oral history interview by David Culbertson, pp. 13–14, LBJ Library. Christian, who discussed the broadcast with Johnson, is also utterly convinced that the influence of Cronkite's broadcast on Johnson has been overstated by some Vietnam histories that suggest "that Cronkite had . . . a major role in changing national policy or something. Well, I don't buy that. It didn't quite happen that way."

76. Johnson, *Vantage Point*, p. 396.

77. Tom Johnson's notes, March 4, 1968, box 2; Rusk to Johnson, March 4, 1968, NS Country file: Vietnam, box 127; Rusk oral history, p. II, 11, LBJ Library. See also Schoenbaum, *Waging Peace*, p. 470; Clifford, *Counsel*, p. 496; and Johnson, *Vantage Point*, p. 399.

78. Tom Johnson's notes, March 12, 1968, box 2, LBJ Library.

79. Tom Johnson's notes, March 6, 1968, box 2; statement with Rusk's name at the bottom, March 5, 1968, in file: Vietnam, March 19, 1970, "Decision to Halt Bombing, 1967, 1968," tab V, box 127, LBJ Library. Clifford seems to refer to the Rusk idea in a brief memo to Wheeler, March 5, 1968, Clifford Papers, box 2, LBJ Library.

80. Rostow to Johnson, "Subject: Decision to Halt Bombing," NS file, Country file: Vietnam, box 127, pp. 8–10, LBJ Library.

81. See the President's daily diary for March 1968, LBJ Library.

82. Johnson's handwriting is on a cover memo from Rostow to Johnson, February 29, 1968, regarding William Douglas's previously cited report to Johnson, in "Vietnam, Mar. 19, 1970, Decision to halt bombing," NS Country file: Vietnam, box 127, LBJ Library. In the same box, see also Rostow to Johnson, March 4, 1968.

83. Isaacson and Thomas, *Wise Men*, p. 690; *Times* quote from *The Pentagon Papers: The Gravel Edition* (Boston: Beacon Press, 1971), vol. 4, p. 588; Rostow quoted in Schandler, *Unmaking*, p. 202; Tom Johnson's notes, March 19, 1968, box 2; Wheeler's description of the impact of such stories is in his cable to Westmoreland, March 12, 1968, Westmoreland Papers, box 16, LBJ Library.

84. Richard Rusk, in an interview with Clark Clifford, tape XX, p. 18, Rusk Papers, Russell Library. The Rusk Papers were the source for Rusk's memoirs, *As I Saw It*, as told to Richard Rusk and edited by Daniel Papp (New York: Norton, 1990). Rusk granted me access to these papers prior to the publication of his book.

85. Schandler, *Unmaking*, p. 202.

86. Hoopes, *Intervention*, pp. 180–181. Hoopes's access to Clifford made the account of this meeting possible. He writes (mistakenly, I think), "with respect to Vietnam nothing was so deeprooted as the President's instinctive bellicosity and will to win." White House speechwriter Harry McPherson shared all Hoopes's doubts about the war but had access to Johnson almost daily in the latter years of the administration—something Hoopes lacked as under secretary of the air force. (After Johnson left office he acted as if he never knew Hoopes—perhaps he did not—and asked friends after the book came out, "Who is this Hoop-eez?" See Richard Helms oral interview, p. II, 28, LBJ Library.) McPherson saw a president who "was trying to summon up just enough martial spirit and determination in the people to sustain limited war, but not so much as to unleash the hounds of passion that would force him to widen it. He was trying to thwart China's purposes, by thwarting its deputy, and to get away with

that without taking on China directly. He was negotiating with the Russians over a nuclear nonproliferation treaty, and hoped to conclude an arms limitation agreement with them; this while Soviet munitions poured down the Ho Chi Minh trail, aimed at America's sons" (*A Political Education*, p. 394).

87. Lodge to Rusk, copy sent to Johnson, March 5, 1968, March 31 speech, vol. 4, NS file, NSC history, LBJ Library. On Lodge's access to Johnson when the ambassador was both in and out of office, Lodge wrote, "during the whole period from the end of 1963 to 1968 that I worked for President Johnson, I never had the slightest difficulty in getting his attention and therefore had no reason to 'complain.' . . . [Johnson] was always courteous and considerate of me. Far from being inaccessible, he gave of himself unstintingly." *New York Times*, May 21, 1972, p. 14. Wheeler to Johnson, March 11, 1968, file: March 31 speech, vol. 4, NS file, NSC history, box 48, LBJ Library.

88. Isaacson and Thomas, *Wise Men*, p. 694; Acheson, "Meeting with the President . . . ," March 14, 1968, in McClellan and Acheson, *Among Friends*, p. 292. Charles Kaiser's *1968 in America* (New York: Weidenfeld and Nicolsen, 1988) is a recent history (drawing on *Wise Men*, which draws on Hoopes's *Intervention*) that pictures Acheson dealing with an angry, emotional Johnson but fails to describe this key unemotional meeting of March 14. See pp. 125–126.

89. Isaacson and Thomas, *Wise Men*, p. 694; Rostow, Memo: "Summary of Dean Acheson's Proposal," March 14, 1968, file: March 31 speech, vol. 4, NS file, NSC history, box 48, LBJ Library. Acheson recalled suggesting that younger figures within the government form such a commission to study the situation in Vietnam rather than employing outsiders. Rostow and Johnson seem to have thought that Acheson had in mind a group made up in part of those no longer in government. Despite Acheson's skepticism, Rostow listened well enough to fairly and unemotionally summarize Acheson's major ideas in his memo to Johnson. See also McClellan and Acheson, *Among Friends*, p. 294.

90. Johnson, *White House Diary*, p. 702.

91. Roche oral history, p. I, 60, LBJ Library; Lewis Chester, Godfrey Hodgson, and Bruce Page, *An American Melodrama: The Presidential Campaign of 1968* (New York: Viking, 1969). Early reports showed Johnson with 49 percent and McCarthy with 42 percent of the votes, but with Republican write-ins included, there was less than a 1 percent difference in the two candidates' vote totals. But even the larger 7 percent victory margin for Johnson was widely perceived as a defeat, since McCarthy had not been expected to do well.

92. Arthur Schlesinger, *Robert Kennedy and His Times* (Boston: Houghton Mifflin, 1978), pp. 914, 926; Clifford, "Memorandum of Conference with Sen. Robert Kennedy . . ."; transcript of telephone conversation (between D. Pierson and T. Sorensen), both March 14, 1968, White House famous names, box 6, LBJ Library.

93. McPherson, *Political Education*, pp. 427–428.

94. Schandler, *Unmaking*, p. 248; Rostow to Johnson, March 11, 1968, March 31 speech, vol. 4, NS file, NSC history, box 48, LBJ Library. About the American people, McPherson wrote to the president, "Maybe they have never had it so good, but neither have they been so uneasy, at least in my lifetime." McPherson to Johnson, March 28, 1968, copy provided to the author by George Christian, Austin, Texas.

95. McPherson says that Rowe was also the first person to whom Johnson offered an apology after becoming president. McPherson oral history, p. I, 27, and II, 27; Rowe to Johnson, March 19, 1968, Reference file: Vietnam, box 2,

both LBJ Library. On Rowe's role in Johnson's political career, see Rowland Evans and Robert Novak, *Lyndon B. Johnson: The Exercise of Power* (New York: New American Library,1966), pp. 110, 346–347.

96. Fortas to Johnson, mailed on March 12, 1968, folder: "Abe Fortas," files pertaining to Abe Fortas and Homer Thornberry, box 1, LBJ Library. Other hawkish proposals were percolating: The Southeast Asia Coordinating Committee (SEACORD), composed of American ambassadors including Bunker plus Admiral Sharp and General Westmoreland, recommended: "Contingency planning for possible limited ground operations by U.S. and/or ARVN forces in Laos should proceed." NS file, NSC history, March 31 speech, vol. 4, tabs N–Z, AA–KK, LBJ Library.

97. Bruce A. Murphy's *Fortas: The Rise and Ruin of a Supreme Court Justice* (New York: William Morrow, 1988) makes this claim, but his analysis sees the president too much in the context of his relationship with Fortas and too little in the context of Johnson's intimate relationships with many others. Fortas, he writes, was Johnson's "one unswerving supporter." The president "would appreciate every word" of Fortas's "incredibly bloodthirsty" advice (see pp. 256–259).

98. Document prepared by Dept. of State, March 7, 1968, at Johnson's request; file: March 31 speech, vol. 4, NSC file: NSC history, LBJ Library.

99. Johnson called Cousins to invite him to the White House. A partial account of the meeting is in Papers of George Christian, Christian notes 1968, box 1, LBJ Library. The meeting with Cousins is described in a March 19, 1968, memo from Edgar Berman to Hubert Humphrey. Berman says that Cousins told him that he pushed Johnson to use Humphrey as his special emissary to meet in any suitable place with representatives of the North Vietnamese. Berman's memo is based on Cousins's description of the meeting in a phone call with Berman, a Humphrey confidant. File: Berman memos to VP, 1968, Minnesota Historical Society.

100. Goldberg to Johnson, sent by Rostow with accompanying remarks to Johnson at his ranch, March 16, 1968, file: Vietnam, March 1970, Memo to President, Decision to halt bombing, NS file, Country file: Vietnam, box 127, LBJ Library. Johnson once compared George Ball's importance as an adviser to that of Goldberg: Ball was a principal, strategic adviser, he said, but "I never felt Goldberg was a strategic adviser at all. I just felt he presented our policy at the United Nations." Lyndon Johnson oral interview with William Jorden, August 12, 1969, LBJ Library.

101. Ibid.; Rostow to Johnson, March 16, 1968, file: March 31 speech, vol. 4, NS file, NSC history, LBJ Library.

102. Rostow to Johnson, March 15, 1968, file: March 31 speech, vol. 4, NS file, NSC history, LBJ Library. Notes from a Tuesday Lunch on November 4, 1967, have Johnson saying that "he does not like to override his man in the field (Bunker) nor does he like to see McNamara and Rusk override him." Meeting notes file, box 2, LBJ Library.

103. Lilienthal, *Journals*, vol. 6, p. 509.

104. Pearson to Johnson, March 11, 1968, and Johnson to Pearson, March 12, 1968, NS file, Country file: Vietnam, box 127, LBJ Library.

105. Rusk to Bunker, March 16, 1968, March 31 speech, vol. 4, NS file, NSC history, box 48, LBJ Library. Rusk even told Bunker that "higher authority" (i.e., Johnson) had not seen the two proposals, which was not true. Regarding the message's "literally eyes only" status, a hierarchy of levels of secrecy was

attached to government memoranda: "Confidential" and "Secret" memoranda were not as secret as "Top Secret," "Eyes Only," and "Literally Eyes Only" documents.

106. Bunker to Rusk, March 30, 1968, file: March 31 speech, vol. 4, NS file, NSC history, box 48, LBJ Library; also Johnson, *Vantage Point*, p. 411.

107. Tom Johnson's notes, March 19, 1968, box 2, LBJ Library.

108. On Johnson's shouting, the story was reported in Hoopes, *Intervention*, p. 185, and repeated in Bernard Kalb and Elie Abel, *Roots of Involvement: The U.S. in Asia* (New York: Norton, 1971), p. 230, and Don Oberdorfer, *Tet: The Turning Point in the Vietnam War* (Garden City, N.Y.: Doubleday, 1971), p. 296. It is discounted by Schandler, *Unmaking*, p. 239.

109. Tom Johnson's notes, March 20, 1968, box 2, LBJ Library.

110. Johnson, *Vantage Point*, pp. 413, 415. On Westmoreland's willingness to accept 13,500 more troops, see Tom Johnson's notes, (March 26, 1968, box 2, LBJ Library) of the president's meeting of Wheeler and Abrams. On the bombing, see the original transcript of "CBS-TV's 'Why I Chose Not to Run,'" p. 44, box 1, LBJ Library. Johnson's memory was as fallible as anyone else's after he left office, but he pinpoints the response from Bunker as virtually clinching his decision on the bombing proposals. Rusk oral history, p. II, 12, LBJ Library.

111. Small, *Johnson, Nixon*, p. 147, n. 60. Small's treatment of Clifford is typical in mistakenly judging him as the almost lone antiescalation adviser of this period.

112. Rostow, interview with the author, January 20, 1989. Rusk oral history II, tape 2, p. 13; Schoenbaum, *Waging Peace*, p. 457; Johnson, *Vantage Point*, p. 428; on Clifford, see McPherson, *Political Education*, p. 438.

113. Schandler, *Unmaking*, p. 242; Hoopes, *Intervention*, p. 207.

114. McPherson, *Political Education*, p. 431; on McPherson's attendance at meetings, see his oral history, interview 4, tape 1, p. 2, LBJ Library.

115. Schandler, *Unmaking*, p. 244.

116. See Tom Johnson's notes, March 19, 1968, box 2, for a discussion in which Clifford and others urged Johnson to hold a meeting with precisely the same men he had met in November 1967. Wheeler told the president, "I would get the views of the same men. A reappraisal might be important indicators of public opinion." See also Clifford oral history, tape 3, p. 2, LBJ Library.

117. Meeting notes file, March 22, 1968, Tuesday Lunch, box 2, LBJ Library. For impressions, see McPherson, *Political Education*, p. 432; Schandler, *Unmaking*, pp. 252–253.

118. McPherson to Johnson, March 23, 1968, file: March 31 speech, vol. 4, NS file, NSC history, box 48, LBJ Library; McPherson, *Political Education*, pp. 431–433.

119. McPherson, *Political Education*, p. 435. McPherson is unclear as to whether Rusk referred specifically to the McPherson memo or the Goldberg/Rusk proposals sent to Bunker earlier that month. See also Johnson, *Vantage Point*, p. 419. On the same day, Rusk reminded Johnson in a memo of his suggestion along those lines earlier in the month and added, "the McPherson suggestion is a very constructive one." Rostow to Johnson, Rusk to Johnson, both March 25, 1968, NS file, NSC history, March 31 speech, vol. 4, tabs N–Z, AA–KK, LBJ Library.

120. Westmoreland, *Soldier*, p. 361. Westmoreland's history notes, March 23, 1968; Johnson to Westmoreland, March 23, 1968, Westmoreland Papers, box 16, both LBJ Library. After the war, Ellsworth Bunker told author Neil

Sheehan that Westmoreland had been "kicked upstairs"; see Sheehan, *A Bright Shining Lie: John Paul Vann and America in Vietnam* (New York: Random House, 1988), p. 720.

121. Westmoreland, *Soldier*, pp. 358–359; Westmoreland's history notes, March 24, 1968, Westmoreland Papers, box 16, LBJ Library.

122. Ibid. See also General Earle Wheeler, oral history, p. II, 9–12, LBJ Library.

123. Humphrey, transcript of tape recording for his autobiography, January 1975, p. 4. Autobiography files, 24 C 9 1B, Minnesota Historical Society.

124. Hubert Humphrey, *The Education of a Public Man* (Garden City, N.Y.: Doubleday, 1976), p. 357. This book speaks of the executive branch becoming "a kind of closed society" as the war went on, but, even judging by Humphrey's own memoir, the president was more open to Humphrey as a member of that "society" in the later stages of the administration than he had been in 1965. See pp. 350–358. But, as Jack Valenti has said, administration members "don't really know why a President came to a certain decision because they're not privy to all that was fed into his mind and heart before the decision was made." Valenti oral interview, p. III-6, LBJ Library. A measure of Humphrey's access to Johnson during early 1968 is Humphrey's calendar, which shows him with Johnson for two hours on the night of January 31 and seeing him again three times on February 1. Humphrey's calendar is in Miscellaneous Unprocessed Materials box, Minnesota Historical Society.

On March 20, 1968, Humphrey gave a memo to Johnson that was written by a Humphrey friend. It advocated stopping bombing above the 20th parallel, sending no more U.S. troops, and allowing the Vietcong to participate in South Vietnam's government. The memo "merits your reading and consideration," Humphrey told Johnson. HHH Memos to LBJ, 1968, VP White House Papers, 24 F 8 2F, Minnesota Historical Society.

125. Johnson, *White House Diary*, pp. 705–706.

126. Temple oral history, p. III, 1, LBJ Library; Johnson, *Vantage Point*, p. 419.

127. Tom Johnson's notes, March 26, 1968, box 2, LBJ Library. The notes show the president referring to the 20th parallel bombing halt as "Clifford's plan." One can only guess if Tom Johnson made a mistake taking notes or if Johnson purposely described what was originally Rusk's idea as actually being Clifford's. On the gold crisis, see Johnson, *Vantage Point*, pp. 317–318, 537.

128. Rusk to Johnson, March 25, 1968, March 31 speech, vol. 4, NS file, NS history, LBJ Library; also the "Mar. 31 speech" report by Robert Ginsburgh, November 8, 1968, p. 23, in March 31 speech, vol. 1, NS file, NS history, box 48, LBJ Library.

129. Rostow to Johnson, March 25, 1968, March 31 speech meeting notes, vol. 7, NS file, NS history, box 49, LBJ Library.

130. On March 22, Bundy wrote another memorandum to Johnson saying, among other things, "I want to put some comments that are just too private to go to anyone else, even Walt [Rostow] and Harry [McPherson]. . . . I agree with those who are worried about the line in Vietnam in your Minneapolis speech. If we get tagged as mindless hawks, we can lose both the election and the war . . . that's what I found dead wrong in Abe Fortas' advice on Wednesday—although he was dead right about the need to avoid empty peace gestures right now." Bundy agreed with Goldberg on the need for a bombing halt, however: "Nothing less will do." At the time he wrote the memo, Bundy "assumed" that

Johnson had decided to send 40,000 more troops to Vietnam but perceptively added, "If I am wrong on this, then I must say I hope you will reconsider it." The Bundy memos show a sensitivity to Johnson's operating style that matches that of Rusk and exceeds Clifford's: Bundy recognized that although Johnson appeared to have made a final decision to send 40,000 more troops to Vietnam, no Johnson decision was final until virtually the moment of its announcement. See Bundy memos to Johnson, March 21 and 22, 1969, Office files of the President: M. Bundy, box 1, LBJ Library.

131. George Ball, *The Past Has Another Pattern* (New York: Norton, 1982), p. 408.

132. Oberdorfer's *Tet* has an excellent account of this meeting (pp. 309–315), which is consistent in tone with my other source, "Mar. 26, 1968 – 3:15 PM, Special Advisory Group," Meeting notes file, box 2, LBJ Library. President Johnson's handwritten notes of the meeting are also available in the same folder. Also see Clifford, *Counsel to the President*, pp. 511–519. On Ball's departure from the administration, see Ball to Johnson, September 17, 1966, NS file, Memos to President, box 10, LBJ Library. Typical of those who were substantively urging Johnson toward a form of disengagement but were uncomfortable with the word itself was Lodge, who wrote to the president after the meeting that he was for a shift in policy toward "organization of South Vietnamese society" generally away from "search and destroy" but that he was against "disengagement." Lodge to Johnson, March 27, 1968, March 31 speech, NS file, NSC history, box 49, LBJ Library. The ambiguity of hawks was typified by Bradley, who favored some sort of bombing halt and sending "only support troops" but told Johnson, "let's not show them that we are in any way weakening."

133. Carver's account of the restaging of the briefing comes from Thomas Powers's *The Man Who Kept the Secrets* (New York: Knopf, 1979), p. 220. Hoopes's account of the meeting shows Johnson less appreciative of Carver's briefing; see pp. 217–218. There is a set of handwritten notes suggesting that the meeting ranged more widely over other topics; see "CIA-DoD Briefing by Gen. Dupuy and George Carver," Tom Johnson's notes, March 27, 1968, box 2, LBJ Library.

134. Johnson, *Vantage Point*, p. 418; see also Johnson's recollection of the briefings in a conversation with Walter Cronkite in "CBS Interview: Why I Chose Not to Run," transcript – original (unedited), box 1, LBJ Library. It was Rusk's and Taylor's view as well that Tet and the media's coverage of it had affected the Wise Men as it had other Americans. See Rusk oral interview II, tape 2, p. 8, LBJ Library, and Taylor, *Swords and Plowshares*, p. 391.

135. Johnson, *Vantage Point*, pp. 419–420; Mansfield to Johnson, March 13, 1968, file: March 26, 1968 – 3:15 PM, Special Advisory Group, Meeting notes file, box 2, LBJ Library. Schandler's *Unmaking of a President* describes the meeting differently, based on correspondence with Mansfield some years after the meeting occurred. There Johnson is portrayed as not having decided in favor of a bombing limitation. But the best contemporaneous account is in the *Congressional Record* of April 2, 1968, p. 8569, which records Mansfield telling fellow senators: "I spent three hours with the President last Wednesday evening . . . the entire speech was read to me that evening, and I recall that in the speech a reference was made to a cessation of the bombing [above] the 20th parallel. . . . The President discussed at that time the cessation of bombing above the 20th parallel to protect the Marines and our troops stationed along the DMZ."

136. 1968 Datebook, Russell Library. The datebook was primarily used by Russell to keep track of the large amount of prescribed medications he was taking daily. Occasionally he would treat the datebook as a diary. Being treated as part of the Johnson family obviously meant a lot to Russell. He was a bachelor and was devoted to many young people, including his own nieces and nephews as well as the Johnson daughters. Back at the White House on April 3, he recorded in his datebook that he stayed after a meeting to have supper with Johnson and Luci and Lynda Bird: "both kissed me on arrival and departure about 1 AM + called me Uncle Dick." Of Russell, Lady Bird Johnson said, "Lyndon would over and over call him and get him to come over to see him, and a number of times, just the two of them." Lady Bird Johnson oral interview, pp. 23, 24, Russell Library. Johnson called Russell to discuss Clifford's appointment in January and had McNamara call Russell on January 30 about the beginning of the Tet Offensive, according to a scrawl made by Russell on an envelope. These notations are in Special presidential file, 1941–1967 and in the XV Gen. Red Line (Winder) file, Russell Library. Similarly, Dean Rusk had the impression that "Johnson talked to Russell probably four or five times a week." Rusk oral interview, p. 45, Russell Library.

137. *Congressional Record*, April 12, 1968, pp. 8570–8573; at Katzenbach's suggestion, specification of the 20th parallel was finally dropped from the speech. Katzenbach thought that it would have no meaning to most people. Johnson always specified the parallel to congressional leaders in their private meetings. See also Johnson, *Vantage Point*, pp. 420–421. The Russell speech foreshadows an imminent break in the intimacy of the Johnson-Russell relationship in the summer of 1968 over a judicial nomination advocated by Russell but pushed too slowly—in Russell's opinion—by Johnson, who had civil rights groups and his own attorney general to contend with on the nomination. See Tom Johnson's letter to Russell, July 3, 1968, White House central files, Name file: "Russell, 1-1-68 — ." The story is told in Chapter 14 of Murphy's *Fortas* with slight exaggeration—Russell and Johnson *did* have personal contacts with each other, though drastically fewer ones, during the remainder of the Johnson administration and by telephone and mail after the Johnson presidency. A year and a half after Russell's death and four months before Johnson died he responded personally to a letter from a little girl in Winder, Georgia: "Did you know that one of the greatest men of all came from Winder, Georgia? His name was Richard B. Russell and he represented Georgia in the United States Congress for many, many years." See the Post-presidential File: Sen. Richard Russell, LBJ Library. See also George Christian's oral history, p. IV, 8, LBJ Library, on the Russell-Johnson relationship after the summer of 1968.

138. "Mar. 20, 1968 Meeting with Advisers," Meeting notes file, box 2, and "Luncheon Meeting, Mar. 22, 1968," Diary backup, box 93, both LBJ Library. The notes of the March 20 meeting appear to be the handwriting of McPherson. At the March 22 meeting, Clifford suggested "a limited cessation of bombing above 20th parallel, with reciprocal action by the enemy by stopping shelling from the DMZ or just north of the DMZ." Rusk agreed but said that there should be no "hard conditions" on the enemy because they would not agree to them. On this issue, as on some others, Rusk was more dovish than Clifford.

139. "Mar. 20, 1968, Meeting with Advisers," and "Mar. 22, 1968 Luncheon Meeting," both Meeting notes file, box 2, LBJ Library.

140. Clifford, quoted in Rostow to Johnson, March 19, 1970, NS file, Country file: Vietnam, box 127, LBJ Library. Clifford recalls in an interview

with Richard Rusk (son of Dean Rusk), "In that morning, the whole tone of that speech was changed. It was not changed over the opposition of your father. I don't understand what was going on that day" (tape XX, p. 14, Rusk Papers, Russell Library). After leaving office, Dean Rusk explained why—if he and the president were tentatively planning a partial bombing halt—the speech draft wasn't changed until such a late date to reflect such a policy: The president's decision wasn't final until late March, "therefore you don't put things in them that the President hasn't decided on; and so it was only in the last two or three days that that particular part was added to the President's speech." Rusk, oral history, p. II, 123, LBJ Library. See also an interview with Rusk conducted by Richard Rusk and William Bundy, pp. 10–12, Rusk Papers, Russell Library. On March 10, 1969, *Newsweek* magazine published an article about the White House deliberations of this period, based primarily on reporter Charles Robert's conversations with Clifford and his former Pentagon associates. Harry McPherson criticizes the article for making "it appear as if Rusk was dragged, kicking and screaming, into a bombing limitation and was overpowered by numbers and that sort of thing." McPherson oral history, p. IV, 2, LBJ Library. See also Clifford, *Counsel*, p. 520.

141. Johnson, *Vantage Point*, p. 420.

142. Rusk to Bunker, March 28, 1968, file: March 31 speech, vol. 4, NS file, NSC history, LBJ Library. Also see William Bundy's conversation with Dean Rusk on the paternity of the March bombing halt in Dean Rusk oral history QQ, pp. 10–12, Rusk Papers, Russell Library. Rusk says that it took no "real effort" to move Johnson toward the bombing halt: "You see, every casualty in Vietnam took a little piece out of Lyndon Johnson. I remember driving with him through a relatively small, Texas town. And people were out on the side-walks to wave and say hello. He looked at them and he said, 'Dean, those are the mommies and daddies of our men in Vietnam.' It was always on his mind."

143. Johnson, *Vantage Point*, p. 421.

144. Wheeler, oral history, p. II, 14, LBJ Library.

145. CIA memo, March 28, 1968, NS file, NSC history, March 31 speech, vol. 4, tabs N–Z, AA–KK, LBJ Library. Jack Valenti, *A Very Human President* (New York: Pocket Books, 1977), p. 271.

146. Johnson, *White House Diary*, p. 708; Turner, *Lyndon Johnson's Dual War*, p. 247. Johnson, *Vantage Point*, p. 431.

147. Johnson, *Vantage Point*, p. 434.

148. Johnson, *Vantage Point*, p. 435. Even on the morning of March 31, John-son showed Humphrey two different endings to the speech—one a retirement announcement, the other a routine close. See Humphrey, *Education*, p. 358.

149. *Congressional Record*, April 2, 1968, p. 8569. On the significance of Johnson's speech for the future of the war, see the final chapter of Schandler's *Unmaking of a President*. After Fulbright's speech, his own wife suggested publicly that perhaps silence was the best policy for politicians to follow at that time. Johnson told a group of legislators the next day, "I agree with Mrs. Ful-bright." He also referred to the Wise Men's meeting. See "Meeting with House/Senate Leadership," April 3, 1968, Tom Johnson's notes of meetings, box 2, LBJ Library. Contrary to Fulbright, most congressional leaders saw Johnson's speech as a significant turning point. See, for instance, *Congressional Record*, April 2, 1968, pp. 8533, 8595–8596, in which Senator Daniel Inouye (D-Hawaii), House Speaker Carl Albert (D-Okla.), and House Minority Whip Hale Boggs (D-La.) speak of Johnson's deescalation of the war.

150. Congressional leaders' breakfast, April 2, 1968, Meeting notes file, box 2, LBJ Library. Johnson made a similar remark to another group of legislators the next day. See the previous note. It is worth noting that Johnson's audience in these congressional meetings included a number of hawkish members and that the Wise Men Johnson cited to them had good hawkish credentials. As always, Johnson's comments have to be put into the context of the audience he was addressing. This is not to suggest that he was lying about the Wise Men having been influential, but that there were many influences; to another audience he would have – and ultimately did – stress other influences. He later told Walter Cronkite that he had pretty much made up his mind before meeting the Wise Men: "the essence of what these men who were counseling with me were saying was not in conflict with what we were then exploring" (CBS Interview "Why I Chose Not to Run," original [unedited], pp. 6–7, box 1, LBJ Library). The archival record laid out in this chapter suggests that this is true – he had signaled key people as to which course of action he was likely (but not certain) to take regarding the bombing and the troop questions prior to the meeting with the Wise Men.

151. See Hoopes, *Intervention*, pp. 219–220, for an account of how Clifford thought he was "making progress" with Rusk at the March 28 meeting.

152. Helms, oral history, p. II, 28, LBJ Library.

153. Kearns, *Lyndon Johnson*, pp. 342–345. McPherson oral history, p. IV, 11, LBJ Library. Dirksen, quoted in Neil MacNeil, *Dirksen* (New York: World Publishing Co., 1970), p. 328.

154. Westmoreland to Wheeler and Sharp, February 13, 1968, Westmoreland Papers, box 16, LBJ Library.

Chapter 5. The Evolution of Johnson's Vietnam Advisory System

1. Acheson to Erik Boheman, July 7, 1965, in David McClellan and David Acheson (eds.), *Among Friends: Personal Letters of Dean Acheson* (New York: Dodd, Mead, 1988), pp. 272–273; emphasis added.

2. "Cabinet Room, July 22, 1965," July 21–27 Meetings on Vietnam, Meeting notes, box 1, LBJ Library.

3. "Views of Clark Clifford" (notes taken by Jack Valenti), July 25, 1965, Miscellaneous Vietnam documents, Reference file, LBJ Library.

4. Maxwell Taylor, *Swords and Plowshares* (New York: Norton, 1972), p. 379; Arthur Schlesinger, *Robert Kennedy and His Times* (Boston: Houghton Mifflin, 1978), p. 833.

5. Lady Bird Johnson, *A White House Diary* (New York: Holt, Rinehart, and Winston, 1970), p. 550.

6. David Humphrey, "Tuesday Lunch at the White House: A Preliminary Assessment," *Diplomatic History* 8, 4 (Winter 1984): 82.

7. Leonard Marks, "Johnson and Leadership," in Kenneth W. Thompson (ed.), *The Johnson Presidency: Twenty Intimate Perspectives of Lyndon B. Johnson* (Lanham, Md.: University Press of America, 1986), pp. 285–286.

8. Notes of meeting with Democratic congressional leadership, February 6, 1968, Tom Johnson's notes, box 2, LBJ Library.

9. *Gallup Opinion Index*, April 1968, p. 3.

10. John E. Mueller, *War, Presidents, and Public Opinion* (New York: Wiley, 1973), p. 54.

11. Notes of meeting with Democratic congressional leadership, February 6, 1968, Tom Johnson's notes, box 2; Meeting notes file, March 22, 1968, Tuesday Lunch, box 2; LBJ Library.

12. Townsend Hoopes, *The Limits of Intervention* (New York: McKay, 1969). These and similar comments are found on pp. 59–61, 150, 181, 207, and 218.

13. Lyndon Johnson, *The Vantage Point: Perspectives of the Presidency* (New York: Holt, Rinehart, and Winston, 1971), pp. 391–393.

14. Johnson, oral history, interviewed by Elspeth Rostow, LBJ Library. Bruce Altschuler, *LBJ and the Polls* (Gainesville: University of Florida Press, 1990), pp. 49, 102.

15. Stephen Hess, *Organizing the Presidency*, 2d ed. (Washington, D.C.: Brookings, 1988), ch. 1.

16. Charles Walcott and Karen Hult, "Organizing the White House: Structure, Environment, and Organizational Governance," *American Journal of Political Science* 31, 1 (February 1987): 110–111.

17. Rusk, interviewed by Richard Rusk and William Bundy, tape OO.1, p. 18, Rusk Papers, Richard Russell Library.

18. Lady Bird Johnson, oral history, pp. 23, 24, Russell Library.

19. On Arthur and Rollins, see Michael Medved, *The Shadow Presidents* (New York: Times Books, 1979), ch. 3, and Thomas Reeves, *Gentleman Boss: The Life of Chester A. Arthur* (New York: Knopf, 1975); on Wilson and House, see Alexander and Juliette George's *Woodrow Wilson and Colonel House* (New York: Dover Publishing, 1964); on Roosevelt and Hopkins, see Robert Sherwood, *Roosevelt and Hopkins: An Intimate History* (New York: Harper and Brothers,1948).

20. As James David Barber writes, "If any 'system' was moving inexorably down the track toward tragedy in Vietnam, it was Johnson's own system—his character—not some structure or set of abstractions." Barber, *The Presidential Character* (Englewood Cliffs, N.J.: Prentice-Hall, 1972), p. 33. Larry Berman, *Lyndon Johnson's War: The Road to Stalemate in Vietnam* (New York: Norton, 1989), p. 37, and in Peter Braestrup (ed.), *Vietnam as History* (Washington, D.C.: University Press of America, 1984), p. 16; similarly, regarding 1968, see Melvin Small, *Johnson, Nixon, and the Doves* (New Brunswick, N.J.: Rutgers University Press, 1988), p. 146: "Characteristically, it seemed, the Wise Men had met only for show, to demonstrate that Johnson listened to all options before acting."

21. Redford and McCulley write, for instance, that Johnson's "direct and feverishly pursued contact with cabinet and other executives, congressmen, trusted advisers, and numerous other persons supplemented the staff system and often left even the top staff assistants uncertain about the sources of his information." *White House Operations* (Austin: University of Texas Press,1986), pp. 42, 69; see also Glenn T. Seaborg and Benjamin S. Loeb, *Stemming the Tide* (Lexington, Mass.: Lexington Books, 1987), pp. 183, 424, and Leslie Gelb and Richard Betts, *The Irony of Vietnam: The System Worked* (Washington, D.C.: Brookings, 1979), p. 158.

22. George M. Kahin's *Intervention: How America Became Involved in Vietnam* (New York: Knopf, 1986) is the best exemplar of this minority view of Johnson, though it reflects only fleetingly on the wider implications of evidence showing an open-minded president confronting the confident interventionism of McGeorge Bundy and Robert McNamara. From nonscholarly literature, see Jack Valenti, *A Very Human President* (New York: Pocket Books,

1977). To a certain extent, George Ball's *The Past Has Another Pattern* (New York: Norton, 1982) fits into this group. Valenti makes the case more strongly, and Ball tends to see himself as more of a lone dissenter than he actually was.

23. Howard K. Smith, "A Strong Thread of Moral Purpose," in James McGregor Burns (ed.), *To Heal and to Build* (New York: McGraw-Hill, 1968), p. 2.

24. Bruce Buchanan, *The Presidential Experience: What the Office Does to the Man* (Englewood Cliffs, N.J.: Prentice-Hall, 1978), p. 58. See also p. 73, n. 2, relaying Barber's description of a "helpless" Robert McNamara contending with President Johnson.

25. Frank Kessler, *The Dilemmas of Presidential Leadership* (Englewood Cliffs, N.J.: Prentice-Hall, 1982), p. 66. Kessler repeats the popular story (recounted earlier in this book) by Chester Cooper, who writes in his memoir, *The Lost Crusade* (New York: Dodd, Mead, 1970), that he could not bring himself to level with President Johnson at group meetings. Barbara Kellerman and Ryan J. Barilleaux, *The President as World Leader* (New York: St. Martin's Press, 1991), p. 123.

26. Bernard Brodie, *War and Politics* (New York: Macmillan, 1973), pp. 139, 141.

27. Here I refer primarily to George Reedy's *Lyndon B. Johnson: A Memoir* (New York: Andrews and McMeel, 1982).

Chapter 6. Secrecy and Openness in the White House: An Interpretation of Johnson's Political Style

1. This thesis was presented at greater length in David M. Barrett, "Secrecy and Openness in Lyndon Johnson's White House: Political Style, Pluralism, and the Presidency," *Review of Politics* 54, 1 (Winter 1992): 72–111. I thank the *Review* for permission to use parts of that article here.

2. An increasingly popular data base for quantifying Johnson's advisory encounters is the daily diary at the Johnson Library in Austin, Texas, but researchers should be cautious: An archivist there told me that secretaries charged with tracking Johnson's meetings became increasingly systematic over the course of the administration. The diary is of questionable reliability in comparing early and late years. Further, I was told that tracking of Johnson's meetings or phone calls with informal advisers, especially during evening hours, was not comprehensive. My research confirms this. For example, John Burke and Fred Greenstein's *How Presidents Test Reality: Decisions on Vietnam, 1954 and 1965* (New York: Russell Sage Foundation, 1989), uses the diary to report remarkably on p. 140 that Johnson—discouraging advisers from exploring critical questions about Vietnam—had *no* one-on-one meetings with Senator Richard Russell (who questioned escalation in Vietnam) in the crucial period from February 6 through July 28, 1965. Papers at the Russell Library, Athens, Georgia, show him at the White House and on the presidential yacht on various evenings during these months. See also Lady Bird Johnson's oral history, Russell Library.

3. Character, says James David Barber in *The Presidential Character*, 2d ed. (Englewood Cliffs, N.J.: Prentice-Hall, 1977), is "the way the President orients himself toward life—not for the moment, but enduringly" (pp. 6–8, 11). I define style as characteristic patterns that are chosen and employed by a president in dealing with his job and interacting with others.

4. Patrick Anderson, *The Presidents' Men* (Garden City, N.Y.: Doubleday, 1969), p. 328. A section of the book is titled "Caligula's Court." Larry Berman, in Chapter 1 of his *Planning a Tragedy* (New York: Norton, 1982), similarly notes and labels such interpretations of the Johnson White House. Barber's *Presidential Character* fits into this group. From the people "under Johnson's control" the president "expected complete conformity to his will—expressed and unexpressed." Barber expresses wonder that Johnson's "assistants stayed as long as they did" (see p. 80). One prominent Caligula-style interpretation of Johnson does not (yet) deal with Vietnam: Robert Caro's multivolume biography, *The Years of Lyndon Johnson, Vol. 1: The Path to Power* (New York: Knopf, 1982) and *Vol. 2: Means of Ascent* (New York: Knopf, 1990). A persuasive critique of Caro is Garry Wills's "Monstre Sacre," *New York Review of Books*, April 26, 1990, pp. 7-9.

5. In a personal interview in October 1990 and in correspondence, Reedy has reemphasized the difference he believes existed between Johnson's advisory interactions during his Senate days and those of his White House years. On April 30, 1992, Reedy wrote to me that Johnson "saw verbal confrontations as contests and the ideas that would arise out of the discussion as weapons. He was too busy conducting warfare during the meeting to pay very much attention to the substantive points that could influence his decisions in any other than a tactical sense." Reedy adds, however, that he does not believe that advisers were "afraid" to tell Johnson "the truth." "What they did, however, was to approach him very respectfully—the wrong way to approach American politicians." Earlier, he wrote that the president "succeeded in closing the debate [on Vietnam] only in the White House and could not understand just why it persisted in the nation as a whole." Reedy, *Lyndon B. Johnson: A Memoir* (New York: Andrews and McMeel, 1982), pp. 18, 142-143, 157. Asked about Johnson's advice-seeking style, former Senator J. William Fulbright replies similarly: "I'm bound to say that President Johnson rarely consulted in the sense of seeking advice and certainly being influenced by it." Fulbright, oral history interview, p. 6, Richard Russell Library, University of Georgia. See also Richard Goodwin, *Remembering America* (Boston: Little, Brown, 1988), ch. 21; Rhodri Jeffreys-Jones, *The CIA and American Democracy* (New Haven, Conn.: Yale University Press, 1989), ch. 9.

6. Chester Cooper, *The Lost Crusade: America in Vietnam* (New York: Dodd, Mead, 1970), p. 223. In truth, as Cooper notes, NSC meetings were not usually important advisory forums for Johnson.

7. Philip Reed Rulon, *Compassionate Samaritan: The Life of Lyndon Baines Johnson* (Chicago: Nelson Hall, 1981); Jack Valenti, *A Very Human President* (New York: Pocket Books, 1977), pp. 52, 58. Further, Valenti writes: It is "a fact that President Johnson was unusually accessible to all his staff."

8. Former CIA Director Richard Helms claims that Johnson would challenge written intelligence reports at times, but "when he finally reealized that the facts were right and had been accurately presented and that his conception was wrong . . . [he would] . . . accept what you had told him and not refer to it anymore—simply go on about his business, having changed his view about what this series of events either portended or what had happened." Helms, oral history, p. I, 13, LBJ Library; see Abe Fortas on this in Kenneth W. Thompson (ed.), *The Johnson Presidency: Twenty Intimate Portraits of Lyndon B. Johnson* (Lanham, Md.: University Press of America, 1986), pp. 9-10; Rusk, oral history, p. I, 37, LBJ Library; see also George M. Kahin, *Intervention: How America Became*

Involved in Vietnam (New York: Knopf, 1986), pp. 348, 362, 366. Emmette Redford and Richard McCulley find that "evidence of confrontation between the President and his top assistants was abundant." They quote speechwriter Harry McPherson, who remembers differing with Johnson by telephone over Vietnam peace talks: "Well, we argued and argued and I, for the first time I think since I'd been working for him, I started shouting. I said, 'Goddamn it, I'm trying to help you! I'm trying to get you out of a fix! If you can't listen to me, go listen to somebody else! I'll take my advice somewhere else!'" See Redford and McCulley, *White House Operations* (Austin: University of Texas Press, 1986), pp. 72, 74.

9. Not that they disagree absolutely: Reedy describes Johnson as "the consummate political leader of his era," who sometimes, "even when his White House setbacks produced a touch of paranoia . . . was willing to give serious consideration to opposing points of view." On the other side of the coin, Valenti admits that the president could be abusive.

10. Doris Kearns, *Lyndon Johnson and the American Dream* (New York: Harper and Row, 1976), pp. 238, 323–324; see also Burke and Greenstein, *How Presidents Test Reality*, pp. 144–145, 214–216, 237, 238, 280.

11. On keeping options open until the last moment, with no decision being final until announced, see Johnson's oral history interview with Elspeth Rostow, p. II, 11, and Benjamin Read's oral history, p. 17, both LBJ Library.

12. David Truman, *The Governmental Process* (New York: Knopf, 1957), pp. 399, 403, 422, 428.

13. Richard Neustadt, *Presidential Power* (New York: Wiley and Sons, 1960), p. 185.

14. Barbara Ward's *The Rich Nations and the Poor Nations* (New York: Norton, 1962) has commonly been cited as one book that Johnson read and reread.

15. Rowland Evans and Robert Novak, *Lyndon B. Johnson: The Exercise of Power* (New York: New American Library, 1966), pp. 10–11. This is one of the finest early studies of Johnson's political career. On Johnson and mentors see Kearns, *Lyndon Johnson*, pp. 214, 239–240; also Reedy, *Lyndon B. Johnson*, pp. 39–44.

16. Evans and Novak, *Lyndon B. Johnson*, p. 148.

17. William Bundy, oral history, p. 31; emphasis in the original. See also Richard Helms, oral history, pp. I, 23, 30, 33, all LBJ Library.

18. McGeorge Bundy, oral history conducted by Richard Rusk, p. 17, Dean Rusk Papers, Richard Russell Library. Bundy isn't quite calling Johnson a liar here; George Reedy writes that Johnson "never told a deliberate lie. But he had a fantastic capacity to persuade himself that the 'truth' which was convenient for the present was the truth and anything that conflicted with it was the prevarication of enemies." Reedy, *Lyndon B. Johnson*, p. 3.

19. Wheeler, oral history, p. II, 8, LBJ Library. Dean Rusk says that Johnson "didn't like to have his hand disclosed before he was ready to announce it." Rusk, interviewed by Richard Rusk, tape QQQQQ, pp. 10–11, Rusk Papers, Russell Library. See also Walter Heller, "President Johnson and the Economy," in James M. Burns (ed.), *To Heal and to Build* (New York: McGraw-Hill, 1968), p. 152. Kearns, *Lyndon Johnson*, p. 225.

20. On Johnson's liberalism, see William Schambra, "Progressive Liberalism and American 'Community,'" *Public Interest* (Summer 1985): 32–37; also David McKay, *Domestic Policy and Ideology: Presidents and the American State, 1964–1987* (Cambridge: Cambridge University Press, 1989), ch. 2.

21. Harry McPherson, *A Political Education* (Boston: Little, Brown, 1972), pp. 263–264. On Johnson and Roosevelt, and Johnson as a "congressional president," see Stephen Hess, *Organizing the Presidency*, 2d ed. (Washington, D.C.: Brookings, 1988), pp. 94–95, 103. Also Earle Wheeler's oral history, LBJ Library.

22. David Truman, *The Governmental Process* (New York: Knopf, 1951), pp. 399, 401–403, 422, 428.

23. Richard Neustadt, *Presidential Power* (New York: Wiley and Sons, 1960), pp. 6, 9–10, 185, 188, and, in general, ch. 6. That theme was even more boldly stated by James MacGregor Burns's *The Deadlock of Democracy* (Englewood Cliffs, N.J.: Prentice-Hall, 1963), pp. 5–7, 257. Grant McConnell found in *The Modern Presidency* (New York: St. Martin's Press, 1967) that the presidency was too weak but uniquely "responsible to *all* of the people" and the "medium for reasserting national values" (see pp. 90–94). In 1986, Samuel Kernell noted such writers and reflected that, at times, "the model of the bargaining president appears to be little more than a generalization of Roosevelt's style. Kernell, *Going Public* (Washington, D.C.: Congressional Quarterly Press, 1986), pp. 10–17.

24. Oral history interviews of Johnson, conducted by William Jorden and Elspeth Rostow for the Johnson Library, contain similar views as those expressed in Lyndon Johnson, *The Vantage Point* (New York: Holt, Rinehart, and Winston, 1971).

25. Johnson, *Vantage Point*, pp. 18, 27, 28, 29.

26. Ibid., p. 433.

27. Truman, *Governmental Process*, p. 403.

28. Johnson, *Vantage Point*, pp. 157–158, 438, 447.

29. Wheeler, oral history, p. I-3, LBJ Library.

30. Roche oral history, p. I, 50, LBJ Library. See also p. I, 9, 54, 63, 72, 73 of this insightful record.

31. Joseph Califano, *Governing America* (New York: Simon and Schuster, 1981), pp. 140–141. This is a very readable comparison of the Carter and Johnson presidencies.

32. Norman Thomas and Harold Wolman, "Policy Formulation in the Institutionalized Presidency: The Johnson Task Forces," in Thomas Cronin and Sanford Greenberg (eds.), *The Presidential Advisory System* (New York: Harper and Row, 1969), pp. 124–143. See also Nancy K. Smith's "Presidential Task Force Operation During the Johnson Administration," *Presidential Studies Quarterly* 15, 2 (Spring 1985): 320–329.

33. Thomas and Wolman, "Johnson Task Forces," p. 127.

34. Kearns, *Lyndon Johnson*, pp. 222–223; see also Smith, "Presidential Task Force Operations"; Paul Conkin, *Big Daddy from the Pedernales* (Boston: Twayne Publishing, 1986). In addition, there were 90 "internal or interagency" task forces. See Conklin, *Big Daddy*, pp. 209–212.

35. Thomas and Wolman, "Johnson Task Forces," p. 128.

36. Ibid., p. 129; Johnson, quoted in Smith, "Presidential Task Force Operations," p. 321.

37. Johnson, *Vantage Point*, p. 433.

38. Thomas and Wolman, "Johnson Task Forces," pp. 131, 135; emphasis added. The Kennedy administration faced pressures to "balance" its task forces.

39. Ibid., p. 136. See also Smith, "Presidential Task Force Operations," pp. 321–322.

40. Thomas and Wolman, "Johnson Task Forces," p. 137.

41. Ibid., pp. 134, 139, 140, 142–143. Thomas and Wolman observe that the Johnson task forces may be "a good example of what Theodore Lowi in *The End of Liberalism* (New York: Norton, 1969) has called 'interest group liberalism,' a phenomenon which Lowi feels has come increasingly to characterize American politics in the 1960s" (p. 143). But Lowi describes a process in which policy-making in government is largely *captured* by the access and influence of interest groups; the Johnson task forces represented a decided effort to escape excessive "access" of interest groups.

42. Glenn T. Seaborg with Benjamin S. Loeb, *Stemming the Tide: Arms Control in the Johnson Years* (Lexington, Mass.: Lexington Books, 1987), p. xix.

43. Seaborg, *Stemming the Tide*, p. 19.

44. Ibid., pp. 20, 23.

45. Ibid., pp. 36, 44–45; Johnson, *Vantage Point*, p. 466.

46. See Eugene Rostow's oral history, p. 1, LBJ Library. Also Kearns, *Lyndon Johnson*, pp. 248–249: "If a reporter learned in advance that the President was going to do something on Thursday, and reported that fact in Tuesday's paper, Johnson would often change his plans in order to embarrass the reporter, who had then to explain his error, and to serve notice on those who leaked the story that such indiscretion was a serious act of insubordination." In this too he may have resembled Roosevelt, who (late in his second term) apparently canceled a planned appointment of Louis Johnson as secretary of war because of a news leak. See Jack Alexander, "Stormy New Boss of the Pentagon," *Saturday Evening Post*, July 30, 1949, pp. 26, 27, 66–70.

47. Seaborg, *Stemming the Tide*, pp. 136, 148.

48. Ibid., pp. 145, 146.

49. Ibid., p. 149.

50. In fairness to Seaborg, the interpretation presented here, of Johnson seeking diverse views while insisting on secrecy about the advisory process, is mine. Seaborg refers to — and implicitly accepts — prevailing views of Johnson as a president who, for complex psychological reasons, "needed to be, or at least to appear to be, in control of events." Nor does Seaborg explicitly differ with interpretations of Johnson as a president who talked with only a small number of advisers. But his account gives considerable evidence that Johnson wanted the best possible kinds of advice on arms control, consulted with a varied group of people on the issue, and sought to keep a veil of secrecy around the advisory process as he considered his options. At least 11 persons, plus the Gilpatric Committee, are listed as advising Johnson on arms control: Rusk, McNamara, Bundy, Rostow, Seaborg, Ball, Helms, Clifford, Fortas, and senators Russell and Jackson.

51. Nor am I suggesting that Johnson's use of this combination of openness and secrecy always "worked." When Senator Richard Russell pressed the president to support his nomination of a man who was apparently conservative on racial issues for a federal judgeship, Johnson consulted not only with Russell but also with civil rights groups and Attorney General Ramsey Clark, who opposed the nomination. Through secret machinations, Johnson tried to achieve agreement that the nominee was not racist or anti–civil rights. This would then allow Johnson to support Russell's nominee. Russell lost patience with the process, castigated Johnson, and saw their friendship severely damaged; this, in turn, damaged the nomination of Abe Fortas as Chief Justice. See files on the Fortas-Thornberry nominations at the LBJ Library, also Gilbert Fite, *Richard B. Russell, Jr., Senator from Georgia* (Chapel Hill: University of North Carolina Press, 1991), pp. 476–482.

On Johnson and civil rights, see Thompson, *The Johnson Presidency*, p. 7; Conkin, *Big Daddy*, pp. 214–217; Vaughn Davis Bornet, *The Presidency of Lyndon B. Johnson* (Lawrence: University Press of Kansas, 1983), p. 97; Evans and Novak, *Lyndon B. Johnson*, p. 377. Johnson's judgment surely included a rational calculation of the civil rights bill's chances for passage in 1964. See Tom Wicker, *JFK and LBJ: The Influence of Personality upon Politics* (New York: Morrow, 1968), pp. 173–174.

52. In 1965, he even took on the language of the civil rights movement, proclaiming to Congress, "We shall overcome." Jack Bell, *The Johnson Treatment* (New York: Harper and Row, 1965), pp. 159–166. It took more than Johnson's lobbying to move Smith. See Charles and Barbara Whalen, *The Longest Debate* (Cabin Lodge, Md.: Seven Locks Press, 1985); Joseph Califano, *A Presidential Nation* (New York: Norton, 1975), p. 215.

53. Barbara Tuchman, *The March of Folly* (New York: Knopf, 1984), pp. 311, 338.

54. Thomas P. O'Neill, *Man of the House* (New York: Random House, 1987), pp. 183–184.

55. William Westmoreland, *A Soldier Reports* (Garden City, N.Y.: Doubleday, 1976), pp. 234, 230, 414; Rusk, oral interview, no. 1, LBJ Library, pp. 42, 37.

56. Ball, oral interview, p. II, 15, and Eugene Rostow, oral interview, p. 11, both LBJ Library. Emphasis in the original.

57. Aiken, oral interview, p. 9; Gruening, oral interview, p. 8, both LBJ Library.

58. Helms, oral interview, pp. 12, 37, LBJ Library.

59. W. Bundy, oral interview, pp. 27–29, LBJ Library. Bundy says that such written characterizations came from former administration officials James Thomson and Richard Goodwin in the late 1960s and were "inherently small minded" and "rather sordid and opportunistic."

60. Maxwell Taylor oral interviews (1969), p. 25, (1981) p. II, 37, LBJ Library.

61. Christian, oral history, p. IV, 27, LBJ Library. See also Henry Cabot Lodge, quoted in the *New York Times*, May 21, 1972, p. 14: "during the whole period from the end of 1963 through 1968 that I worked for Johnson, I never had the slightest difficulty in getting his attention and therefore had no reason to 'complain' . . . [Johnson] was always courteous and considerate of me. Far from being inaccessible, he gave of himself unstintingly." See also White House aide Larry Temple, oral history, on Johnson's reputation for "chewing people out": "I must say I didn't experience that very much. He always was nice to me, treated me with complete deference, even at times I knew he was unhappy with me." See p. III, 36, and, for Temple's quotation of Lawrence O'Brien on Johnson, p. II, 18, LBJ Library. See also Larry Berman, "The Evolution and Value of Presidential Libraries," in Harold C. Relyea et al. (eds.), *The Presidency and Information Policy* (New York: Center for the Study of the Presidency, 1981), dealing on pp. 88–89 with Budget Director Kermit Gordon and Johnson.

62. Redford and McCulley, *White House Operations*, pp. 72–75.

63. Roche oral history, p. I, 42, LBJ Library.

64. Other published works that move us toward a new understanding of the Johnson presidency include Hugh Davis Graham, *The Uncertain Triumph: Federal Education Policy in the Kennedy and Johnson Years* (Chapel Hill: University of North Carolina Press, 1984); David Humphrey, "Tuesday Lunch at the White House: A Preliminary Assessment," *Diplomatic History* 8, 4 (Winter 1984): 81–101; Emmette Redford and Marlan Blissett, *Organizing the Executive*

Branch: The Johnson Presidency (Chicago: University of Chicago Press, 1981); Bernard J. Firestone and Robert C. Vogt (eds.), *Lyndon Baines Johnson and the Uses of Power* (New York: Greenwood Press, 1988); David M. Welborn and Jesse Burkhead, *Intergovernmental Relations in the American State: The Johnson Presidency* (Austin: University of Texas Press, 1989); Vaughn Davis Bornet, "Reappraising the Presidency of Lyndon B. Johnson," *Presidential Studies Quarterly* 20, 3 (Summer 1990): 591–602; John Schwarz, *America's Hidden Success* (New York: Norton, 1983); William J. Jorden, *Panama Odyssey* (Austin: University of Texas Press, 1984).

Afterword: On Rationality, Johnson's Worldview, and the War

1. On Johnson's view of history and Vietnam, see his *The Vantage Point* (New York: Holt, Rinehart, and Winston, 1971), pp. 150–151, 531; also Doris Kearns, *Lyndon Johnson and the American Dream* (New York: Harper and Row, 1976), pp. 345–347.

2. W. W. Rostow, *The United States and the Regional Organization of Asia and the Pacific, 1965–1985* (Austin: University of Texas Press, 1986). Norman Podhoretz, *Why We Were in Vietnam* (New York: Touchstone Press, 1983), pp. 197, 210. Guenter Lewy, *America in Vietnam* (New York: Oxford University Press, 1978), p. 441. In a similar vein, former CIA Director Richard Helms says that the American effort in South Vietnam permitted "Indonesia, Malaysia, Singapore, and the Philippines to maintain their independence, to get themselves straightened out from the effects of World War II. And now look at the economic prosperity of that part of the world . . . they owe that to the United States." Helms, oral history, p. II, 26, LBJ Library.

3. Henry Steele Commager, Samuel E. Morison, and William E. Leuchtenburg, *A Concise History of the American Republic*, 2d ed. (New York: Oxford University Press, 1983), p. 753. Philip Reed Rulon, *The Compassionate Samaritan: The Life of Lyndon Baines Johnson* (Chicago: Nelson Hall, 1981), p. 256. Rusk, interviewed by Richard Rusk and Thomas Schoenbaum, tape C, p. 1, Rusk Papers, Russell Library. Yet Rusk thought that the war was winnable, "if we had been able to maintain greater solidarity on the home front here." See tape T, p. 25.

4. *Webster's Seventh New Collegiate Dictionary* (Springfield, Mass.: Merriam Co., 1967), s.v. "wisdom."

5. Especially in the field of public administration, the distinction between process and outcome seems commonplace. George Gordon writes in *Public Administration in America*, 2d ed. (New York: St. Martin's Press, 1982), of a "widespread tendency, even among some political scientists, to scornfully dismiss or downgrade as 'irrational' any behavior or decision not clearly directed toward achieving the 'best' results" (p. 259). Much public administration scholarship stresses the "rationality of the process of making decisions, without reference to whether one's goals are also 'rational'" (p. 238; see also p. 577). In part, process/outcome rationality distinctions are a legacy of Max Weber, who distinguished between "formal rationality" (instrumental rational action that adapts to prevailing circumstances) and "substantive rationality" ("rationalization of life-conduct oriented by certain 'ultimate' or 'otherworldly' ideals"). Weber came to believe increasingly in his later years that rationality could mean many

different things and was a hazardous concept if not related to a particular vantage point. See Wolfgang J. Mommsen, *The Political and Social Theory of Max Weber* (Chicago: University of Chicago Press, 1989), pp. 160-165.

6. *Webster's Third New International Dictionary* (unabridged) (Springfield, Mass.: Merriam Co., 1981), s.v. "rationality."

7. Roger Scruton, *A Dictionary of Political Thought* (New York: Hill and Wang, 1982), p. 393.

8. J. William Fulbright, *Old Myths and New Realities* (New York: Random House, 1964), pp. 4-8.

9. "Conversation with former Chancellor Adenauer, June 22, 1965," file: Kissinger, NS file, Files of M. Bundy, box 15, LBJ Library.

10. Walt Rostow, interview with the author, January 20, 1989. Rostow believes that Johnson was anything but ignorant about international relations and was guided by a theory of emerging regionalism in world politics; see also Johnson, *Vantage Point*, p. 42; Philip B. Geyelin, *Lyndon B. Johnson and the World* (New York: Praeger, 1966). Geyelin portrays a president unsophisticated in his understanding of world affairs and uninterested in the subject, "except as a practical need to be interested rose" (p. 17; see also pp. 18-20, 62, 71-73, 302-303). Michael Hunt, *Ideology and U.S. Foreign Policy* (New Haven, Conn.: Yale University Press, 1987), ch. 5; Gabriel Kolko, *Anatomy of a War* (New York: Pantheon, 1985), especially p. 168. George M. Kahin, *Intervention: How America Became Involved in Vietnam* (New York: Knopf, 1986), p. 394, finds domestic politics "one of the president's paramount considerations" in 1965 Vietnam decisionmaking, but adds that Johnson was "deeply concerned about the international implications" of proposed "all-out" escalation.

11. The "Fulbright" in this section refers to the senator and his 1964 analysis; his later views espoused a more personalistic explanation of the war. For a discussion of the worldview-policy link, see Harold and Margaret Sprout, *The Ecological Perspective on Human Affairs, with Special Reference to International Relations* (Princeton, N.J.: Princeton University Press, 1965), pp. 28-30. An application to one issue in international relations is found in Daniel Frei, *Perceived Images: U.S. and Soviet Assumptions and Perceptions in Disarmament* (Totowa, N.J.: Rowman and Allanheld, 1986). See also Robert Axelrod (ed.), *Structure of Decision* (Princton, N.J.: Princeton University Press, 1976); John D. Steinbruner, *The Cybernetic Theory of Decision* (Princeton, N.J.: Princeton University Press, 1974); and Barry Buzan, *People, States, and Fear: The National Security Problem in the International Relations* (Chapel Hill: University of North Carolina Press, 1983).

12. Hannah Arendt, "Lying in Politics," in *Crises of the Republic* (New York: Harcourt Brace Jovanovich, 1972), p. 32.

13. W. Bundy, oral history, pp. 27, 29, LBJ Library.

Bibliography

Books and Articles

Anderson, James. "President Johnson's Use of the Cabinet as an Instrument of Executive Action." *Journal of Politics* 48, 3 (1986): 529–537.

Anderson, Patrick. *The President's Men.* Garden City, N.Y.: Doubleday, 1969.

Altschuler, Bruce. *LBJ and the Polls.* Gainesville: University of Florida Press, 1990.

Arendt, Hannah. *Crises of the Republic.* New York: Harcourt Brace Jovanovich, 1972.

————. "Lying in Politics." *New York Review of Books* 18 (November 1971): 30–39.

Arnold, James R. *The First Domino: Eisenhower, the Military, and America's Intervention in Vietnam.* New York: William Morrow, 1991.

Axelrod, Robert, ed. *Structure of Decision.* Princeton, N.J.: Princeton University Press, 1976.

Baldwin, Louis. *Hon. Politician: Mike Mansfield of Montana.* Missoula, Mont.: Mountain Press, 1979.

Ball, George. *The Past Has Another Pattern.* New York: Norton, 1982.

Barber, James David. *The Presidential Character: Predicting Performance in the White House.* Englewood Cliffs, N.J.: Prentice-Hall, 1972.

Barrett, David M. "Communications: Sen. Russell and the Tonkin Resolution." *Georgia Historical Quarterly* 73, 3 (Fall 1989): 698–699.

————. "Doing 'Tuesday Lunch' at Lyndon Johnson's White House: New Archival Evidence on Vietnam Decisionmaking." *P.S.: Political Science and Politics* 24, 4 (1991): 676–679.

————. "The Mythology Surrounding Lyndon Johnson, His Advisers, and the 1965 Decision to Escalate the Vietnam War." *Political Science Quarterly* 103, 4 (1988–89): 637–663.

————. "Secrecy and Openness in Lyndon Johnson's White House: Political Style, Pluralism, and the Presidency." *Review of Politics* 54, 1 (Winter 1992): 72–111.

Bassett, Lawrence J., and Stephen E. Pelz. "The Failed Search for Victory: Vietnam and the Politics of War." In *Kennedy's Quest for Victory*, edited by Thomas G. Paterson, pp. 223–252. New York: Oxford University Press, 1989.

Bell, Jack. *The Johnson Treatment.* New York: Harper and Row, 1965.

Benjamin, Burton. *The CBS Benjamin Report.* Washington, D.C.: Media Institute, 1984.

Bensman, Joseph, and Robert Lilienfeld. *Between Public and Private.* New York: Free Press, 1979.

Berger, Raoul. *Executive Privilege: A Constitutional Myth.* New York: Bantam Books, 1975.

Berman, Larry. "The Evolution and Value of Presidential Libraries." In *The Presidency and Information Policy*, edited by Harold C. Relyea et al. New York: Center for the Study of the Presidency, 1981.

————. *Lyndon Johnson's War: The Road to Stalemate in Vietnam.* New York: Norton, 1989.

————. *Planning a Tragedy: The Americanization of the Vietnam War.* New York: Norton, 1982.

Berman, William. *William Fulbright and the Vietnam War.* Kent, Ohio: Kent State University Press, 1988.

Best, James. "Who Talked to the President When? A Study of Lyndon B. Johnson." *Political Science Quarterly* 103, 3 (Fall 1988): 531–546.

Blum, John M. *Years of Discord: American Politics and Society, 1961–1974.* New York: Norton, 1991.

Bock, Joseph G. *The White House Staff and the National Security Assistant: Friendship and Friction at the Water's Edge.* Westport, Conn.: Greenwood Press, 1987.

Bornet, Vaughn Davis. *The Presidency of Lyndon B. Johnson.* Lawrence: University Press of Kansas, 1983.

————. "Reappraising the Presidency of Lyndon B. Johnson." *Presidential Studies Quarterly* 20, 3 (Summer 1990): 591–602.

Braestrup, Peter, ed. *Big Story: How the American Press and Television Reported and Interpreted the Crises of Tet.* Boulder, Colo.: Westview, 1977.

————. *Vietnam as History.* Washington, D.C.: University Press of America, 1984.

Brands, Henry W. "Johnson and Eisenhower: The President, the Former President, and the War in Vietnam." *Presidential Studies Quarterly* 15, 3 (Summer 1985): 589–601.

Brodie, Bernard. *War and Politics.* New York: Macmillan, 1973.

Buchanan, Bruce. *The Presidential Experience: What the Office Does to the Man.* Englewood Cliffs, N.J.: Prentice-Hall, 1978.

Burke, John P. "Responsibilities of Presidents and Advisers: A Theory and Case Study of Vietnam Decision Making." *Journal of Politics* 46, 3 (1984): 818–845.

Burke, John P., and Fred I. Greenstein, with the collaboration of Larry Berman and Richard Immerman. *How Presidents Test Reality: Decisions on Vietnam, 1954 and 1965.* New York: Russell Sage Foundation, 1989.

Burns, James MacGregor. *The Deadlock of Democracy.* Englewood Cliffs, N.J.: Prentice-Hall, 1963.

————, ed. *To Heal and to Build.* New York: McGraw-Hill, 1968.

Buzan, Barry. *People, States, and Fear: The National Security Problem in the International Relations.* Chapel Hill: University of North Carolina Press, 1983.

Byrd, Robert. *The Senate, 1789–1989: Addresses on the History of the United States Senate.* Washington, D.C.: Government Printing Office, 1988.

Cable, Larry E. *Conflict of Myths: The Development of American Counterinsurgency Doctrine and the Vietnam War.* New York: New York University Press, 1986.

————. *Unholy Grail: The U.S. and the Wars in Vietnam, 1965–8.* New York: Routledge, 1991.

Califano, Joseph. *Governing America.* New York: Simon and Schuster, 1981.

————. *A Presidential Nation.* New York: Norton, 1975.

Caro, Robert. *The Years of Lyndon Johnson: The Path to Power.* New York: Knopf, 1982.

———. *The Years of Lyndon Johnson: Means of Ascent.* New York: Knopf, 1990.
Chester, Lewis, Godfrey Hodgson, and Bruce Page. *An American Melodrama: The Presidential Campaign of 1968.* New York: Viking, 1969.
Chomsky, Noam. *American Power and the New Mandarins.* New York: Pantheon, 1969.
———. "The Logic of Withdrawal." In *American Power and the New Mandarins,* edited by Noam Chomsky, pp. 246–269. New York: Pantheon, 1969.
Clifford, Clark (with Richard Holbrooke). *Counsel to the President.* New York: Random House, 1991.
———. "A Viet Nam Reappraisal: The Personal History of One Man's View and How It Evolved." *Foreign Affairs* 47, 4 (July 1969): 605–627.
Coffin, Tristram. *Senator Fulbright: Portrait of a Public Philosopher.* New York: E. P. Dutton, 1966.
Cohen, Warren. *Dean Rusk.* Totowa, N.J.: Cooper Square Press, 1980.
Commager, Henry Steele, Samuel E. Morison, and William E. Leuchtenburg. *A Concise History of the American Republic.* 2d ed. New York: Oxford University Press, 1983.
Congressional Quarterly Almanac, 1965–1968.
Congressional Quarterly Weekly Report, 1965–1968.
Cooper, Chester. *The Lost Crusade: America in Vietnam.* New York: Dodd, Mead, 1970.
Conkin, Paul. *Big Daddy from the Pedernales.* Boston: Twayne Publishing, 1986.
Corwin, Edward S. *The President: Office and Powers, 1787–1957.* New York: New York University Press, 1957.
Cronin, Thomas. *The State of the Presidency.* 2d ed. Boston: Little, Brown, 1980.
Cronin, Thomas, and Sanford Greenberg. *The Presidential Advisory System.* New York: Harper and Row, 1969.
Destler, I. M. *Presidents, Bureaucrats, and Foreign Policy.* Princeton, N.J.: Princeton University Press, 1974.
Dickerson, Nancy. *Among Those Present.* New York: Ballantine Books, 1977.
Dietz, Terry. *Republicans and Vietnam, 1961–1968.* Westport, Conn.: Greenwood Press, 1986.
Divine, Robert, ed. *Exploring the Johnson Years.* Austin: University of Texas Press, 1981.
Eckstein, Harry. "Case Study and Theory in Political Science." In *The Handbook of Political Science.* Vol. 7, *Strategies of Inquiry,* edited by Fred Greenstein and Nelson Polsby. Reading, Mass.: Addison-Wesley, 1975.
Edelman, Murray. *The Symbolic Uses of Power.* Urbana: University of Illinois Press, 1967.
Eisele, Albert. *Almost to the Presidency.* Blue Earth, Minn.: Piper, 1982.
Evans, Rowland, and Robert Novak. *Lyndon B. Johnson: The Exercise of Power.* New York: New American Library, 1966.
Firestone, Bernard J., and Robert C. Vogt, eds. *Lyndon Baines Johnson and the Uses of Power.* New York: Greenwood Press, 1988.
Fite, Gilbert. *Richard B. Russell, Jr., Senator from Georgia.* Chapel Hill: University of North Carolina Press, 1991.
Frei, Daniel. *Perceived Images: U.S. and Soviet Assumptions and Perceptions in Disarmament.* Totowa, N.J.: Rowman and Allenheld, 1986.
Fulbright, William. *The Arrogance of Power.* New York: Vintage Books, 1966.
———. *Old Myths and New Realities.* New York: Random House, 1964.
Gallup Opinion Index, 1965–1968.

Geertz, Clifford. *The Interpretation of Cultures: Selected Essays.* New York: Basic Books, 1973.

Gelb, Leslie, and Richard Betts. *The Irony of Vietnam: The System Worked.* Washington, D.C.: Brookings, 1979.

————. "Vietnam: Some Hypotheses about Why and How." Presented to the annual meeting of the American Political Science Association, 1970.

George, Alexander. "Case Studies and Theory Development: The Method of Structured, Focused Comparison." In *Diplomacy: New Approaches in History, Theory, and Policy,* edited by Paul G. Lauren, pp. 43–68. New York: Free Press, 1979.

George, Alexander, and Juliette George. *Woodrow Wilson and Colonel House.* New York: Dover Publishing, 1964.

Geyelin, Philip B. *Lyndon B. Johnson and the World.* New York: Praeger, 1966.

Goldhamer, Herbert. *The Adviser.* New York: Elsevier Press, 1978.

Goodwin, Richard. *Remembering America.* Boston: Little, Brown, 1988.

Gordon, George. *Public Administration in America.* 2d ed. New York: St. Martin's Press, 1982.

Goulding, Phil. *Confirm or Deny.* New York: Harper and Row, 1970.

Graham, Hugh Davis. *The Uncertain Triumph: Federal Education Policy in the Kennedy and Johnson Years.* Chapel Hill: University of North Carolina Press, 1984.

Gray, J. Glenn. *The Warriors: Reflections on Men in Battle.* New York: Harcourt Brace, 1959.

Greenstein, Fred. "Change and Continuity in the Modern Presidency." In *The New American Political System,* edited by Anthony King, pp. 45–86. Washington, D.C.: American Enterprise Institute, 1978.

————. *The Hidden Hand Presidency: Eisenhower as Leader.* New York: Basic Books, 1982.

————, ed. *Leadership in the Modern Presidency.* Cambridge, Mass.: Harvard University Press, 1988.

————. *Personality and Politics: Problems of Evidence, Inference, and Conceptualization.* Princeton, N.J.: Princeton University Press, 1987.

Greenstein, Fred, and Nelson Polsby, eds. *The Handbook of Political Science.* Vol. 7, *Strategies of Inquiry.* Reading, Mass.: Addison-Wesley, 1975.

Halberstam, David. *The Best and the Brightest.* New York: Random House, 1972.

Hall, David K. "The National Security Assistant as Policy Spokesman, 1947–1981." Presented at annual meeting of the American Political Science Association, 1981.

Harris, T. George. "A Policy-Maker's Views: Experience vs. Character." *Psychology Today,* March 1975, p. 39.

Hart, John. *The Presidential Branch.* New York: Pergamon, 1987.

Hartke, Sen. Vance. "Vietnam Costs More Than You Think." *The Saturday Evening Post,* April 22, 1967, pp. 10–11.

Hatcher, Patrick L. *The Suicide of an Elite: American Internationalists and Vietnam.* Stanford, Calif.: Stanford University Press, 1990.

Heclo, Hugh. "The Changing Presidential Office." In *Politics and the Oval Office,* edited by Arnold Meltsner, pp. 161–184. San Francisco: Institute for Contemporary Studies, 1981.

Heller, Walter. "President Johnson and the Economy." In *To Heal and to Build,* edited by James MacGregor Burns, pp. 151–206. New York: McGraw-Hill, 1968.

Herring, George. *America's Longest War.* New York: Wiley, 1979.

———. "The War in Vietnam." In *Exploring the Johnson Years*, edited by Robert Divine, pp. 27–64. Austin: University of Texas Press, 1981.

Hess, Stephen. *Organizing the Presidency*. 2d ed. Washington, D.C.: Brookings, 1988.

Hill, Walter, and Douglas Egan. *Readings in Organization Theory*. Boston: Allyn and Bacon, 1967.

Hoekstra, Doug. "Presidential Power and Purpose." *Review of Politics* 47, 4 (1985): 566–587.

Hoopes, Townsend. *The Limits of Intervention*. New York: McKay, 1969.

Humphrey, David. "Tuesday Lunch at the White House: A Preliminary Assessment." *Diplomatic History* 8, 4 (Winter 1984): 81–101.

Humphrey, Hubert. *The Education of a Public Man*. Garden City, N.Y.: Doubleday, 1976.

Hunt, Michael. *Ideology and U.S. Foreign Policy*. New Haven, Conn.: Yale University Press, 1987.

Isaacson, Walter, and Evan Thomas. *The Wise Men*. New York: Simon and Schuster, 1986.

Janis, Irving. *Groupthink: Psychological Studies of Policy Decisions and Fiascoes*. 2d ed. Boston: Houghton Mifflin, 1982.

Jeffreys-Jones, Rhodri. *The CIA and American Democracy*. New Haven, Conn.: Yale University Press, 1989.

Johnson, Haynes, and Bernard Gwertzman. *Fulbright: The Dissenter*. Garden City, N.Y.: Doubleday, 1968.

Johnson, Lady Bird. *A White House Diary*. New York: Holt, Rinehart, and Winston, 1970.

Johnson, Lyndon. *The Vantage Point: Perspectives of the Presidency*. New York: Holt, Rinehart, and Winston, 1971.

Jones, Bruce E. *War without Windows*. New York: Vanguard Press, 1987.

Jones, Bryan D., ed. *Leadership and Politics: New Perspectives in Political Science*. Lawrence: University Press of Kansas, 1989.

Jones, Charles O. *Introduction to the Study of Public Policy*. 3d ed. Monterey, Calif.: Brooks/Cole Publishing, 1984.

Jorden, William J. *Panama Odyssey*. Austin: University of Texas Press, 1984.

Kahin, George M. *Intervention: How America Became Involved in Vietnam*. New York: Knopf, 1986.

———. "The Pentagon Papers: A Critical Evaluation." *American Political Science Review* 69, 2 (1975): 675–684.

Kaiser, Charles. *1968 in America*. New York: Weidenfeld and Nicolsen, 1988.

Kalb, Bernard, and Elie Abel. *Roots of Involvement: The U.S. in Asia*. New York: Norton, 1971.

Karnow, Stanley. "Giap Remembers." *New York Times Magazine*. June 24,1990, pp. 22–23, 36–39, 57–62.

———. *Vietnam: A History*. New York: Viking Press, 1983.

Kattenburg, Paul. *The Vietnam Trauma in American Foreign Policy, 1945–1975*. New Brunswick, N.J.: Transaction Books, 1980.

Kaufman, Herbert. "Organization Theory and Political Theory." *American Political Science Review* 58, 1 (March 1964): 5–14.

Kearns, Doris. *Lyndon Johnson and the American Dream*. New York: Harper and Row, 1976.

Kellerman, Barbara, and Ryan J. Barilleaux. *The President as World Leader*. New York: St. Martin's Press, 1991.

Kendall, Willmoore. *Dialogues in Americanism*. Chicago: Henry Regnery, 1964.
Kernell, Samuel. *Going Public*. Washington, D.C.: Congressional Quarterly Press, 1986.
Kessel, John. *The Domestic Presidency: Decision-making in the White House*. North Scituate, Mass.: Duxbury Press, 1975. Kessler, Frank. *The Dilemmas of Presidential Leadership*. Englewood Cliffs, N.J.: Prentice-Hall, 1982.
King, Anthony. *The New American Political System*. Washington, D.C.: American Enterprise Institute, 1978.
Kinnard, Douglas. *The Certain Trumpet: Maxwell Taylor and the American Experience in Vietnam*. New York: Brassey's, 1991.
Kissinger, Henry. *The White House Years*. Boston: Little, Brown, 1979.
Koenig, Louis W. "The Invisible Presidency." In *The Presidential Office*, edited by Sidney Wise and Richard Schier, pp. 29–41. New York: Thomas Crowell, 1968.
Kolko, Gabriel. *Anatomy of a War*. New York: Pantheon, 1985.
Komer, Robert. *Bureaucracy at War: U.S. Performance in the Vietnam Conflict*. Boulder, Colo.: Westview Press, 1986.
Kowet, Don. *A Matter of Honor*. New York: Macmillan, 1984.
Lewy, Guenter. *America in Vietnam*. New York: Oxford University Press, 1978.
Lilienthal, David. *The Journals of David Lilienthal*. Vol. 6, *Creativity and Conflict, 1964–1967*. New York: Harper and Row, 1976.
———, edited by Helen Lilienthal. *The Journals of David Lilienthal*. Vol. 7, *Unfinished Business, 1968–1981*. New York: Harper and Row, 1983.
Lowi, Theodore. *The End of Liberalism*. New York: Norton, 1969.
McClellan, David, and David Acheson, eds. *Among Friends: Personal Letters of Dean Acheson*. New York: Dodd, Mead, 1980.
McConnell, Grant. *The Modern Presidency*. New York: St. Martin's Press, 1967.
McKay, David. *Domestic Policy and Ideology: Presidents and the American State, 1964–1987*. Cambridge: Cambridge University Press, 1989.
MacNeil, Neil. *Dirksen*. New York: World Publishing Co., 1970.
McPherson, Harry. *A Political Education*. Boston: Little Brown, 1972.
March, James, and Herbert Simon. *Organizations*. New York: Wiley and Sons, 1958.
Marks, Leonard. "Johnson and Leadership." In *The Johnson Presidency: Twenty Intimate Perspectives of Lyndon B. Johnson*, edited by Kenneth Thompson, pp. 285–286. Lanham, Md.: University Press of America, 1986.
Matthews, Lloyd J., and Dale E. Brown, eds. *Assessing the Vietnam War*. New York: Pergamon Press, 1987.
Medved, Michael. *The Shadow Presidents*. New York: Times Books, 1979.
Mommsen, Wolfgang. *The Political and Social Theory of Max Weber*. Chicago: University of Chicago Press, 1989.
Morgenthau, Hans. "We Are Deluding Ourselves in Vietnam." In *The Vietnam Reader*, edited by Marcus Raskin and Bernard Fall, pp. 37–44. New York: Random House, 1965.
Mueller, John E. *War, Presidents, and Public Opinion*. New York: Wiley, 1973.
Murphy, Bruce Allen. *Fortas: The Rise and Ruin of a Supreme Court Justice*. New York: William Morrow, 1988.
Neustadt, Richard. *Presidential Power*. New York: Wiley and Sons, 1960.
Neustadt, Richard, and Ernest May. *Thinking in Time: The Uses of History for Decision Makers*. New York: Free Press, 1986.
Newman, John M. *JFK and Vietnam*. New York: Warner, 1992.

Nolting, Frederick. *From Trust to Tragedy: The Political Memoirs of Frederick Nolting, Kennedy's Ambassador to Diem's Vietnam.* New York: Praeger, 1988.

Oberdorfer, Don. *Tet: The Turning Point in the Vietnam War.* Garden City, N.Y.: Doubleday, 1971.

O'Neill, Thomas P. *Man of the House.* New York: Random House, 1987.

Palmer, Bruce. *The Twenty-five Year War: America's Military Role in Vietnam.* Lexington: University Press of Kentucky, 1984.

Paterson, Thomas G., ed. *Kennedy's Quest for Victory.* New York: Oxford University Press, 1989.

Patterson, Bradley H. *The Ring of Power: The White House Staff and Its Expanding Role in Government.* New York: Basic Books, 1988.

Patterson, Eugene C. "Sen. Richard Russell: A Study in Division." *Washington Post,* January 25, 1971. Report in U.S. Congress, *Richard Brevard Russell: Memorial Tributes in Congress,* pp. 86–87. Washington, D.C.: Government Printing Office, 1971.

The Pentagon Papers: The Gravel Edition. Boston: Beacon Press, 1971.

Pfeffer, Jeffrey. "Management as Symbolic Action: The Creation and Maintenance of Organizational Paradigms." In *Research in Organization Behavior,* edited by L. L. Cummings and Barry Stow, vol. 3, pp. 1–52. Greenwich, Conn.: JAI Press, 1981.

———. *Organizations and Organization Theory.* Boston: Pitman, 1982.

Podhoretz, Norman. *Why We Were in Vietnam.* New York: Touchstone Press, 1983.

Powers, Thomas. *The Man Who Kept the Secrets.* New York: Knopf, 1979.

———. *The War at Home.* New York: Grossman Publishers, 1973.

The President's Special Review Board. *The Tower Commission Report.* New York: Bantam Books and Times Books, 1987.

The Public Papers of the Presidents: Lyndon Baines Johnson, 1967. Washington, D.C.: Government Printing Office, 1968.

Quill, J. Michael. *Lyndon Johnson and the Southern Military Tradition.* Washington, D.C.: University Press of America, 1977.

Raskin, Marcus, and Bernard Fall, eds. *The Vietnam Reader.* New York: Random House, 1975.

Redford, Emmette, and Marlan Blissett. *Organizing the Executive Branch: The Johnson Presidency.* Chicago: University of Chicago Press, 1981.

Redford, Emmette, and Richard McCulley. *White House Operations: The Johnson Presidency.* Austin: University of Texas Press, 1986.

Reedy, George. *Lyndon B. Johnson: A Memoir.* New York: Andrews and McMeel, 1982.

———. *The Twilight of the Presidency.* New York: World Publishing, 1970.

Reeves, Thomas C. *Gentleman Boss: The Life of Chester A. Arthur.* New York: Knopf, 1975.

Roberts, Charles. *LBJ's Inner Circle.* New York: Delacourt Press, 1965.

Rostow, W. W. *The Diffusion of Power: An Essay in Recent History.* New York: Macmillan, 1972.

———. *Essays on a Half Century: Ideas, Policies, and Action.* Boulder, Colo.: Westview, 1983.

———. *The United States and the Regional Organization of Asia and the Pacific, 1965–1985.* Austin: University of Texas Press, 1986.

Rulon, Philip Reed. *The Compassionate Samaritan: The Life of Lyndon Baines Johnson.* Chicago: Nelson Hall, 1981.

Rusk, Dean (as told to Richard Rusk, edited by Daniel Papp). *As I Saw It*. New York: Norton, 1990.

Schambra, William. "Progressive Liberalism and American 'Community.' " *Public Interest* (Summer 1985): 32–37.

Schandler, Herbert. *Lyndon Johnson and Vietnam: The Unmaking of a President*. Princeton, N.J.: Princeton University Press, 1983.

Schlesinger, Arthur. *The Bitter Heritage*. Boston: Houghton Mifflin, 1967.

———. *The Imperial Presidency*. Boston: Houghton Mifflin, 1973.

———. *Robert Kennedy and His Times*. Boston: Houghton Mifflin. 1978.

Schoenbaum, Thomas. *Waging Peace and War: Dean Rusk in the Truman, Kennedy, and Johnson Years*. New York: Simon and Schuster, 1988.

Schwarz, John. *America's Hidden Success*. New York: Norton, 1983.

Scruton, Roger. *A Dictionary of Political Thought*. New York: Hill and Wang, 1982.

Seaborg, Glenn T., with Benjamin S. Loeb. *Stemming the Tide: Arms Control in the Johnson Years*. Lexington, Mass.: Lexington Books, 1987.

Sharp, Ulysses S. G. *Strategy For Defeat*. San Rafael, Calif.: Presidio Press, 1978.

Sheehan, Neil. *A Bright Shining Lie: John Paul Vann and America in Vietnam*. New York: Random House, 1988.

———. "Not a Dove, But No Longer a Hawk." *New York Times Magazine*, October 9, 1966.

———, ed. *The Pentagon Papers: The New York Times Edition*. New York: Quadrangle Books, 1971.

Sherwood, Robert. *Roosevelt and Hopkins: An Intimate History*. New York: Harper and Brothers, 1948.

Shogan, Robert. *A Question of Judgment: The Fortas Case and the Struggle for the Supreme Court*. Indianapolis: Bobbs-Merrill, 1972.

Sloan, John W. "President Johnson, the Council of Economic Advisers, and the Failure to Raise Taxes in 1966 and 1967." *Presidential Studies Quarterly* 15, 1 (1985): 89–98.

Small, Melvin. *Johnson, Nixon, and the Doves*. New Brunswick, N.J.: Rutgers University Press, 1988.

Smith, Howard K. "A Strong Thread of Moral Purpose." In *To Heal and to Build*, edited by James McGregor Burns, pp. 1–15. New York: McGraw-Hill, 1968.

Smith, Nancy Kegan. "Presidential Task Force Operation during the Johnson Administration." *Presidential Studies Quarterly* 15, 2 (Spring 1985): 320–329.

Solberg, Carl. *Hubert Humphrey: A Biography*. New York: Norton, 1984.

Spalding, Jack. "Senator Richard Russell." *Atlanta Journal*, January 26, 1971. Reprinted in U.S. Congress, *Richard Brevard Russell: Memorial Tributes*. Washington, D.C.: Government Printing Office, 139.

Sparks, Will. *Who Talked to the President Last?* New York: Norton, 1971.

Sprout, Harold, and Margaret Sprout. *The Ecological Perspective on Human Affairs, with Special Reference to International Relations*. Princeton, N.J.: Princeton University Press, 1965.

Steinbruner, John D. *The Cybernetic Theory of Decision*. Princeton, N.J.: Princeton University Press, 1974.

Stoessinger, John. *Crusaders and Pragmatists: Movers of Modern American Foreign Policy*. New York: Norton, 1985.

———. *Why Nations Go to War*. 4th ed. New York: St. Martin's Press, 1985.

Summers, Harry G. "Lessons: A Soldier's View." In *Vietnam as History*, edited by Peter Braestrup, pp. 109–114. Washington, D.C.: University Press of America, 1984.

———. "A Strategic Perception of the Vietnam War." In *Assessing the Vietnam War*, edited by Lloyd Matthews and Dale Brown, pp. 35–42. New York: Pergamon, 1987.

Taylor, Maxwell. *Swords and Plowshares*. New York: Norton, 1972.

Thomas, Norman, and Harold Wolman. "Policy Formulation in the Institutionalized Presidency: The Johnson Task Forces." In *The Presidential Advisory System*, edited by Thomas Cronin and Sanford Greenberg, pp. 124–143. New York: Harper and Row, 1969.

Thompson, Kenneth, ed. *The Johnson Presidency: Twenty Intimate Portraits of Lyndon B. Johnson*. Lanham, Md.: University Press of America, 1986.

Thomson, James C. "How Could Vietnam Happen?" *Atlantic*, April 1968, pp. 47–53.

Trewhitt, Henry. *McNamara*. New York: Harper and Row, 1971.

Truman, David. *The Governmental Process*. New York: Knopf, 1951.

Tuchman, Barbara. *The March of Folly*. New York: Knopf, 1984.

Turner, Kathleen. *Lyndon Johnson's Dual War: Vietnam and the Press*. Chicago: University of Chicago Press, 1985.

U.S. Congress. *The Congressional Record*. 89th to 90th Congress. Washington, D.C.: Government Printing Office, 1964–1968.

U.S. Congress. *United States–Vietnam Relations, 1945–1967: Study Prepared by the Department of Defense*. Washington, D.C.: Government Printing Office, 1971.

U. S. State Department. *Aggression from the North*. Washington, D.C.: Government Printing Office, 1965.

Valenti, Jack. *A Very Human President*. New York: Pocket Books, 1977.

VanDeMark, Brian. *Into the Quagmire: Lyndon Johnson and the Escalation of the Vietnam War*. New York: Oxford University Press, 1991.

Walcott, Charles, and Karen Hult. *Governing Public Organizations: Politics, Structure, and Institutional Design*. Pacific Grove, Calif.: Brooks/Cole, 1990.

———. "Organizing the White House: Structure, Environment, and Organizational Governance." *American Journal of Political Science* 31, 1 (February 1987): 109–125.

Waltz, Kenneth. *Man, the State, and War*. New York: Columbia University Press, 1959.

Ward, Barbara. *The Rich Nations and the Poor Nations*. New York: Norton, 1962.

Welborn, David M., and Jesse Burkhead. *Intergovernmental Relations in the American State: The Johnson Presidency*. Austin: University of Texas Press, 1989.

Westmoreland, William. *A Soldier Reports*. Garden City, N.Y.: Doubleday, 1976.

Whalen, Charles, and Barbara Whalen. *The Longest Debate*. Cabin Lodge, Md.: Seven Locks Press, 1985.

Wiarda, Howard. *Foreign Policy without Illusion*. Glenview, Ill.: Scott, Foresman, 1990.

Wicker, Tom. *JFK and LBJ: The Influence of Personality Upon Politics*. New York: Morrow, 1968.

Wills, Garry. "Monstre Sacre," *New York Review of Books*, April 26, 1990, pp. 7–9.

Wise, Sidney, and Richard F. Schier, eds. *The Presidential Office*. New York: Thomas Y. Crowell, 1968.

Wood, Gordon S. "Intellectual History and the Social Sciences." In *New Directions in Intellectual History*, edited by Paul Conkin and John Higham, pp. 27–41. Baltimore: Johns Hopkins Press, 1979.
Ziemke, Caroline. "Senator Richard B. Russell and the 'Lost Cause' in Vietnam, 1954–1968." *Georgia Historical Quarterly* 72, 1 (1988): 30–70.

Archival Materials

Lyndon B. Johnson Library, University of Texas, Austin.
Richard B. Russell Library, University of Georgia, Athens.
Dwight D. Eisenhower Library, Abilene, Kans.
Minnesota Historical Society (the papers of Hubert Humphrey), St. Paul, Minn.
National Archives, Washington, D.C.
Library of Congress, Washington, D.C.

Personal Interviews

George Christian
W. W. Rostow
Dean Rusk
George Reedy

Oral History Interviews

LBJ Library

George Aiken, George Ball, William Bundy, George Christian, Clark Clifford, Abe Fortas, Andrew Goodpaster, Ernest Gruening, Richard Helms, Lyndon Johnson, Harry McPherson, Powell Moore, Benjamin Read, John Roche, Eugene Rostow, Dean Rusk, Bromley Smith, Maxwell Taylor, Larry Temple, Jack Valenti, William Westmoreland, Earle Wheeler.

Russell Library

McGeorge Bundy, Clark Clifford, Sam Ervin, J. William Fulbright, Lady Bird Johnson, Dean Rusk.

Library of Congress, Manuscript Division

J. William Fulbright.

Index

Abrams, Gen. Creighton, 145, 147–148, 151
Acheson, Dean, 8, 39–40, 61, 84, 136, 140, 141, 149, 150, 161, 166–168, 184
  adviser, as informal, 128–129, 158
  on Johnson, 43, 128, 129, 136, 144
  Rostow, relationship with, 137, 141
Adenauer, Konrad, 58, 193
Adviser, The (Goldhamer), 7
Advisers
  definition of, 7–9
  evolution of systems of, 9–11, 160–161, 168, 203n32
  informal, 7–9, 59, 84, 99, 101, 108, 158, 162, 164, 166–169
Afghanistan, compared to Vietnam, 36
Africa, 31, 58, 123
Aiken, Sen. George, 98–99, 187, 231n141
Air Force, U.S., 88, 110
American Medical Association (AMA), 179–180
Americans for Democratic Action (ADA), 76
Anatomy of a War (Kolko), 6
Anderson, Patrick, 28, 173
Anderson, Robert, 108
Anti-infiltration barrier, 91, 92–93
Antiwar movement, 12, 107. *See also* Demonstrations, antiwar
Arendt, Hannah, 193
Army, U.S., 52, 75, 88, 105. *See also* Vietnam War
Army of the Republic of Vietnam (ARVN), 27, 53, 121, 122
Arrogance of Power, The (Fulbright), 94
Arthur, Chester, 169
Asia, 91–92, 126, 191, 193
Associated Press, 184
Australia, 41, 103, 109

Balance-of-payments crisis, 127, 147–148, 149
Ball, George, 3, 8, 31, 33, 34, 38, 42, 45, 49, 41, 54, 55–60, 85, 128, 138, 144, 152, 192, 193

access to Johnson, 28–29, 58, 85, 150–151, 186, 209n57, 214n105
  on bombing, 21, 149
  and McGeorge Bundy, 149
  and Rusk, 29
  on Rusk and McNamara, 24–25, 59
  on withdrawal, 6, 27–30, 32, 52–54, 150, 162
Barber, James David, 5–6, 170–171
Barilleaux, Ryan, 170
Bay of Pigs incident, 55
Beliefs, impact of on foreign policy, 190–194
Berlin, 129
Berman, Larry, 6, 42–43, 171
Betts, Richard, 5, 6, 14, 44, 190
Bingham, Rep. Jonathan, 64
Bornet, Vaughn Davis, ix
Bradley, Gen. Omar, 39, 40, 106, 150, 156
Britain, 41, 130, 133, 147
Brodie, Bernard, 170–171
Brooke, Sen. Edward, 87
Buchanan, Bruce, 170
Bundy, McGeorge, 8, 24, 26, 30, 32, 40, 51, 54, 55, 58, 73–74, 138, 142–144, 150, 162, 185, 207n28
  adviser, as informal, 85, 111, 149, 158, 222n35, 245n130
  background of, 22
  described by others, 22, 222n35
  on Eisenhower, 21
  escalation, urging, 16, 21
  on French in Vietnam, 29
  and Johnson, 22, 59, 73, 149, 167, 176, 185
  and John Kennedy, 21–22
  and Mansfield, 17
  and Moyers, 28
  as national security adviser, 22, 33, 73
  and Pleiku incident, 17, 22
  and withdrawal, 21–22, 29, 53
Bundy, William, 26, 33, 43, 104, 125, 143
  advisory status of, 31, 142, 210n63, 227n93

Bundy, William, *continued*
  background of, 30–31
  on Johnson, 32–33, 60, 187, 194
  on Mansfield and Johnson, 17–19
  "middle way," 30–32, 38
  on Rusk and McNamara, 31
  on withdrawal, 126
Bunker, Ellsworth, 74–76, 91, 92, 112,
  121, 122, 125, 142, 143, 145, 154
  influence of, 91, 229n107
  on war, 104, 141, 157
Burke, John, 34–35
Burma, 58
Busby, Horace, 53–54, 122, 155
Byrd, Sen. Robert, 117–118, 165

Califano, Joseph, 125, 138, 179–180,
  187, 188
Cambodia, 58, 76, 78, 87
Carver, George, 151
Castro, Fidel, 36
Central Intelligence Agency (CIA), 7, 30,
  39, 51, 84–85, 89–90, 116, 129, 135,
  182
  analyses of war, 88–90, 116, 151, 155,
  228n100
  See also Foreign Intelligence Advisory
  Board; Helms, Richard; Intelligence
  Reports
Channing, Carol, 119
China, People's Republic of, 5, 13, 18,
  20, 31, 45, 46, 53–55, 57–58, 81, 82,
  85, 86, 88, 101, 107, 123
Chomsky, Noam, 71–72, 80
Christian, George, 85, 111, 132, 187
Church, Sen. Frank, 51
Clark, Sen. Joseph, 50, 51, 65, 106
Clark, Ramsey, 142
Clifford, Clark, 8, 43, 54, 72–73,
  115–116, 118–119, 122, 134, 135,
  139–141, 145, 148, 149, 152–154,
  158
  on bombing, 100, 142, 143, 153
  and Clifford Group, 126–127, 129–133,
  136, 147, 167
  described by others, 56, 100, 121,
  156–157, 239n40
  and escalation, 33–34, 55–57, 58, 60,
  100, 110–111, 126, 131, 136, 144,
  162
  and Johnson, 33–34, 72, 100, 121, 130,
  135–136, 143–144, 146, 153, 167
  and Robert Kennedy, 138
  mission with Taylor, 101–102
  as secretary of defense, 121, 144, 153
Cohen, Wilbur, 179
Cold War, 7, 13, 15, 45

Commager, Henry Steele, 191
Compassionate Samaritan, The (Rulon),
  174
Congo, 123
Congress, U.S., 7, 8, 10, 15, 33, 39, 55,
  57–58, 60, 62–69, 71, 72, 79, 80, 84,
  98, 103, 104, 106–107, 111–114,
  116–118, 127, 135, 138, 139, 148,
  154–157, 173–178, 181, 183, 185,
  189, 194
  access of members to Johnson, 69,
  106–107, 221n26
  appropriations for war, 48–51, 64–67,
  69
  debates on war: in 1965, 48–51,
  161–162; in 1967, 63–69, 163–165;
  in 1968, 109–110, 112–113, 165–167
  and declarations of war, 13, 218n143
  and military reserves, 131
  See also House of Representatives,
  U.S.; Senate, U.S.
Congressional Record, 69, 107, 111, 163,
  166
Containment doctrine, 193–194
Conyers, Rep. John, 51
Cooper, Chester, 173
Cooper, Sen. John Sherman, 15, 50
Corwin, Edward, 7
Cousins, Norman, 140, 244n99
Cronkite, Walter, 132, 241n75
Cuba, 36, 45
Czechoslovakia, 183

Dean, Arthur, 150
Dean, Patrick, 133, 156
Defense, U.S. Department of, 7, 30, 32,
  51, 64, 84, 86, 93, 105, 125, 130,
  135, 136, 143, 144, 153
DeGaulle, Charles, 43
Democratic party, 49, 62, 63, 65, 72, 94,
  106, 111–113, 117, 138, 139, 154,
  175
Demonstrations, antiwar, 10, 12, 62,
  71–72, 83. *See also* Antiwar
  movement
Detroit, riots in, 1, 100, 102
Dewey, Thomas, 22
Diem, Ngo Dinh, 14
*Dilemmas of Presidential Leadership,
The* (Kessler), 170
Dillon, Douglas, 149, 150
Dirksen, Sen. Everett, 67, 68, 113, 157
Dominican Republic, 40, 99
Domino theory, 5, 46, 58, 60–61, 193.
  See also Containment doctrine
Douglas, Sen. Paul, 176
Dulles, John Foster, 35, 168

Eisenhower, Dwight D., 8, 11, 22, 31, 36, 60, 83, 108, 168, 175, 177
and Goodpaster, 40–41
and Johnson, 40–41, 83, 105, 123
Vietnam policies of, 14, 35, 50, 60, 203n2
on Wheeler and Westmoreland, 123
Ellison, Ralph, ix
Environment, American political, 9–10, 23, 46–51, 62–74, 106–108, 111–114, 157, 160–168, 171. *See also* Public opinion
Ervin, Sen. Sam, 37
Europe, 40, 58, 107, 123, 125, 193
Evans, Rowland, 176

Federal Bureau of Investigation (FBI), 185
Ford, Rep. Gerald, 51, 60, 113
Foreign aid, U.S., 2
Foreign Intelligence Advisory Board, 33, 72, 122
Forrestal, James, 127–128
Fortas, Abe, 8, 84, 99–100, 138, 141, 142, 158
Lady Bird Johnson on, 100
and President Johnson, 99–100, 139–140, 168, 169
views on war, 100, 111, 140, 143, 150, 155, 157
Fowler, Henry "Joe," 127, 129, 142
France, 43
and colonial Vietnam, 13–14, 27, 29, 35
Fraser, Rep. Donald, 64
Fulbright, Betty, 44, 46, 249n149
Fulbright, J. William, 4, 8, 33, 57, 58, 65–67, 75, 80, 87, 103, 112, 117, 123, 135, 140, 192–193
and *Arrogance of Power*, 94
on bombing, 2–3, 94
described by others, 2, 106, 124
friendship with Johnsons, 1–2, 44, 46, 192
and Lilienthal, 45, 93
and Mansfield, 67
meetings with Johnson, 1–3, 44–46, 94, 102, 107, 134, 164
and *Old Myths and New Realities*, 192
reaction to March 31, 1968, speech, 156
relationship with Johnson, 44–46, 93–94, 102, 124, 132
on Russell, 36–37
and Tonkin Resolution, 15, 66, 102
on withdrawal, 44–45, 71, 164

Galbraith, John Kenneth, 92
Gallup Organization, 70, 105, 113
Gardner, John, 178–179
Gelb, Leslie, 5, 6, 14, 190
Geneva Accords, 67, 124
Germany, West, 58, 193
Giap, Gen. Vo Nguyen, on Johnson, 6
Gilpatric, Roswell, 40
Gilpatric Report, 184–185
Goldberg, Arthur, 8, 9, 144, 209n57
de-escalation proposal, 140–143, 145
meetings with Johnson, 142, 143, 158, 166
Goldhamer, Herbert, 7
Goldwater, Sen. Barry, 186
Goodpaster, Gen. Andrew, 40–41, 105
Goodwin, Richard, 6, 69–70, 171
Gore, Sen. Albert, 49–50, 51
Governmental Process, The (Truman), 176–177, 180
Great Britain, 41, 130, 133, 147
Greenstein, Fred, 34–35
Greece, 58
Groupthink (Janis), 170–171, 199n12
Gruening, Sen. Ernest, 50, 67, 187
Gruenther, Gen. Alfred, 184
Guam conference, 74–79

Habib, Philip, 151
Halberstam, David, ix
Harriman, Averell, 8
Hartke, Sen. Vance, 92
Harvard University, 16, 22, 58
Hayden, Sen. Carl, 37
Helms, Richard, 8, 84–85, 88–90, 116, 117, 122, 129, 135, 151, 228n100
on Johnson and Clifford, 156–158
relationship with Johnson, 88–89, 187, 192
on Tuesday Lunch Group, 84
See also Central Intelligence Agency; Intelligence reports
Hess, Stephen, 9
Ho Chi Minh, 3, 13, 31, 52, 60, 64, 118
Holt, Harold, 109
Hoopes, Townsend, 110, 111, 121, 135, 157, 170–171, 242n86
Hopkins, Harry, 169
House, Col. Edward, 108, 169
House of Representatives, U.S., 11, 49, 51, 64–65, 106, 113, 186
Appropriations Committee, 65
Armed Services Committee, 25
Rules Committee, 185
See also Congress, U.S.
How Presidents Test Reality (Burke and Greenstein), 34–35

Hult, Karen, 9, 168
Humphrey, David, 84–85, 162
Humphrey, Hubert, 8, 34, 58, 60, 85,
  91–92, 111, 127, 132, 137, 138, 143,
  151, 155, 158
  described by others, 18, 20
  McNamara and, 25
  opposition to bombing, 18–19, 92, 162
  relationship with Johnson, 19–21,
  91–92, 142, 146–147, 149, 230n112
  withdrawal, advocacy of, 19–20

India, 58
Intelligence reports, 116, 118, 119, 122,
  146, 151, 192, 228n100, 239n43. *See
  also* Central Intelligence Agency;
  Helms, Richard
International Control Commission, 124
International law, 120
International system, 6, 23, 25, 192–194
Irony of Vietnam, The (Gelb and Betts),
  190
Israel, 96, 100

Jackson, Andrew, 169
Jackson, Sen. Henry, 68, 157, 183
Janis, Irving, 170–171, 199n12
Japan, 58
Johnson, Gen. Harold K., 105, 115
Johnson, Lady Bird, 8, 23, 35, 72, 95,
  99, 103, 117, 147, 156
  and Eartha Kitt incident, 119
  on President Johnson, 44, 62, 106,
  137, 147, 155
  on Johnson and Fulbright, 44, 106, 192
  on Johnson and Humphrey, 21
  on Johnson and Russell, 37, 152, 169
  nightmares described, 120
  on Rusk, 130
  with wounded soldiers, 119–120
Johnson, Lyndon B.
  advisers: "using" them, 42–43,
  214n105, 215n106; informal, 32–33,
  42, 73, 108, 138, 139, 162, 164,
  167–169
  arms control and, 182–185
  character of, 5–6, 9–10, 11, 24, 60,
  170–174, 185–188, 254n18
  daily diary of, 201n25, 216n116,
  252n2
  described by others, 19, 23, 41, 42, 56,
  59, 60, 63, 64, 67, 75–77, 82, 84,
  89, 91-93, 97-99, 105, 108, 110-111,
  117, 120, 124, 128, 141, 146, 147,
  151, 155-158, 169-171, 178-180,
  185-188, 194, 232n141, 253n5
  Diem, views of, 14

domestic agenda of, 6, 21, 23, 24, 49,
  56–57, 59–60, 63, 106, 127, 128,
  180–182, 197n1
  on history, 190
  hopes to avoid war, 15–16, 161
  on leaks, 31, 176, 184–186, 256n46
  March 31, 1968, speech, 134, 135,
  147, 154–155, 156, 157
  nightmares of, 120
  openness/resistance to diverse advice,
  16–17, 58, 60, 63, 67, 85, 110–111,
  117, 119, 161-162, 164, 166, 168,
  173-174, 181, 182, 185-188, 192,
  194, 221n26, 232n141, 243n87,
  257n61
  political style of, 11, 43, 108, 111,
  134, 167, 172-189, 193-194
  pre-presidential years of, 11, 35, 92,
  98, 173, 175-176
  presidential leadership, "theory" of,
  175-180
  public memories of, ix
  published accounts of, 3, 63, 110, 161,
  166, 169-171, 173-174, 191, 193,
  257nn59, 64
  on retirement, 137-139, 147, 154-157
  role in shaping advisory system,
  168-171
  South Vietnam, and predictions of
  "fall" of, 24, 194
  troop deployments announced: 1965,
  59; 1967, 104; 1968, 154, 156
  as vice president, 19
  visits troops, 122-123
Johnson, Tom, notes of, 105, 197n2,
  236n1
Joint Chiefs of Staff (JCS), 7, 19, 35, 38,
  40, 81, 84-86, 104, 107, 129, 151,
  199n15
  support for 1965 troop request, 26-27,
  32, 54-55
  at 1968 meetings with president, 115,
  118-119

Karnow, Stanley, 25
Katzenbach, Nicholas, 85, 92, 125, 129,
  131, 227n93
Kearns, Doris, 37, 85, 117, 157, 171,
  174, 176, 181
Kellerman, Barbara, 170
Kennedy, Sen. Edward, 51, 138, 140
Kennedy, John F., ix, 11, 30, 33, 40, 89,
  101, 149, 180-181, 183
  assassination of, 14, 22, 171
  McGeorge Bundy and, 22
  Diem and, 14
  Mansfield and, 17

Kennedy, John F., *continued*
  Rusk and, 22, 191
  Taylor and, 38
  Vietnam policies of, 6, 14–16, 21, 22, 50, 171, 191, 204nn4,6
Kennedy, Sen. Robert, 38, 51, 65, 69, 75, 80, 87, 93, 105, 112, 138–140, 185
  announces presidential candidacy, 138
  and McNamara, 105, 127
  meetings with Johnson, 68, 107, 164
Kessler, Frank, 170
Khan, Ayub, 58
Khe Sanh, battle of, 114, 116, 124, 129, 131
Khrushchev, Nikita, 184
King, Rev. Martin Luther, 83
Kissinger, Henry, 7, 58, 168, 193
Kitt, Eartha, 119
Kolko, Gabriel, 6, 193
Komer, Robert, 74, 90–91, 101, 103
Korean War, 55, 81, 128, 129. *See also* North Korea; South Korea
Kosygin, Aleksei, 70, 88
Ky, Nguyen Cao, 29–30, 74, 78, 86, 91, 96, 122

Laos, 58, 76, 78, 81, 82, 87, 91
Lausche, Sen. Frank, 2
Leaks, 7, 84, 130
  Johnson and, 20, 31–32, 135, 256n46
Lewy, Guenter, 191
Life magazine, 140
Lilienthal, David, 45, 74–75, 77, 90, 93, 103, 112
  on Clifford, 100
  on Johnson, 75, 77, 105
  on McNamara, 128
Limits of Intervention, The (Hoopes), 110–111, 157, 170–171
Lippmann, Walter, 96
Lodge, Henry Cabot, 8, 51, 53, 136, 144, 149, 156, 167, 243n87
Long, Sen. Russell, 111–112, 117
Lovett, Robert, 40, 184
Lyndon B. Johnson: A Memoir (Reedy), 173
Lyndon Johnson and the American Dream (Kearns), 174
Lyndon Johnson and Vietnam (Schandler), 110–111

MacArthur, Gen. Douglas, 128, 129
McCarthy, Sen. Eugene, 51, 112, 137–139
McCarthy, Sen. Joseph, 176
McCloy, John, 39

McConnell, Gen. John, 88
McCulley, Richard, 187
McGovern, Sen. George, 80–81
McNamara, Robert, 8, 17, 22, 28, 31, 38, 46, 59, 61, 73, 76, 78–81, 85–87, 88, 90–92, 96, 97, 100–102, 106, 116–117, 120, 121, 125–129, 152
  bombing and, 25, 78, 86, 104, 115, 164
  McGeorge Bundy and, 25
  described by others, 25, 36, 97, 127–128
  disillusionment with war, 78, 105, 128
  domestic policy and, 128, 181
  escalation: urging, 16, 25, 30, 36, 51–58, 162, 208n39; opposing, 86–87, 126
  "fall" of Vietnam, and predictions of, 24–25
  hostility to dovish advice, 25
  Humphrey and, 25
  Johnson and, 24–26, 105, 128
  Robert Kennedy and, 68–69, 105
  missions to Saigon, 41–43, 78, 100–101, 103–104
  optimism on war, 100–101, 104
  resignation of, 105, 127
  Rostow and, 165
  Rusk and, 24–25, 115
  Russell and, 37, 97
  Westmoreland and, 103–104
McNaughton, John, 1, 24, 90
McPherson, Harry, 8, 74, 92, 94–97, 112, 122–123, 125, 126, 138–139, 141, 154–156, 158
  background of, 95
  on bombing, 96, 123, 145, 148
  and Clifford, 144–145
  and Johnson, 95–96, 157, 166, 176
  and Moyers, 95
  role in administration, 96, 142, 144
  and Rostow, 112
  and Russell, 96–97
  trip to Vietnam, 96
Mahon, Rep. George, 65
Malaysia, 58
Mansfield, Sen. Mike, 3, 8, 34, 50, 51, 57, 60, 65, 67, 92–93, 158
  amendment proposed by, 67–69
  background of, 17
  on bombing, 17–18, 92, 152
  McGeorge Bundy and, 17
  on inevitability of Vietnam war, 4–5, 58
  and Johnson: judgments of, 4–5; meetings with, 17–18, 57–58, 67, 118, 152, 157, 166; letters to, 4–5, 18, 36, 56–57, 59, 92–93
  Russell and, 36

Mao Tse-tung, 13
Marcos, Ferdinand, 101
Marks, Leonard, 98-99, 164, 232n141
Marshall, Gen. George, 39, 87, 105
May, Ernest, 16
Middle East, 73, 88
Morse, Sen. Wayne, 69, 71, 80, 93, 140
  in debates, 50, 62, 65-67
  and Johnson, 44
  on Tonkin Resolution, 50
Moyers, Bill, 8, 20, 162, 179, 209n52
  McGeorge Bundy and, 28
  McPherson and, 95
  resignation of, 95
  role in Johnson administration, 28, 59
Murphy, Robert, 150

National Guard, 52, 124
National Security Act, 7
National Security Council (NSC), 7, 82, 84, 91, 109
  meetings of, 17-19, 99, 173-174
  staff, influence of, 22
Navy, U.S., 54, 112
NBC news, 147
Nelson, Sen. Gaylord, 50, 67
Neustadt, Richard, 16, 177
New Hampshire primary, 137-138, 243n91
News media, 10, 69, 71, 72, 75, 78-79, 84, 103-106, 110-112, 118, 122, 124, 132, 135, 136, 140-141, 146-147, 151, 157, 165, 166, 179, 181, 185, 186, 184
Newsweek, 140
New York Times, 1, 71, 105, 135-136, 141, 147, 183
Ngo Dinh Diem. *See* Diem, Ngo Dinh
Nguyen Cao Ky. *See* Ky, Nguyen Cao
Nguyen Van Thieu. *See* Thieu, Nguyen Van
Nitze, Paul, 54, 129
Nixon, Richard, 7, 139, 168
Non-Proliferation Treaty, 183
North Atlantic Treaty Organization (NATO), 43, 75, 184-185. *See also* Europe
North Korea, 13, 109, 111, 128
North Vietnam (People's Republic of Vietnam), 14, 57, 64, 72, 78-80, 89, 109, 110, 116, 119, 124-125, 137, 151
  accepts offer to negotiate, 156
  bombing of, U.S., 2-3, 15, 17-19, 21-26, 38-39, 78, 86, 115, 123, 134, 154
  Johnson on, 116

and Tonkin incident, 15
  victory in 1975, 13
Novak, Robert, 176
Nuclear weapons, use considered, 116, 140
Nugent, Lyn, 150
Nugent, Pat, 132, 151, 155

O'Brien, Lawrence, 69, 179
Old Myths and New Realities (Fulbright), 192
O'Neill, Thomas P. "Tip," 186
Organization theory, 7, 168-169
Organizing the Presidency (Hess), 9

Pacification programs, 90, 151
Pakistan, 58
Palmer, Gen. Bruce, 75-76
Pastore, Sen. John, 2
Paul VI, Pope, 64
Pearson, Drew, 141
Pell, Sen. Claiborne, 8, 69, 98
Pentagon Papers, 27, 31, 41-43, 74, 86, 200n18, 208n39
Planning a Tragedy (Berman), 6, 42
Pluralism, 175-178, 188-189, 193
Podhoretz, Norman, 191
Powers, Thomas, 89
President as World Leader, The (Kellerman and Barilleaux), 170
Presidential Character, The (Barber), 5-6, 170-171
Presidential Experience, The (Buchanan), 170
Presidential Power (Neustadt), 177, 180
Public opinion, 10, 46-48, 69-72, 79, 86, 90, 100, 103, 105-107, 111, 113-114, 127, 140-141, 145, 147, 150, 152, 157, 161-167, 194. *See also* Environment, American political
Pueblo incident, 109-112, 117, 118

Raborn, Adm. William, 51
Radford, Adm. Arthur, 35
Rationality, 106, 170, 190-194
  definitions of, 9-10, 191, 258n5
Rayburn, Sam 11, 97-98
"Realists," 192-193
Redford, Emmette, 187
Reedy, George, 171, 173, 174, 253n5
Republican party, 60, 63, 65, 83, 93, 106, 113, 117, 140, 154
Reston, James, 26, 71
Ridgway, Gen. Matthew, 128, 138, 150, 156, 158, 166
Robb, Charles, 132, 155

Robb, Lynda Johnson, 119, 155
Roche, John, 76, 94, 137, 178–179, 187–188
Rogers, William, 168
Rollins, Daniel, 169
Roosevelt, Franklin D., 11, 43, 49, 75, 139, 169, 173, 175–177, 179
Roosevelt, Theodore, 178
Rostow, Eugene, 186
Rostow, Walt W., 8, 64, 72, 73, 76, 79, 80, 84–85, 89, 91, 92, 98, 106, 109, 111, 116, 125, 129, 134, 135, 140, 142, 145, 148, 150, 154
    and Acheson, 137
    background of, 82
    on bombing, 103, 105, 141
    and Clifford, 126, 143–144
    described by others, 82, 110, 117
    and McNamara, 103, 105, 165
    as national security adviser, 82, 117
    views on war, 90, 103, 105, 112, 131, 132, 155, 190–191, 193
Rowan, Carl, 51
Rowe, James, 139
Rulon, Philip, 174, 191
Rusk, Dean, 8, 17, 35, 37, 43, 61, 68, 75, 80, 82, 83, 85, 87–88, 91, 92, 94, 97, 105, 111, 116, 118, 120, 124, 125, 127, 129, 135, 140, 143–146, 149, 152, 158, 183
    advisers, on presidential, ix, 82, 88, 130, 169, 174
    advisory role, on his, 32
    and Ball, 29
    on bombing, 87–88, 115, 130, 133, 134, 140, 142, 148, 153, 154, 227n93, 241n66
    and Clifford, 130, 132, 153, 154, 156, 167
    described by others, 31, 54, 102, 110
    and escalation, 31, 87–88, 130, 148, 167
    and "fight and talk" strategy, 130, 133
    and Johnson, 31–32, 87, 117, 130, 133, 156, 186
    and President Kennedy, 22, 191, 227n93
    and McNamara, 24–25
    on his responsibility for the war, 191, 227n93
    troop deployments, on purpose of initial, 26
    on Tuesday Lunch Group, 84, 130
Rusk, Richard, 135
Russell, Sen. Richard, 2, 8, 51, 58, 59, 65–66, 68–69, 80, 81, 84, 96–98, 112, 147, 153, 155, 157
    advisory status, 34–35, 37, 43, 97–98, 158, 166, 168
    Afghanistan and Vietnam, compares, 36
    and Appropriations Committee, 37
    archival records of, 37, 98
    battleships, and refitting of, 97
    described by others, 35, 36–37
    on escalation, 35, 60, 65, 97–98, 123, 135, 146, 152
    and Fulbright, 45
    and Johnson, 11, 35–37, 96, 123, 152, 248nn136,137, 256n51; meetings with, disputed frequency of: 34–35, 201n25, 211n76, 252n2
    and President Kennedy, 35
    and McNamara, 36, 97
    and Mansfield, 36
    and 1954 Vietnam controversy, 35

Saturday Evening Post, 92
Schandler, Herbert, 110–111
Schlesinger, Arthur, 71, 92, 106, 163
Schultze, Charles, 179
Seaborg, Glenn, 182, 183, 185
Senate, U.S., 11, 36–37, 45, 49–51, 55, 65–69, 83, 93, 97, 98, 102, 106, 109, 112–113, 152, 156, 161, 164, 175–176, 181, 183, 187
    Appropriations Committee, 37, 66, 178
    Armed Services Committee, 34, 37, 66
    Finance Committee, 112, 179
    Foreign Relations Committee, 2, 33, 44, 67, 102, 124
    leadership of, 1–3, 111
    and Mansfield amendment, 67–69
    See also Congress, U.S.
Senior Advisory Group. See Wise Men
Shannon, William, 1
Sharp, Adm. U. S. Grant, 26, 106, 121, 234n164
Sheehan, Neil, 71
Situation Room (White House), 22, 113, 186
Six Day War, 70, 88, 92, 96, 100
Smith, Bromley, 83
Smith, "Judge" Howard, 185
Smith, Howard K., 74
Sorensen, Theodore, 138
Southeast Asia Treaty Organization (SEATO), 14
South Korea, 13, 41, 103, 120, 128
South Vietnam (Republic of Vietnam), 14, 23, 32, 33, 34, 48, 73, 76, 86, 87, 99, 110, 114, 115, 122, 124, 126, 127, 130–131, 141, 142, 145, 148, 154–155, 163–166, 190–191, 194

South Vietnam (Republic of Vietnam),
  continued
  defeat of: in 1975, 13, 191; U.S. fears
    about, 23-24, 26-27, 31, 38, 51, 53,
    60, 72, 127, 161
  described by Ball, 29-30
  strategic value of, 35, 40, 45, 60
Soviet Union (USSR), 5, 13, 14, 18, 36,
  45, 57, 82, 107, 112, 117, 123,
  183-184, 192
State, U.S. Department of, 31, 32, 55,
  82, 84, 125, 130, 140, 186, 187
Stennis, Sen. John, 146, 157
Stevenson, Adlai, 18, 44, 46
Stimson, Henry, 22
Strategic Arms Limitation Treaty
  (SALT), 183

Taylor, Gen. Maxwell, 8, 26, 34, 62,
  129, 141, 144, 150, 155-158
  on bombing, 38-39, 80, 102, 162
  on ground troops, 38-39, 80, 116, 132
  and Johnson, 38, 101, 187, 232n141
  mission with Clifford, 101-102
  resigns ambassadorship, 101
  U.S. options in Vietnam, 80, 158-159
  on withdrawal, 38, 163
Temple, Larry, 147
Tet Offensive, 63
  beginning of, 109-110, 112-113
  intelligence regarding, 239n43
  outcome of, 110, 119, 122
Thailand, 58
Thant, U, 123
Theories of international
  relations, impact on foreign
  policy, 190-194
Thieu, Nguyen Van, 74, 91, 122
Thinking in Time (Neustadt and May), 16
Thomas, Norman, 180
Thurmond, Sen. Strom, 109, 113
Time magazine, 140
Today Show, 106
Tonkin incident, 15, 62, 204n9
Tonkin Gulf Resolution, 3, 15, 44, 50,
  56, 62-63, 66, 68, 102
Tower, Sen. John, 51, 65, 106
Truman, David, 176-177, 178, 179
Truman, Harry, 5, 22, 39-40, 43, 75,
  127, 129, 177
  Vietnam policies of, 13-14, 190
Tuchman, Barbara, 185
Tuckner, Howard, 147
Tuesday Lunch Group, 59, 73, 76,
  83-85, 87, 91, 103, 105, 107, 108,
  109, 115, 118, 122, 124, 130, 133,
  135, 142, 145, 224-225n72
  early history of, 84, 164
  frequency of meetings, 85, 158, 164,
    166, 167
  members of, 85, 142, 146, 164
Turkey, 58
Twenty-five Year War, The (Palmer),
  75-76

United Nations, 44, 99, 123
United States Information Agency
  (USIA), 51, 98-99, 164
USSR. *See* Soviet Union
U Thant, 123

Valenti, Jack, 8, 56, 57, 74, 95, 117,
  155, 174, 186
Van Buren, Martin, 97
Vance, Cyrus, 128, 141, 150
  cable to McNamara, 41-43, 54, 59
Van Dyke, Ted, 19
Vantage Point, The (Johnson), 60-61, 180
Viet Cong, 15-16, 24, 31, 37, 41, 52-53,
  57, 77, 94, 109, 110, 112, 115, 116,
  118, 122
  and Pleiku incident, 17-19, 21-22
"Vietnam Group," 84
Vietnam War
  before Johnson's presidency, 13-14
  bombing of North Vietnam, U.S.,
    38-39, 63, 64, 68, 69, 73, 80-82,
    85-87, 92, 94, 96-97, 100-101, 103,
    105, 106, 115, 123, 135, 139-141,
    145, 149, 152-153, 154, 162,
    205n11; civilian casualties from, 89,
    115, 157; initial, 15, 17-19, 21-23,
    25; purpose of, 17, 23, 26, 38, 86;
    results of, 24, 62, 72-73, 86-89,
    105, 149
  casualties in, U.S., 62, 119-120, 157
  causes of, 5-6, 169-171, 190-194
  enemy body counts disputed, 235n181
  enemy troop levels disputed, 223n48
  ground troops, U.S.: decisions on, 26,
    58-61, 103-106, 116, 131, 132, 148,
    154; defensive enclave strategies for,
    26-27, 37-38; deployments sug-
    gested, 25-26, 30, 52, 63, 77-78,
    81-82, 86, 125, 130, 143; levels of
    in Vietnam, 26, 52, 59, 62, 78, 102,
    104, 116, 150; reserves, 43, 52,
    59-60, 81, 103, 124, 127, 128, 130,
    131, 135, 146
  peace negotiation plan accepted by
    Hanoi, 156
  Pleiku incident, 17, 18, 19, 21-22, 25
  purposes in, U.S., 25, 31, 35, 40, 53,
    55, 58, 73, 87, 94, 161, 163, 190-194

Vietnam War, *continued*
  regarded as a mistake, 3, 13, 60, 105,
    106, 113–114, 157, 163, 165, 190,
    192, 232n141
  results of, 13, 68–69, 72–73, 90, 104,
    105, 148–150, 151, 157
  withdrawal from, difficulties of U.S.,
    16, 21–22, 45, 53, 54, 98–99, 107,
    150, 161, 164, 190, 194, 205n15
  See also Khe Sanh, battle of; Tet
    Offensive
Vo Nguyen Giap. *See* Giap, Gen. Vo
  Nguyen

Walcott, Charles, 9, 168
War and Politics (Brodie), 170–171
Ward, Barbara, 133
Warnke, Paul, 131, 239n40
Westmoreland, Gen. William, 3, 8, 25,
    32, 37–39, 41, 42, 59, 64, 86, 91,
    100, 102–104, 109, 121, 145–146,
    148, 151, 152, 156, 157
  appointment to Vietnam command, 23
  background of, 23, 124
  on bombing, 23, 86
  and civilian leaders in Washington, 23,
    77, 103–104, 158
  Eisenhower and, 83, 123
  enemy troop levels, allegedly dis-
    torted, 223n48
  "fall" of South Vietnam, predictions
    of, 24
  ground strategy and Johnson, 224n57

  and Johnson, 23, 104, 158, 169, 186,
    207n32, 224n57
  promotion to Army Chief of Staff,
    133, 145
  requests more troops, 26–28, 52, 54,
    63, 74–79, 81–82, 121, 124–125
  Tet Offensive, early response to, 112,
    114–116, 121
  visits Washington, 80–83, 104
Wheeler, Gen. Earle, 8, 51, 73–74, 85,
    101, 103, 109, 111, 114–116, 123,
    129, 134, 136, 145–148, 151, 155,
    157, 158
  Clifford on, 56
  "fall" of Vietnam, fears of, 23–24
  and Johnson, 81, 155, 176, 178,
    207n32, 231, 141
  and McNamara, 104
  mission to South Vietnam, 121,
    124–125, 127
  troop requests, supports: 1965, 27,
    52–53, 56; 1967, 81–82; 1968,
    124–125, 127
White House Operations (Redford and
  McCulley), 187
Whitten, Rep. Jamie, 69
Wilson, Woodrow, 169
Wise Men, 108, 128, 136, 141, 158,
    184–185
  impact of 1968 meeting, 110, 152, 156
  meetings with Johnson, 39–40, 73,
    110, 111, 142, 144–146, 148–152, 166
Wolman, Harold, 180–182

CPSIA information can be obtained
at www.ICGtesting.com
Printed in the USA
BVHW082129250822
645549BV00016B/124